Outdoors in the Southwest

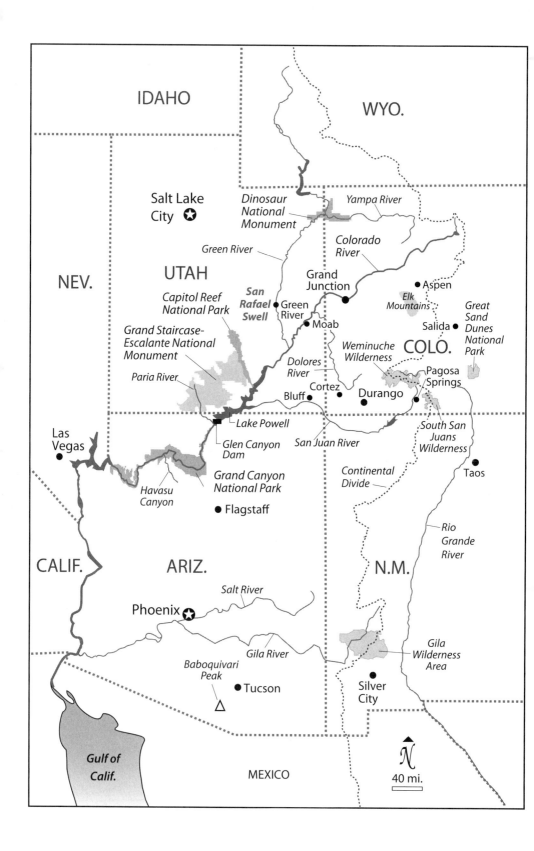

Outdoors in the Southwest

An Adventure Anthology

Edited by
Andrew Gulliford

University of Oklahoma Press : Norman

Also by Andrew Gulliford
America's Country Schools, Washington, D.C., 1984
Boomtown Blues: Colorado Oil Shale, Niwot, Colo., 1989
Sacred Objects and Sacred Places: Preserving Tribal Traditions, Niwot, Colo., 2000
Preserving Western History, Albuquerque, 2005

Library of Congress Cataloging-in-Publication Data

Outdoors in the Southwest : an adventure anthology / edited by Andrew Gulliford.
  pages cm
  Includes bibliographical references and index.
  ISBN 978-0-8061-4260-9 (paperback : alkaline paper) 1. Southwest, New—Description
and travel. 2. Southwest, New—Environmental conditions. 3. Wilderness areas—Southwest,
New. 4. Nature conservation—Southwest, New. 5. Outdoor life—Southwest, New. 6. Adventure and adventurers—Southwest, New. I. Gulliford, Andrew.
  F787.O97 2014
  979—dc23
                        013038045

Copyright © 2014 by the University of Oklahoma Press, Norman, Publishing Division of the
University. Manufactured in the U.S.A.

2 3 4 5 6 7 8 9 10

Dear Ed,

You were so good about supporting young writers. Look at this post-card you wrote me in March 1989. You were ill, yet you took the time to write about a book of mine you never got to review. Within three weeks you had passed on. You always said you'd come back as a turkey vulture and ride the thermal updrafts. How's the view from up there?

I hope you like Outdoors in the Southwest *and that it inspires young environmentalists as much as you have.*

We still miss you, Ed.

Cheers,

Andy

Dear Mr. Gulliford:

15 II 89

Yes. Ask your publisher to send me an advance copy of your book, in bound galley form, and I'll be happy to read it. Your subject sounds interesting. Best, Edward Abbey

Tucson

This postcard is one of the last things Ed Abbey wrote.

Edward Abbey, nicknamed "Cactus Ed," wrote many books, both fiction and nonfiction, about the Southwest. Some of his memorable phrases include, "Society is a lot like stew. If you don't stir it up scum rises to the top" and "Wilderness needs no defense, only more defenders." Drawing of Abbey © Mike Caplanis.

Dedicated to those quiet use adventurers
who open their eyes and ears
and learn with their hearts

and to Ed Abbey
who was never quiet
about defending America's wild lands

"I belong to the wondrous West
and all the West belongs to me."
—Boatman Bert Loper

May your trails be crooked, winding, lonesome, dangerous, leading to the most amazing view. May your mountains rise into and above the clouds. May your rivers flow without end, meandering through pastoral valleys tinkling with bells, past temples and castles and poets' towers into a dark primeval forest where tigers belch and monkeys howl, through miasmal and mysterious swamps and down into a desert of red rock, blue mesas, domes and pinnacles and grottos of endless stone, and down again into a deep vast ancient unknown chasm where bars of sunlight blaze on profiled cliffs, where deer walk across the white sand beaches, where storms come and go as lightning clangs upon the high crags, where something strange and more beautiful and more full of wonder than your deepest dreams waits for you—beyond that next turn of the canyon walls.

—Edward Abbey, "Benediction"

CONTENTS

PREFACE

> I am glad I shall never be young without wild country to be
> young in. Of what avail are forty freedoms without a blank
> spot on the map?
>
> —Aldo Leopold, *A Sand County Almanac*

This is a book about exploring the Southwest and the Colorado Plateau in a reasonable, sane, and meaningful way. It's not about how many peaks you can bag in a day or the number of river miles paddled. Rather, it's about learning from expeditions, outdoor leadership, and the Southwest landscapes we enjoy. *Outdoors in the Southwest* is about public land policies, the value and aesthetics of wilderness, hard-earned lessons of solo experiences, and the need for public land stewardship.

All too often we "take" a hike in the desert or climb a mountain without thinking about "giving back" to our national treasure: public lands. The Colorado Plateau, with 85 million acres in the Four Corners states of Colorado, Utah, Arizona, and New Mexico, has more national parks, national monuments, national forests, and federally and tribally designated wilderness areas than anywhere on earth. But it needs public land advocates. In the words of poet Gary Snyder, "Find your place, dig in, defend it."[1]

In *Wild Thoughts from Wild Places,* David Quammen writes, "In the course of a life a person could travel widely but could truly open his veins and his soul to just a limited number of places."[2] For me, my place is the American Southwest and the spectacular landscapes of the Colorado Plateau.

Ed Abbey opened his classic book *Desert Solitaire* with the line, "This is the most beautiful place on earth." He went on, "There are many such places. Every man, every woman carries in heart and mind the image of the ideal place, the right place, the one true home, known or unknown, actual or visionary."

"For myself I'll take Moab, Utah," said Abbey. "I don't mean the town itself, of course, but the country which surrounds it—the canyonlands. The slickrock desert. The red dust and the burnt cliffs and the lonely sky—all that which lies beyond the end of the roads."[3]

Actually, Cactus Ed came to ramble far and wide across the Southwest, eventually making his home near Tucson, Arizona, but his writing reached out to fire towers on Grand Canyon's rim, ranchers in central New Mexico, urban sprawl, and that damn dam Glen Canyon. Congress passed the Wilderness Act in 1964, and four years later Abbey published *Desert Solitaire*. In the following decades the country watched as the West's extraction-based economy sputtered and died. Behind the fall of mining, lumbering, and grazing emerged a new recreation- and amenity-based economy. Nineteenth-century mining towns survived only as tourist attractions. Then a new generation, a thrill-seeking one, propped up economies located near recreational landscapes to hike, ski, mountain bike, and live in the Southwest.[4] And why not? The Southwest and the Colorado Plateau present ample opportunities to find a deep and abiding sense of place. Think of yourself surrounded by the mesas and monoliths of Monument Valley. As you set your mind to be present in the splendid surroundings, lightning begins to strike the landscape. It begins to rain. You breathe deeply, smelling the earthy freshness of the rain-soaked land. According to Navajo tradition, rain can either be the hard-driving, fast-moving male rain of summer or the slower, softer female rains of spring and fall. The Kiowa writer and poet N. Scott Momaday admonished:

> Once in his life a man ought to concentrate his mind upon the remembered earth, I believe. He ought to give himself up to a particular landscape in his experience, to look at it from as many angles as he can, to wonder about it, to dwell upon it. He ought to imagine that he touches it with his hands at every season and listens to the sounds that are made upon it. He ought to imagine the creatures there and all the faintest motions of the wind. He ought to recollect the glare of noon and all the colors of the dawn and dusk.[5]

For me, that place is the Four Corners, where Arizona, Colorado, New Mexico, and Utah meet, and the broader Colorado Plateau. No other part of the United States has a wider variety of mountains, canyons, and rivers. Within these ecosystems is the Henry Mountains, the last mountain range discovered and named in the lower forty-eight states, and the Escalante River, the last river to receive a name. These remote places provide rare opportunities to experience what has been lost to us in the business of the twenty-first century: to find silence, solitude, and darkness with plenty of stars. To walk for miles without seeing a single town.[6]

In our region of the Southwest, we can hike among sandstone cliffs that are clearly the beds of ancient oceans, where waves lapping against beaches millions of years ago left still-visible marks. For decades of American history, the Colorado Plateau was an island of unexplored and impassable rock, its geography unknown until after the Civil War. Then the mystery of Grand Canyon became unraveled by the heroic Colorado River expedition of John Wesley Powell in 1869. Not until after World War II was the region much traversed. Travel was by vague trails and dirt roads. Paved roads, especially across the seventeen-million-acre Navajo Reservation, remained virtually nonexistent until the 1950s.[7]

With low desert to high alpine terrain, the Southwest is blessed with a wide variety of topography and climate zones. In one area of southwestern New Mexico, most of earth's climatic zones can be found near and within the Gila Wilderness. In the Southwest we can hike, bike, and climb varied terrain and float mild to wild rivers, including the Colorado River through Grand Canyon. No wonder Frank Waters called the Colorado Plateau the "last great wilderness of America, its spiritual heartland."[8] Now, after millennia of supporting native inhabitants, and a few hundred years of fur traders, trappers, ranchers, miners, loggers, and cowboys, a new kind of resident has moved to the Southwest. This one wants to explore the peaks and canyons and be challenged by steep mountains, swift rapids, and backpacking trips.

According to the *New Yorker* magazine, more undergraduate college students are interested in outdoor recreation or adventure education than in foreign language or literature.[9] Extreme sports have introduced a new array of personal challenges to students. They are kayaking down steep mountain creeks at high-water flows, bagging several peaks in a single day, or endurance running or hiking. Those challenges and goals are important, but this book is also about understanding the natural landscapes of those pursuits.

The book is also about expeditionary learning and achieving as a group, without a "me first" attitude. Personal responsibility in wild and remote settings is essential, as is the notion of human power and quiet use without relying on machines or battery-powered technologies. My version of *Outdoors in the Southwest* is not about mountain biking or ATV riding, nor is it about hunting and fishing, which are admirable pursuits. Instead, it's about the lessons behind using oars or paddles on the Green and Yampa Rivers, taking group hikes to the top of southwestern peaks, and a meditation on *place*.

This isn't a guidebook. There are plenty of those in print, perhaps too many. Nor is this a series of nature essays extolling the virtues of desert or southwestern landscapes, though such praise is important and sampled in the book. As Jim Stiles wrote in *Brave New West*, "I will not regale you with tales of inspiring hikes to seldom-visited secret places, though I've had more than my fair share. Go find your own goddamn secret places, and when you do, don't tell anyone what you've found. . . . Earn the right to be overwhelmed. Create your own special corners of the world. It's so much more satisfying."[10]

I am a professor of history and environmental studies at Fort Lewis College, a four-year public liberal arts school in Durango, Colorado, where we have adventure education and environmental studies majors. I teach classes on wilderness, environmental history, and national parks, and I'm excited about the students who are coming to class dedicated, fit, and eager to learn, with that far-off look in their eyes that probably means they'll skip class at the end of the week to climb spires in Canyonlands, paddle rapids in the San Juan River, or hike towering peaks in the adjacent San Juan Mountains.

Fort Lewis College and Durango are blessed with close proximity to the largest wilderness area in the state: the Weminuche Wilderness. At half a million acres, the Weminuche straddles both the San Juan and Rio Grande National Forests. The South San Juans Wilderness has habitat so wild that it saw the last Colorado grizzly killed.

It is easy to see that this new generation is different from mine. It contains members who are fearless in the water in kayaks and in deep avalanche-prone snow on both snowboards and backcountry skis. This generation is connected and wired in new ways, but all their connectedness doesn't mean they understand the landscapes they traverse.

Hence this book, an adventure anthology that draws from personal stories. I edited *Outdoors in the Southwest* because this reader includes themes not covered in textbooks. I see this book as a supplemental reader useful for orienting groups and stimulating discussion of Southwest issues, in particular ecological and environmental issues linked to human use of the landscape and group exploration. If the nineteenth- and mid-twentieth-century West was about extractive industries such as mining, grazing, and lumbering, the late twentieth-century and early twenty-first-century West is about recreation, spending time outdoors, and personal growth through the acquisition of skills such as rafting, hiking, climbing, and backpacking. Learning through doing. Experiential education in the field.

Outdoors in the Southwest: An Adventure Anthology begins with an introduction that describes our need for nature and a definition of outdoor adventure based on the history of experiential education and the insights of Kurt Hahn, British-born founder of Outward Bound.

The introductory pages also chronicle the current disconnection from the outdoors by today's wired generation of Internet and social network users.

In chapter 1, a case study of the Gila Wilderness sets up an explanation of why we need wilderness. This New Mexico wilderness was set aside in 1924 as the first administratively designated wilderness in the world. Aldo Leopold, one of our nation's first ecologists, recommended the designation because he wanted to preserve a stretch of country big enough to absorb a two-week horse pack trip without crossing a single road.

Leopold and others felt, as I do, that visits to wilderness are essential to maintaining our unique American character. As a nation we were forged by our relationship to wild lands at the edges of canyons, mountains, plains, or forests. Edited wilderness essays for chapter 1 include naturalist Terry Tempest Williams discussing Aldo Leopold, Howard L. Smith writing about a backpacking trip in the Gila Wilderness, and canyoneering expert Steve Allen explaining wilderness values and canyoneering.

"Looking for History" is the theme for chapter 2. This chapter enables readers to better understand cultural resources in the Southwest, including cliff dwellings, archaeological artifacts, historic homesteads and fences, and cowboy corrals. I write about my own fascination with ancient handprints found high on canyon walls as well as finding a large *olla* or water jar in a mountain lion's den in New Mexico. I describe "catch and release" arrowhead hunting because no artifact found on public land can be kept. Instead, after finding an arrowhead, spearpoint, or ancient knife blade, put it back where you found it and push it deeper into the soil. I also discuss Native American peeled ponderosa pines and Hispanic aspen tree carvings or arborglyphs as well as a brief definition of Native American sacred sites.

Readings include Barbara Kingsolver on the Eagle Tail Mountains in an excerpt from *High Tide in Tucson*; Greg Gordon on the Fremont Indian culture; and Jack Turner's "The Maze and Aura—Canyonlands." I describe finding blood red rock art on the San Rafael Swell from the Barrier Canyon people. Bill and Beth Sagstetter offer the proper etiquette for entering backcountry cliff dwellings, and a similar protocol or etiquette for visiting historic mining sites is explained by Frederick Athearn.

Mountain hiking and climbing are featured in chapter 3 with my explanation of hiking and discovering the Ute Indian Trail on Colorado's Western Slope and then descriptions of tribal sacred places on public lands such as the San Francisco Peaks and Hesperus Peak, one of the four Navajo sacred mountains. Essayists include "Aussie Dave" on hiking the 3,200-mile Continental Divide Trail; Janice Emily Bowers describing her climb of Arizona's Baboquivari Peak; and Dean Cox on being hit by lightning. Jane Koerner, the first woman to climb the hundred highest peaks in Colorado, describes a hiking accident, and search and rescue first responder and registered nurse Leo Lloyd explains "Backcountry Travel and the Darwin Effect." The chapter concludes with a remarkable survival story. Fred Hutt fell nine hundred feet off Colorado's Engineer Peak when a cornice gave way during a spring ascent. Leo Lloyd was the Durango-based nurse who helped get him to the hospital. For the first time, the two recount in vivid detail what happened in this true-to-life cautionary tale.

Chapter 4 features stories on canyons and deserts, beginning with the time a friend and I got lost in Canyonlands on a hike where a spring day turned cold at night. I also describe a trip down to Havasu Canyon below the rim at Hualapai Hilltop, and a near-disastrous flash flood on a horse pack trip into Ute Mountain Tribal Park.

Ann Zwinger describes the Honaker Trail above the San Juan River. Chip Ward writes about being too close to a flash flood, and Steve Susswein and Susan Agranoff tell their canyon country epic of getting stuck in a slot canyon. Wayne Ranney offers advice in his essay "Grand Canyon Trail Guides: A Job Worth Living For." I visit the legendary Katie Lee in her hometown of Jerome, Arizona.

"Running Western Rivers" is the title of chapter 5, with my descriptions of canoeing the Dolores River, rafting the Green through the Gates of Lodore, and running the Yampa at high water. I explain how important it was in 1956 to stop a dam in the bottom of Echo Park—an event that inspired the modern American environmental movement. I also write about river running in Grand Canyon. Chad Niehaus tells tales of being a Westwater Canyon river ranger. The chapter concludes with insights from Dr. William Karls, a boatman and psychiatrist. He comments on how a psychiatrist looks at group dynamics on river trips in Grand Canyon and how to be a better boatman.

Chapter 6 chronicles important issues about solo trips and the importance of going out and coming back. In this chapter I deal with "re-entry" and how hard it is to be in wilderness for an extended time period and then return to "civilization" with all its crass consumerism. I describe my first solo hike into a lonely area of southern Colorado and the structure of accidents: how they happen and how survivors respond.

Katie Lee begins with getting trapped in Glen Canyon. River runner and writer Ellen Meloy loses her raft on the Green River and has moments of panic trying to recover it. From Ed Abbey's classic *Desert Solitaire* is the story of his solo adventure turning sour in a side canyon off Havasu in Grand Canyon. I write about mapping and hiking the Continental Divide Trail, which is known as "the king of trails" because of its distance, isolation, and long miles between resupply points.

Wilderness hiking would be far less meaningful without the presence of animals. Seeing deer, elk, bear, and mountain lions in the wild adds spice, and sometimes fear, to any extended trek. Chapter 7 on animal encounters begins with Aldo Leopold's epiphany after shooting a wolf in the Southwest. Because of that action he rethinks the idea of ecological balance and the value of predator-prey relationships. In this section I write about the successful reintroduction of California condors into northern Arizona and also difficulties reestablishing the Canadian lynx in the Southern Rockies. I describe "feathered Ice Age memorials" and a wonderful encounter with condors at the historic Marble Canyon Bridge on the Arizona Strip.

Essays include Creek Hanauer's story "Pirates of the Granite Gorge," about smart ravens in Grand Canyon; David Petersen writing on mountain lion tracks at his campsite; and Lynell Schalk's story about counting and vaccinating desert bighorn sheep from a rare herd living on the Navajo Reservation. I explain my search for Colorado grizzlies and a hike we made to where the last grizzly bear death occurred.

The anthology concludes with Chapter 8 and the concept of wilderness tithing or giving back to public lands. We *take* a hike, but what do we give back? Public lands stewardship needs to be an essential part of any outdoor recreation program, as well as for individuals who use public lands. I write about picking up trash at Lake Powell in hundred-plus-degree summer heat. At Glen Canyon National Recreation Area we use a sixty-five-foot-long houseboat, an aging motorboat, and an even older National Park Service barge, which we routinely fill with bags of trash as well as refrigerators, microwaves, tires and rims, and rusting propane bottles.

In this final chapter I describe the work of Great Old Broads for Wilderness and their efforts to protect public lands. Another example is the Colorado Fourteeners Initiative, whose motto is "Get out, get up, give back." All too often the literature these days is about extreme sports and a young generation climbing, rappelling, rafting, and kayaking for the adrenaline rush of getting into and out of difficult situations. But most of that recreation occurs on public lands, and we need to practice sensitive use, not abuse, and learn the satisfaction that comes from public land stewardship.

Lynn Hamilton, executive director of the Grand Canyon River Guides Association, writes about their successful "adopt-a-beach" program and science and stewardship along the Colorado River. Harry Bruell, executive director of the Southwest Conservation Corps, writes about connecting youth to the landscape through training and hard, physical work on useful public lands projects. Whitman College professor Phil Brick concludes with "Walking the Distance: Finding the Advocate's Path in a Warming West."

So enjoy this book. Learn from it, and may these chapters make your travels across the Southwest more meaningful. I've tried to follow Ed Abbey's advice to "Write right; write good; right wrong; write on!" Let me know how I did.

Andrew Gulliford, Durango

Gulliford_a@fortlewis.edu

Notes

1. Gary Snyder quoted in Timothy Egan, *Living in the Runaway West: Partisan Views from Writers on the Range* (Golden, CO: Fulcrum Publishing and High Country News, 2000), ix.

2. David Quammen, *Wild Thoughts from Wild Places* (New York: Scribners, 1998), 256.

3. Edward Abbey, *Desert Solitaire* (New York: McGraw-Hill, 1968), 1.

4. To understand recent tourism in the Southwest, see Hal K. Rothman, *Devil's Bargains: Tourism in the Twentieth-Century American West* (Lawrence: University Press of Kansas, 1998), and David M. Wrobel and Patrick T. Long, eds., *Seeing and Being Seen: Tourism in the American West* (Lawrence: University Press of Kansas, 2001).

5. N. Scott Momaday, *The Way to Rainy Mountain* (Albuquerque: University of New Mexico Press, 1969), 83.

6. Natural Bridges National Monument in Utah has been named the first Dark Sky Park by the International Dark-Sky Association. See Verlyn Klinkenborg, "Our Vanishing Night," in *National Geographic*, November 2008.

7. See H. Jackson Clark, *The Owl in Monument Canyon* (Salt Lake City: University of Utah Press, 1993), especially chapter 1, "Exploring Navajoland," and Art Gomez, *Quest for the Golden Circle* (Albuquerque: University of New Mexico Press, 1994).

8. Frank Waters, *The Colorado* (reprint, Athens: Ohio University Press, 1984), xiv.

9. The May 21, 2007, issue of the *New Yorker* stated, "There are more bachelor's degrees awarded every year in Parks, Recreation, Leisure and Fitness Studies than in all foreign languages and literatures combined" (28).

10. Jim Stiles, *Brave New West: Morphing Moab at the Speed of Greed* (Tucson: University of Arizona Press, 2007), 5. For the change from the Old West of resource extraction to the New West outdoor recreational playground, see Lisa Nicholas, Elaine M. Bapis, and Thomas J. Harvey, eds., *Imagining the Big Open: Nature, Identity and Play in the New West* (Salt Lake City: University of Utah Press, 2003).

ACKNOWLEDGMENTS

I want to gratefully acknowledge the following for providing research funds for this book: the John Topham and Susan Redd Butler Faculty Research Award, the Charles Redd Center for Western Studies, Brigham Young University, and the Ballantine Family Foundation of Durango, Colorado. I also received financial support from Ginger Harmon, the Fort Lewis College Faculty Development Fund, and the Fort Lewis College Foundation. In addition, the Ballantine Family Foundation provided financial support to the University of Oklahoma Press for assisting with the design and publication of this book.

I am indebted to the Fort Lewis College Board of Trustees for a fall 2008 sabbatical that provided time to research, write, run rivers, and bag a few peaks. On the FLC campus, Dr. Robert Stremba in the Adventure Education Program encouraged this anthology and gave me the enjoyable opportunity of speaking to his classes. The staff in our Outdoor Pursuits Program has also been wonderful to work with. I owe a debt of gratitude to Jay Dew and Chuck Rankin at the University of Oklahoma Press, who understood this book's potential and stood by it through all stages of the publication process.

In researching this book I've benefited from interviews with colleagues at colleges, universities, and federal agencies, including Pam Foti, Department of Geography, Planning, and Recreation at Northern Arizona University; Bruce Kime, Department of Outdoor Education at Colorado Mountain College in Glenwood Springs; Kevin Nelson, Department of Outdoor Leadership at Western State College; Nathan Nelson, School of Environmental Studies, Apple Valley, Minnesota; Steve Munsell, Outdoor Education Program at Prescott College; Ed Franz, outdoor recreation planner for the Bureau of Land Management; Rick Boretti, San Juan river ranger; Marie Tuxhorn, BLM law enforcement at Monticello, Utah; Scott Edwards, backcountry ranger at the Kane Gulch BLM Ranger Station, Cedar Mesa, Utah; and archaeologist Michael Selle, who introduced me to Canyon Pintado. Other interviewees are credited in the book's text.

Some of these essays were previously published in my *Durango Herald* newspaper column "Gulliford's Travels," and also in *Inside/Outside Southwest*,

Mountain Gazette, Utah Adventure Journal, and the "Writers on the Range" syndicated column of *High Country News.* Thank you to Betsy Marston of *HCN* for your wit and grace. I've also updated essays from my edited book *Preserving Western History,* my article from the *Encyclopedia of American Indian Religious Freedom,* and my contribution to *Going Green,* edited by Laura Pritchett (University of Oklahoma Press, 2009). I also want to thank the authors for letting me reprint their work in this volume and for the outdoorsmen and women I interviewed throughout the Southwest. A special thanks to Patrick Gaughan at Fort Lewis College for his computer assistance and to adventure education majors Kate Shavel and Ryan Moore for writing study questions for each chapter.

For illustrations I want to thank the artists and photographers whose work is utilized in this book. Credit is given in the captions. I have also enjoyed working with mapmaker Robert Garcia, graphics editor at the *Grand Junction Daily Sentinel.* A debt of gratitude goes to editors John Peel and Jan Nesset, who taught me to tighten my flabby prose. Thanks to Tom Noel, "Dr. Colorado," who inspired me to lead trips and tell campfire stories even when it was too damn hot for fires in "Leave No Trace" fire pans. I have been encouraged by Gina and Hugh Bingham, whose Mark Twain monologues are a storyteller's inspiration.

Dr. Alfred Koumans enjoyed my lectures on the Linblad cruise ship *M/V Sea Lion.* He insisted we ride horseback into the Weminuche Wilderness, which we did up to La Ventana and across to La Rincon de la Ossa, one of the last hiding places for grizzly bears in the Colorado Rockies. Tony Gurzik of the Colorado Division of Wildlife reviewed the animal encounters chapter.

Numerous friends and colleagues have helped me with this book. I would like to thank Roland Stone for showing me the Gila; Steve Jones for backpacking with me into the South San Juans Wilderness; David Vackar for teaching me about wilderness policy; Steven Allen for helping me descend an Anasazi route down a slot canyon; and Ronni Egan for her leadership of Great Old Broads for Wilderness. Katie Lee is my hero and a great person to interview, and I learned much about cultural resource protection from Lynell Schalk. Bill and Beth Sagstetter have taught me about mining camps as well as cliff dwellings, and I'll never forget our hike into Thanksgiving House and the narrow ledge with the three-hundred-foot drop-off.

Bill Grant and Bill Harding have been constant hiking companions for more than thirty years, and Tiffany Mapel is showing me the best and worst about Lake Powell. I miss my hunting buddy John Heyer because he taught me to read animal signs. Thank you to Darlene Reidhead, Ken McNutt, Bob and Emily Atwood, and Tom McBride of the Rim Huggers, who showed me the Vermilion Cliffs National Monument with day hikes into the Paria Wilderness. Thank you to Vince and Martha Wilcox for letting me use their casita in Bluff, Utah, for precious time to read, write, think, and hike. Jim and Jeannette Petersen of Bluff and Boulder have also shared their special cliff dwelling finds with me. Tom West read the manuscript and had useful suggestions.

My son Tristan David has been fun to hike with on the Flat Tops Wilderness, and we have many miles to go. A special thanks to my son Duncan for losing or wearing out enough camping gear so that I've had to buy more. It's been great to hike, mountain climb, paddle, canoe, and duckie with Amy and Nik Kendziorski, but we still don't camp enough.

As a guide, historian, interpreter, and storyteller, I want to acknowledge the many clients I have learned from and shared ideas with. I've led tours across the West by canoe, raft, horseback, van, cruise ship, private train, and private jet. I am grateful for having worked with staff at Adrift Adventures, Jensen, Utah; Arizona Raft Adventures, Flagstaff, Arizona; Centennial Canoe Outfitters, Centennial, Colorado; History Colorado, Denver; Great Old Broads for Wilderness, Durango, Colorado; Off the Beaten Path, Missoula, Montana; and national organizations such as National Geographic Expeditions, the National Trust for Historic Preservation, Rocky Mountain Public Broadcasting Service (PBS), and the Smithsonian Associates Program. On each tour I've learned more about the landscape and I've benefited from extraordinary conversations with people who also love the American West.

Of course, I need to acknowledge my hero, President Theodore Roosevelt, for without him there would be far fewer acres of public lands. He saved 230 million acres for us all to enjoy. I also want to thank my Fort Lewis College environmental studies and history students in HIST 313 American Wilderness, HIST 181 Environmental History, HIST 323 National Parks, ENVS 496 Senior Seminar, and ENVS 410 Internship. My students have been, and continue to be, an inspiration.

Without my wife Stephanie Moran's patience and encouragement this book never would have happened. After thirty-six years of marriage I'm still trying to remember to clean the camp stove when we get home . . .

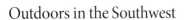

Outdoors in the Southwest

Introduction
Our Need for Nature and Adventure

In the end, we will conserve only what we love, we will love only what we know, and we will know only what we have been taught.[1]

—Baba Dioum

Adventure is worthwhile in itself.

—Amelia Earhart, pilot lost over the Pacific

Children and their families need to spend more time outdoors learning the value of quiet recreation. This is true in the Southwest and across the nation. The 1960s generation successfully advocated for the national Wilderness Act and environmental laws and protections. Now a new generation must also become eco-advocates. Getting families outdoors must become a priority. Environmentalists—the so-called greens—are graying. We've saved many spectacular landscapes in the American Southwest, but saving wild places isn't enough; visiting them is equally important.

College students with outdoor recreation and education programs may be engaging in the outdoors, but few public-school kids get beyond their fenced-in, concrete playgrounds. A number of disturbing trends in American schools, including childhood obesity, attention deficit disorders, and juvenile depression, are the symptoms of insufficient outdoor education.[1]

Glued to computer screens, video games, and cell phones, children seem to have no knowledge of nature and no way to slow down, lie in the grass, and look for dragons emerging in afternoon clouds. Nature writer David Petersen explains, "As students of human ecology have so well documented, and our increasingly virtual culture so blithely ignores, a childhood deprived of nature leaves one hell of a hole to pull yourself out of."[2]

Reed Karaim reports, "According to a Kaiser Family Foundation study, American kids age 8 to 18 average 44.5 hours per week in front of some kind of screen. The only thing that they do more is sleep."[3] Across the country we have plenty of asphalt playgrounds with chain-link fences, but not enough places for children to play in woods and along streams, to make homemade forts. Children need wild places and wild landscapes—where they can use their imaginations and think quietly about the world rather than be bombarded with fast-paced media images. They need nature and the opportunity for sustained thought to manipulate things in a three-dimensional environment, not just on a screen.

In *The Geography of Childhood*, Gary Paul Nabhan writes, "To counter the historic trend toward the loss of wildness where children play, it is clear that we need to find ways to let children roam beyond the pavement, to gain access to vegetation and earth that allows them to tunnel, climb, or even fall."[4] Now it seems we have a major crisis involving urban and suburban American children who do not understand nature, who do not know their place in the natural world, and who do not enjoy all the comforts and mysteries that come from outdoor exploration.

For those of us keenly involved with environmental issues, this is a deeply disturbing trend. How can we teach and mentor a new generation of eco-advocates if they never walk in wild landscapes? Stephen Trimble explains, "By forging connections with plants, animals, and land, by finding ways to experience some relationship to the Earth, individuals can gain a sense of worth. Herein lies security."[5] In one of the most famous catchphrases of the environmental movement, Henry David Thoreau stated, "In wildness is the preservation of the world."[6] What he meant more than 150 years ago continues to be debated, but unquestionably we need wild places where children can find themselves and feel connected to the larger world. Yet Nabhan adds, "The percentage of children who have frequent exposure to wildlands and to undomesticated species is smaller than ever before in human history."[7]

I'm a former fourth grade teacher from Silt, Colorado, where for years I was the only male elementary school teacher in a community of farm and ranch kids who understood nature, hunted deer and elk with their fathers and uncles, and enjoyed the outdoors as much as I do. On the lawn outside our classroom I would read to the children after lunch from outdoor-themed books such as *Brighty of the Grand Canyon; Danny, the Champion of the World;* and *Where the Red Fern Grows.* My boys and girls loved sitting in the grass, dreaming, playing with ants, breaking sticks into smaller and smaller pieces, and watching those white, puffy Colorado cumulus clouds sail over the mesas and mountaintops.

In order for a younger generation to become interested in conserving the environment, children need to spend more time outdoors learning about nature in the company of their parents and adults. Drawing © Krista Harris.

Every year our principal would ask me if I wanted curtains for my south-facing windows, and every year I'd say no. Who would want to obscure the expansive view south across the Colorado River to Mamm Peak, Dry Hollow, Divide Creek, and the White River National Forest, the second oldest such forest in the United States?

In our school district the first Monday of the fall elk-hunting season was routinely a day off from school, because so many children and teenagers would have taken the day off anyway to help their families hunt. We lived in a rural, remote area blessed with rivers, creeks, mountains, and thousands of acres of national forest. To the north lay the Flat Tops Wilderness Area, which is one of the largest in the state. This wilderness area is home to Trappers Lake, which inspired Arthur Carhart to make it the cradle of the American Wilderness movement.[8]

At Silt Elementary School, kids got outside every day. When I taught science we'd collect insects, and now, more than twenty-five years later, some of those ranch kids still have their insect collections—butterflies pinned to cardboard, black stinkbugs with red pins through their abdomens. Educating fourth graders in Silt was a great way to begin a teaching career, and I bonded to our community by hunting, fishing, and riding horseback with my students' parents and grandparents. When children walked home from school in the late fall, amid a swirl of cottonwood leaves, they'd break branches off the tall willow trees on the path above the Cactus Valley ditch, and they'd lean over the fence to steal fruit from the decades-old heirloom Italian plum trees in our backyard. I didn't mind. Better them than the raccoons.

Paul Nabhan explains, "The earth allows children to be themselves, to be active rather than passive, to take control of their play, their time, their imaginations."[9] Yet children are simply not getting enough time outdoors, which has a striking impact on their personal development. In his book *Last Child in the Woods*, author Richard Louv describes a "nature-deficit disorder" as one of the causes of obesity and poor academic performance in children. He explains that being in nature "improves the capacity to pay attention" and that a nine-year study of Outward Bound–like wilderness programs found that "during these treks or afterward, subjects reported experiencing a sense of peace and an ability to think more clearly."[10] Louv states, "Direct exposure to nature is essential for physical and emotional health," yet nationally since 1987 we have seen decreases in the use of outdoor spaces, the frequency of family camping and backpacking trips, and national park attendance, while children become more and more likely to learn from computer screens what they should be learning in the field.[11]

Attendance is also down at national forests. Recreational visits slipped 18 percent since 2001 in every one of the U.S. Forest Service's nine regions.[12] However, some family outdoor traditions continue. *New York Times* columnist Nicholas Kristof, hiking with his eleven-year-old daughter, writes, "Time in the wilderness is part of our family's summer ritual, a time to hit the 'reset' switch and escape deadlines and BlackBerrys." He adds, "We spend the time fretting instead about blisters, river crossings and rain, and the experiences offer us lessons on inner peace and life's meaning—cheap and effective therapy without the couch."[13]

Writing in the *Denver Post*, Nancy Lofholm discusses "nature-deficit disorder" and explains, "The phenomenon is epidemic in a generation that spends more time indoors than out and is more familiar with YouTube and Guitar Hero than with tadpoles and pine cones." She adds, "Studies show that American children now spend an average of 30 minutes of unstructured time outdoors weekly but watch as much as four hours of television daily."[14] Hunting and fishing licenses for children have dropped, and backpacking and camping permits are down. "We need to grow more stewards," believes former Colorado National Monument superintendent Joan Anselmo. "We need

At the south rim of Grand Canyon a young boy plans to take his first steps down the Bright Angel Trail. Statistically, of the more than 4 million people to visit Grand Canyon, only 10 percent hike below the rim, and only 1 percent make it to the bottom and the Colorado River. Photo courtesy of Wayne Ranney.

to introduce them to the ethics of taking care of public lands while they're young."[15]

Peter Fish reports in *Sunset* magazine that visitation at Carlsbad Caverns National Park in New Mexico decreased to 45 percent of what it was twenty years ago, and Olympic National Park in Washington State has seen a decline of 15 percent in annual visitors. For the Intermountain Region of the Rockies, visitation has declined eleven years out of the last thirteen, with backpacking decreasing 23 percent between 1998 and 2005.[16]

Jeff Osgood writes, "Forget the park; where's the remote control?" in an essay that uses the phrase "videophilia" to explain how observation in nature has given way to nature observation on television. Osgood comments, "Why go searching in the Rocky Mountains for the sight of a bighorn sheep, marmot or a pika when you can tune into . . . Animal Planet?"[17] Of course, watching wildlife on television requires neither the patience nor the skill that seeing wildlife in wild settings does.

This problem is serious enough that Congress has proposed "No Child Left Inside" legislation that would create incentives for states and schools to expand outdoor education and nature programs. The U.S. Forest Service also has monies available for cooperative partners through its "Take It Outdoors" national campaign to help children develop environmental values. Louv believes, "For a new generation, nature is more abstraction than reality. Increasingly, nature is something to watch, to consume, to wear—to ignore."[18] Journalist Froma Harrop sees the long-term results of a generation not being out in nature. She writes, "Environmentalists worry that the loss of direct contact with the natural world will eventually weaken Americans' commitment to conservation and biodiversity."[19]

Children need nature in their backyards, in their neighborhoods, and down the street, but they also need truly wild landscapes and wilderness areas. As the curmudgeon Ed Abbey admonished, "Every Boy Scout deserves a forest to get lost, miserable and starving in."[20] Exploring wildlands teaches us what we can't control— getting lost, the weather, mosquitos in the high country, no-see-ums at lower elevations, and snowslides. Being outdoors is about risks and rewards, and adults and children need both. Dr. Seuss wrote:

> *On and on you will hike.*
> *And I know you'll hike far*
> *and face up to your problems*
> *whatever they are.*
> *You'll get mixed up, of course,*
> *as you already know.*
> *You'll get mixed up*
> *with many strange birds as you go . . .*
> *Today is your day!*
> *Your mountain is waiting.*
> *So . . . get on your way!*[21]

As Americans we come from wild landscapes, and understanding our relationship to nature has set our culture apart. Now more than ever, children need to get off the phone, off the Internet, away from text messaging, and outdoors. Our future, and theirs, depends upon it.

∽

But if this is an adventure education reader, what is adventure, anyway? And why are there so many new school and college programs in outdoor pursuits, wilderness pursuits, adventure education, and outdoor leadership? What is this adventure impulse for children, young adults, and corporate groups? At Zion National Park the Zion Adventure Company takes clients canyoneering, which involves backcountry travel, swimming, rappelling, climbing, hiking, and problem solving. Their brochure states, "There's nothing like being together at the rock for the day. We see climbing as more than just something you 'do,' it's a lifetime experience. One day on the rock offers immeasurable opportunity for growth, challenge, and perspective."[22]

Yet Arctic explorer Vilhjalmur Stefansson believed that "adventures are a mark of incompetence." Jeff Renner, writing about lightning encounters for mountaineers, states, "Adventures are a mark of inexperience and poor information."[23] What is the appropriate definition of adventure in an educational or experiential context? Writing in the periodical *Adventure Guide to the Western San Juans*, Lance Waring states, "Among outdoor enthusiasts, an epic is an adventure that becomes a misadventure and which requires some fortitude." He adds, "In the mountains, epics typically involve being high on the flanks of a frigid peak, pinned down by a raging storm. One typically runs short on food and fuel, and frostbite or hypothermia may set in."[24] That doesn't sound like fun, but it does provide the opportunity for personal growth, albeit at a possibly high cost.

The goals for adventure education, beginning with Kurt Hahn's Outward Bound program, which came to the United States in 1961, are laudatory. Hahn wrote, "I regard it as the foremost task of education to insure the survival of these qualities: an enterprising curiosity, an undefeatable spirit, tenacity in pursuit, readiness for sensible self-denial, and, above all, compassion."[25] Outward Bound programs have exemplified expeditionary learning and whole group success as opposed to a "me first" attitude characteristic of an extreme sports mentality where public lands are taken for granted. Arden Anderson, former recreation and wilderness specialist for the Bureau of Land Management (BLM), explains that for some members of the new outdoor generation, "Nature's just a dirty gym where we go to climb the highest peak or speed down the trail. The entire sense of appreciating nature has been lost in the world of extreme sports."[26]

Successfully concluding lengthy experiences in the outdoors does result in transformed lives, and peak experiences do come from risk taking, problem solving, and dealing with uncertainty. Upset over a college girlfriend's interest in someone else, at age eighteen I drove west from the Colorado College campus into the Colorado Rockies and decided to freehand climb a granite cliff near Wilkerson Pass. Angry at myself, confused about my girlfriend, I scampered up the rock free soloing only to find myself stuck—rimrocked. Unable to go up, down, or sideways, I clung to a stony ledge feeling sorry for myself. No one knew where I was. No one cared. As my self-pity began to affect my decision making, a strong gust of wind from a microburst blew me off the ledge and I lost my secure handhold. Instead of having two hands and two feet on granite, I waved in the wind like a tattered flag with only my right hand and right foot attached to the cliff. No ropes. No helmet.

When the wind stopped a minute later—a minute that seemed like an eternity—I was able to cling to the rock with both hands and feet, overjoyed, tearful, and deeply grateful. I was on the same ledge, but within an instant I had become a new person, more confident, composed, and able to think clearly about how to get off the rock. I considered the possible routes and within a short time made it to the top of the cliff and back to my car. A dumb decision as a college freshman had almost caused me to have a serious accident. Had I fallen I'm sure I would have broken something—maybe even my neck. I had an adventure that I hadn't counted on. As Arden Anderson explains, "When the curve of rising confidence crosses the curve of declining skill, the stage is set for a monumental learning experience."[27] I agree. My adventure was such a learning experience that I've been more humble hiking ever since.

Self-reliance has always been an American virtue, and there's no place better to practice common sense and to learn about nature than in outdoor wilderness settings. Outdoor recreation and outdoor leadership programs can change lives, especially with the concept of "challenge by choice." Within this precept, individuals stretch themselves beyond their comfort level but on terms that they accept. Low-impact, nonmechanized, human-powered activities can be deeply satisfying in our technologically dependent world. Project Adventure editors Dick Prouty, Jane Panicucci, and Rufus Collinson explain, "Adventure education can be defined as direct, active and engaging learning experiences that involve the whole person and have real consequences."[28] And adventure travel is on the increase. Dave Brewster for ABC News claims that "one of the biggest, baddest, boomingest slices of the ever-swelling travel pie [is] adventure travel."[29] Why? Because, says Brewster, it offers a brush with death. Peter Stark explains that in dangerous, outdoor settings,

> Another part of what compels me—a big part of it, and one that accentuates all the others—is the sense of the nearness of my own mortality. . . . In a difficult or risky situation in the wilderness, the total reliance on oneself and trust in one's teammates and the need for total focus—whether climbing a rock face, skiing a steep chute, or paddling a whitewater canyon—brings a crystalline awareness of the world around one at the same time a kind of obliteration of the separateness of the self. . . . One hears it again and again: that at moments like this the participant feels acutely alive.[30]

Adventure is also about personal discoveries and unknown outcomes. "Does anyone have an interest in not knowing what lies around the next bend? Maybe not, but I know for a fact that my most memorable experiences were the ones I hadn't planned," writes Jim Stiles.[31]

In his book *The Wilderness Within*, outdoor educator Daniel L. Dustin writes, "Maybe that's what is so special about wilderness to me. It offers the kind of challenge that is increasingly rare, a paring down to the essentials, a stripping away of the civilized veneer that shields us all so that we can once again experience the basic nature of our existence."[32] Thanks to Henry David Thoreau, John Muir, Aldo Leopold, Robert Marshall, and others, we've saved important American wilderness landscapes, but what we do on those public lands, and our attitudes while using them, needs further clarification.

This anthology is about adrenaline-laced adventure opportunities, but it's also about humility. We don't conquer mountains. We climb them. My concern is how outdoor programs and personal experiences interface with public lands, particularly in the Southwest. Here students need to understand the environmental consequences of backcountry travel, as well as the magnificent cultural and historical contexts embedded in the landscape: Ancestral Puebloan cliff dwellings, cowboy camps, mining sites, and contemporary Native American sacred places. A new outdoor ethic, based on Kurt Hahn's belief in curiosity and compassion, must include ecological literacy, an understanding of natural resource management and human impacts, and environmental stewardship. That's what this book is about, with its focus on personal perspectives from the Southwest. Within the long, broad history of American conservation and the environmental movement that emerged in the 1960s, we have the historic evolution of national parks, public land policies, and quality wilderness experiences, which must include silence, solitude, and darkness—away from the noise, clamor, and lights of civilization.

It's time to put our "outdoor ego" back in a box and think more clearly about where we are and the lessons we need to learn from nature. We also have to know how to cooperate with each other in difficult, dangerous, and remote settings—and we need to give back. Now in her early 80s, Ginger Harmon, a climber, canyoneer, and trekking guide in Nepal, believes we need "wilderness tithing."[33] We need outdoor adventures, but we also need to do what we can for the public land playgrounds we use in the American West. One of her contributions has been to help create Great Old Broads for Wilderness, a true environmental advocacy group. Some organizations concern themselves only with access, but other issues are more important, especially if we are to have a sustainable Southwest and human-powered recreational opportunities into the next century. What will you do to share Kurt Hahn's compassion? Bertrand Russell wrote, "A life without adventure is likely to be unsatisfying, but a life in which adventure is allowed to take whatever form it will is sure to be short."[34] Have adventures, but have a long life, and along the way, practice wilderness tithing.

It only seems right to end with an eloquent admonition from that old curmudgeon Ed Abbey. So here is his advice to frustrated environmentalists and a credo for my classes:

> Do not burn yourselves out. Be as I am—a reluctant enthusiast . . . a part-time crusader, a half-hearted fanatic. Save the other half of yourselves for pleasure and adventure. It is not enough to fight for the West; it is even more important to enjoy it. While you can. While it is still here. So get out there and hunt and fish and mess around with your friends, ramble out yonder and explore the forests, encounter the griz, climb the mountains, bag the peaks, breathe deep of that yet sweet and lucid air, sit quietly for awhile and contemplate the precious stillness, that lovely mysterious and awesome space. Enjoy yourselves, keep your brain in your head and your head firmly attached to the body, the body active, and alive, and I promise you this much: I promise you this one sweet victory over our enemies, over those deskbound men with their hearts in a safe deposit box and their eyes hypnotized by desk calculators. I promise you this: You will outlive the bastards.[35]

Notes

1. Nancy Hellmich, "Childhood Obesity Levels Off—but a Third Still at Risky Weight," *USA Today*, May 28, 2008. The story clarifies, "About 32% of children and teens ages 2 to 19—about 23 million—were either overweight or obese in 2003–2006 compared with 29% in 1999. The increase is not considered statistically significant." A National Public Radio story on May 28, 2008, confirmed that a third of American children are overweight or obese and that childhood obesity has tripled since the 1980s. Also see Marc Ambinder, "Beating Obesity," *The Atlantic*, May 2010.

2. David Petersen, *Writing Naturally* (Boulder, CO: Johnson Books, 2001), xxii.

3. Reed Karaim, "A New Era in Play," *USA Weekend*, Dec. 14–16, 2007.

4. Gary Paul Nabhan and Stephen Trimble, *Geography of Childhood: Why Children Need Wild Places* (Boston: Beacon, 1994), 9.

5. Ibid., 22.

6. For discussions on this important phrase and Thoreau's thinking, see Jack Turner, "In Wildness Is the Preservation of the World," in *The Abstract Wild* (Tucson: University of Arizona

Writer and wilderness proponent Edward Abbey inspired a generation of
eco-advocates in the Southwest while protesting many forms of technology
including television and ATVs. Here he proudly poses with a television he has
just shot. Photo © Suzi Moore McGregor.

Press, 1996), and Ed Abbey, "Down the River with Henry Thoreau," in *Down the River* (New York: E. P. Dutton, 1982).

7. Nabhan and Trimble, *Geography of Childhood,* 85.

8. For a new biography of Carhart and the importance of Trapper's Lake to his thinking, see Tom Wolf, *Arthur Carhart: Wilderness Prophet* (Boulder: University Press of Colorado, 2008).

9. Nabhan and Trimble, *Geography of Childhood,* 74–75. For an additional perspective, see Ken Wright, *The Monkeywrench Dad* (Durango, CO: Raven's Eye Press, 2008).

10. Richard Louv, *Last Child in the Woods*: *Saving Our Children from Nature-Deficit Disorder* (New York: Algonquin Books of Chapel Hill / Workman Publishing, 2005), 102–103. Also see S. M. Kroger and D. Du Nann Winter, *The Psychology of Environmental Problems,* 3rd ed. (New York: Psychology Press, 2010), esp. chapter 9, "Developmental Psychology: Growing Healthy Children in Nature."

11. Louv, *Last Child,* 34. Also see Michael Hodgson, *Wilderness with Children: A Parent's Guide to Fun Family Outings* (Harrisburg, PA: Stackpole Books, 1992), and Thomas Power Loweay, *Camping Therapy* (Springfield, IL: Charles C. Thomas, 1974). Loweay discusses the advantages of groups and families working together to "plan and prepare their own meals, explore and use their natural surroundings, and plan and carry out their own program of adventurous living."

12. Will Sands, "Vanishing Visitors: Forest Service Reports Drop in Recreation," *Durango Telegraph,* July 30, 2009, 9.

13. Nicholas Kristof, "American Kids Are Raised Far Too Disconnected from Nature," *Durango Herald,* August 4, 2009. Also see George W. Burns, "The Path of Happiness: Integrating Nature into Therapy for Couples and Families," in Linda Buzzell and Craig Chalquist, eds., *Ecotherapy: Healing with Nature in Mind* (San Francisco: Sierra Club Books, 2009).

14. Nancy Lofholm, "Into the Wild," *Denver Post,* May 9, 2008, 1A, 21A. For a contrary view on why "Americans are retreating from outdoor activities," see "Out of the Wilderness," *The Economist,* July 10, 2008.

15. Quoted in Lofholm, "Into the Wild."

16. Peter Fish, "Old Faithful versus the Xbox," *Sunset Magazine,* July 2007, 104–106. Additional data can be found in Oliver R. W. Pergams and Patricia A. Zaradic, "Is Love of Nature in the US Becoming Love of Electronic Media?" *Journal of Environmental Management* 80, no. 4 (September 2006): 387–93. The authors report that Americans now spend 327 hours annually playing video games, surfing the Web, or watching movies.

17. Jeff Osgood, "Forget the Park; Where's the Remote Control?" Writers on the Range, *Durango Herald,* March 13, 2008. The phrase "videophilia" originated in Pergams and Zaradic, "Love of Nature," where they propose that infatuation with video games and the Internet is responsible for a "per-capita decline in nature recreation." They also examined visitation rates on public lands and published their results in the *Proceedings of the National Academies of Science.* See "Online Trend," *Nature Conservancy,* Autumn 2008, 15.

18. Louv, *Last Child,* 2.

19. Froma Harrop, "Treating Nature-Deficit Disorder May Prevent Other Ailments," *Durango Herald,* February 15, 2008. Also see Theodore Roszak, Mary E. Gomes, and Allen D. Kanner, eds., *Ecopsychology: Restoring the Earth, Healing the Mind* (San Francisco: Sierra Club Books, 1995), and Robert Greenway, "The Wilderness Experience as Therapy: We've Been Here Before," in Buzzell and Chalquist, *Ecotherapy.*

20. Ed Abbey, *The Journey Home* (New York: Plume, 1991), 229. Abbey's writing was always tongue-in-cheek. But to really understand environmental education and its value, see Larry

Crenshaw, ed., *The Outward Bound Earth Book* (Asheville: North Carolina Outward Bound School, 1990); Ruth Baetz, *Wild Communion: Experiencing Peace in Nature* (Center City, MN: Hazelden Press, 1997); and Michael K. Stone and Zenobia Barlow, eds., *Ecological Literacy: Educating Our Children for a Sustainable World* (San Francisco: Sierra Club Books and Collective Heritage Institute, 2005).

21. Dr. Seuss, *Oh, the Places You'll Go* (New York: Random House, 1990).

22. Zion Adventure Company Activity guide, 2007–2008. See www.zionadventures.com.

23. Both quotations from Jeff Renner, *Lightning Strikes: Staying Safe under Stormy Skies* (Seattle: Mountaineers Books, 2002), 24.

24. Lance Waring, "A San Juan Mountains Mini-Epic: Scouting the Hardrock 100," *Adventure Guide to the Western San Juans*, Summer 2008, 13.

25. Kurt Hahn quoted in Prouty et al., *Adventure Education*, 3.

26. Interview with BLM recreation specialist Arden Anderson at the May 2008 meeting of the Southwest Colorado BLM Resources Advisory Council. Uncited quotations come from articles and essays previously published by the editor. See the bibliography for Andrew Gulliford's prior publications.

27. Arden Anderson, recreation and wilderness specialist, Gunnison, Colorado Field Office, Bureau of Land Management, interview with author, November 12, 2008.

28. Dick Prouty, Jane Panicucci, and Rufus Collinson, eds., *Adventure Education: Theory and Applications* (Champaign, IL: Human Kinetics and Project Adventure, 2007), 12. Also see Simon Priest and Michael A. Gass, *Effective Leadership in Adventure Programming* (Champaign, IL: Human Kinetics, 1997).

29. Cited in Jim Stiles, *Brave New West: Morphing Moab at the Speed of Greed* (Tucson: University of Arizona Press, 2007), 173. Stiles claims that "a quick Google search for 'Moab' and 'Adventure' provided almost 480,000 hits" (176).

30. Peter Stark, *Last Breath: The Limits of Adventure* (New York: Ballantine Books, 2001), 3, 8.

31. Stiles, *Brave New West*, 92.

32. Daniel L. Dustin, *The Wilderness Within: Reflections on Leisure and Life*, 2nd ed. (Champaign, IL: Sagamore, 1999), 12.

33. "Wilderness tithing" was a phrase used by Ginger Harmon on a multiday southeastern Utah Ancestral Puebloan field trip donated and led by the author as a fund-raiser for Great Old Broads for Wilderness. For more on Ginger Harmon, see Chip Ward, *Canaries on the Rim* (New York: Capra Press, 2000).

34. Bertrand Russell quoted in Renner, *Lightning Strikes*, 15.

35. In the late 1970s Abbey made these remarks in a speech to a meeting of environmental activists, but exactly where is unclear—some sources states it was a Vail, Colorado, conference in 1976 and others that it was at a meeting in Missoula, Montana, in 1978. Cited in Steve Van Matre and Bill Weiler, eds., *The Earth Speaks* (Greenville, WV: Institute for Earth Education, 1983), 57.

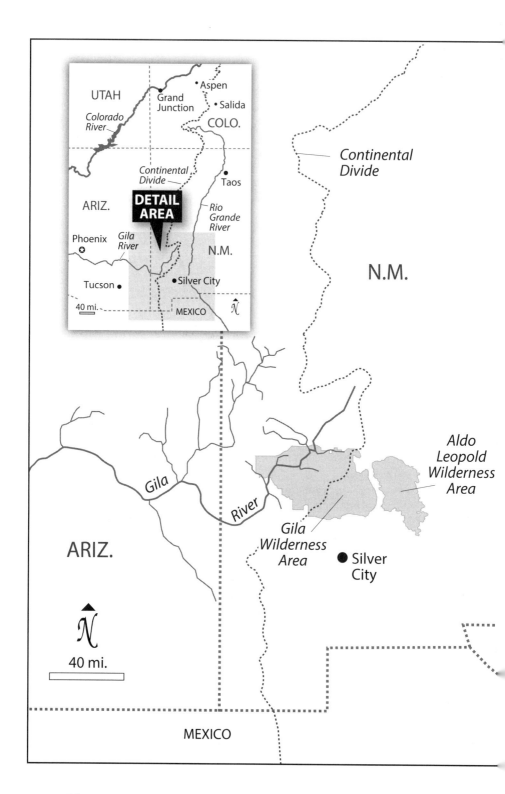

UTAH

COLO.

ARIZ.

N.M.

Colorado River

Grand Junction

• Aspen

• Salida

Continental Divide

Taos

Rio Grande River

DETAIL AREA

Phoenix

Gila River

Tucson •

• Silver City

40 mi.

MEXICO

$\hat{N}$

Continental Divide

N.M.

Aldo Leopold Wilderness Area

Gila

River

Gila Wilderness Area

● Silver City

ARIZ.

$\hat{N}$

40 mi.

MEXICO

CHAPTER 1

Why We Need Wilderness

All America lies at the end of the wilderness road, and our past is not a dead past, but still lives in us. Our forefathers had civilization inside themselves, the wild outside. We live in the civilization they created, but within us the wilderness still lingers. What they dreamed, we live, and what they lived, we dream.
—T. K. Whipple, *Study Out the Land*

We must save wilderness because in saving it we will be saving part of ourselves. We have been shaped by the wild lands we have lived in, and because they are still part of our landscape, they continue to live within us. When they are gone, many of the fundamental values that created America will also vanish. Take away the wilderness and the American Dream will lose its authenticity.

—Karen Shepherd, *Testimony*

I'm never as happy as when I step across a wilderness boundary and into a federally protected wilderness. Once across that magical border I know that I will encounter only hikers or horseback riders, because motorized vehicles are not allowed in wilderness. Behind me is a world of machines and roads, and ahead a landscape as wild as can be found in America, a place where natural systems and processes are allowed to maintain nature's balance.

With my first step into wilderness, everything changes. I have heightened awareness of my responsibility for my own actions, and that includes taking the risks that could result in a medical emergency. Ed Abbey wrote in *Desert Solitaire*, "There are special hazards in traveling alone. Your chances of dying in case of sickness or accident are much improved, simply because there is no one around to go for help."[1] In *The Practice of the Wild*, Gary Snyder defines wilderness as "a place of danger and difficulty: where you take your own chances, depend on your own skills, and do not count on rescue." "The wilderness can be a ferocious teacher," he adds, "rapidly stripping down the inexperienced or the careless. It is easy to make the mistake that will bring one to an extremity."[2] But without risk, there is little to no reward, and little revelation.

Leo McAvoy writes, "Adventure programs use wilderness areas because of the opportunities there to have participants experience the beauty and grandeur of nature, and also because of the risk, challenge and opportunity for self-sufficiency that the wilderness provides." To further that opportunity, on federal lands he has suggested creating "rescue-free wilderness areas" where visitors "could experience the self-growth that comes from the challenge of testing themselves and taking full responsibility for their actions."[3] Not a bad idea, and Abbey agrees. In describing Grand Canyon in *Down the River*, Abbey wrote, "Let each person who enters the Canyon, whether on foot, on mule, or by boat, clearly understand that some risk is involved, some rather elementary and fundamental risk and that nothing can guarantee your safety but your own common sense. Nor even that. Nothing should be guaranteed. Nothing can be."[4]

It's exhilarating to be in a canyon or on a forest trail free from the technological tedium of the twenty-first century. I'm back to basics with what's on my feet, in my pack, and in my heart. A destination in mind, the trek begins and I've found through the years that the heaviest thing I carry into wilderness isn't in my backpack but in my head. The cluttered thoughts and ideas I carry, that mental baggage, can take a day or two on the trail to unload. "Simplicity in all things is the secret of the wilderness and one of its most valuable lessons," wrote Sigurd Olson. "It is what we leave behind that is important. I think the matter of simplicity goes further than just food, equipment and unnecessary gadgets; it goes into the matter of thoughts and objectives as well." He adds, "When in the wilds, we must not carry our problems with us or the joy is lost."[5]

I've enjoyed hikes in many Colorado wilderness areas, such as the Uncompahgre, Weminuche, Lizard Head, Flat Tops, Lost Creek, West Elk, and Maroon Bells. In New Mexico, the Bisti, the Gila, and the Aldo Leopold wildernesses are others I have trekked, but there are so many more places to go, so many more hikes to make. I cut my teeth in the Gila, the place where I began to understand the true meaning and value of wilderness and the valiant fight of conservationists to protect large landscapes for their natural processes but also as part of our American tradition. Huck Finn said it best: "I reckon I got to light out for the territory ahead of the rest, because Aunt Sally she's going to adopt me and sivilize me, and I can't stand it. I been there before."

We need wild spaces. We need them to get away from the stress and strain of daily life, the rampant consumerism, the crowded cityscapes—for their refuge. Alone in their vastness, we need to unzip from our sleeping bags and breathe freely of the morning air, waking only to the soft twitter of birds and the glow of sunrise streaming through aspen groves and creeping over canyon walls.

What I love about wilderness is that it's egalitarian. One's possessions, one's career, one's concerns all are left behind at the trailhead. In wilderness you are who you are and what you carry—both in and out. The concept of "Leave No Trace" has real meaning as both an ethic and a way of traveling through natural landscapes. For students of adventure education and outdoor leadership disciplines who aspire to become guides, one reward is that wilderness will be home away from home. Canoeist Sigurd Olson wrote, "We all have a pronounced streak of the primitive set deep within us, an instinctive longing that compels us to leave the confines of civilization and bury ourselves periodically in the most inaccessible spots we can penetrate . . . and what makes guiding the sport of kings is just that. No two men react alike. There is always variety in human nature."[7]

As Americans, our ancestors pioneered a wild continent that was not ruled by kings. In learning to survive in the new land, the challenges of nature to body and mind built within us the essential values that make us uniquely American. Our American character was hewn out of wilderness. The frontier spirit that drove us westward, into and across vast wilderness, forged within us American pride. Keeping wildlands and wilderness areas intact, and learning to use them well, is thus the essence of American patriotism.

$\sim$

Many of my students hike into wilderness to learn about the landscapes but also to learn more about themselves, their friends, and their future. Wilderness tests them, not just their endurance but also their understandings of community, sharing, and getting along with others, whether the climate is hot, wet, or cold, or if the trail is difficult. It's about discovering in their own way that possessions can clutter our lives and that inside each of us are inner reserves and strengths. Wilderness teaches us not about comfort but about new levels of understanding both within and without ourselves—life lessons, learned in the outdoors.

As Craig Childs explains in *Soul of Nowhere*, "It wasn't heroism or glory that I hoped to find in these places. Rather, it was the odor of rain, it was encountering animals alone in the heavy woods, or the moment in trackless country when I realize that I am utterly lost and suddenly there is no separation between me and the ground beneath me."[8] Dave Foreman agrees. He writes in *Confessions of an Eco-Warrior*, "Our passion comes from our connection to the Earth and it is only through direct interaction with the wilderness that we can unite our minds and our bodies with the land, realizing that there is no separation."[9]

I once had a student say in class, "Everybody talks about finding themselves in wilderness, but can't I find myself in the mall?" Dead silence spread through the classroom. I spoke up, saying, "Well, yes, you could find yourself in a mall, I guess, but malls are about buying things, about material possessions that come and go. What we're discussing are enduring values, the sorts of strengths and insights that can't be bought but have to be earned." That didn't resonate with her, not right away. But later, after a weekend river trip, she seemed to be getting it. She had enjoyed floating the San Juan River, sleeping in a tent, and paddling a duckie solo. In class, she wore less make-up.

I knew I had succeeded when at the end of the semester another student stated that the course had clarified her goals to spend an extended amount of time outdoors. She became inspired, wanting to rearrange her life to hike the entire Pacific Crest Trail. As her professor, I felt deep gratification because I knew she'd take into the field what she learned in our classroom.

And what are those lessons we learn with the heart and lungs as well as the head? They're personal truths about self-reliance, independence, and risk taking. About going to the edge and challenging oneself not just in miles hiked but also in sleeping under the stars. We learn to let our body adjust to natural rhythms rather than the routines of work and home. Wilderness teachings can and should be deeply personal, but there are also skills to learn such as orienteering, low-impact camping, map reading, water filtration, and meal planning. Students of wildlands should also know the sweep of American environmental history and how we came to have our precious public lands in the first place.

~

One of the greatest advocates for wildlands was my hero, President Theodore Roosevelt. He worked to set aside more public land than any other president before or since. Though born in New York City, in a brownstone in Manhattan, he came to truly know the West. He wrote, "The man should have youth and strength who seeks adventure in the wide, waste spaces of the earth, in the marshes, and among the vast mountain masses, in the northern forests, amid the steaming jungles of the tropics, or on the desert of sand or of snow. He must long greatly for the lonely winds that blow across the wilderness, and for sunrise and sunset over the rim of the empty world."[10]

When we hike in the Southwest we owe a great debt to the early conservationists who understood the need to protect wildland as part of the American experience. For in many ways our American character was not forged in cities or on factory floors but in contact with vast landscapes. "In the wilderness you learned what was authentic and what was not," writes Kim Heacox in *The Only Kayak*. "To 'boot up' meant to put on your boots, not turn on your computer. A mouse was still a mouse. Hardware was your kayak. . . . You slept on the ground until you were uncomfortable in a bed," explained the former backcountry ranger. "You breathed fresh air until you suffocated indoors. You laughed from your toes and flew in your dreams. . . . You found that you could sing the high notes; that true wealth was not a matter of adding to your possessions but of subtracting from the sum of your desires. You understood what was enough and what was too much and why the prophets went into the desert alone."[11]

~

The concept of wilderness comes to us as part of the Judeo-Christian tradition. The word appears 246 times in the Old Testament of the Bible. Originally considered to be desert, worthless and without water, wilderness also came to be considered a place for savage men and wild beasts. Later it became a place for solitude and sanctuary.[12] A century and a half after the first farms had been planted along the Atlantic seaboard, Henry David Thoreau proclaimed in his 1851 lecture at the Lyceum in Concord, Massachusetts, "In wildness is the preservation of the world." But for a nation bent upon industrialization, his was a voice crying in the wilderness.

In 1862 Congress passed the Homestead Act, which realized Thomas Jefferson's dream of providing for a nation of yeoman farmers. Any head of household, male or female, could travel west and claim 160 acres if they lived on the land for five years and cultivated it, but the West had neither the water nor deep enough soils to sustain agriculture without irrigation. Thousands of farms failed.

As the nation began to perceive the loss of its public land and wild landscapes, a conservation movement emerged in the 1890s. Rather than carving up the entire public domain for private ownership, the government assigned some of the land to the U.S. Forest Service, led by the talented Gifford Pinchot, while other lands were designated national parks. What was left became, in 1946, the domain of the Bureau of Land Management. A broader-based environmental movement in the 1960s focused on the value of not just public land for human uses but also ecosystems.

Wallace Stegner argued eloquently that the American character had been "hewed" out of wilderness, and the frontier spirit had spurred the creation

of America. Stegner called wilderness "the geography of hope," and in his famous 1960 wilderness letter he wrote, "Something will have gone out of us as
a people if we ever let the remaining wilderness be destroyed."[13]

In 1964 Congress passed the Wilderness Act, one of the significant pieces
of legislation coming from the "Conservation Congress" and President Lyn-
don B. Johnson. At last America had come to terms with its vanishing wild
landscapes and sought to preserve small vestiges of the continent as it had
existed when the colonists arrived at Jamestown, Virginia, in 1607. But much
of the public estate that belongs to all Americans, including many thousands
of acres of federally protected wilderness areas, can be attributed to the pen of
President Theodore Roosevelt.

~

In our bedroom we have two photos of strangers. In one image, John Wesley Powell, the leader of the first documented exploration of Grand Canyon,
points off into the distance while a Ute friend looks on. I am inspired by Powell and his courageous 1869 boat trip into Grand Canyon. In the second photo,
President Teddy Roosevelt sits in the morning sunlight in a cabin south of
Silt, Colorado. In his lap sits a small terrier—an aspiring hunting dog—and
the president seems engrossed in an open book, light glinting off his spec-
tacles. He wears dusty lace-up boots and an old hunting jacket. His work shirt
is buttoned to the collar, and his pants are frayed.

This photo of Roosevelt never fails to draw my attention. Here was an east-
erner from Manhattan, a Harvard graduate, a member of the New York leg-
islature and later governor of New York, who would come to know the West
unlike any other American president. Teddy hunted across the United States,
and he set aside millions of acres of public lands. He protected 234 million
acres or a whopping 8,400 acres a day during his presidency. Other presidents
have presidential libraries and museums, but Roosevelt has none. His real legacy is the millions of acres of western lands he saved from overzealous timber
barons and cattle ranchers. I wish more presidents hunted deer and elk, read
books in Colorado log cabins, and had frayed pants cuffs and dusty boots.[14]

~

The concept of wilderness, an idea with deep meaning for thinkers such as
Aldo Leopold, Bob Marshall, and Olaus and Mardy Murie, finally coalesced
into federal legislation with congressional passage of the Wilderness Act of
1964. Later, federal agencies inventoried select roadless areas as Wilderness
Study Areas (WSAs). They currently sit in legal limbo awaiting definitive decisions from Congress, who has not acted on many of those lands in years.

But we need additional wilderness for many reasons. John Muir, that talented Scotsman who founded the Sierra Club, wrote in 1898, "Thousands of nerve-shaken, overly civilized people are beginning to find out that going to the mountains is going home, and that mountain parks and reservations are useful not only as fountains of timber and irrigating rivers, but as fountains of life."[15] Today, we do not have enough acreage designated as wilderness. The percentage of wilderness in the continental United States actually equals the percentage of the country's land that is paved, or about 4 percent.[16] As a nation we have yet to adopt a land ethic, though Aldo Leopold recommended it in *A Sand County Almanac*, his conservation classic.

Wilderness areas protect watersheds. They act as refuges and sanctuaries for humans and as genetic banks for flora and fauna. Federal wilderness areas also inspire strong statements and political passions. Edward Abbey wrote in *Desert Solitaire*:

> Wilderness invokes nostalgia. . . . It means something lost and something still present, something remote and at the same time intimate, something buried in our blood and nerves and something beyond us and without limit. . . . But the love of wilderness is more than a hunger for what is always beyond reach; it is also an expression of loyalty to the earth, the earth which bore us and which sustains us, the only home we shall ever know, the only paradise we ever need— if only we had the eyes to see. . . . No, wilderness is not a luxury but a necessity of the human spirit, and as vital to our lives as water and good bread.[17]

In Stephen Trimble and Terry Tempest Williams's book *Testimony*, compiled in defense of the Southern Utah Red Rocks Wilderness Act, many authors wrote eloquently about our need for wild places. Rick Bass argued, "The unprotected wilderness of the West is one of our greatest strengths as a country. Another is our imagination, our tendency to think, rather than accept—to challenge, to ask why, and what if; to create, rather than to destroy. This questioning is a kind of wildness, a kind of strength, that many have said is peculiarly American. . . . We all know that what is rare is always valuable, and wilderness is our rarest and most imperiled resource of all."[18] As a case study in wilderness preservation, let's look at the Gila in southwestern New Mexico.

Geronimo, Aldo, Earth First! and the Gila Wilderness

One of the least visited and most pristine environments in the United States is in the mountains of southwest New Mexico. Here, where the Continental Divide stretches north from Mexico, a spectacular country of canyons, hot springs, mesas, and mountaintops survives as an ecological island: the 800,000-acre Gila and Aldo Leopold Wildernesses, within the 3.3-million-acre Gila National Forest. From Sonoran desert and exotic cactus below to spruce, fir, and aspen above, rising to 10,892 feet at the summit of Whitewater Baldy, the Gila River region is rich in biological and cultural diversity. But it is the wilderness itself that survives as a truly unique ecosystem, though it is less whole without the return of its wolves.[19]

Set aside in 1924 as the nation's first designated wilderness, the Gila Wilderness is both a physical reality and the culmination of a distinctly American ideal to preserve a landscape and an environment in its original unspoiled condition. Yet even the Gila is not as natural as it seems.

Aldo Leopold's Plea for a Primitive Gila

In 1909, after graduating from Yale with a degree in forestry, young Aldo Leopold headed to the mountains of Arizona and New Mexico. He hunted, fished, and surveyed on horseback this forest domain. All the while, he observed where man's encroachments had resulted in the land getting portioned into mere vestiges of what had been a true wilderness. He called these patches "tag-ends" of the once boundless American landscape and "fly-specks on the map." An erudite philosopher and creative thinker who helped invent the concepts of wild ecology and wildlife management, he wanted all Americans to experience the awesome space that had overwhelmed the first western pioneers.[20]

Deeply appreciative of the clear vistas, sparkling days, and rich opportunities for solitude in the Gila, Leopold proposed setting aside acres of the Gila National Forest as a wilderness or primitive area. In explaining the proposal to the Gila management team, he said the area would be "a continuous stretch of country preserved in its natural state, open to lawful hunting and fishing, big enough to absorb a two weeks' pack trip, and kept devoid of roads, artificial trails, cottages, or other works of man."[21]

To say that Aldo Leopold was ahead of his time is an understatement. He understood the human need for solitude and sanctuary. He argued eloquently, "Of what avail are forty freedoms without a blank spot on the map?" In 1924 Leopold's wilderness proposal was accepted by the Southwestern regional office of the U.S. Forest Service, but there was still no federal law protecting roadless areas, nor was there a congressionally accepted philosophy on wilderness and the value of wild landscapes.

Although three-quarters of a million acres had been set aside as a "primitive area," white settlement had already occurred deep within it along the forks of the Gila River. Until the Great Depression of the 1930s collapsed farm prices, Anglo settlers and Hispanic farmers were earning a meager living in the Gila's isolated canyons and narrow river valleys. Gradually, the settlers drifted away, as had the prehistoric Mimbres Indians who had lived in the same valleys. The U.S. Forest Service had owned the mountainsides; now, thanks to unpaid property taxes, it gradually began to own the river bottoms.

Wilderness without Rules

In the mid-1920s the Forest Service drafted L20 regulations to keep primitive areas wild with regard to "environment, transportation, habitation, and subsistence." However, the "primitive" designation did not include protections for wildlife. The federal government continued to carry out its predator control policy of hiring bounty hunters to shoot mountain lions, grizzly bears, and wolves. In 1931 the last grizzly in the Southwest wandered out of the Gila Wilderness and was shot to death by a rancher.

During the Depression the Civilian Conservation Corps (CCC) came to the Gila National Forest and the Gila Wilderness. The CCC workers built some of the first trails into the wilderness, making steps toward Leopold's vision of two-week pack trips. They also created the first campgrounds outside the wilderness. These campgrounds, merely level places in the woods without facilities, were built adjacent to the new North Star Road, completed in 1934, which connected the Mimbres River Valley with Beaverhead Ranger Station. The North Star Road split the Gila Wilderness into two wildernesses, with the Gila to the west and the Aldo Leopold Wilderness to the east. This dirt and gravel road, known today as New Mexico 61 and the Outer Loop, bisected the wilderness to create access for fire control and extended into the northern part of the vast forest, "but with due regard to the preservation of wilderness values."

World War II brought an end to the CCC and to mining camps near the wilderness areas. Towns that supported them, such as Mogollon and Graham, began to wither. The end of World War II also resulted in a surplus of Jeeps. Because they were accessible to all Americans, it didn't take long for the use of the rugged four-wheel-drive vehicles to expose a flaw in the wisdom of Aldo Leopold's plan for a roadless wilderness area. The vast Gila National Forest,

Designated in 1924 as the first wilderness in the world big enough for a two-week-long horse-pack trip without crossing a road, the Gila Wilderness, carved out of the Gila National Forest, now includes the Aldo Leopold Wilderness on its east side. Photo by author.

home to elk, mule deer, mountain lions, javelina, and wild turkey, became a hunter's paradise. Hunters used Jeeps to make their own roads, and because no guidelines had been established for wilderness management, the Forest Service accessed wilderness using Jeeps, tractors, and even small airplanes. Though the Gila received protection in 1924, few rules or regulations existed for the wilderness, and no regulations restricted miners from building Jeep trails to their remote mining claims.

In 1952 the Southwestern regional forester suggested reducing the area of the wilderness to open Iron Creek Mesa to lumbering, prior to transferring the reserve to permanent wilderness status under the new U1 regulation. A full third of the wilderness was on the chopping block. Citizens of Silver City, New Mexico, balked and, in order to fight the plan, formed an unlikely coalition that included the Sierra Club, the American Legion, the Lions Club, the Chamber of Commerce, and sportsmen's organizations. The group succeeded, serving notice to the Forest Service that the Gila Wilderness should not be reduced in size. Then in 1964, with the passage of the Wilderness Act, national legislation set specific guidelines on wilderness use and created new challenges for the Gila's district rangers.

New Rules Create New Challenges

The 1964 Wilderness Act proclaimed that "a wilderness . . . is hereby recognized as an area where the earth and community of life are untrammeled by man, where man himself is a visitor who does not remain." But humans had been living in the Gila Wilderness for the last thousand years. With the act's passage, zealous Forest Service employees burned historic corrals and log cabins that may have endured as valuable cultural resources.

While the Forest Service sought to return the wilderness to its natural state, angry four-wheelers sought to test the new law. A four-wheel-drive club from El Paso, Texas, arrived to drive their Jeeps—against federal policy—through the Gila River and into the wilderness. Stalled in unexpected floodwaters, the Jeeps were abandoned. Later, when club members petitioned the Forest Service to permit them to retrieve their stuck vehicles and drive them out of the wilderness, the Gila responded with a steadfast "no." The Jeep owners had to pay dearly to have mules pull out their vehicles because no motor or engine can be turned on in a federal wilderness area.

Despite the demise of grizzly bears and Mexican wolves, plant and animal life has thrived in the Gila. Raptors abound, including a variety of hawks, eagles, and ubiquitous turkey vultures. The Mexican spotted owl lives quietly among thick stands of ponderosa pine. Biological survey teams have sought out the reclusive owls as part of a baseline study of their nocturnal travels. The Gila River Valley is home to several endangered plant species, such as grama grass cactus, grayish-white giant hyssop, Mogollon whitlowgrass, the threadleaf false carrot, and the Pinos Altos flamethrower.[22] The Sonoran mountain kingsnake and the narrow-headed garter snake are among the endangered animal species in the Gila, which is the only known home for the rare spikedace and loach minnows.

The native Gila trout are also endangered, thanks to the addition of other trout species. During the Great Depression of the 1930s, New Mexico's Fish and Game Department introduced game trout into the Gila's streams. But the rainbows, cutthroats, and German browns came to dominate the natural habitat of the native Gila trout, which led to its listing as an endangered species half a century later. After years of complicated fish studies and a careful reintroduction plan, biologists thought they might have been looking at a success story. At one point they even considered downgrading the Gila trout from endangered status to threatened. But all the efforts and a carefully executed reintroduction program were washed away in a week of heavy rains coming on the heels of massive forest fires in the late 1980s. The silt and dirt washing into remote Gila streams clogged the gills of the rare fish, and they suffocated and died. Dazed and disappointed but undaunted, teams of biologists are now in the midst of new programs to reintroduce the Gila trout into other creeks.

Cattle grazing has been one of the most controversial issues of contemporary wilderness management. A congressional compromise in the 1964 Wilderness Act authorizes cattle in wilderness areas where grazing had been historically practiced.[23]

It is believed that the presence of cattle in wilderness has altered natural vegetation patterns and destroyed communities of plants. Alligator juniper trees are now in close proximity to ponderosa pine habitat. The piñon-juniper advance, known by range and conservation staff as the PJ invasion, may be the result of extensive overgrazing in the Gila. Since the early 1900s the number and range of grassy meadows in the Gila has been reduced, along with the ability of native grasses to sustain wildfires because the grasses are no longer naturally thick and luxuriant. They've been cropped short by grazing.

Also, a dearth of grasses and a misguided Forest Service fire suppression policy begun in 1910 have changed the natural cycles of fire and plant rebirth.[24] Fires burn as part of the natural process in the Gila ecosystem, but excessive dry years and large out-of-control fires have altered fire ecology in the Gila. "Prescribed burns" may be possible to mitigate the problem, but the fuel wood cycle is off balance. In some areas of the Gila there is too much downed wood from previous fires to let a fire burn "naturally" without creating a catastrophe.

The Mogollon Rim, which stretches a wild, ragged line across Arizona to New Mexico, has one of the highest incidents of lightning-caused fires in the world. On one June night in 1989, more than three thousand lightning strikes hit the Gila National Forest. By dawn ninety fires were ablaze. Because wilderness regulations restrict mechanized equipment, access to the Mogollon's steep canyons and uneven terrain presents a challenge to firefighters and smokejumpers. But they have adjusted. Fire management techniques now include rappelling out of helicopters into fire zones.

By the 1970s visitor usage of the Gila Wilderness had increased dramatically, and in one case, massively. In 1977 the Rainbow Family of Living Light applied for a permit to hold its annual Rainbow Gathering in the East Fork of the Gila. The permit was granted, despite the probability of severe resource damage, and five thousand members of the Rainbow family converged to camp in a quiet side canyon of the Gila. A baby was born during the event and died there. He and countless Native Americans, early settlers, and former U.S. Cavalry soldiers are buried in unmarked graves in the wilderness.

Other Human Impacts on the Gila Wilderness

Pothunters saw the Gila as a land of opportunity for robbing graves. On benches above the Gila's flood line, the prehistoric Mimbres Indians had left their dead buried in the floor of their homes with elaborate black-and-white painted bowls placed over the heads of the deceased. Eight hundred years later, grave robbers routinely dug up Mimbres burial sites for bowls worth thousands of dollars on the black market. Despite stiff penalties and fines, pothunting and illegal excavation of Indian sites continue in the Gila and other southwestern wilderness settings.[25]

In the 1980s new backpacking ethics and strict regulations concerning the number of people and animals in a group helped preserve the pristine values of wilderness. The demographic of backpacking couples and families who enjoyed wilderness areas year round had given way to organized education groups who come primarily during summer months and practice low-impact camping. These groups also cleaned up after themselves, following the ethic of leaving a place better than it was found.

In the 1990s students from Texas A&M University hiked the trail to White Water Baldy and scattered more than fifty fire rings at abandoned camp sites. These efforts heal land from the scars of thoughtless campers who "civilized" a site by building fire pits and lean-tos, stacking firewood, and letting horses paw the ground near trees. It's just one good sign that wilderness continues to offer peace and healing for all well-intentioned souls who venture in and practice the new etiquette of keeping the landscape free of anything manmade.

Celebrating Wilderness: The Twenty-fifth Anniversary

The author of the Wilderness Act, Howard Zahniser, dedicated his life to the passage of the act, but he died before it was signed into law. He rewrote it sixty-six times before Congress gave it final approval. The passage of the act bolstered protections at the Gila, too, which had been an administratively designated wilderness since 1924. Forest supervisors held authority to alter its protections, but the federal law mandated that all land managers abide by the will of the people as expressed through Congress.

In 1989 the Gila National Forest celebrated the twenty-fifth anniversary of the Wilderness Act. Perhaps the most important aspect of the celebration was a five-day trail ride deep into the Gila Wilderness by retired foresters. It had been their job to implement the specific charges laid out in the Wilderness Act. Despite being older and stiff in the joints, these dauntless seniors swung into the saddle to see what lessons the area could provide after a quarter century of mandated wilderness management.

Former Gila forest supervisor Richard C. Johnson expressed dismay with the piñon-juniper invasion and widespread outbreak of giardia in all the streams and tributaries. "Used to be," he said, "that I could get off my horse and cup my hands and drink out of any stream I wanted to, but no more." Today's backpackers must carry water filters. Though the swift-flowing Gila River and other creeks look fresh and sparkling, the protozoa *Giardia lamblia* is in every stream, and giardia in one's intestines can cause painful diarrhea and dehydration. But the natural landscape still has a powerful attraction for today's visitors, just as it did for the Apaches who came to the Gila by the mid-seventeenth century.

The nation's first wilderness is doing quite well decades after its designation. Campsites are cleaner and backpackers are more "ecologically house-broken"—they know how to use biodegradable soaps and gas stoves instead of green-branch campfires. Though the Gila Wilderness is a physical entity with legal boundaries and regulations governing its use, it carries on the idea from which it began. It's wild. Ponderosa pines soar on either side of the wilderness boundary; no fence separates the Gila National Forest from the Gila Wilderness.

The Gila River flows freely through the wilderness. I can imagine Aldo Leopold standing along its banks nearly a century ago, receiving inspiration from its wild flow. Leopold argued that we need wilderness because it "is the raw material out of which man has hammered the artifact called civilization."[26] What better place to explore and to practice wilderness skills than in the Gila? Inspiration to Aldo Leopold, home to the nation's first wilderness, the Gila remains an ecological island in a sea of pollution and change.

⁓

We need wilderness. Wallace Stegner wrote, "We simply need that wild country available to us, even if we never do more than drive to its edge and look in."[27] We need wilderness for plants and animals, but also because wilderness and access to wildlands helped shape our American character. Who we are as a nation, and who we became as a people, is a direct result of our intimate contact with wild landscapes. Hiking and camping on wildlands, "where man is a visitor who does not remain," to quote from the 1964 Wilderness Act, is one of America's most enduring traditions.

We need to venture into wilderness because we need to understand wild-lands in order to become better stewards of our environment. Aldo Leopold understood that. He wrote in *A Sand County Almanac,* "We abuse land because we regard it as a commodity belonging to us. When we see land as a community to which we belong, we may begin to use it with love and respect."[28]

In an age of prolific ATV and off-road vehicle use, Jim Stiles notes, "Wilderness as a spiritual and moral issue has been replaced by economic and political considerations, from both ends of the ideological spectrum. Passion is what we need right now." He adds, "We need the acetylene torch that Abbey lit beneath us thirty-five years ago, not the scented candles and reams of lawsuits and injunctions that have replaced the fire and Ed."[29] We need wilderness as a sanctuary, as a place of retreat, where we can withdraw, refresh, and possibly even start over again if civilization crumbles. Edward Abbey saw wilderness as a vital place for plants, animals, and patriots—a hideaway for Americans seeking refuge from political madness. Perhaps that's an extreme view, but as the poet Robinson Jeffers wrote,

> But for my children, I would have them keep their distance
>   From the thickening center; corruption
> Never has been compulsory, when the cities lie
>   At the monster's feet there are left the mountains.[30]

Environmental organizations have successfully lobbied Congress to designate more than 100 million acres of federally protected wilderness—only 4 percent of the nation's land. The fight continues. But if we've been winning on acreage, we're losing on visitation. The number of recreational visits to national parks in 2010 was lower than in 1987, and there were 35 percent more backcountry campers in 1979. *New York Times* columnist Nicholas D. Kristof argues, "Conservationists need to expand their focus from preserving nature to encouraging the public to experience it. The only way to protect wilderness in the long run is to build a constituency for it, to grow the number of people who revel in camping under the stars."[31]

Wilderness visits provide solitude, if that's what you're looking for, but they are also about building community, sharing the outdoors, and learning significant lessons about the ties that bind us—to the land and to each other. What follows are essays about the value of wilderness in the American Southwest, personal accounts of experiencing nature and why, as Ed Abbey wrote, "The wilderness idea needs no defense—only more defenders."[32]

Notes

1. Ed Abbey, *Desert Solitaire* (New York: Ballantine Books, 1968, 1988), 226.
2. Gary Snyder, *The Practice of the Wild* (Berkeley: Counterpoint Press, 1990), 11, 25. Also see Mathew G. McDonald, Stephen Wearing, and Jess Ponting, "The Nature of Peak Experience in Wilderness," *Humanistic Psychologist* 37, no. 4 (2009).

3. Leo H. McAvoy has advocated for "Rescue-Free Wilderness Areas" in a variety of publications and conference presentations. See McAvoy and Daniel L. Dustin, "The Right to Risk in Wilderness," *Journal of Forestry* 79, no. 3 (1981), and McAvoy, *The Wilderness Within* (San Diego: San Diego State University Press, 1993). For another perspective, see Charles Farabee, *Death, Daring, and Disaster: Search and Rescue in the National Parks* (Lanham, MD: Taylor Trade Publishing, 2005).

4. Edward Abbey, *Down the River* (New York: Dutton, 1982), 147.

5. Sigurd Olson, *Reflections from the North Country* (New York: Alfred A. Knopf, 1976), cited in Joseph Cornell, *Listening to Nature* (Nevada City, CA: Dawn Publications, 1987), 27.

6. Mark Twain, *The Adventures of Huckleberry Finn* (New York: Bantam Books, 1981), 281.

7. Quoted in David Backes, ed., *Sigurd Olson: The Meaning of Wilderness: Essential Articles and Speeches* (Minneapolis: University of Minnesota Press, 2001), 6.

8. Craig Childs, *Soul of Nowhere* (Boston: Little, Brown, 2002), 24.

9. Dave Foreman, *Confessions of an Eco-Warrior* (New York: Harmony Press), 6.

10. Theodore Roosevelt, *Wilderness Writings* (Salt Lake City: Gibbs Smith, 1986), 31. Also see Paul Russell Cutright, *Theodore Roosevelt: The Making of a Conservationist* (Urbana: University of Illinois Press, 1985), and H. Paul Jeffers, *Roosevelt the Explorer* (New York: Rowman & Littlefield, 2003).

11. Kim Heacox, *The Only Kayak: A Journey into the Heart of Alaska* (Guilford, CT: Lyons Press, 2006), 30.

12. The Jews wandered forty years in the wilderness, and Jesus spent forty days in the wilderness seeking revelations. A modern account of a wilderness hike with spiritual intent is David Douglas, *Wilderness Sojourn: Notes in the Desert Silence* (San Francisco: Harper & Row, 1987).

13. Wallace Stegner, "Wilderness letter," December 3, 1960, reprinted in *Marking the Sparrow's Fall: The Making of the American West,* ed. Page Stegner (New York: Henry Holt, 1998), 111.

14. See Andrew Gulliford, "Where's Teddy When You Need Him?" *High Country News*, October 13, 2003, and Gulliford, ed., *Preserving Western History* (Albuquerque: University of New Mexico Press, 2005), 235–38.

15. Muir quote from *Our National Parks* cited in Doug Scott, *The Enduring Wilderness* (Golden, CO: Fulcrum, 2004), 21.

16. Scott, *Enduring Wilderness*, 2.

17. Abbey, *Desert Solitaire* (New York: Ballantine Books, 1988), 189–90, 192.

18. Rick Bass in Stephen Trimble and Terry Tempest Williams, eds., *Testimony: Writers of the West Speak on Behalf of Utah Wilderness* (Minneapolis, MN: Milkweed Press, 1996), 36–38.

19. For the failure of Mexican wolf reintroduction, see articles in *High Country News* and Michael J. Robinson, *Predatory Bureaucracy: The Extermination of Wolves and the Transformation of the West* (Boulder: University Press of Colorado, 2005).

20. For an earlier version of this essay, see Andrew Gulliford, "Geronimo, Aldo, and Earth First! All Basked in the Nation's First Wilderness Area," *Trilogy Magazine,* May/June 1991. Also see Christopher J. Huggard, "America's First Wilderness Area," in Christopher J. Huggard and Arthur R. Gomez, eds., *Forests under Fire* (Tucson: University of Arizona Press, 2001).

21. Part of the issue with wilderness is "wilderness management," as odd as that sounds. See John C. Hendee, George H. Stankey, and Robert C. Lucas, *Wilderness Management*, USDA Forest Service, Publication No. 1365, Oct. 1978, USDA Forest Service, Wilderness Management School Notebook, May 21–25, 1990, Gila Wilderness/Willow Creek, New Mexico; and J. Baird Callicott and Michael P. Nelson, *The Great New Wilderness Debate* (Athens: University of Georgia Press, 1998). Also see Sarah Pohl, "Technology and the Wilderness Experience," *Environmental Ethics* 28, no. 2 (2006).

22. Gulliford, "Geronimo, Aldo, and Earth First!"

23. For an excellent overview of the 1964 Wilderness Act and the compromises involved in its legislative passage, see Steven C. Schulte, "Where Man Is a Visitor: The Wilderness Act as a Case Study in Public History," in Gulliford, *Preserving Western History*. For an overview of wilderness perspectives in America, the classic reference is Roderick Nash, *Wilderness and the American Mind*, 4th ed. (New Haven, CT: Yale University Press, 2001). Also see Michael Lewis, ed., *American Wilderness: A New History* (New York: Oxford University Press, 2007).

24. To understand the impacts of the 1910 fire and subsequent fire suppression, see Timothy Egan, *The Big Burn: Teddy Roosevelt and the Fire That Saved America* (Boston: Houghton Mifflin, 2009).

25. See Andrew Gulliford, *Sacred Objects and Sacred Places: Preserving Tribal Traditions* (Boulder: University Press of Colorado, 2000).

26. Aldo Leopold, *A Sand County Almanac* (New York: Ballantine Books, 1970), 264.

27. Stegner, "Wilderness letter."

28. Leopold, *A Sand County Almanac*, 237–64.

29. Jim Stiles, *Brave New West* (Tucson: University of Arizona Press, 2007), 6. For information on off-road vehicle abuse see the Government Accounting Office report on OHV use on public lands mentioned in Susan Montoya Bryan, "Off-highway Vehicle Use Increasing on Public Lands," *Durango Herald*, July 31, 2009, and George Wuerthner, ed., *Thrillcraft: The Environmental Consequences of Motorized Recreation* (White River Junction, VT: Chelsea Green Publishing/Foundation for Deep Ecology, 2007).

30. Robinson Jeffers, "Shine, Perishing Republic," in Louis Untermeyer, ed., *Modern American and Modern British Poetry* (Harcourt, Brace & World, 1955), 194.

31. Nicholas D. Kristof, "Recognize America's Greatest Asset—Its Public Lands," *Durango Herald*, September 13, 2011.

32. Abbey, *Down the River*, 120. Also see Andrew Gulliford, "Ed Abbey: One of the Last Things He Ever Wrote," *Inside/Outside Southwest*, August/September 2006.

Wilderness and Intellectual Humility: Aldo Leopold

Terry Tempest Williams

I can remember exactly where and when I read *A Sand County Almanac* for the first time: Dinosaur National Monument, June 1974. My mother and grandmother were talking comfortably in their lawn chairs, my brothers were playing on the banks of the Green River, and I was sitting beneath the shade of a generous cottonwood tree. Aldo Leopold spoke to me. With a yellow marker in hand, I underlined the words: "Wilderness is the raw material out of which man has hammered the artifact called civilization. . . . The rich diversity of the world's cultures reflects a corresponding diversity in the wilds that gave them birth." And a few pages later: "The ability to see the cultural value of wilderness boils down, in the last analysis, to a question of intellectual humility."

I closed the book having finished the last two chapters, "Wilderness" and "The Land Ethic." I wanted desperately to talk to someone about these ideas, but I kept quiet and tucked Leopold into my small denim pack, not realizing what the personal impact of that paperback copy with a flaming orange sunset over wetlands would be.

I was eighteen years old.

Almost twenty-five years later, I can honestly say it is Aldo Leopold's voice I continue to hear whenever I put pen to paper in the name of wildness.

The essays of *A Sand County Almanac* were published in 1949. They were revolutionary then and they are revolutionary now. Leopold's words have helped to create the spine of the American wilderness movement.

The vision of Aldo Leopold manifested itself on the land in 1924, when he convinced the National Forest Service to designate twelve hundred square miles within the Gila National Forest as a wilderness area forty years before the Wilderness Act of 1964 was signed into law.

Aldo Leopold perceived the value of wilderness to society long before it was part of the public discourse. He has inspired us to see that in the richness of biological systems all heartbeats are held as one unified pulse in a diversified world. He understood this as a scientist and land manager, and he understood it as a natural philosopher.

When Leopold writes about "the community concept" and states, "All ethics so far evolved rest upon a single premise: that the individual is a member of a community of interdependent parts," he instinctively elevates the discussion above what one typically hears in wilderness debates—that the land is meant for our use at our discretion, that profit dictates public lands policy.

And when he takes this notion of interdependent parts one step further and proposes that we "[enlarge] the boundaries of community to include soils, waters, plants, and animals, or collectively: the land," he challenges us. In a politically conservative and theocratic state like Utah, this kind of thinking can be grounds for heresy, evidence of paganism, the preemptive strike before black helicopters fueled by the United Nations move in to defend public lands from the people who live there.

But what I love most about Aldo Leopold is that he keeps moving through his lines of natural logic with an eloquent rigor and persistence. Finally, he ruptures our complacency and asks simply, "Do we not already sing our love for and obligation to the land of the free and home of the brave? Yes, but just what and whom do we love?" Wilderness.

In the American West, there may not be a more explosive, divisive, and threatening word.

Wilderness.

The place of a mind where slickrock canyons hold a state of grace for eons whether or not human beings make an appearance.

Wilderness.

The mind of a place where perfection is found through the evolutionary path of a mountain lion slinking down the remote ridges of the Kaiparowits Plateau like melted butter.

Roadless.

　Ruthless.

　　Wilderness.

"A resource which can shrink but not grow." Shrink but not grow. Aldo Leopold's words echo throughout the wildlands of North America.

Why is this so difficult for us to understand? Why as we enter the twenty-first century do we continue to find the notion of wilderness so controversial?

Perhaps Leopold would say wilderness is becoming more difficult to understand because there is less and less wilderness to be found.

Wilderness is threatening as a word because it is now threatened as a place. How can we begin to understand what wilderness is if we have never experienced a place that is unaltered and unagitated by our own species? How are we to believe in the perfect mind of the natural world if we have not seen it, touched it, felt it, or found our own sense of proportion in the presence of wildness? If there is a greatness to the American spirit, a spirit aligned with freedom and faith, surely its origin is to be found in the expanse of landscapes that have nurtured us: coastlines, woodlands, wetlands, prairies, mountains, and deserts.

"Shall we now exterminate this thing that made us American?" writes Leopold. The extinction of places we love may not come as a result of global warming or a meteor heading in our direction, but as a result of our lack of imagination. We have forgotten what wildness means, that it exists, here, now. If we continue to cut, whittle, and wager it away, stone by stone, tree by tree, we will have turned our backs on bears, wolves, cougars, mountain goats and mountain sheep, martens, fishers, wolverines, caribou, musk oxen, otters, sea lions, manatees, alligators, Gila monsters, blue-collared lizards, roadrunners, song sparrows, milkweeds and monarchs, spring peepers and fireflies and the myriad other creatures with whom we share this continent.

When Leopold speaks of silphium, sedge, leatherleaf, tamarack, buffalo, bluebirds, cranes, geese, deer, and wolves, he recognizes them as family. His language of landscape evokes an intimacy born of experience. And his experience in nature, on the land, allowed him to test his ideas, to change and grow, to alter his opinions, and to form new ones. We are the beneficiaries of his own philosophical evolution.

In 1925, Aldo Leopold wrote in "A Plea for Wilderness Hunting Grounds,"

> There are some of us who challenge the prevalent assumption that Christian civility is to be measured wholly by the roar of industry, and the assumption that the destruction of the wild places is the objective of civilization, rather than merely a means providing it with a livelihood. Our remnants of wilderness will yield bigger values to the nation's character and health than they will to its pocketbook, and to destroy them will be to admit that the latter are the only values that interest us.

Brave words to an America that was on the verge of the dust bowl, the Depression, and the postwar buildup. Leopold held the long view in a country spoiled by its abundance of natural resources and whose native gifts were viewed as infinite. He took his stand in the wilderness.

We continue to learn from Leopold that wilderness is not simply an idea, an abstraction, a cultural construct devised to mirror our own broken nature. It is home to all that is wild, "blank places on a map" that illustrate human restraint.

There are those within the academy who have recently criticized "the wilderness idea" as a holdover from our colonial past, a remnant of Calvinist tradition that separates human beings from the natural world and ignores concerns of indigenous people. They suggest that wilderness advocates are deceiving themselves, that they are merely holding on to a piece of America's past, that they are devoted to an illusory and "static past," that they are apt to "adopt too high a standard for what counts as 'natural.' " These scholars see themselves as ones who "have inherited the wilderness idea" and are responding as "Euro-American men" within a "cultural legacy ... patriarchal Western civilization in its current postcolonial, globally hegemonic form."

I hardly know what that means.

If wilderness is a "human construct," how do we take it out of the abstract, and into the real? How do we begin to extend our notion of community to include all life-forms so that these political boundaries will no longer be necessary? How can that which nurtures evolution, synonymous with adaptation and change, be considered static? Whom do we trust in matters of compassion and reverence for life?

I believe that considerations of wilderness as an idea and wilderness as a place must begin with conscience.

I come back to Leopold's notion of "intellectual humility." We are not alone on this planet, even though our behavior at times suggests otherwise. Our minds are meaningless in the face of one perfect avalanche or flash flood or forest fire. Our desires are put to rest when we surrender to a grizzly bear, a rattlesnake, or goshawk defending its nest. To step aside is an act of submission, to turn back an act of admission, that other beings can and will take precedence when we meet them on their own wild terms. The manic pace of our modern lives can be brought into balance by simply giving in to the silence of the desert, the pounding of a Pacific surf, the darkness and brilliance of a night sky far away from a city.

Wilderness is a place of humility.

Humility is a place of wilderness.

Aldo Leopold understood these things. He stepped aside for other wild hearts beating in the Gila National Forest, in the Boundary Waters, in the wetlands of the sand counties, and in the fields of his own home, where he must have puffed his pipe in admiration as the sandhill cranes circled over him at the Shack.

When contemplating Aldo Leopold and wilderness, I believe we need both intellectual humility and political courage in the days ahead. We need humility to say we may not know enough to intrude on these wildlands with our desire for more timber, more coal, more housing and development. We may have to bow our heads and admit our intellectual ceiling may be too low to accommodate the vast expanse above and inside the Grand Canyon. We will need political courage to say we need to honor and protect all the wilderness that is left on this continent to balance all the wilderness we have destroyed; we need wilderness for the health of our communities and for the health of the communities we acknowledge to exist beyond our own species. We will need both intellectual humility and political courage to say, for example, we made a mistake when we dammed Hetch Hetchy and Glen Canyon; let us take down with humility what we once built with pride. Political courage means caring enough to explain what is perceived at the time as madness and staying with an idea long enough, being rooted in a place deep enough, and telling the story widely enough to those who will listen, until it is recognized as wisdom—wisdom reflected back to society through the rejuvenation and well-being of the next generation who can still find wild country to walk in.

This is wilderness—the tenacious grip of beauty.

In 1974, as a self-absorbed teenager, I was unaware of the efforts made twenty years earlier on my behalf by people like Howard Zahniser, Margaret and Olaus Murie, David Brower, and Wallace Stegner to keep the Green River free-flowing through Split Mountain in Dinosaur National Monument.

Nor did I realize as I sat on its banks that summer day that it had ever been threatened by the Bureau of Reclamation's efforts to dam Dinosaur as part of the Colorado River Basin Storage Project. It was a history no one told us in Utah's public schools. All I knew was that I felt safe enough here to continue dreaming about wildness. Aldo Leopold was tutoring me sentence by sentence in how ecological principles are intrinsically woven into an ethical framework of being. Historians have said the defeat of the dam on the Green River in Dinosaur National Monument marked the coming of age of the conservation movement. Conservationists of my generation were born under this covenant. The preservation and protection of wilderness became part of our sacred responsibility, a responsibility that each generation will carry.

In order to protect that which is original in the land and in ourselves, we can draw on the intellectual humility, the political courage, the wisdom and strength of character of Aldo Leopold. His lifelong stance toward wilderness inspires us not to compromise out of expediency and social pressure in considering lifestyles over life zones. Rather, as Leopold states in *The River of the Mother of God,* "In this headlong stampede for speed and ciphers we are crushing the last remnants of something that ought to be preserved for the spiritual and physical welfare of future Americans, even at the cost of acquiring a few less millions of wealth or population in the long run. Something that has helped build the race for such innumerable centuries that we may logically suppose it will help preserve it in the centuries to come."

The Gila Wilderness—Southwestern New Mexico

Howard L. Smith

One of life's great joys is a long trip deep into wilderness, disengaged from the intrusions of technology and immersed in a spellbinding natural environment. Every person should have an opportunity to make such a journey at least once in life. Not only would this build a deep appreciation for the wild, but it would also help others to form a better understanding of the value underlying community. Cut off from the comforts of home; freed from the computer, television, radio, or CD player; unable to shower or bathe easily; reliant on others to assist in the fundamental tasks of purifying water, gathering firewood, and preparing meals; and bound together in the interests of safety, you find that it does not take very long to forge strong bonds with fellow travelers. You develop a sense of community, an almost forgotten thread of American society. . . .

The longer the trip, the deeper into the wilderness, and the more hazardous the situations, the more rewarding are the gifts of community. Wildness, therefore, can contribute to deeply enriched relations among people and a sense of togetherness that is being lost in urban society. A culture that loves the earth will benefit from and build upon community among those who treasure the wild.

∼

Coming from Flagstaff, where highs typically reached the low to mid-seventies and the high thirties at night, I was most concerned about being too hot. Consequently, my pack was definitely on the light side.

The first stop would be in Phoenix at the Holubar store. Once famous for high-quality, featherweight equipment, Holubar made a very lightweight sleeping bag rated to plus fifteen degrees. The bag had 60 percent fill on top to maximize its efficiency. Looking at the long trek in the Gila with substantially higher temperatures than Flagstaff, I thought it only natural to shed pounds. The sales associate had disappointing news, indicating that they did not have any fifteen-degree bags with a right-hand zipper in stock. This was definitely not good, but also not a problem. I had brought an "elephant's foot" as a backup. An elephant's foot is a bivouac bag that covers approximately two-thirds of your body. A thick down coat would complement the bag and ensure sound sleep. . . .

Into the Gila (Day One)

At the Gila Hot Springs, the road levels out and curves dissipate. The valley, though at nearly six thousand feet, is generally quite warm. We stopped at the visitor center to fill our water bottles and inquire about trail conditions. It was still too early in the season for much news to have made its way back to the deskbound rangers. Most people just leave after finishing a major hike and do not share information about trail conditions with them, so the news they receive is often spotty and not up to date. From the scant reports, it appeared that the Gila was experiencing normal water flows—an important consideration since much of the trail was across, in, and around the river.

Parking at the road's end by the cliff dwellings, we shouldered our packs. The temperature was in the mid-eighties, and thus quite comfortable on the shady sections of the trail. I was especially glad for this warmth in view of my sleeping equipment. A trail sign indicated the way to several of our destinations—Hell's Hole was a bit over twelve miles and White Creek sixteen miles from our vehicle. Although we did not have any specific target for each day, we did plan on averaging about six miles per day in order to complete the loop. There, among the box elder, locust, New Mexico privet, and scrawny pine, we took our first steps on the sandy trail.

Soon the shade ran out and we were walking through the sandy canyon bottom. Hills rose gradually on each side, sparsely covered in juniper, some piñon, and some pine. Deciduous trees spread out along the canyon bottom, the most prevalent being varieties of cottonwoods. Tall, elderly pines occasionally shaded the trail. We could not see the West Fork, but we knew it was over to the west. A channel of stagnant water bound in rocky shores suggested that this canyon carried heavy water at other times of the year. The bed of the pond was covered in green scum, verdant with life living in the shallows.

Within half an hour we came to our first obstacle—a crossing of the West Fork. Since everyone was wearing leather hiking boots, we stopped and took them off to ford the river. This was a time-consuming task with a dubious reward of having to cross the stream barefooted. The cobblestones were just small enough and covered in scum to present real problems for maintaining balance, but the cool water felt refreshing. The minute we exited a problem arose—with our feet covered in sand, we then had to put socks and boots back on. Now, on the west bank of the river, we climbed up among a scattered pine forest only to drop down to several river crossings in succession.

It was at this point that two important decisions were made by consensus. First, it was clear that it would take several years to walk the route if we kept removing our boots. Thus, we simply waded through the water in our boots—there were so many crossings that our boots and socks would remain perpetually wet. Boots offered better traction and protection from the rough stones than bare feet. Second, Bill, Claus, and Tim decided that a walking stick would provide balance in crossing the river. Tim began recording our crossings by cutting a notch in his staff.

At three miles we came to an Indian ruin across the West Fork. Up off the river about forty feet were the remains of what appeared to be a granary. One wall was still quite evident with tree posts used in building the structure in place. Off to the right was another depression, almost a cave, which had fallen into decay. Remnants had apparently slid down into the West Fork. Ancient people had trod these very paths, and we wondered whether they saw this wilderness as a comforting home.

Continuing through twisting canyons with walls rising steeply above us, tentlike rock formations came into view. The colors were mesmerizing, with red and ivory formations abounding. We were entering the fabled canyons of the Gila, where access out of the maze can be quite difficult, especially at points where the walls rise more than a thousand feet above the valley. Close inspection suggested avenues that provide a way out if needed, but then there was the problem of traversing the broad mesas.

Looking for a campsite in the dark canyon with a mild cooling wind, we found a suitable level site that had been used by others in the past. Bare ground and fire rings surrounded by logs are the common indicators of preferred campsites. Normally there are good reasons why others have camped in a specific spot before—level ground, availability of water and firewood, difficult terrain ahead that makes camping problematic.

There is a great amount of pleasure in finally realizing that you are at the end of the trail for the day. With an appealing campsite, your community begins to unfold. We set up our tents amid the brush and trees—enough privacy for each, yet closeness to build the bonds of friendship—and started a fire for cooking. This first night out was going to be extra special because our meal included filet mignon, baked potatoes, and salad. This was the last good meal we would see for a week.

Retiring early, I unfurled the elephant's foot and fluffed up the down coat. How would this high-tech combination work? An answer was forthcoming within an hour of settling into bed. I discovered that I was too hot, but that was comforting. Lying in bed, looking up through the mesh fabric of the little blue tent, 1 saw that the closeness of canyon walls and dense forest canopy obscured the stars despite almost total darkness and the crystal clarity of the air at six thousand feet.

Tent Rocks to Mountain Forest (Day Two)

The morning dawned fresh and bright, with a slight chill in the wind blowing down the canyon. Tim was first up and off to seek bird sightings. The rest of us assembled our packs after a quick breakfast. My staples for the next week would be hot chocolate, oatmeal, and breakfast bars. That sounds unappealing now, and it was unappealing then, but there was method to our madness. Our group was more interested in making miles than spending great effort on making breakfasts and lunches for which we were individually responsible. Dinner was a communal affair, with each person allotted two meals. Shared meals not only saved weight, but they also built camaraderie when replaying the events of the day—the highs and the lows along the trail.

After breakfast we headed up the West Fork, and at the first crossing Jim was able to navigate across a downed tree without getting his boots wet. He only delayed the inevitable. His bright red Kelty pack, with a faded yellow tent perched precariously atop it, swayed dangerously as he balanced on the beam. Bill followed gracefully without disaster. Claus and Tim just decided to get it over with and plowed through the water to the other side.

With twelve miles to go to White Creek, we cautiously walked, hopped, and jumped over and around rocks, tree limbs, and shrubs, exercising great caution owing to the urgent warnings of rangers. Rattlesnakes are prevalent in the Gila and must be given due respect. Consequently, much of the time our sight was focused on the ground looking for snakes, or at the rocky river bottom when crossing. Still, there were plenty of opportunities to appreciate the beauty of the Gila. In the narrow canyons pines tended to dominate with willows, box elders, locusts, and cottonwoods along the water's edge. Fords across the river seldom saw water rising above our knees, but the water was clear and cold.

The West Fork murmurs along as a constant companion providing the central character of the canyon. High on the steep rocky walls, especially in the shade of the canyon, spruce and fir dominate the cliffs. In spots tent rocks assemble and add a riot of red color to the scene. The river bottom itself is mostly cobblestone, and fish fled when we splashed across the current, creating a bow-wave with our legs. Waiting on the other bank of every ford is a path of sand that soon balls up on boots and momentarily makes walking difficult. Meanwhile, the air temperature varies depending on the shade and vegetation. Not surprisingly, the farther up the canyon we went, and the higher the walls soared, the cooler it became.

One hour after breaking camp, we happened upon another campsite with its signature fire ring and logs. Glancing over to the fire pit, Claus noticed that smoke was rising almost imperceptibly in the air. We walked over to put the fire dead out and were shocked to discover that the previous campers had thoroughly doused their fire. Somehow, the fire had progressively smoldered underground and was heading toward dense brush. We rapidly dug out around the smoldering fire, only to find that the ground was extremely hot to touch. If it had reached dense vegetation there would have been a serious conflagration.

Pail after pail of water was poured on the fire resulting in billowing clouds of ash, steam, and smoke, but potential disaster was averted. We certainly did not blame the previous campers. They had poured plenty of water on the coals and ashes, but it just was not enough. This experience touched us deeply and we left committed to stirring all ashes and seeking hidden hotspots in the duff around fire rings.

By lunch we had arrived at Hell's Hole—a canyon with magnificent walls and tent rocks. The West Fork lingers in this grotto with deep, clear pools that make fine swimming holes for the intrepid. It had been a pleasant walk to this point; however, the trail was seldom level. The ups and downs added together requiring a more strenuous effort than anticipated. Our full packs presented an additional challenge. Thus, at lunch we all were ready for a break. Nibbling away at our food supply, we jointly commented on the Gila as we found it versus the Gila as we thought we would find it. Tim remarked on how disappointed he was in the bird life. He expected to see many more birds and much greater variety.

Beyond Hell's Hole the trail wove through a wonderfully quiet forest of tall ponderosa pines. After wallowing through sand and river, the soft tread caressed our feet. A balsamy fragrance and rich scent of pitch swept over us as we continued to gain elevation. Now a little more than six hundred feet higher than when we first started, the forest and vegetation were changing significantly. Shrubs and deciduous trees were definitely not leafed out and the forest possessed that stark look so typical in winter. As we crossed the West Fork at Pine Flat, the stream had diminished considerably since first stepping out on the trail. Formerly thirty feet wide at crossings, the river had narrowed to less than twenty feet across. The water was still crystalline clear with enticing pools, but its character was markedly different than down by the cliff dwellings. It was becoming a mountain stream rather than a canyon stream.

Jumping across the river to convenient rocks with the top-heavy pack swaying dangerously behind, I paused to look up at the sky. A clear turquoise had faded, and in its place was a white hazy overcast. There appeared to be no threat of rain, but the sun was obscured and the temperature was dropping without the intensity of sunny rays that had sought us out in the open stretches of the canyon. Even fewer bird sightings were occurring as we climbed up to White Creek Flat at seven thousand feet, our camp for the night.

On reaching the campsite our group went into action again. I went off in search of firewood and had to go a considerable distance to find even modest pieces of dry wood. Coming back with a meager load cupped in my arms, I looked up to see two tents already erect and a haggard-looking crew stretching their sore muscles. My first thought was, "What's wrong with this picture?" Jim had put on his trusty red vest. Tim was in a powder-blue down parka. Bill and Claus had on their dark mountain shell parkas. It then dawned on me that there was a discernible coolness in the air. What a difference a thousand feet can make in the mountains.

Jim, Claus, and Bill went off to fish, I set up my tent, and Tim chased birds. Above camp was a broad tranquil pond impounded by a beaver. The house made of weathered sticks was well sited near the eastern edge of the pond, but still far from shore and predators. Thirty- to forty-foot pines of modest girth flanked the West Fork. Tomorrow the trail would lead us up on Cub Mesa toward Turkeyfeather Pass, but for the moment we enjoyed the fruits of a long day and our mutual effort to negotiate the wilderness.

Trout that Jim, Bill, and Claus had caught supplemented dinner. Although you cannot deny how good trout taste after being pulled fresh from the stream, they do take a lot of effort to eat. These were not plump trout steaks that offered a lot of meat per bite. I spent more time picking bones out than seemed worthwhile—still hungry, I went looking for extra helpings of the macaroni and cheese. Given the meager breakfasts and lunches in my pack, I had a different expectation about dinner, envisioning a grand meal that filled you up—a woods person's meal. Instead, the portions were way too slim, and five hungry men were competing for extra servings. We went to bed hungry.

This combination of a modest dinner, gain in elevation, and the increasing cold of the high plateau and frigid air dropping down off 10,770-foot Mogollon Baldy Peak made for a very long night. I was hungry going to bed, and the situation was certainly not going to change during the night. Consequently, sleep eluded me because I was cold and uncomfortable. The skimpy sleeping bag and down coat were insufficient to keep me warm. While not in danger of becoming hypothermic, I was just uncomfortable enough to remain awake.

Sleepwalking with Friends (Day Three)

When morning arrived I felt completely exhausted, and the rush to down a meager breakfast did not help matters. Per camp custom, we boiled water and ate quickly in order to be on our way. I was dragging from the beginning, and my friends could tell that something was wrong. At one point or another along the trail that morning they would chat with me when walking or at a rest stop, offering their sympathies. I might be miserable, but at least I knew that others were looking out for me. . . .

Turkeyfeather Pass is beautiful parkland of open meadow and spacious, towering ponderosa pine trees. Spruce and fir are spread throughout the taller ponderosas and rich green grass carpeted the ground beneath the pines. This is the Gila at its best. Judging by the limited undergrowth beneath the trees, this area does not receive much moisture. By now the day had mellowed and the pass provided the perfect opportunity to relax and enjoy the sun. It simply felt good to be warm again, and we sat in the sun soaking up its radiance. At 8,250 feet, the pass marked the high point of the trip.

The trail dropped down for another two miles toward Cooper Canyon where we found an idyllic camp among the spruce and confluence of Cooper Canyon and Iron Creek. An entire afternoon was still ahead of us so out came the fishing poles to catch diminutive and elusive trout in this creek. After fishing we stripped down for a bath in the icy waters of Iron Creek. It was cold but refreshing, and we romped like children until Jim brought out his camera and started taking pictures of the frolic. There were a lot of full moons on the rise. Over a lingering dinner, Jim and Claus raised the issue about helping me catch up on sleep. Their concern was well received, although I stood there in a rather numb state, unable to enjoy the soft grandeur of the Gila. The group decided that I should sleep with Bill in his tent and Jim would switch to mine. They expected that I would sleep much better with increased warmth in the tent thanks to two people sharing the narrow confines. This was a gracious idea on my friends' part, but Bill snored up a storm, and although warm, I could not fall to sleep until well after midnight. But it was definitely much better being warm and sleepless than cold.

Cold Turkey(s) (Day Four)

The following day we headed east across a shoulder of the Jerky Mountains to the Middle Fork of the Gila River. We were all in a good mood, and the relatively level stroll offered fine views of the newly green oak-covered slopes of the Jerky Mountains and various canyons running east from their shoulders. Tim was in the lead ahead of me when he rounded a copse of trees and stopped to look back at us impatiently, wanting us to move faster. There ahead of him was a group of seven turkeys that he had not noticed. Pointing at Tim, I cried, "Turkeys, turkeys." Tim just thought I was kidding him, calling him a turkey. Fortunately, he turned around at the last minute as the turkeys soared over the edge of Clayton Mesa down into the forested valley below Clayton Spring. Tim was so excited. This was a bird he had been repeatedly trying to add to his life list. We all felt a deep sense of happiness for Tim and his achievement.

From the edge of Clayton Mesa we looked east to the distant Black Range and the Middle Fork, and then south to the Middle Fork's meandering course. Hillsides of the mesas and canyons were covered in oak and pine. Vegetation was sparse with lots of rough rock formations in this very rugged country. You could see the distinct change in microclimates between the higher pine- and fir-covered mesa and the lower oak and pine canyons. We would lose another six hundred feet to the Middle Fork, putting us a thousand feet lower in elevation than last night. Judging by the dry scene unfolding before us, I was certain that the cold nights would be left behind—deep sleep seemed a guarantee.

I took one last look to the ridges of the Jerky Mountains and Mogollon Baldy Mountain before dropping down to the Middle Fork. The high parks were just greening up and the new foliage was a shocking green. Below on the Middle Fork, huge cottonwoods were just beginning to leaf out. We zigzagged down the switchbacks and selected a campsite amid the lofty cottonwoods and green grass. Life suddenly opened up.

By the campsite I found a dead bald eagle. It was difficult to determine the cause of death, but we suspected that it had been shot. It must have been a magnificent bird in life, given its size. We continued across the Middle Fork drawn by a fantastic clump of claret cactus. Its deep red flowers served as a beacon, and bees were drawn in battalions to them. It gradually dawned on us that we were now in much warmer territory and might expect to see rattle-snakes. Our alertness went up a notch or two.

After dinner I retired to my tent under the cottonwoods. I loved this site because it was open and much warmer. I just knew that my troubles were behind me. Of course, that's when the slight, but persistent, breeze began to blow down the canyon. It seemed like the breeze just cut through the flimsy nylon tent. Sleeping by myself because we thought that the elevation was sufficiently low to ensure a warm night, I experienced a third night of sleep deprivation.

In fact, it became so cold that I simply arose and started the campfire going, much to the distress of my companions. I kept a fire going all night long and was thankful for the lightening sky at dawn. In the course of those early morning hours, freezing my tail off, I had plenty of time to think about this go-light ethic. My pack was superlight; I simply did not have sufficient clothing, bedding, or food for the Gila at this time of year.

These days the go-light fascination and fast-packing are the rage. Who can quibble with the thought of taking less rather than more so long as you do not suffer as a consequence? Mark Jenkins has argued in *Outside* magazine that no one purposefully wants to be a pack mule. Even from my initial days of hiking I always thought that the image of people trudging along with enormous weight on their backs was not the way to go. I cannot think of a backpack trip on which weight was minimal enough that I actually enjoyed the experience and at the same time was totally comfortable throughout the trip. Admittedly, my pack on this Gila trip was quite light, but for what good purpose? . . .

The point is to be prudent. For the Gila this would mean very light clothing for the day, but a down parka or vest for night and the early morning. This should save weight over a fleece jacket and long-sleeve shirt. In the San Juan

Mountains of Colorado, you would increase the weight of your sleeping bag and add additional clothes, such as a light fleece jacket, that you would not take to the Gila. . . .

Friends to the Rescue (Day Five)

The following morning was a blur. We headed down the Middle Fork, and increasingly the canyon deepened. Trail and river meandered along, gradually losing elevation. Open, sparsely vegetated flats of Flying V Canyon and Swinging Cross Canyon were hot, dusty, and painful to cross. In my sleeplessness, I was having a tough time because the day's warmth made me want to stop for a nap. After more foot plodding, Clear Creek came into view and with it additional water volume that enlarged the Middle Fork. In my daze we came upon Trotter Cabin standing in an open meadow with sparse tall pines, cottonwoods, and junipers. Homesteaders must have been extremely hardy folk. My worries about sleeping at night would have made them laugh.

Trotter Cabin itself was returning to the earth. It had lost its roof and seemed to be stuck out in a fairly dry and unattractive setting. Rocky hills surrounding the cabin may have held the treasure that attracted this homestead, or this site was selected because it was the last large meadow before the canyon closed in. Over in the Middle Fork several blue herons gracefully stalked a pool for nourishment. There was wildness to the scene that tugged at your heart, even if you were too tired to enjoy it.

We finally reached a campsite deep in the canyon of the Middle Fork, and what a lovely scene it was. Tall ponderosa pines reached to the sky from the canyon's depth. They had a perfect climate of sun, shade, and water. The ground was covered in pine needles that added further to the ambiance. Down in the canyon, the harsh light of the upper Middle Fork was lost. Even in my drowsy state I felt blessed with the beauty of this wilderness canyon. Robust clumps of purple lupine blossomed victoriously in spots. Tentlike rock formations added colorful variety to the canyon depths. Shallow caves and intriguing depressions were everywhere. Things were looking up again.

After dinner my community of support came to the rescue. They informed me that I would sleep in the same tent with Claus in order to prevent me from being too cold. Bill loaned me an extra Pendleton shirt. Wow! What a night it was! I slept like the rocks that made up this canyon cathedral. In the morning Claus said, "You went to sleep the minute you put your head down. You started snoring right away and I was afraid to wake you seeing that you really needed the sleep." What a great sacrifice from a friend. At 6,500 feet, the night was much warmer than the previous night, even though we were sheltering in a canyon through which cold air was constantly flowing. Whatever the recipe, I slept the sleep of the dead. Morning was tremendous.

Encounter of the Fatal Kind (Day Six)

We continued to lose elevation as we approached an open area in the Middle Fork known as the Meadows. By now the canyon was enchanting, with the river twisting and turning constantly. Water levels had progressively risen as we dropped down the canyon. At twenty-five feet across, and with occasional deep pools, the river afforded us just plain fun. Here was the classic Gila. Walls towered above us for more than seven hundred feet. Tent rocks—pinnacles—provided a beauty that everyone could appreciate. A bright blue sky and blazing yellow sun were tempered by the constant interplay of shade in the bends. Tall pines provided coverage overhead. We continued to walk through refreshingly cool pools and crossings as the trail was often forced down into the middle of the canyon. . . .

I opened my pack to find two lunches left, and neither amounted to very much. A small aluminum can of meat and crackers was about it for this lunch. I was so hungry after finishing this meager meal that I broke into a Snickers bar as a way to fill up. Our only hope was that the fishermen would have better luck with trout. To this point the fishing efforts had produced dozens of the many suckers that scoured the stream's rocky bottom. Given their many bones and their penchant for bottom dwelling, we routinely threw these plentiful fish back.

The aluminum can crushed easily beneath my Vibram-soled boot. This was the sixth day out in the Gila Wilderness, and our remaining food was becoming not only sparse but also boring. Crackers that had begun the trip so fresh and neat in their plastic bags were now broken and crumbling due to the hot and dry conditions as well as having been loaded and reloaded within my pack. The chicken salad had tasted okay, but there just wasn't enough to satisfy that lingering hunger. I stuffed the trash bag back into my pack and tried to catch up with Bill. He was only fifty yards ahead of me, but he was moving fast, drawn by the progressive opening of the canyon. We were searching for the Meadows, which would be our camp for the night.

Bill turned around and paused for me to catch up. Ahead was the 113th river crossing of the trip. Every crossing had been notched onto his walking staff. By now it was just plunge ahead with rapid steps whenever the trail crossed the river. What a difference this was to the first tentative crossings where we carefully examined the riverbed, gauged the river's flow, and took precautions in the event of a slip.

Bill finished notching his walking staff as I bulldozed my way across the stream with a wake of rolling water pushed ahead by my passing. He took the lead and commented on the number of crossings and then looked back at my reaction just as he approached a gnarled white-gray cottonwood blocking the trail. He hesitated to lift his foot, and I almost walked into him. As he swung his foot over the log that terror of terrors sounded. Rattlesnake! The next few seconds passed in extreme slow motion as we tried to sort out the situation.

"Where is he? Where is he?" Bill cried. "It is over to your left. It is over to your left," I shouted. Bill was hung up on the log, having straddled it partially before coming to a stop. I tried to lift him and his pack back toward me. All we could hear was this loud sinister buzzing. Panic-stricken, his feet were flailing in the air, trying to get a purchase on anything that would get him away from the deadly rattle. After what seemed like hours, I finally pulled Bill back and we hastily retreated away from the log. Hearts were beating faster than we could believe. We were shaking—that was too close. Claus, Jim, and Tim came running up.

We retold the story over and over again with much laughter to ease the high anxiety. Then, we all walked over to take a look at the seven-foot-long monster as it slithered off toward the river. By the time the snake was well away from the log, we could see that it was more on the order of four feet rather than seven feet, but it was a thick specimen. The story was replayed once again from Bill's perspective and we all laughed. Then I said, "I'm glad that you took the lead after lunch, Bill. If it had been me with my longer stride, I would have walked right over the log onto the snake." The more I thought about it, the more I realized how close I had been to a potentially fatal encounter.

Tim notched yet another crossing while we stood silently, shifting our nervous feet, coming down from the event. Then, we slowly took off toward the Meadows. It was almost comical to see Tim and Claus in the lead with their walking staffs. They beat the grass and path furiously to detect snakes. After all these many days and nights in the Gila we had grown complacent about the prospect of running into a snake. Now we had encountered the reality that so many people have come to know in these canyons and mesas. . . .

Having arrived at the Meadows just after lunch, we had most of the afternoon to fish, hang out, and explore. In many ways it was nice to be out of the dark canyon again and in a more spacious setting. The troops returned with enough fish to supplement the dinner because with only one more communal dinner left, the pickings were getting pretty slim.

Since we had dropped to almost six thousand feet, the day was extremely warm, and I guessed that night would be warm as well. It was, and I slept alone in my tent that night—or at least tried to sleep. We all were kept awake by a vociferous whippoorwill. A bright moon was out, and the bird just would not shut up. At first the calls were a novelty brimming with life and melody, but then they became a nuisance. It was acknowledging its territory and interest in establishing a family.

The Draw Toward Home (Day Seven)

The next day we climbed a thousand feet out of the Meadows to Woodland Park. The views to the north were beautiful with a clear, cool morning. We could see almost the entire way up to Snow Lake where we had begun the trip down the Middle Fork. Over to the east was a great view of Indian Creek and its tortuous, rocky, and winding canyon. Views to the south and the Middle Fork were all pine and fir on the mountainsides. As we looked west the expansive views of Mogollon Baldy and the West Fork drainage were well in view.

We walked along Woodland Park mesa to the south and came upon a great bald spot that heightened our ability to gain distant views. Walking was very mellow, with tread that was softened by needles from the junipers, piñon, and smaller ponderosa. The way dropped down several hundred feet into Big Bear Canyon. Here the ponderosa were more prevalent, thanks to an intermittent stream. A profusion of wild flowers, especially lupine, spread among the trees.

We hoisted our puny packs after a rest break; they had virtually nothing in them by this point. Climbing out of Big Bear Canyon, we came to a trail junction. One route led to the visitor center and the other to the West Fork. We took the latter. . . . About two and a half miles from the trailhead, we sat down in the shade of some trees and crudely slaked our thirst. We had to go up the trail about a mile and a half to reach our first campsite. Sitting there sprawled out in the shade, our group had seen better days. Suddenly Jim suggested that it might be good to end our trip now rather than use another day in a site we had already enjoyed. Agreement was enthusiastic and unanimous.

There we sat for a few more minutes, a filthy bunch with scrapes on our legs and arms. Everyone's hair was greasy beyond belief. Collectively we were tired from the noisy whippoorwill night. The thought of cold drinks, hot showers, and substantial, tasty meals was overpowering. We were saturated with camping and quite honestly did not want another minute more. These are great moments to look back upon. You have had your fill of wildness and now want the best that civilization can offer. Home was all we could think about.

~

Looking back across the length of our trip in the Gila Wilderness, I recognize the presence of community. Woven throughout the fabric of our wilderness experience was this fundamental reality—we looked after each other and shared, deeply, in many ways that are otherwise lost in city settings. . . .

Our Gila adventure is more than a tale of community focusing on one person. It is about how the beauty, and challenges, of the wild brings people together. Community was present in those last nostalgic moments around a fading campfire, when the red-hot coals formed a beacon in the night. The presence of the wild; the warmth of the coals; the sights, sounds, and smells of the Gila; and the bonds of friendship among those who know and love the earth drew us together around that campfire. . . .

In sum, wilderness trips, particularly multiday adventures, inevitably provide a ripe medium for the growth of communities. Not too surprisingly, in wild areas people are drawn out of their cloistered urban lives. There is cause to celebrate the bounty of nature, and there are immediate, tangible reasons to band together for the common good. This bonding creates community, and from it a culture that deeply loves the earth.

Wilderness Values and Canyoneering in Southern Utah

From an oral history interview with Steve Allen,
author, eco-activist, and legendary canyoneer

If we are going to talk about Wilderness, first, let's define the word so we have a common language. This is Wilderness with a capital "W" instead of a lowercase "w." It is an important distinction. A small "w" wilderness is a vague and nearly meaningless word that can encompass a lot of definitions, from a backyard wilderness to the Alaskan wilderness. It is wilderness in the eye of the beholder. But a big "W" Wilderness as used here has a very specific definition provided by Congress in 1964 as a part of the Wilderness Act. That act defines Wilderness as "an area where the earth and its community of life are untrammeled by man, where man himself is a visitor who does not remain." It also states that the area has to be five thousand acres or larger, it must provide opportunities for primitive and unconfined recreation, and motorized and mechanical vehicles and tools (off-road vehicles [ORVs], bicycles, snowmobiles, chain saws, etc.) are not allowed.

I think it is hard for people who don't have a historic sense of this land to see what we have lost and what we are continuing to lose. They don't understand what the fight is all about. As far as the Wilderness debate goes in

Utah (and other states as well), Wilderness-eligible lands are disappearing at an alarming rate. As an example in the last twenty years, we've seen fully a quarter of the San Rafael Swell's million acres be removed from Wilderness consideration because of the destructive nightmare of ORVs. That is 250,000 precious acres that we'll never get back.

It is not only the San Rafael; huge areas of the East Tavaputs Plateau and the adjacent Book and Roan cliffs have fallen to oil and gas exploration and production. In San Juan County—the county that includes the archaeologically rich Cedar Mesa, Comb Ridge, Grand Gulch, and Mancos Mesa areas— the powers that be are allowing the illegal building of ORV roads and trails that are leading to the decimation of what in almost any other state, or country, would be considered national treasures.

On Mancos Mesa an oil company built an illegal road across Moqui Canyon in the 1970s. Instead of closing the road, the Bureau of Land Management (BLM)—the federal entity charged with overseeing the management of this land—has "officially" opened the road to motorized vehicles. This canyon, made famous by the archaeological expeditions of John Wetherill and Charles Bernheimer in the 1920s, is quickly turning into an ORV playground.

As of this writing, the BLM is considering opening an illegally constructed road in Recapture Canyon near the town of Blanding in San Juan County. The road did irreparable damage to archaeological sites, including an Ancestral Puebloan (Anasazi) burial ground. After the road construction was discovered, the BLM did close the road and the perpetrators went to court and were fined. But the BLM is now considering opening the road, certainly sending a message that illegal road construction on federal lands is okay in Utah. The list of areas we have lost and are losing goes on and on. And these aren't second-rate areas; they are some of the best.

I know that the other side says that it is the rich easterners who want to save the land for their own private recreation. There might be a tiny smidge of truth to that, but it is really much more. What scientists are now finding is that a lack of intact ecosystems often has downstream effects that we are just now finding out about. A good example can be found in the relationship between cattle grazing and ORV use in Utah and Arizona and water problems in Colorado. The cattle and ORVs have destroyed the microbiotic crust that essentially holds the desert soils together and prevents erosion. The frequent winter and spring winds now blow the loose sand onto Colorado's snowpack. Instead of the snow melting slowly, the sand covering makes the snow melt a month or more earlier than in the past. This has affected water retention, making less water available for domestic supplies, agriculture, and recreation.

The San Rafael Swell is bisected by Interstate 70 in central Utah and contains a variety of stunning slot canyons, petroglyphs, pictograms, and wilderness study areas, which are threatened by increasing off-road ATV use. Photo by author.

This is an example of why we need to protect land as Wilderness. It is not just so we'll have a pretty place to recreate. We need to protect the land for its own sake. The critters and the grasses and the flowers and the trees have to come first. And they cannot be saved in small "islands" surrounded by development. Large contiguous chunks of land are needed for ecosystems to survive and thrive. Animals need to be able to migrate. Streams and rivers need to be intact from start to finish.

Scientists are finding out more and more about the interconnectedness of landscapes, and the more they learn, the more it becomes obvious that what we don't save now, and soon, will be much more than just the loss of a place to go hiking or climbing or canyoneering. The loss of wild areas will directly affect not only our physical well-being but our spiritual happiness as well.

～

Now, let's talk about recreation and Wilderness. I do think that "quiet" recreation can and should be a part of the Wilderness equation. Here, I often disagree with some of my environmentalist friends, who think that the back-country is already too crowded. And in some places it is. But the reality is that it is the recreationists who are our best advocates for saving the areas that they've come to love. I know it happens, but I think it is rare that people go into the canyons of Utah and come out unaffected by what they've seen and experienced.

It is interesting, too, to see what the trends are with recreation. Times have changed and the way we use the land has changed, a lot. Recreationists use either the frontcountry or the backcountry—or both. The standard definition of "frontcountry" is an area that can be reached in a day. You do not stay out overnight. Frontcountry users include mountain bikers, rock climbers, canyoneers, and, of course, day hikers. The casual tourist who goes from scenic pullout to a short nature hike would be using the frontcountry.

"Backcountry" is defined as any place that takes multiple days to get to, where you actually camp in the backcountry away from vehicles and roads. I think that it's very important to clarify that difference, because the uses of the frontcountry and the backcountry have changed significantly over the past twenty years. My generation (the baby boomers of the 1960s and 1970s) led the exodus into the backcountry. We were influenced by the writings of Renny Russell in *On the Loose*, and Colin Fletcher in *The Thousand Mile Summer, The Man Who Walked Through Time*, and *The Complete Walker* (still the how-to bible on backpacking). We wanted to get away from it all, to find peace and quiet as far from the noise of society as we could get. And we did. It was not unusual to find like-minded folks in the most remote places in the mountains or on the desert.

With the newer generation (Gen X and the Millennials) the focus has changed from backcountry use to frontcountry use. Today we are finding that frontcountry use has skyrocketed while backcountry use has declined measurably, not only statistically but from what we see on the land. Younger folks are more interested in the thrill of right now. They are mountain biking, rock climbing, canyoneering, and river running, all in the frontcountry. It is the immediacy that people like, the physical rush you get climbing a good route in Indian Creek or clambering through a slot canyon, or running a hard river.

Nowadays, unless it's Outward Bound or National Outdoor Leadership School or a university trip, we rarely see groups of young friends out in the backcountry anymore. If you do see groups, it's usually older folks in their fifties and even into their sixties and seventies. In a way it's good that people are using the frontcountry, because we get a lot more people looking at the land and enjoying the land. In a way it's bad because I think visitors are missing what the backcountry has to offer.

But there is no right or wrong way of seeing the land. Everyone enjoys the landscape in their own way, whether it is communing on the top of a slickrock dome or cranking a hard move on a vertical wall. Who is to say if a bird-watcher is enjoying the land more than a climber sitting on a high ledge looking out over the same landscape? Everyone has their own way and their own motivations. Sometimes people (myself included) get criticized for using the outdoors and wilderness as a big gymnasium. As long as they aren't destructive, I think that's just fine. In the mountains some people will bag a peak and the next guy will go fly-fishing—all great stuff, with one big caveat. That is, if you use the land, you must also join the fight to protect it.

The younger folks haven't seen what's happened to the land over the years. I've read articles on the canyoneering blogs where people ask, "Why are we trying to save this country? There's nothing out there trying to destroy it." I've been hiking hard in Utah for more than forty years, and I can tell you that the land has changed so much. Some of the change has been inevitable, such as the paving of dirt roads. But much of it has been destruction for destruction's sake, and little has come of it.

And some of it just seems so senseless, like the paving of the Burr Trail (actually a road) between the town of Boulder and Capitol Reef National Park. Meant to be a faster way for tourists to get from Bull Frog Marina to Boulder, it is now only partially paved (the National Park Service refuses to pave their part), so it is a paved road to nowhere. And if it was completely paved, it would mean tourists would avoid the small towns they now have to pass through, such as Hanksville and Torrey, and wouldn't spend their money there. So why did they want to pave it in the first place?

⁓

The younger generation, as they start to build their own history in canyon country, will see the diminishment of the land and will find that those opportunities for quiet recreation get fewer and fewer and the places they go get smaller and smaller. After all, they didn't see Glen Canyon before the dam or the San Rafael Swell before Interstate 70 was blasted through it in the 1970s.

Do rock climbers realize that it was only a generation ago that a nuclear waste dump was planned adjacent to perhaps the premier climbing area in canyon country, Indian Creek? Do river runners know that dams have been proposed for Ruby/Horsethief Canyons, for Labyrinth/Stillwater Canyons, for Cataract Canyon? That one would have backed water all the way up to Moab, and that town would have had to move! Do canyoneers know that proposed dams on the Escalante River, and in North Wash, would have inundated some of their best slots? And most importantly, do they know that it took a lot of people a lot of hard work over many years to stop each one of those proposals? And that each and every day, people are still working hard, perhaps harder than ever, to protect the land that we all have come to love and cherish?

Choosing a Wilderness Vocation

I am a backcountry guide. I started doing this in Telluride in the 1960s. That was before the ski area. I enjoyed it. I took a twenty-year break to get an education and to start a couple of businesses. One day I woke up and said to myself that I wasn't happy. All I really wanted to do was go hiking, see pretty places, explore the desert, stop answering telephones, and stop having people depend on me for their livelihood and for their fun.

One September I put all of my belongings, except my tools and my books, on the front lawn of my house with a sign that said "Free." In an hour my old life was gone; students made it disappear. I lived in my van for nearly twenty years. It was heaven. I got it all; I'd spend months alone, then months with groups, then months with a traveling road show of close friends, often all of us living out of my van.

We hiked, we ran rivers, we climbed, we canyoneered, and then we'd hike some more. Season after season, year after year. One year I wore out a half dozen pair of big mountaineering boots; the desert sandstone takes its toll. I slept out in 120-degree weather and 30-below weather, was eaten by deer flies, swam potholes in the dead of winter, hiked off the Kaiparowits Plateau with a broken leg, bivouacked on high ledges in the middle of huge walls, and along the way I saw things that few had seen and, in some instances, things that I was the first to see.

But all along I was working with various environmental groups intent on protecting the land that was giving so much to me. For a short while I worked with the federal agencies who are charged with managing and protecting the land. I found out pretty quickly that while their mandate was multiple use, in reality it was all about multiple abuse. It wasn't about land preservation; it was about kowtowing to the oil and gas industries, to the mining industries, and to the ORV industry. Big industry versus a couple of hundred tree huggers.

I soon realized that working with the agencies was a waste of time; the only thing that really worked was lawsuits, and the only way you could sue the federal government was to have a lot of money. So I made a niche for myself: I take groups out on week-long backpack trips to all the unprotected areas of southern Utah. As we wind our way through the canyons and across the uplands in between, we talk about the land and its preservation. It is fun for me to take people to areas that they've perhaps never heard of and hear them say, "That is as good as Zion National Park," or Arches National Park, or any of the areas that already have protection. I tell them about the proposal to make most of southern Utah into a national park years ago [in the 1930s], the

Escalante National Park. And how we are fighting now for the last vestiges of what that would have been.

$$\sim$$

I think what we are seeing now in the sport of canyoneering is that fun comes first and safety is second. The environment hardly registers at all, which is shortchanging the participants. Many of the canyons are becoming what Bill Hatcher calls "viaferetta canyons," where much of the canyon is fixed with gear; with bolts, with cables and chains to help get out of potholes, with cables stretched across the hard places so they aren't hard anymore. What this really does is force the canyoneer to *not* look at the canyon, to *not* think and to *not* analyze and find what Mother Nature has to offer. It forces you to *not* feel the rock and get to know her and her many moods.

A continuing issue in canyoneering is the use of inappropriate anchors, and that ends up being bolts. This is very controversial, of course. On one side, they deface the rock, which I don't think is great stuff, especially because bolts are never, ever needed in canyoneering. On the other side, bolts are easy and they do allow people without skills to go through canyons. Of course, I don't object at all to people in canyons; I heartily approve of it. But those people must have the requisite skills. And by fixing canyons with climbing gear, people aren't building those skills, and they are getting in trouble.

One of the most common emails I get is from people asking about the hardest canyon I've done because they want to do it. The first thing I do is run through their résumé. Mostly it is short: fifty canyons, a hundred canyons. They are beginners and yet they feel like they have the skills to do the "hardest" thing around. Yikes. It is depth of experience that keeps you alive in the canyons. It is the judgment accrued from years of not only going through technical slots but hiking the slickrock, seeing and recognizing weather patterns, getting a feel for the different sandstones and formations and what their characteristics are, and finding out about yourself and what your strengths and weaknesses are. It is also about learning who your companions are and what they do to complement your strengths and bolster your weaknesses. And to learn what type of people they are deep down inside; are they going to be the person you want around when it all goes to hell?

Over the past couple of years it's made me very sad to see people get badly hurt or dead in canyons that I call my own: Quandary, Knotted Rope, Blue John, Choprock, Larry, No Mans, among many. When we look at the details of the accidents in those canyons, it invariably comes down to inexperience; people think they are better than they are, they don't have experienced companions along, and they don't have the judgment to be there in the first place.

In one case, a person was swept away in a flash flood: they entered the canyon while it was raining. In another, two people entered the same pothole at the same time without leaving themselves a way out; in several, people died because they didn't know the ABCs of ropework.

Reasons for Tragedy

Most of those accidents, and the innumerable near misses posted on the canyoneering blogs, indicate several reasons for tragedy.

1. *There is little depth of experience.* From what I've seen recently, very few slot canyoneers actually have much canyoneering experience. They've been down slot canyons, but they've never really had to deal with country, terrain, time, water, heat, cold, and complex route finding. For some canyoneers, just the idea of having to walk to the top of the canyon in order to go down it is anathema to them; they do car shuttles so they can do the canyon going only downhill. Talk about shameful, and talk about a missed opportunity to learn more about the land. The reality is that if you get back to your vehicle every night, there is a long list of skills that you don't develop but would wish you had when it all falls apart.

2. *There are not enough technical skills.* I remember years ago going down a canyon with some "experienced" canyoneers, all of whom had long résumés. At one drop we stuck a rope while pulling it after a rappel. I tossed some "jugs" (jumars or ascending devices) to one of my companions so he could go up the rope and reset the anchor and pull the rope. He'd never used jumars before. Didn't have a clue.

   When people ask how to get into canyoneering, I tell them to take a course in canyoneering, but only after taking a really good course in basic rock climbing, where you learn the knots and the safety procedures and protocols. Without taking courses or clinics, you only learn what you need to learn at the time, if you have time. That doesn't help if you are in the middle of a huge, free-hanging rappel and it is the first time you've had to get over a knot. A fellow in Big Bend National Park ran into that exact problem on a four-hundred-foot-long rappel. He didn't know how to get over the knot. His buddy was down below trying to scream directions up to him. He died. I know "good" canyoneers who don't know how to do sitting hip belays, tie off weighted ropes, or make jug lines, or don't understand the very real problems with biner blocks, or with a "fireman's belay" on manky anchors. The list goes on.

3. *The mindset that a canyon has to be done on a particular day or weekend.* How many times have we seen folks come down to the canyons with a particular agenda for a specific time frame and, by darn, they'll do that canyon no matter what. Big clouds building up over the mountains ten miles away? Who cares, I might not ever get back to do that canyon! So what if it rains, I'll beat it!

I can think of driving North Wash at the north end of Lake Powell, a favorite canyoneering area, with the clouds building, but knowing, by the numbers of cars at every canyon mouth, that there are scores of people in those canyons. I have a feeling that many of those folks, faced with a rainy day in the slots, would rather go home than do a nice hike. They're more interested in testosterone than nature.

4. *It won't happen to me, because I'm special.* Reminds me of a story from a fellow guide, my friend Wendy. She was leading a group up a peak in Colorado. As they came up over the final ridge, they got a clear view of the sky to the west, and it did not look good. Wendy immediately had the group turn around and head down, just a couple of hundred yards from the summit. But one person thought that the rules about lightning didn't apply to them, and they continued toward the top; they never made it; they were hit by lightning. The moral of the story is that lightning, flash floods, loose rock, and uncaring companions, are all equilateral killers; they don't give a darn about who you are or how good you think you are.

Perhaps the most important publication one can read is the yearly *Accidents in North American Mountaineering*. Reading about the accidents and the analysis that follows is a good start on finding that a high percentage of accidents are avoidable. Above, I mention the four things that I think tell you *why* accidents happen. *Accidents in North American Mountaineering* tells you *how* they happen. It is homework worth doing.

~

I said before that I'm a guide and have been one—on and off—for more than forty years. But that is not the only type of trip that I do. I think that there are three types of trips: solo, me and my buddies, and guiding others.

I've got a real problem with solo trips. They can be dangerous, they account for a lot of deaths and accidents in the backcountry, and I've done hundreds of them, from hard technical slots to month-long hikes in remote regions where another human footprint is never seen. So I have a hard time telling people the standard mantra about never going out alone. As well, it seems to me that

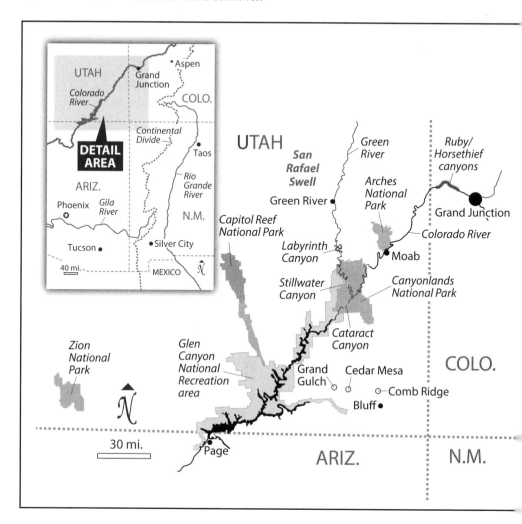

in order to become accomplished in the backcountry, you have to solo. It is too easy to go with others and share the decision making. By yourself, it is all you, all the time. I think that your learning curve escalates rapidly when you solo. You get to revel in your own good decisions and bark at your bad ones.

Having said that, I have to throw in some caveats—really important caveats. You truly have to understand the risk ethic, and you have to understand that you may die and that you may go through incredible pain before you do. And you and your family have to be all right with that decision. An injury by yourself is far different than an injury while with people who can take care of you, summon help, and otherwise get you home alive. I hate it when I read about some mountaineer or rock climber, married with children, who was doing something totally at the edge. They die and everyone says that they died doing what they loved. One magazine even quoted a child of the dead man saying that! NO NO NO. At some point you have to back off the hard stuff—until the kids are grown, out of college, off of your health and car insurance—and then you can go back to being on the edge.

My buddy trips are, to me, perhaps the best. Sometimes it is two of us, sometimes ten. Nothing's better than a shared passion acted on. The best is that you get to choose the people and you know there won't be any duds, anyone who will drive you crazy, and you'll know from past trips that they have the strength, both physically and mentally, to do well and to be a positive addition to the group.

It is a real art to put the right people together for a long trip. When I'm putting the trips together, I have a rule of thumb on deciding who gets invited. If I have to seriously think about a person fitting into the trip, then I don't invite them. If I just absolutely know that they will be perfect, then they will be.

The longer the trip, the better. On a weeklong trip it takes about three days to start getting into the groove of it—the terrain, the camping, the routine, your companions—and to feel really comfortable. Day four is absolute bliss, with the cares of the real world a long way away, both physically and metaphorically. Then day five comes and you are starting to think about getting out and back to the real world—work, responsibilities, kids, relationships. One day of bliss. Now extend the length of that trip and the same rule applies—three days at either end, but now the bliss lasts for days, or weeks, or more. You settle into a routine. You lose track of the days and the weeks. You get used to the routines of your companions, their noises and peculiarities and similarities. The talk goes from superficial to deep and back a hundred times. You start looking for the fun in the small things; you ignore the things that bother you. Sometimes you have to be bigger than you thought you could ever be.

So You Want to Be a Wilderness Guide . . .

Then there is guiding. A whole different set of rules. You don't get to pick the clients, they pick you. Oh yes, you do those phone interviews, find out about their experience, tell them what you expect of them, how you run your trips so there are no surprises, and then you hope for the best. And they lie: yes, they run five miles a day, but what they really mean is that they'd really like to run, but they don't have the time so they are horribly out of shape and you carry half their gear for most of the trip.

One fellow arrived on a trip having just had a four-way heart bypass; it had been done after his medical forms had been turned in. Another fellow showed up on a Muddy Creek (appropriately named) wading trip with a catheter inserted because of some sort of urinary problem. He claimed that his doctor had okayed a week-long wading trip down a river with muddy, waist-deep water. I don't think so!

Another person showed up with an "amazing" outdoor dog who was wonderful, ancient, with a belly that dragged on the ground, and didn't make it a half mile down the trail before hiding under a bush and refusing to go anywhere but back home. The most poignant was the fellow who showed up for a trip with an incurable disease in its end stages. Forgot to tell the leader about that one! His comment after having him helicoptered out was that he picked my trip because he knew that if it all went awry with him, I'd somehow get him out okay. I did, but at how much risk to the rest of the group?

I especially liked the fellow who told the group endless tales of derring-do on big rock walls and frozen waterfalls. Day four and we were pretty well into the boonies and the first rappel, which admittedly had a hard start, and he was frozen solid to terra firma. He wasn't going down that rope for anything, until I reminded him that we'd have to retrace our rather difficult route for four days unless he went down the one-hundred-foot cliff. I think it was the tired faces of his companions that finally persuaded him to make that first step.

Every guide has stories, endless stories. Any of the old-time guides will tell you that when they first meet a group, they'll know within the first hour (or within minutes) who they'll have problems with. Some people just exude incompetence. But there are also those who "get it." They step up to the plate, or the cliff's edge, to help. They recognize problems before you mention them and are right on top of them. The really good ones do it with such aplomb and grace that those in need barely realize that they've been helped. These are the ones you pray for, and usually end up hiking with time and again.

Guiding is fun, but it is also hard work. You are the one who is up early to get things going, and you are the one who goes to bed late after everything is tidied up at the campsite. You are the one crossing your fingers that the next water hole that has always had water will be full this time. Blisters? Drinking enough electrolyte replacements? Nailed by a scorpion? Wind blew something in someone's eye? Broken leg? Boot fell apart? Tent shredded in those eighty-mile-an-hour winds? Yep, you have to be able to handle all of them, and with an outward sense of competence that you sometimes don't really feel. It is all part of the job.

Truly the best part of guiding is the people. I watch people change as their perceptions of this incredible desert start to sink deep into their souls. There are no vehicles, or iPods, or cell phones. The noise of everyday life is suddenly gone. People have to engage, with the terrain, with the group, with you. You can spend a year with someone in the outside world, but you'll never get to know them as well as on a week-long backpack trip. And the mix of people on a trip can be incredible. I've hiked with the heads of major corporations, and a California salmon fisherman. I spent a day with the fellow who invented Corn Nuts, and years with a carpenter from Cambridge.

On our trips it's environment first, safety second, and fun third. Our philosophy is that, of course, you have to be safe, but that safety can't come at the cost of the environment. If you do everything right and you do it well and you do it in a thoughtful, knowledgeable way, you will be safe and that leaves room for fun. We are total sticklers about "Leave No Trace," a philosophy that promotes a slew of techniques for leaving as little sign of passage as possible on the land.

We always talk about the environment and Wilderness on my trips. It is essential that people realize that the land they are walking does not have permanent protection. I have a *modus operandi* here. I wait until I get them on the end of a rope and halfway up a cliff, then we have "The Talk." The talk is about what their experience has meant to them and what they can do to help preserve these areas for all time. We talk about the many battles we have won in the past because people like them supported our cause. And, without exception, they donate . . . then the knife goes back into my pack, away from the rope they are dangling on, and up they come!

So my advice is to come on out to the canyonlands of southern Utah. Before you come, read about the history, visit the environmental websites, enjoy what you see and experience, and then go home and join the battle to protect what you've seen. Join the groups, donate money, write letters, volunteer. We call it "tithing for wilderness." People will spend hundreds or thousands of dollars coming out to visit and enjoy the land. At the end of every trip they should send a couple of bucks to the environmental groups who made it possible. Nothing comes for free, nor should it.

Study Questions

1. Do you support the idea of a rescue-free wilderness? Why or why not? If they did exist, would you go in? Would you take friends or clients in?
2. Andrew Gulliford writes that it usually takes one to two days to leave all that mental baggage behind. Do you agree? What is your ideal time for "leaving it all behind"? What do you think the ideal times are for different client groups?
3. Why is the learning curve on a solo so high? What do you need to know before going solo?
4. What do cattle and ORVs have to do with avalanches and the San Juan snowpack?
5. With frontcountry use on the rise and backcountry use on the decline, how do we get people interested in the backcountry? Why do we need to?

CHAPTER 2

Looking for History

There is no zest like exploration, no longing like that for the
desert places, no call like that of the unknown.
　　　　　　　—Clyde Kluckhohn, *Beyond the Rainbow*

In Grand Gulch we are moving into an era of managed remoteness, of planned romance. I think that is probably how it has
to be if we are to preserve the qualities of the area at all in an
increasingly mobile and exploitative society. The challenge is
to have effective management that does not itself overwhelm
the values it is designed to protect.
　　　　　　　—William D. Lipe, "Grand Gulch: Three Days
　　　　　　　　　　　　　　on the Road from Bluff"

All across the Southwest hikers and backpackers encounter the Old Ones.
Almost anywhere in the Four Corners, walking in the backcountry means
coming across Anasazi or Ancestral Puebloan ruins, cliff dwellings, trails, or
shrines. Discovering and understanding these remote sites gives hiking on
the Colorado Plateau a special sense of significance, a true connection to the
past and the people who have gone before us. What did humans do here? Why
did they do it?

While hiking I appreciate finding subtle clues of human presence, whether
prehistoric or historic. I always carry a small pair of binoculars to scan cliff
tops, canyons, alcoves, or historic mines high on ridge tops. I look in order
to learn how people used what nature provided. The editors of *Adventure
Education* explain that with expeditionary learning, "Leaders also have the
responsibility to convey cultural information to participants. If a leader is
traveling in the Four Corners region of the southwestern United States, being
able to impart knowledge about the peoples who lived there before Europeans
came to the United States is important."[1] Although much literature is available

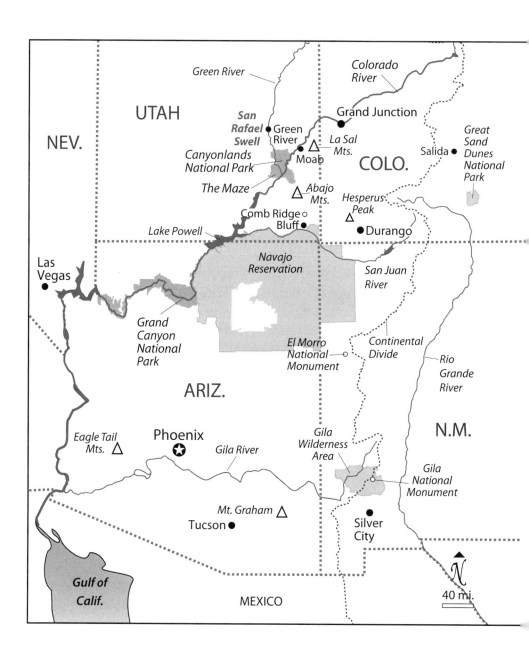

about southwestern Native Americans, this section is about how to look for history and how to read the landscape itself.[2]

These signs of the past are legally protected on public lands. From hard-to-visit cliff dwellings, which under new public land management plans cannot be accessed with climbing ropes, to small black-on-white pottery sherds and arrowheads found in sand, every cultural artifact, or an object made by human hands, must be left in place. Items can be picked up and photographed, but they should then be put back or, better yet, buried two to four inches in the dirt where they are found. Over the last decades far too many arrowheads, flakes, scrapers, and broken potsherds have been removed to sit on shelves or in drawers with their original provenance long since forgotten and their archaeological value destroyed.

Under the Archaeological Resources Protection Act (ARPA), it is *illegal* to surface collect arrowheads on federal/Indian lands *without an archaeological permit*. Arrowheads are considered *archaeological resources,* and to collect them one must be an archaeologist with a federally issued permit. A law enforcement officer can issue a citation under the Theft of Government Property statute, 18 USC 641. And there are federal regulations for all land-owning federal agencies that can also apply.

Practice "catch and release" arrowhead hunting as editor Andrew Gulliford did with this five-thousand-year-old Archaic spear point from southeast Utah, which he photographed and then re-buried on the spot. Photo by author.

In some cases, those who have taken artifacts or human-placed stones have then had a string of bad luck, and they've gone to great lengths to try to return what they took. The "Leave No Trace" ethic is not just about clean campsites. It's also about not removing items, especially cultural resources that are irreplaceable and only have meaning in context—whether it's an eleventh-century Anasazi white quartz knife or a nineteenth-century cowboy coffee cup. If you're with a group and you find something, do not walk across a prehistoric or historic site to show it to others in your party; have them come to you. Then put it back exactly where you found it. What's protected on public lands? Everything, from prehistoric and historic sites to all associated artifacts. Specific federal laws include the Antiquities Act (1906), the National Historic Preservation Act (1966), and the Archaeological Resources Protection Act (1979).[3]

Human traces on the landscape give depth and meaning to backcountry travel. On one hike I went looking for cliff dwellings, only to find something more subtle.

$\sim$

Handprints in the Canyon

The shadows grew long. I knew I had to get off the slickrock and out of the canyon soon or I'd never cross the wash in the proper place, then find my way through the mud and the tangle of tamarisks and up the other side to my truck. Shadows lengthened. Impatient and a bit depressed, I descended the canyon. I had been trying to glean some sign from the ancient inhabitants.

I'd spent a glorious spring afternoon high atop Comb Ridge in San Juan County, Utah, breathing in the wind from far across the Navajo Reservation and walking slowly, deliberately, to the top of the sixty-five-million-year-old uplift with Charlie, my Border collie mix. He eagerly led the way, tail up, nose down, eyes bright. We had napped close to the top of the Comb in sand beneath a juniper and I'd seen a few small petroglyphs or prehistoric rock carvings on the massive sandstone fins. I'd picked up a few pottery sherds and some red chert flakes, which I put back down on the ground and covered with a thin layer of dirt. I walked without maps, wanting to discover the landscape on my own.

The weather had been splendid, the temperature just right, perfect for hiking the Comb, but despite looking and searching, scanning the horizon and the cliff walls with my small birder's binoculars, I had not seen much of consequence. Among the dozens of Ancestral Puebloan sites along the Comb,

I had found nothing special. I wanted to find a spectacular site that would reach out to me across time and space and jolt me out of the present, but no luck. I was tired, a little hungry, irritable, and late getting down to the truck. I hadn't gleaned anything from the landscape.

And then I saw it. High up. Higher than I could reach. My hiking sticks had been clicking down the canyon floor as I moved quickly looking for small barrel cactus, tree roots, and bends in the trail. The light was gone and though the air was not yet cool, night was coming. I approached a long south-facing alcove. Suddenly, for no reason I can remember, I looked above a low Basketmaker wall from more than a thousand years ago. This early Ancestral Puebloan site had been severely pothunted or looted by vandals looking for bowls, baskets, anything. The desecration meant there were no standing ruins and no need to stop, but for some reason I looked up, and what I saw rooted me to the spot.

My blood pulsed through my body. As silence and shadow became darkness, I saw the row of exquisite handprints, ochre red and fifteen feet high. I was not alone.

In the canyons and broken terrain of southeast Utah, one frequently hikes in solitude and silence. Hours and even days go by with only the mesmerizing beauty of clouds scuttling above the tops of the La Sals or the Abajo Mountains vivid against red rocks and layers of sandstone from ancient beaches. The solitude soothes and softens, but one is never alone. The Ancient Ones are present and palpable.

That day I had found no stunning rock art panels or defensive, difficult-to-access cliff dwellings. Instead I walked and hiked and napped, shook off a few sorrows, talked to a few family ghosts, and crossed from one drainage south to another. Hurrying back against the darkness I had forgotten to look up, but now something compelled me to shift my weight, align my shoulders, and there like a message from the Old Ones arched the handprints. Magnificent, they spoke as clearly as if an Anasazi, long, dark hair flowing, water dripping from cupped hands, had raised his head from the small pour-over pool I had passed moments ago.

I stopped. My dog Charlie stopped. He sniffed the air. I stared at the gallery of handprints, some adult size, many from small children. This is what I had sought all day—that moment of discovery, the thrill of finding something not on any map. A village had left its mark in this low, deep alcove centuries ago as families giggled and laughed and stood on the rooftops of their small stone rooms. Now the ceilings were gone, rooms had toppled; only a few low walls remained of rectangular, dressed stones. But still in place, protected from wind and rain and sun, handprints spread across the alcove, a silent

Of all the rock art symbols in the Southwest, some of the most striking are handprints that have been either painted or pecked on stone. These are negative handprints from southeast Utah. Photo by author.

gesture of kinship in the universal sign of peace and presence, an open hand pressed upon hard stone.

In the shadows as I gleaned the red hands, large and small, I looked down the alcove. A few yards away were more handprints, white this time around the edges, negative handprints made from paint held in a young man's mouth then blown against the wall by using a small reed tube. In this style of pictogram the shape of the hand and each distinct finger was outlined in white, unlike the red prints where the hands had simply been dipped in ochre paint. I stood stunned, my dog burrowing into the sand, ready to spend the night.

I had not been stopped by a high cliff dwelling or an etched petroglyph, but rather by the simplicity and humanity of handprints waving to me across time, frozen forever in a moment of playfulness asserting, "This is us. We are here. These are our hands."

Downcanyon the stars came out one by one. The evening star appeared and then the others shone. When I could see the handprints no more I finally started walking, more slowly now, at peace. I did not worry about finding my way to the truck.

The Old Ones had been there. They would always be there. The presence of the handprints in the canyon, their subtlety and intimacy struck me more deeply than if I had stumbled upon an unknown cliff dwelling. Though they had been made a thousand years ago, the red and white hands, particularly the children's prints, reached across time and space to my heart.

I came out of the canyon into a brilliant rising moon. I was flush with warmth and affection for a people who had left their telltale sign in such careful, colorful patterns. I was humbled and grateful. My dog and I stepped off the steep bank into the mud and tamarisks as moonlight glinted on my truck's windshield above us and through the trees. Then I understood the wisdom of the Old Ones. I stopped again and smiled.

I had come down through the canyon too fast, in too much of a hurry, caught up in all the modern pettiness and busyness that burdens our lives. Had I not paused to study the handprints I would have hit the arroyo in the dark with no moon to guide me. Despite my canine companion, we probably would have gotten lost. But with the moon reflected upon my windshield, I found my truck on the arroyo's opposite bank.

What had drawn me to that alcove precisely when I needed to slow down and wait for the rising moon? What had made me look up at that exact moment? I'll never know, but in Utah canyon country, as across the West, there are always secrets in the landscape, silent signs from those who went before. There are messages from the past to the present. Stories on stones.[4]

The many types of prehistoric sites on southwestern public land include ancient trails, road systems (particularly Chacoan roads in the San Juan Basin), *herraduras* or shrines, and cliff dwellings. A cliff dwelling can accommodate a variety of sites, such as habitation sites—rooms that once had doorways, level floors, and smoke on the ceilings—and sites for storage areas and granaries, which can be much smaller, higher, and tucked into narrow crevices above alcoves.[5]

Stacked stones often indicate a wall. Built hundreds if not thousands of years ago, walls are often found toppled and blocks scattered. But each needs to be left as is, untouched and definitely with all stones in place, regardless of the wall's state of disrepair. Many walls were originally built by craftsmen fitting loose rubble into structures. Others were intricately designed with eight-hundred-year-old clay masonry and stone chips used as filler to give the walls more strength when the clay or adobe mud dried. Some cliff dwellings have dressed stone walls, meaning the stones themselves were cut and shaped, squared off, and hammered to create dimpled surfaces so that plaster would bond more completely. On narrow ledges, standing walls near an approach to a cliff dwelling can be considered choke points to block entry—then and now.[6]

Across the Southwest are petroglyphs or rock art pecked into dark desert varnish on long cliff faces. The various symbols include animals, humans, anthropomorphs (figures that are both human and animal), objects such as sandals and necklaces, and the ever-present Kokopelli, the flute-playing fertility deity. Rock art from the Basketmaker era, two thousand years ago or more, includes pictograms, or symbols painted on rock, depicting shamans, desert bighorns, and a variety of creatures, often in vivid red hues.[7]

The personal traces left behind by prehistoric peoples offer an irresistible draw for modern-day humans. Many prehistoric sites have been looted by pothunters who secretly dig holes in ancient villages and cliff dwellings, seeking pots, blankets, baskets, game pieces, and anything else that can be sold on the thriving black market. Not everyone who enters such sites has bad intentions, however. Once I went with a team of archaeologists into the Gila National Forest in New Mexico to remove a large clay water jar that had been found by a young teenager in a mountain lion's den. To this day I wonder if we did the right thing; perhaps we should have left it alone. Instead of removing found objects, we should consider leaving items where they are, creating an "open museum" for backcountry hikers.[8]

~

Into the Mountain Lion's Den

It was a fantastic story, really. A young teenager from Texas, hiking in the Gila National Forest, had begun a game of hide and seek with his brother. While running over rocks and through Gambel oak, he found a cave, where he discovered a large *olla,* or prehistoric Mimbres Indian storage jar. This extremely rare artifact was larger than anything on display at the Gila Cliff Dwellings National Monument.

The boy had left a crude map leading to his find. As a historian and university museum director, I was part of the five-person team of archaeologists and cultural resource staff who set out to find the cave and see if the tale was true. I will never forget that day. In many ways what happened changed my life.

Fall is a beautiful time of year in southwestern New Mexico. The air is crisp and clean in the morning, and the oak and aspen leaves change from green to shades of golden yellow. It was cool enough to wear jeans and a fleece jacket as we drove into the Mimbres River Valley from U.S. Forest Service headquarters in Silver City. My archaeologist friend was in charge of our mini-expedition. We had high hopes but no particular expectations for an outcome. It was just good to be in the ponderosa pines, walking over decades of fallen pine needles, peering under rocks, and imagining how hard it would be to find the right cave in hundreds of thousands of acres of national forest.

As we scrambled over boulders and peered around ledges, the local district forest ranger accompanying us let out a shout. We came back to where Jan had been climbing; with a broad smile, she lifted up in her gloved hands a small, mug-sized plainware Mogollon jar about the size of a tall coffee cup. She'd just found it. There. On the rock. Where someone had placed it eight hundred years ago.

A rush of energy ran up my spine. Like any boy growing up in the West, I'd always wanted to hunt for arrowheads but had little luck. When I started my teaching career in western Colorado and had begun deer hunting, I once found a broken white quartz Ute arrowhead on a high mountain game trail. I'd called back to my hunting partner and said, "Hey, there've been hunters ahead of us on this trail." He came over and looked at the point in my hand, smiled, and said, "Yes, but they're not after our game."

Over years of hiking, climbing, and camping across the West, I'd never found any other Indian relics or artifacts, but that was about to change. I was living in southwestern New Mexico, where the presence of the prehistoric Mimbres people was palpable. They had lived everywhere in river valleys and had built small room blocks or houses near where they farmed at different elevations.

As director of the Western New Mexico University Museum, I was in charge of the largest permanent exhibit of Mimbres black-on-white pottery on display in the world, but someone else had found or dug those pots. I felt honored to curate the collection, but I was equally interested in how the prehistoric Indians had lived, and where. That afternoon I reveled in being outdoors and off campus, and I was astonished that Jan had simply found an ancient jar sitting on a stone ledge. But there were more revelations to come.

One member of our group had a sixth sense. I don't know how to describe it. She was an Anglo archaeological technician who had not completed her full four-year degree, but she understood Indian sites and artifacts intuitively. Something in her background gave Vicki an ability to find sites that other experts could not locate. She was gifted, she was good, and she found the cave. And just like me she would feel sick and uneasy, downright ill, for the next day or two, because we had disturbed something that we should not have touched. We removed something that we should not have moved. My Pueblo Indian friends clearly understood; the archaeologists did not.

Vicki found the cave and with flashlight in hand crawled and slid down over centuries of dust and leaves. It had another opening nearby where we could peer in from a different direction, but there was only one real entrance. Eventually, one at a time, we all slid down the narrow opening. There on the cave floor, undisturbed for centuries, was the largest Mogollon olla ever found in New Mexico. Long ago packrats had devoured the contents, and a small piece of the corrugated rim was missing, but overall it was an astonishing find, a true museum piece, a one-of-a-kind storage jar that could have contained enough dried corn to feed an entire village for months or provided seed corn for several villages.

Shafts of light illuminated the dust. Once our eyes adjusted we didn't really need flashlights. There in the soft soil we found the rim of another jar and a few large broken pieces too big to be called sherds. Slowly I scanned the small space, perhaps as large as a good-sized closet or pantry, and as I leaned back on my haunches I saw just a trace of bone. Startled, I wasn't sure what to do.

Finding prehistoric artifacts on public land is one thing, but finding human bone is a completely different case involving consultation with tribes and potential repatriation and reburial. I looked again and realized it was a claw buried under dusty leaves. Gingerly, I pushed the leaves aside to find the skeletal forearm of a mountain lion, withered tendons still attached.

I stepped back and took a deep breath. Not only had this large olla been resting for centuries in this small hidden passage, but over time mountain lions had also used this cave. Clearly, it was a special place, perhaps even sacred. It was time to go. I wanted to leave everything there, in situ or in place, undisturbed. I was already aware of ethical issues surrounding found Indian artifacts on public land and the commercial looting of sites by thieves who dug ancient villages by moonlight and sold their finds on the black market. But the archaeologist in charge said we should take everything out. I felt no better than one of those looters working in the dark of night.

Carefully the Forest Service staff cradled the items and pulled them up. We had to both push and pull the large olla through the cave's narrow keyhole entrance. We even retrieved the lion's claw. I'll never forget the archaeologist cradling the immense olla and walking slowly down through the pine forest toward the trucks. We held our breath that he wouldn't slip on the pine needles and break the olla that had lain undisturbed for hundreds of years and even been protected by mountain lions. I felt uneasy then and I feel uneasy today.

That night I went home to tell my wife and my wide-eyed boys about the fantastic pot we'd found in a lion's den. Thinking about the day's events, I felt ill with severe depression and a strange stomachache. Within a day or two, however, the feelings had passed and I was able to hold and photograph the olla, caressing it as if gently rubbing the belly of a beautiful pregnant woman. When I tapped the side, the jar rang perfectly, like a bell. It represented a masterpiece, probably crafted by a village elder, who sculpted delicate corrugated details along the rim of an otherwise smooth and perfect jar almost three and a half feet tall.

The find created a publicity coup and a major southwestern news story that focused on the young man, fourteen-year-old Mark Imhoff, and his willingness to tell authorities about the large pot he'd found. The New Mexico governor sent the state jet to Texas to retrieve the boy and his family for a special ceremony in Santa Fe, where the lad received a lifetime membership to the New Mexico Archaeological Society. The story made it into a junior edition of *National Geographic,* and modern potters created a small-scale replica of the olla for the governor to present to the teenager who did the right thing.

Gila National Forest archaeologist Robert Schiowitz poses with a large Mimbres olla that fourteen-year-old Mark Imhoff found in a mountain lion's den in the Gila Wilderness. Rather than keep the jar, Imhoff notified authorities of its location and received a special reward from the governor of New Mexico. Photo by author.

All in all it was an important, satisfying statement against the fierce pot-hunting wars and the ongoing looting of Mimbres sites. Even so, I felt uneasy that we had removed objects from the site. I did not attend the ceremony, and within a year or two I'd left my job as museum director. I don't know where the jar is now. I don't want to know. It's probably in storage somewhere on a metal shelf, hidden from view and far from the cave where it was safe for eight hundred years.

I remember sitting in the cave staring at the jar and realizing that my knowledge of our nation's history, the entire span of wars and events, of movements west, of victories and defeats, of forests leveled and farms created, the rise of cities and the birth of highways, had been encompassed in the life of this one jar. It had sat undisturbed in a quiet cave for centuries, and then in the course of a few weeks it had been discovered, removed, publicized, put on display, and now stored somewhere.

I now feel that there are too many things in museums. Too many prehistoric, handmade items—baskets, blankets, pots, lithics, sandals—tucked away in storage, safe and secure but in the wrong place. I believe in a new ethic of leaving things be, a cultural resources corollary to the "Leave No Trace" hiking ethic. This is called the "outdoor museum" concept, and it's a good one. I wish we'd left this magnificent jar alone. For whatever knowledge was gained from finding the jar, there's even more wisdom in leaving things be. That's a lesson we have yet to learn.

$\sim$

Peeled Ponderosa Pines

Like the artifacts that tell their stories in museums and visitor centers, trees also tell stories. While prehistoric Ancestral Puebloans left thousands of archaeological sites across the Southwest, the historic Ute Indian presence is harder to determine. The secret lies in tall ponderosa pine trees that have been culturally modified or peeled, resulting in oval scars. Where Ancestral Puebloans left stone structures, Utes and other tribal peoples left a living legacy among the pines.

Lightning strikes on ponderosa pines also leave scars—usually longer, narrower ones that demonstrate evidence of fire. These scars are sometimes called cat's eyes because felines have dark vertical irises. Ute medicine trees have much wider scars and show evidence of ax cuts horizontally along the bottom of the tree. On tall ponderosas the scars can be centuries old and six feet high. They represent a unique cultural and archeological resource proving Native American use of forested land from the nineteenth century and earlier.

When the trees were young, Ute bands on horseback would have visited forests and cut into the pines in early spring to extract the protein-rich cambium layer underneath the bark as an emergency food source. During times of dietary stress, often in early spring when game was scarce, Ute women and children used special debarking sticks, axes, or knives to peel down to the cambium layer, which tastes like soft cookie dough. The cambium layer of living cells between the inner tree and outer bark help with tree growth and, depending on the soil, contain a range of sugars, starches, and minerals. Archaeologist Marilyn Martorano notes that one pound of cambium is the equivalent of 600 calories and is high in fiber, calcium, protein, carbohydrates, magnesium, iron, zinc, and vitamin C. It provides a food value equivalent to nine glasses of milk. Now that's a health food!

Fragments of animal horn and metal, including baking powder can lids, which were peeling tools used by Native American women, have been found at the base of peeled trees. Peeled ponderosas also acted as medicine trees to create poultices for deep cuts and scrapes, allowing human skin to heal without infection or scars. Tribal peoples also used the trees to make a drink that could treat disorders such as tuberculosis, colds, heart trouble, and rheumatism.

The resource-savvy Utes used selected ponderosas for food and medicine and to sustain and nurture their young children by creating ponderosa pine cradleboards to keep infants warm and tightly secured. Ute women pulled the inner layer of the tree from the bottom up and then cut the soft wood with knives to make cradleboards for infants. Pine became the backboard with leather later sewn onto a willow framework. Peeled pine also served as food trays.

Although Utes used ponderosas for multiple purposes, such culturally modified trees are known today as medicine trees. Some of the trees have numerous scars indicating repeated use over years. Martorano explains, "If a tree was peeled once and then peeled again at a later time, the existence of the first scar probably affected the decision to peel the same tree again. Perhaps it was easiest to begin peeling the bark adjacent to an existing scar, or if the bark substances were used as food or medicine, it is likely that an existing scar would indicate that the bark of the tree was useful or edible."

One place where the Utes returned again and again is now a public campground. At Target Tree Campground on the San Juan National Forest, forty-year veteran forester Lloyd O'Neill worked with Ute Mountain Ute, Southern

Ute, and White Mesa Ute elders to dedicate and rename the campground. They told him, "Yes, this was definitely a Ute campground. We camped here on our way from the winter grounds to our summer area where we gathered berries and fruits." The name of the campground, translated from the Ute word *ivikukuch*, means "target tree or tree you shoot at," which was a large peeled pine.

The peeling practice is centuries old, with peeled tree core dates varying from the late 1700s to the early 1900s. However, identifying and mapping these peeled pines by Forest Service archaeologists and cultural consultants is relatively recent. Groves of such trees have been found at Florissant Fossil Beds National Monument behind Pikes Peak west of Colorado Springs; at Great Sand Dunes National Park and Preserve near Alamosa; in the Upper Rio Grande Basin; and along the La Plata River near Old Fort Lewis, as well as in many other places.

At Great Sand Dunes, Fred Bunch, chief of resources for the National Park Service, states, "As park managers it is quite a challenge to manage living artifacts. These trees have been culturally modified and have a story to tell. They will go through their life cycle and then return to the earth." The Indian Grove site within the national park has seventy-two mature ponderosa pines, many with large scars peeled between 1816 and 1848, and it is listed on the National Register of Historic Places. Bunch adds, "It is important to collect as much information about these trees now to share with future generations."

Modifying ponderosa pines may not be an exclusive Ute tradition. Dr. Adrienne Anderson, archaeologist for the National Park Service's Intermountain Region, cautions that other native groups are documented to have used the Great Sand Dunes and Florissant Fossil Beds National Monument areas, not just the Utes. She explains, "In Great Sand Dunes, we have Puebloan, Apachean, Ute, and Plains Woodland ceramics from the same site. So who is to say which group produced which CMTs or culturally modified trees?" She notes, "The Jicarilla Apache continue to use the park for traditional collecting activities, and their Elders indicate that the tribe has a long history of utilizing the Ponderosas."

Medicine trees are also found in the Red Rock Forests of southeastern Utah, sometimes as single trees close to the Bear's Ears, and also in groups of twos or threes near Allen Canyon on the west side of the Abajos. Dr. Robert McPherson, historian at the Eastern–San Juan campus of Utah State University, writes, "Utes used the plants and animals in the Abajo and La Sal mountains extensively during late spring and summer months before descending to the canyons and river to avoid approaching cold and snow in late fall. These were major hunting and camping areas which saw Ute group activity into the early twentieth century."

Groves of such trees need protection and should be included on resource management plans for fire mitigation. They need to be mapped so the pines are not accidentally cut down in timber sales or damaged in prescribed burns or fuel reductions. Ute medicine trees can teach us much about the age-old Ute use of the forest, and they forge a living link from the present to the past. In the Southwest, Ancestral Puebloans left us stacked stone walls and dozens of cliff dwellings, but deep in the bottoms of canyons and in quiet meadows at higher elevations are more subtle links to American Indians and the living landscape.

$\sim$

Southwestern Sacred Sites for Tribal Peoples

For traditional native peoples the landscape includes not only the physical world of rocks, trees, mountains, and plains, but also the spirit world. Native Americans felt obligated to protect and defend the graves of their ancestors and sacred locations where the Great Spirit both resides and communicates with them, such as Mount Graham in Arizona and Hesperus Peak in Colorado. Thousands of years living in the Southwest has brought about a deep love and understanding of the landscape in which Indians believe themselves inseparable from the land and sky.

We need to understand southwestern landscapes in the context of traditional Native American religion and the powerful, enduring presence of sacred geography. For most tribes a sacred place is a location made holy by the Great Creator, by ancient and enduring myth, by repeated rituals such as sun dances, or by the presence of spirits who dwell in deep canyons, on mountain tops, or in hidden caves. An entire landscape may be sacred because for thousands of years Indians migrated from place to place in search of food on seasonal rounds that took them into the high country in the summer and to lower elevations in the winter. Sacred sites remain integral to tribal histories, religions, and identities.

Indians honor oral traditions linked to specific sites such as Ribbon Falls in the bottom of the Grand Canyon, where the Zunis believe they emerged from the center of the earth as a people. A sacred site is always sacred, and human burials or village sites remain hallowed ground. If shamans carved rock art panels to evoke spirits in southern Utah or at the bottom of Echo Park in Dinosaur National Monument in Colorado, then those places remain special and should not be disturbed. They are sacred sites where the living communicate with the dead or with powerful animal spirits of desert bighorn, elk, and mountain lions that the rock artist came to see in his visions.

Repetition, tradition, and unbroken continuity define traditional Indian spirituality, whether a young man seeks a vision, a tribe conducts a sun dance, or a tribal leader goes on a pilgrimage to collect plants for religious purposes. Indian religions are intricately bound to a tight web of place and an intimate, subtle, even secret understanding of landscape.

⁓

Native Americans and Anglo pioneers have all left their marks upon the western landscape. In the twenty-first century we try to interpret and understand their messages from centuries and even millennia past. Like us today, they were awed and inspired by the landscape, and they left marks to prove their passing. They also left marks to connect earth and land and spirits. For Indian cultures there were connections to other times and other dimensions; for Anglo-Europeans the marks were often meant to mark their passing through the mountains and the canyons of the West. As fur trappers, scouts, ranchers, and settlers moved across the West, prehistoric painted handprints in southwestern canyons evolved into historic inscriptions—dates, initials, full names, and finally flowery phrases etched into stone.

Wallace Stegner wrote, "Describing a place, we inevitably describe the marks human beings have put upon a place, the uses they have put it to, the things they have been taught by it."

To describe human history and the West, Stegner notes, "is quaintly begun in the completely human impulse to immortalize oneself by painting or pecking or carving one's private mark, the symbol of one's incorrigible identity, on rocks and trees."[9] Writing about Dinosaur National Monument in northeastern Utah and northwestern Colorado, Stegner described archaeological sites from the Fremont culture. He chronicled remote habitation sites of these northern Anasazi cousins along the Green and Yampa Rivers, "and—most wistful and most human of all—the painted hand prints and footprints, the personal tracks that said, and still say: 'I am.'"[10]

Across the vastness of southwestern deserts, on mesas on the Colorado Plateau, or in mountain meadows beneath Rocky Mountain peaks are traces of human presence over ten thousand years. Rocky Mountain National Park has prehistoric Ute Indian game drive fences of brush and stone used to herd mountain sheep into ravines where they could be killed by atlatls and later bows and arrows. The remnants of Ute piñon-juniper small brush shelters or wickiups, tree platforms, and occasional cedar mats exist on the Uncompahgre Plateau on Colorado's Western Slope and in the White River National Forest. Far to the south are Pueblo shrines and *herradura* stone placements for leaving offerings and *paho* sticks. Along the base of Comb Ridge in Utah and on the top of the Vermilion Cliffs in Arizona are old forked stick Navajo hogans, facing east. There are also smaller Navajo piñon-juniper sweat lodges, just large enough to be covered by a blanket or two, where a man could light a small fire and have a cleansing sweat bath.

Everywhere in the West, signs—silent, subtle, significant—can be gleaned from the landscape—not from a faraway vantage point, but by walking slowly and coming to know the creeks and canyons, sandstone ledges, and trails through tall timber.

∼

Stories on Stones

About western inscriptions James Knipmeyer notes,

> In the Colorado Plateau region I have found them lightly scratched, with perhaps a knifepoint or horseshoe nail, pecked in with some sort of metal tool, possibly a miner's pick, and sometimes carved deeply with a chisel. Some have been painted with an actual pigment, but most of this type have been made with axle-grease from a wagon, wet charcoal, a fire blackened stick, or even the lead of a bullet. . . . But all of them proclaim to the world in one form or another that "I was here. I am a part of history."[11]

These types of marks, inscriptions, or modifications to the landscape are human ways of showing "we were here." In the vastness of the West, humans have always left their marks. In the twenty-first century we need to glean what those messages might be and what meaning they might have for us.

In the eighteenth and nineteenth centuries, explorers and settlers carved on stone. In the twentieth century the impulse to leave a mark continued with Hispanic herders who brought thousands of sheep into high-country meadows and valleys. As their sheep bedded down in the aspen groves, their herders carved everything from horses, pistols, and self-portraits to profiles of women they longed for. Hikers and backpackers who travel among the aspen trees today can continue to delight in the aspen art or arborglyphs those Hispanic herders left behind.

~

Reading the Trees

Imagine being an artist working alone in a grove of shimmering white aspens carving a portrait that you will never see. A full decade will pass before the design will appear—subtle, serene. Like the quick stroke of a skilled calligrapher drawing on parchment, the Hispanic carver leaves the gentlest mark for the tree to embrace. As the aspen grows the bark expands and the art appears like magic, but the artist never sees his work. Now, half a century later, the sheepherders are gone, and soon the trees will fall, too.

Deep in southwestern forests, beneath barren ridges but above the sides of creeks, stand aspen groves, some a century old. Among these smooth trees at the edge of mountain meadows can be found thousands of carvings etched by sheepherders who passed through the groves beside their bleating sheep. Carving symbols on trees, known as arborglyphs or dendroglyphs, is a revered tradition among high-country herders. A type of male occupational folklore, this cultural tradition is vanishing along with the trees themselves, lost to drought, blight, and other unknown impacts that are decimating the West's aspen forests. The issue is acute for Colorado, which grows half of the aspen trees in the Rocky Mountain states.

Aspen trees tell stories. When we read the trees we glean a new understanding about the lost and lonely life of Basque and Hispanic herders, some from the Pyrenees in Spain and others from northern New Mexican villages. Within thousands of square miles on the Colorado Plateau, certain sections of aspen groves are covered with art. In special places, herders and cowboys left messages for their *compañeros* and created a sense of community.

On the Pine Piedra Stock Driveway at Beaver Meadows and Moonlick Park in the San Juan National Forest, where the trail begins to climb at the ecotone boundary between aspen and fir trees, the carving becomes profuse. Names on the trees include Trujillo, Montoya, Bates, Isgar, Aragon, Archuleta, Gonzalez, Sanchez, Jacquez, and Valdez. Herders bringing sheep from one grazing area to another and back again as the seasons changed moved north from Ignacio, Colorado, along Spring Creek on the edge of the HD Mountains and up Yellow Jacket Pass to Moonlick Park. They spent a few days resting sheep in the park, and as the light played upon the aspen groves they left their marks. Inscriptions include the poignant "Thanks to God" and the comment by cowboy Jim Bates: NO LUCK, DAMN HORSES GONE! SNOW WALKING OUT DAMN!

Calligraphy decades old and inscriptions in flowing script nestle among the aspens clawed by bears and rubbed by elk antlers. Proud of their literacy and the ability to write their names, herders carved who they were, where they were from, and the date they carved the tree so that other herders would know of them. Some herders added a subsequent date each succeeding year they herded to explain to anyone who read the trees that they had returned. Rival herders occasionally vandalized each other's names.

Carving categories included inscriptions; portraits of males with heads in profile and females from a frontal view; religious art such as crucifixes and churches; poems; political slogans; and artistic expressions of mermaids, rifles, burros, sheep, maps, a flying saucer, and even a lifelike Elvis. Women were depicted artistically. "Aspen porn" became a significant subset of these artworks. Retired archaeologist Linda Fainsworth describes "a cultural form

In the Southwest lonely male sheepherders often carved erotic images on aspen trees, which were known as arborglyphs. Many such images can be found in concentrations or galleries along stock driveways or designated corridors that were used to move thousands of sheep through national forests. Photo by author.

of expression" set back in groves "almost like a private gallery," with her favorite glyph reading: VIDA INFERNAL, MAL VITAS SEAN LAS BORREGAS, or in English, INFERNAL LIFE, CURSED BY THE FEMALE SHEEP. One memorable contemporary carving is of a female forest ranger complete with badge and braids.

The key to finding aspen carvings is to know the route the herders took through the forest. In the 1940s these traditional routes were marked with yellow signs stating "stock driveways" to help herders who may have varied from year to year. Some of those signs still exist.

On the Groundhog Trail near Dunton, Colorado, carvers competed not only to leave their name and date but to do so in exquisitely fine penmanship as they carved the smooth skin of the aspens. The best carvers used a light touch, a lover's touch, to caress the trees as they remembered caressing their women so many months ago and miles away. Now decades later, the herders' flourishes stand out in vivid, beautiful detail. The best carvers never gouged or cut but rather made a gentle scratch, a pinprick with the sharp point of a knife, and their ephemeral art lingers upon trees beginning to age and die.

This technique is one of the primary distinctions between historic aspen art and contemporary graffiti, which, because of brutal gouges, can damage and even destroy trees. The ethic now for all forest campers and hikers should be to "leave no trace," including on the trees.

In the summer of 1955 New Mexican Joe R. Martinez was one of the best carvers. Folk art is generally anonymous and speaks to members of a select community or group, but Joe's style was unique and can be seen in marvelously simple cowboys with hats, women with hats, nudes, and other tableaux. He was good, and he signed his work. On July 2, 1955, he carved one of the most amazing images in the forest. A woman in profile wears a fancy feathered hat, and below her, at chin level, appears another woman, this one a crone. Is this *La Llorona* in an amazing double portrait? Is this a herder's version of the beautiful Hispanic seductress who lures men with her body but who is really a witch?

Statistical analysis from one national forest reveals that 75 percent of the carvings were inscriptions with names or initials, hometowns and dates; 5 percent were phrases or comments; and 20 percent were drawings in the category of nature, buildings, portraits, guns, and symbols, including crosses and hands, and erotica such as images of "Venus of the Forest." Who knows how many carvings are yet to be found? How many forest folk artists, with a light touch and a sharp knife, etched images as yet undiscovered?

As the sheep bedded down for the night, shepherds carved. Now fewer and fewer bands of sheep munch on forest grasses, and the herding tradition is declining as are stands of older aspens. Most of the men are gone now. They went back to their villages and small towns. On winter nights, sitting in small kitchens with coffee in hand, they must have looked out their windows and thought of their trees—white in the moonlight, soft and silky to touch, silent except for the rhythmic rustling of leaves. They remembered the incessant bleating of their sheep and the way a herd moves through the forest slowly in a meadow and faster through the trees like a river flowing around rocks. The herders remembered their quiet evenings smoking, carving, dreaming of home. The trees remember. Now we must read the trees to glean and understand a western tradition that's almost gone.[12]

~

Reading the southwestern landscape should be a hiker's delight. It's not how many miles you make in a day, but what you learn as you walk. Across Utah can be found Mormon pioneer trails, especially the 1879 Hole-in-the-Rock Trail built by Mormon families as they moved from Escalante to Bluff, Utah, through some of the most complicated canyons on the continent.

The descent of their wagons down through Hole-in-the-Rock to cross the Colorado River is an epic tale of design and personal daring. Occasionally the Mormon scouts even made use of Anasazi or Ancestral Puebloan roads as they struggled to go east off Cedar Mesa. Their final challenge was to use their weary and bruised horses to pull wagons up steep San Juan Hill. Despite all the hardships in this extraordinary pioneer journey, no one died; babies were born. An inscription at the top of the hill reads, "We thank thee Oh God."[13]

Subtle historic resources found on southwestern trails include logs and stones laid perpendicular to the trail as water barriers or water bars to prevent erosion. There are hundreds of stone cairns, some stacked by native peoples, some built by sheepherders on promontories above meadows, and others from nineteenth-century surveyors. Prospectors staked mining claims with stone piles, some of which can be found above 11,000 feet in elevation in the San Juan Mountains.[14]

The U.S. Geological Survey also left its mark on mountaintops and canyon rims. They placed brass plaques with dates on the tops of peaks to certify height and elevation; on canyon rims they placed plaques, sometimes on iron rods, to show section lines at the corners of square miles. Within national forests some trees also serve the same function of indicating boundaries between sections, or 640 acres of land. Finding these traces of the past makes hiking and backpacking more worthwhile.

All across the Southwest are remnants of travelers, pioneers, miners, settlers. There are log cabins, stone cabins, mining camps, mine shafts, and

Visiting Historic Mining Sites

Rick Athearn

As we visit historic mining locations, we should remember that we are always a guest here, not the owner of the property. There is no such thing as an "abandoned mine" or town. Someone owns the property, be they a private citizen or the government. Therefore, it is protected from theft and destruction by law.

In the case of sites known to be on public lands, they are protected by numerous laws. Places in national forests, national parks, or Bureau of Land Management, state, county, or city lands are subject to protection from damage or destruction under the law. By treating each historic site as a special place that is still "owned" by someone, it becomes a matter of courtesy to behave in the same way you would if you were in a friend's home. Would you take artifacts from your friend's or neighbor's house? Would you steal items from the garage or backyard?

Of course not. So the same principle applies to visiting "abandoned" mining towns and sites. When enjoying a historic mining location, remember to leave only footprints and take only photographs. You simply should not remove property that is not yours. You should also take your trash out with you, so the next person to visit can enjoy this place, too.

Some of the most important information that can be gained from a historic site is in the architecture and archaeology. If a building is vandalized, the data is lost. If a trash dump is dug up, the scientific information contained in it is gone forever. That's why it is critical to leave things the way you find them. Here are a few etiquette tips that are useful when visiting historic sites:

- Standing wooden structures are very fragile. They can be severely damaged by removing parts from them. They are also extremely vulnerable to fire. Never smoke in or around a wooden building. Never remove wood ("barnwood") from a building.
- Historic trash dumps, outhouses, pits, and surface scatter can be scientifically valuable. Never dig up dumps, pits, or outhouses. Doing so not only damages the scientific value of the site, but it is almost always illegal.
- While using metal detectors might be fun, picking up artifacts or digging them up is not only destructive to the scientific value of the resource but is also likely illegal.

- Take out the trash you bring in. Nothing spoils a visit for the next person more than to have aluminum cans, plastic wrappers, and other trash spread around a historic site. If you bring it in, take it out.
- Don't be a vandal. Vandalism is one of the worst things you can do to a historic site. Painting graffiti on buildings ruins them forever. Carving your name in the wood destroys the site for other visitors and degrades the quality of the site. Taking a four-wheel-drive vehicle and pulling down buildings for fun not only destroys our heritage but is illegal. Shooting interpretive and directional signs only ruins everyone else's visit and destroys property. Leave a place as you found it. Would you do the above things to your own home? If not, then treat a historic place as you would your house.

It is important to note that the above behavior is, in general, illegal. Whether you are on private or public property, trespassing and destruction laws protect private lands. Equally, theft and destruction laws provide civil and criminal penalties for damaging federal, state, and county/city properties.

By thinking ahead, planning your visit, and simply showing a little courtesy for others, you can help preserve and protect our fragile historic mining sites.

tram towers for hauling gold and silver ore from mines down to mills. Rusted equipment lies about, along with segments of twisted cable, stone walls that formed the edges of blacksmiths' shops, broken glass, nails, and fragments of tin roofs. Hikers can even find drafty, windswept outhouses with holes below the wooden seats that went straight down off cliffs.

Cowboy and sheepherder line camps also dot western lands. When late winter weather rolls in I think of cowboys waiting out storms huddled in their line shacks drinking hot coffee from blue metal cups. Rode hard and put away wet, with ice-encrusted mustaches, frozen cowboy boots, and red bandannas stiff as cardboard, slowly the herders thawed out in remote winter camps stocked with survival rations of beans, jerked meat, biscuit fixings, matches, dry wood, and thin wool blankets atop mouse-infested wooden bunks.

Tales of line shacks filter down through pioneer memories. Writing about Dominguez and Escalante Canyons and the Uncompahgre Plateau, Muriel Marshall described "stoop-door cabins" with just enough room for a cowboy to lay out his bedroll and build a cook fire. Higher up in the quakies were more

Hikers on public land in the Southwest may encounter not only prehistoric cliff dwellings and archaeological sites, but also historic Native American sites such as this east-facing, forked-stick, male Navajo hogan from southeast Utah. Sweat lodges are similar to this in construction, but smaller. Photo by author.

substantial cowboy camps, never locked, with doors secured by a wooden peg on a latchstring. No padlock—just a whittled stick in the hasp where the lock should have been. Marshall explains, "Traditionally cow camps were never locked and were kept stocked with a minimum of things vital to life for anyone caught out by sudden deep snow or by injury. Stovewood and kindling, chopped and dry. Matches and staple groceries in tight-lidded lard buckets to keep the wood mice out. Lamp and lantern, coal oil, ax, shovel and a bit of rope. Kettles, skillet, tin plates, and cups, cutlery in apple-box cupboards nailed to the logs. Bedding."[15]

So I respect these old camps when I find them on public lands. The vertical board and tar-paper camp in Devils Canyon sits in a stunning location beneath red-rock cliffs west of Colorado National Monument. A white porcelain enamel reservoir held water, and bunk beds crowd the tiny cabin against the north wall. A plank-board table has seen plenty of pointed elbows and playing cards. Homemade shelves jut from rough two-by-four walls. The front door has lost its porcelain enamel handle, and a rusty horseshoe is nailed to the wood for good luck.

Black Ridge Wilderness, part of McInnis Canyons National Conservation Area, is in turn part of the Bureau of Land Management's new National Landscape Conservation System of "treasured lands" important for their natural and cultural resources. I respect that designation and our responsibility to protect the few remaining livestock grazing camps on public lands. When spring storms hit, sheepherders and cowboys needed those lonely cabins. Stories linked to landscapes tell the history of the West.

Remote cowboy camps are strewn with rusted horseshoes, distinctive wooden gates built out of old vehicle parts, corrals, remnants of lean-tos, decrepit shacks for saddles and tack, and numerous food cans with knife holes sliced in the tops. The condensed milk cans with hole-in-top punctures were used with cowboy coffee, said to be strong enough to float a horseshoe.

In canyons in San Juan County of both New Mexico and Utah, and in Montezuma County, Colorado, are historic petroglyphs of Navajo horses, cowboys with six-shooters, prized bulls, and even a Model A Ford car etched in sandstone.

Painted handprints, rock art, inscriptions carved into cliffs and trees— they all represent the lives of humans of varying cultures and backgrounds engaged directly with the southwestern landscape. The messages they left behind mark their presence, their passing, and their existence as travelers and inhabitants of the land. The rock inscriptions and tree carvings give form to our sense of place in the West and the human urge to seek identity in a changing landscape.

Notes

1. Dick Prouty, Jane Panicucci, and Rufus Collinson, eds., *Adventure Education: Theory and Applications* (Champaign, IL: Human Kinetics, 2007), 98.

2. See Bob Greenlee, *Life among the Ancient Ones: Two Accounts of an Anasazi Archaeological Research Project* (Boulder, CO: Hardscrabble Press, 1995); Brian Fagan, *Chaco Canyon:*

Archaeologists Explore the Lives of an Ancient City (New York: Oxford University Press, 2005); Frederick W. Lange and Diana Leonard, *Among Ancient Ruins* (Boulder, CO: Johnson Books, 1985); E. Steve Cassells, *The Archaeology of Colorado* (Boulder, CO: Johnson Books, 1988); David E. Stuart, *Anasazi America* (Albuquerque: University of New Mexico Press, 2000); Stephen Plog, *Ancient Peoples of the American Southwest* (London: Thames & Hudson, 1997, 2001); and Linda S. Cordell, *Prehistory of the Southwest* (New York: Academic Press, 1984).

3. See Andrew Gulliford, *Sacred Objects and Sacred Places: Preserving Tribal Traditions* (Boulder: University Press of Colorado, 2000), and ARPA. Other laws relevant to artifacts and human remains founds on public lands include the American Indian Religious Freedom Act (1978); Archaeological Resources and Protection Act (1979, amended 1989); Native American Graves Protection and Repatriation Act (1990); and Presidential Executive Order 13007 Protecting Native American Sacred Sites (1996). For publications see National Register Bulletin #38 defining traditional cultural properties and articles in *CRM* (*Cultural Resources Management*), especially the special issue "What You Do and How We Think" on Native American perspectives.

4. An earlier version of this essay appeared in Laura Pritchett, ed., *Going Green* (Norman: University of Oklahoma Press, 2009). For an excellent fiction and nonfiction anthology related to the Anasazi, see Ruben Ellis, *Stories on Stone: Tales from the Anasazi Heartland* (Boulder, CO: Pruett, 1997), and to learn more about Comb Ridge, see Robert S. McPherson, *Comb Ridge and Its People: The Ethnohistory of a Rock* (Logan: Utah State University Press, 2009).

5. To learn more about shrines and Ancestral Puebloan trails and roads in the Bluff, Utah, area see Catherine Cameron, *Chaco and After in the Northern San Juan* (Tucson: University of Arizona Press, 2009).

6. For the most comprehensive and understandable source on cliff dwelling architecture, see Bill and Beth Sagstetter, *The Cliff Dwellings Speak* (Denver: Benchmark, 2010). For historic mining camps in the Southwest, see the Sagstetters' earlier book, *The Mining Camps Speak* (1998).

7. See Sally Cole, *Legacy on Stone: Rock Art of the Colorado Plateau and Four Corners Region* (Boulder, CO: Johnson Books, 1995); Scott Thybony, *Rock Art of the American Southwest* (Portland, OR: Graphic Arts Center Publishing, 2002); Alex Patterson, *Rock Art Symbols of the Greater Southwest* (Boulder, CO: Johnson Books, 1992); Polly Schaafsma, *The Rock Art of Utah* (Cambridge, MA: Harvard University Press, 1971); Polly Schaafsma, *Warrior, Shield, and Star* (Santa Fe: Western Edge Press, 2000); and Winston B. Hurst and Joe Pachak, *Spirit Windows: Native American Rock Art of Southeastern Utah* (Blanding, Utah: Spirit Windows Project, 1989).

8. To learn more about the "open museum" concept, see chapter 7, "The Future of the Past," in Fred Blackburn and Ray A. Williamson, *Cowboys and Cave Dwellers* (Santa Fe: School of American Research, 1997), and David Roberts, *In Search of the Old Ones* (New York: Simon & Schuster, 1996).

9. Wallace Stegner, ed., *This Is Dinosaur* (Boulder, CO: Roberts Rinehart, 1985), 4.

10. Ibid., 5.

11. James H. Knipmeyer, *Butch Cassidy Was Here: Historic Inscriptions of the Colorado Plateau* (Salt Lake City: University of Utah Press, 2002), x.

12. An abbreviated version of this essay appeared in Andrew Gulliford, "Reading the Trees: Colorado's Endangered Arborglyphs and Aspen Art," *Colorado Heritage*, Autumn 2007.

13. See Stewart Aitchison, *A Guide to Southern Utah's Hole-in-the-Rock Trail* (Salt Lake City: University of Utah Press, 2005), and William B. Smart, *Old Utah Trails* (Salt Lake City: Utah Geographic Series, 1998).

14. New mining claims are marked with white PVC pipe and claim descriptions in small sealed plastic prescription bottles.

15. Muriel Marshall, *Red Hole in Time* (College Station: Texas A&M University Press, 1988), 208.

Blood-Red Rock Art on the San Rafael Swell

Of the thousands of Indian rock art panels in the Southwest, none are older than Barrier Canyon pictographs found throughout the San Rafael Swell. From tiny five-inch animal figures to stunning seven-foot-tall human shapes with no arms or legs and alienlike bug eyes, Barrier Canyon–style images are almost always a dark blood-red color. They may have been painted eight thousand years ago; many panels are at least five thousand years old.

For a week friends and I drove 4WDs and then hiked into remote locations in Emery County, Utah, to photograph these spectacular ochre-red paintings. The images of eerie, elongated figures with shortened arms and legs are hard to decipher. The anthropomorphs, or human figures, often have overly large eyes, no ears or noses, and no way to distinguish gender. Snakes writhe in their hands or above their heads. Yet circling these fierce, faceless creatures are delicate menageries of exquisitely painted birds, ducks, geese, deer, and occasionally free-floating eyeballs with wings.

Our guide Steve Allen, who wrote one of the first guidebooks on the San Rafael Swell, said, "There may be a thousand rock art sites in the Swell, but only twenty of them are truly spectacular." We set out to find a few of those sites, and in side canyons and small slot canyons, we found them.

I'll not forget the blustery spring day with a storm front moving across Utah and we seven hiking all morning to finally find a few red symbols high on a cliff face shaded by a small alcove. We scrambled up and there in the silence of the Swell the few symbols seen below blossomed into small panels of intricate images expertly drawn in the Barrier Canyon style's signature red paint.

Standing just a few feet from the panels, we could study the masterful brushstrokes, the lyrical zoomorphs or animal-like creatures, and the red paint's perfect preservation. The artist had added a few white dots and faint white streaks. Seated on a sandstone ledge, looking south across a vast canyon landscape, rare pictographs just behind my shoulder, the

Some Barrier Canyon rock art on the San Rafael Swell in Utah is blood-red and up to five thousand years old. This close-up image from Sinbad Wash shows a shaman-like figure holding a snake while birds and designs that look like flying eyeballs whirl around his head. Photo by author.

twenty-first century melted away. Time ceased. I thought if we waited, with luck the artist might return. Instead, there was only the wind.

Another afternoon hike up an unnamed canyon seemed fruitless. Perhaps one of our guides had made a mistake. Then when we were almost across from it, we saw a panel of human figures with the largest one, maybe eight feet tall, painted in a somber red, almost brown. We stared in wonder. The ghostlike images without arms or legs could only be shamanistic art created by medicine people/artists who were powerful shamans communicating across time, space, and different realities.

The most famous Barrier Canyon panel is the Great Gallery in a remote section of Canyonlands National Park named Horseshoe Canyon. But we wanted to hike in wilderness study areas to see ancient art generally not visited. In the vastness of the Swell we could do that. On the fifth day we came across a finger-painted panel of four figures that looked as fresh as if it had been painted that week. One of our party quipped, "If this paint can last five thousand years, why can't the paint on my house?"

Barrier Canyon paint is only one of the mysteries. Probably mixed from vegetable and mineral compounds, the paint is 10 percent blood (whether human or animal is uncertain). The sophistication of the art, which seems to represent a vibrant and complex spirit world, is made more mystifying by the fact that the artists were Archaic period (8500–2000 B.C.) mobile hunters and gatherers who did not plant corn and who lived a precarious subsistence lifestyle. They hunted with spears, and yet when we returned to the famous Buckhorn Wash panel to study it in afternoon shade using binoculars and long camera lenses, I felt I was in the presence of sacred art as powerful as anything on the ceiling of the Sistine Chapel.

"My grandfather put his name here on the panel, and I spent thousands of hours restoring it," said Utah coal miner and rancher Bert Oman, who acts as the site's official greeter. "I wanted to see this art like it was when the pioneers saw it," he added. In 1995, in an award-winning Utah State Centennial Legacy Project, dozens of citizens and volunteers worked to remove bullet holes, graffiti, crayon, and chalk from the Buckhorn Wash Rock Art site's eight panels. They moved the road farther from the site, and added fencing, parking, landscaping, an interpretive trail, and restrooms. Special erasers, jeweler's tools, watercolor paints, and pastels were used in the restoration. Now visitors can see scenes of rituals, celebrations, and homage to Native American gods painted thousands of years ago by artists using brushes of hair, feathers, and yucca fibers.

Oman tipped back his cowboy hat, rubbed his two-day-old beard, and said quietly, "This is one of the most sacred panels in the western United States. I have twenty great-grandchildren, and I want them to see these panels just like this when they're in their seventies." I respect his wishes and admire his stewardship, but all is not well on the Swell, which is a BLM Special Recreation Management Area of 938,500 acres.

The Southern Utah Wilderness Alliance and ATV groups continue to squabble over wilderness designation and boundaries for seven wilderness study areas. ATV use and illegal roads increase yearly. The underfunded Bureau of Land Management has few staff to enforce regulations on backcountry travel, and rock art vandalism is an ongoing problem. Far too many panels have been shot at or scratched over.

One site we visited, not as impressive as the Buckhorn Panel but still possessing ancient Barrier Canyon rock art, was beneath a small cliff face at Molen Seep. For many yards the base of the cliff was covered in cow poop. Steve Allen became visibly upset and commented to our group,

"This site represents rock art thousands of years old, and yet visitors have to walk through cowshit to photograph it! Under federal law the BLM is mandated to protect cultural resources. Looks like we need fences within our outdoor museums."

I'd like to forget that afternoon but I can't—just as I can't forget the rare feeling of hiking into remote canyons to discover five-thousand-year-old paintings. Exploring the Southwest is why many of us live here, and yet personal self-discovery isn't enough. We must advocate for public lands and do our best to protect the natural and cultural treasures we enjoy.

I wrote a letter to the BLM. I told them I'm happy to put on leather gloves and volunteer to string fence at Molen Seep. No one ever replied. Meanwhile, I keep thinking of those blood-red Barrier Canyon figures in the unnamed canyon wash. How much longer will they be safe?

High Tide in Tucson—Eagle Tail Mountains

Barbara Kingsolver

Not long ago I went backpacking in the Eagle Tail Mountains. This range is a trackless wilderness in western Arizona that most people would call God-forsaken, taking for granted God's preference for loamy topsoil and regular precipitation. Whoever created the Eagle Tails had dry heat on the agenda, and a thing for volcanic rock. Also cactus, twisted mesquites, and five-alarm sunsets. The hiker's program in a desert like this is dire and blunt: carry in enough water to keep you alive till you can find a water source; then fill your bottles and head for the next one, or straight back out. Experts warn adventurers in this region, without irony, to drink their water while they're still alive, as it won't help later.

Several canyons looked promising for springs on our topographical map, but turned up dry. Finally, at the top of a narrow, overgrown gorge we found a blessed *tinaja,* a deep-shaded hollow in the rock about the size of four or five claw-foot tubs, holding water. After we drank our fill, my friends struck out again, but I opted to stay and spend the day in the hospitable place that had

Excerpt from *High Tide in Tucson: Essays from Now or Never* by Barbara Kingsolver © 1995 by Barbara Kingsolver, 10–13. Reprinted by permission of HarperCollins Publishers.

slaked our thirst. On either side of the natural water tank, two shallow caves in the canyon wall faced each other, only a few dozen steps apart. By crossing from one to the other at noon, a person could spend the whole day here in shady comfort—or in colder weather, follow the winter sun. Anticipating a morning of reading, I pulled *Angle of Repose* out of my pack and looked for a place to settle on the flat, dusty floor of the west-facing shelter. Instead, my eyes were startled by a smooth corn-grinding stone. It sat in the exact center of its rock bowl, as if the Hohokam woman or man who used this mortar and pestle had walked off and left them there an hour ago. The Hohokam disappeared from the earth in A.D. 1450. It was inconceivable to me that no one had been here since then, but that may have been the case—that is the point of trackless wilderness. I picked up the grinding stone. The size and weight and smooth, balanced perfection of it in my hand filled me at once with a longing to possess it. In its time, this excellent stone was the most treasured thing in a life, a family, maybe the whole neighborhood. To whom it still belonged. I replaced it in the rock depression, which also felt smooth to my touch. Because my eyes now understood how to look at it, the ground under my feet came alive with worked flint chips and pottery shards. I walked across to the other cave and found its floor just as lively with historic debris. Hidden under brittlebush and catclaw I found another grinding stone, this one some distance from the depression in the cave floor that once answered its pressure daily, for the grinding of corn or mesquite beans.

For a whole day I marveled at this place, running my fingers over the knife edges of dark flint chips, trying to fit together thick red pieces of shattered clay jars, biting my lower lip like a child concentrating on a puzzle. I tried to guess the size of whole pots from the curve of the broken pieces: some seemed as small as my two cupped hands, and some maybe as big as a bucket. The sun scorched my neck, reminding me to follow the shade across to the other shelter. Bees hummed at the edge of the water hole, nosing up to the water, their abdomens pulsing like tiny hydraulic pumps; by late afternoon they rimmed the pool completely, a collar of busy lace. Off and on, the lazy hand of a hot breeze shuffled the white leaves of the brittlebush. Once I looked up to see a screaming pair of red-tailed hawks mating in midair, and once a clatter of hooves warned me to hold still. A bighorn ram emerged through the brush, his head bent low under his hefty cornice, and ambled by me with nothing on his mind so much as a cool drink.

How long can a pestle stone lie still in the center of its mortar? That long ago—that recently—people lived here. *Here,* exactly, and not one valley over, or two, or twelve, because this place had all a person needs: shelter, food, and permanent water. They organized their lives around a catchment basin in a granite boulder, conforming their desires to the earth's charities; they never expected the opposite. The stories I grew up with lauded Moses for striking the rock and bringing forth the bubbling stream. But the stories of the Hohokam—oh, how they must have praised that good rock.

At dusk my friends returned with wonderful tales of the ground they had covered. We camped for the night, refilled our canteens, and hiked back to the land of plumbing and a fair guarantee of longevity. But I treasure my memory of the day I lingered near water and covered no ground. I can't think of a day in my life in which I've had such a clear fix on what it means to be human.

Want is a thing that unfurls unbidden like fungus, opening large upon itself, stopless, filling the sky. But *needs,* from one day to the next, are few enough to fit in a bucket, with room enough left to rattle like brittlebush in a dry wind.

∽

Navajo Sandstone Revisited—The San Rafael Swell

Greg Gordon

This excerpted story is from a book describing a professor and his long walk with students camping across Utah's "waste" lands. Note that students have adopted trail names.

After class we explore one of the neighboring canyons. Along the way students stop off to work on their journals, essays, or projects. Soon only Seeker, Huckleberry, and Patience accompany me up the canyon. We halt below an intriguing-looking alcove scooped out of the Navajo sandstone.

"Think there's anything up there?" Seeker asks as I scan the alcove with binoculars. "I doubt it; just a pile of rubble. Still, only one way to find out." Despite the heat we zigzag up the slickrock, and before long we are standing before an alcove much bigger than it looked from below. The pile of rubble at the entrance is undoubtedly a wall constructed to provide protection from the wind and cold.

The four of us stroll through the alcove in silence. Our footfalls raise the soft sand like moondust. Others have been here before us and left their boot prints, which remain undisturbed and protected from the elements.

A series of stacked sandstone blocks denotes rectangular sleeping quarters. A beehive-shaped structure squats at the back of the alcove. A block of sandstone leans against the beehive. It would fit perfectly into the opening as a door to guard the precious contents. I run my hand over the mud-plastered walls and let my fingers slide into the indentations left by a man unaware that the Normans were invading England. My fingers are too big, and they spill out of the mud furrows. Smaller rocks are impressed into the mortar in a line like decorative jewels. I peer inside. The floor is littered with corn cobs.

Originating in Mexico about four thousand years ago, corn cultivation spread north, becoming established along Muddy Creek by the dawn of Christianity. At first these nomadic hunters and gatherers supplemented their diet with corn, squash, and beans, but then became increasingly more reliant on agriculture. In time they developed their own variety of corn, capable of resisting the extremes of cold and drought, called "Fremont dent" after the indented kernels and the name we've bestowed upon this group of Native Americans.

Anthropologists have belatedly recognized the cliff dwellers of the Four Corners region as the ancestors of today's Pueblo Indians and now refer to the Anasazi as Ancestral Puebloans. However, we continue to use the term "Fremont" (after the river where they were first described in 1937) to distinguish this particular group. . . .

A mano and metate lie nearby. I heft the mano in my hand; this grapefruit-sized river rock plucked from the benches below would easily serve to crush corn kernels. I place it back on the smooth surface of the metate, a slab of sandstone worn smooth by generations of Indians using it for grinding. The mano and metate predate corn by several centuries and were originally used to grind seeds of Indian rice grass and acorns. I can't help but wonder how much sand ended up in the flour.

I then spy a large piece of pottery sticking out of the sand, a solid black shard marked with indentations forming short vertical lines all around the rim. Agriculture required an increasingly settled lifestyle, which in turn facilitated the development of pottery. Because of their distinctive pottery style, anthropologists are uncertain whether the Fremont acquired pottery independently from Mexico or adopted it from their Anasazi neighbors. Anthropologist David Madsen writes, "An internally consistent and widely accepted definition of the Fremont has never been developed. Given the lack of elaborate ceremonial kivas, polychrome pottery, detailed basketry designs, and other hallmarks of 'higher' social organizations, the Fremont have always been considered to be some sort of poor, out-back Anasazi."

Anthropologists distinguish the Fremont from the Anasazi based upon pottery and basketry styles, clay figurines, rock art, and footwear. Unlike the yucca sandals typical of the Anasazi, the Fremont wore a unique type of moccasin. These were fashioned from three pieces of hide from a deer's foreleg with the dewclaws intact. Likely this provided a distinctive footprint so tribal members could readily identify each other. Through minor modifications of the sole, one might even be able to distinguish family groups or clans. I wonder if future anthropologists will categorize us as cowboy boot culture, high heel culture, or Birkenstock culture.

Because the Fremont defy categorization, archaeologists continue to debate just who they were and how they were related to each other. Further complicating matters was the discovery of small villages scattered along Bull Creek, south of Hanksville on the flank of the Henry Mountains. This site shows continuous occupation from 6000 b.c. The Fremont occupied this complex of rock-lined pit houses, camps, and storage areas between eight hundred to twelve hundred years ago. Archaeologists have uncovered a potpourri of Fremont as well as Anasazi artifacts, including both classic Fremont and Anasazi pottery.

Some archeological evidence suggests that the Fremont and Anasazi shared geographical regions but occupied different niches, so to speak. The Anasazi confined themselves to lower elevations conducive to agriculture while the Fremont practiced hunting and gathering at higher elevations, living in groups of five to twelve extended families. Certainly the two groups were in frequent contact and may have shared both language and religion, surely a stronger cultural glue than footwear.

Furthermore, Fremont is a rather porous category encompassing both Great Basin hunter-gatherers and these Puebloan farmers. Fremont designates the people who from a.d. 650 to 1300 lived in the area from Grand Junction to Ely, Nevada, north to Pocatello, Idaho, and south to Cedar City, Utah. Likely those living in the Great Basin had more in common with other hunter-gatherers than they did with those here on the plateau who adopted a lifestyle similar to the Anasazi. These people doubtfully categorized themselves as a single group and may have even spoken different languages. Madsen speculates that what we call the Fremont were really three separate groups of different origins that shared a few minor traits acquired through trade and the spread of a religious cult. "Today we call these scattered groups of hunters and farmers the Fremont, but that name may be more reflective of our own need to categorize things than it is a reflection of how closely related these people were," writes Madsen.

Seeker waves me over to a corner of the alcove. By unspoken agreement, none of us have uttered a sound since entering. Seeker places a large spearpoint in my hand when I reach him. I stare at him in amazement. He points to the soft sand just past his feet. I hold the spearpoint in my hand, running my finger along the razor-sharp edge. Made from green chert, the spearpoint is notched slightly at one end where it was laced onto a spear with sinew. I sit at the edge of the alcove staring out to the canyon beyond, holding the spearpoint and puzzling over it.

The corn, pottery, and ruins all suggest that the Fremont lived here about a thousand years ago. The years A.D. 700 to 1300 marked the most widespread and dense indigenous population on the Colorado Plateau. Perhaps the climate was especially conducive to agriculture at that time. The Anasazi and Fremont cultures flourished, but agriculture demanded that people remain in one place, at least seasonally. Thus the game in an area was soon eliminated. The bow and arrow appropriate for small game replaced the atlatl and spear. Yet here was this spearpoint. The juxtaposition of seemingly different lifestyles is indicative of the Fremont who adopted strategies appropriate to the location. In some places and times they practiced agriculture, and in others they depended upon hunting and gathering. Some groups shifted seasonally between the two. In the fall, these shifting groups would harvest crops then quickly head to the highlands to gather pine nuts and hunt deer and sheep. In the winter they retreated to the rock shelters and subsisted off stored food supplemented by hunting. Spring brought planting and gathering. In summer they continued to gather wild plant crops, such as acorns and rice grass, as they came into season.

Other groups would be settled agriculturalists for a few years then take up hunting-gathering again, perhaps moving to another locale to settle. This harsh environment required a diversity of lifestyle strategies in order to survive. Perhaps some individuals simply preferred hunting to farming. Often we get trapped in our thinking, assuming a society *progresses* from hunting-gathering to agriculture.

About the time the Crusades ended, a watershed was reached among people in the Colorado Plateau. The Ancestral Puebloans had abandoned their villages in Utah and Colorado and consolidated into the Hopi, Zuni, Acoma, and Pueblo peoples along the Rio Grande, focusing nearly exclusively on agriculture. These villages are now the oldest continuously inhabited settlements in the United States, dating back to A.D. 1250.

The Fremont took the other route, abandoning agriculture. What actually became of them is speculative. A large proportion of Fremont sites show concurrent use by Shoshone and Paiute with a total replacement of Fremont-style artifacts. This, combined with the fact that the most recent artifacts (dating back five hundred years) are found the farthest away from the Shoshone-Paiute expansion, led Madsen to believe that the Fremont were pushed out of the region. Some argue that the Fremont moved south, integrating with the Pueblo Indians and losing their separate identity. Others hold that the Fremont, having originally come from the plains, simply moved back. Or that they were absorbed into the Shoshone-Paiute culture; I once met a Paiute man who claimed Fremont ancestry.

Nonetheless, this spearhead pointed backward, not forward. Could it be an artifact of the Archaic Indians who preceded the Fremont and also used this alcove? Could it be that humans have been visiting this particular alcove off and on for the past several thousand years? A similar alcove just east of here called Cowboy Cave contains thirteen thousand years' worth of sediments that can be radiocarbon dated. The oldest layer contains dung from mammoth, ground sloth, horse, and camel. The earliest human artifacts date back to 7000 B.C. These people left little evidence besides fires, kill sites, and stone tools. At some point (precise dating is difficult), they began painting and carving figures on rock surfaces. Then they began making things for us to discover: arrowheads, animal figurines from willows, humanoid figurines from clay, baskets, awls, and other bone tools. This Desert Culture traveled about in small bands of twenty-five to fifty individuals, engaging in a sustainable economy for thousands of years until agriculture arrived and the population exploded. Artifacts flourished as well: pottery, burial sites, jewelry, moccasins, and of course buildings, ranging from tiny granaries tucked into a cliff to entire villages.

I hold the spearpoint before me admiring the handiwork and skill it took to fashion it. Suddenly I'm filled with a desire to possess this artifact. I could easily slip it into my pocket and no one would be the wiser. I test out several rationalizations: if I don't take it, someone else will; the museums already have more spearpoints than they know what to do with; it's of no value, really. But they all ring false. This spearpoint has been here for several centuries, and in another thousand years it will still be here where it belongs. Who am I to disturb it? Antiquity bears its own authenticity. I will always have the satisfaction of knowing that it lies here unmolested. That in itself is worth far more than mere possession.

As I turn back to the alcove to replace the spearpoint, I remind myself that removing artifacts not only destroys any archeological value the artifact may hold but also robs the public of what is rightfully public property. It is akin to going into an art museum, cutting up the paintings, and taking all the pieces. I notice for the first time that the alcove is pockmarked with shallow pits where pothunters have been active. An unbroken pot will fetch more than $40,000 on the black market, and every accessible site on the Colorado Plateau has been raided.

Out of the corner of my eye, I notice a brown circle on a pink rock. Stepping closer, my eye perceives a tight coil of concentric circles radiating outward, and it takes a moment before my mind recognizes it as the bottom of a basket. I kneel down. Rock and pottery are so durable they should last a thousand years, but to find something as delicate as a basket comes as a surprise. Aridity, however, is a wonderful preservative and early archaeologists and settlers have found numerous baskets, moccasins, rope, sleeping mats, headdresses, and even buffalo hide robes and shields. This basket is one of the distinctive features of the Fremont. The Fremont had a unique style of basketry called rod and bundle where stripped willow rods were bound with yucca cordage. This method of construction allowed the yucca fibers to swell, and, combined with a bit of mud, rendered the basket virtually waterproof. Baskets and pottery were not only used for hauling water but also for cooking. A hot rock was dropped into the basket and quickly heated the water inside. Unlike their Anasazi neighbors, the Fremont never abandoned basketry in favor of pottery. Baskets were quicker and easier to make and could be readily constructed on site, important for a people clinging to their nomadic roots.

Made valuable by time alone, this treasure was uncovered and exposed by men intent upon quick profit. Reduced to a fragment, it was tossed aside as worthless. I lean over the basket fragment, and my strong scent permeates the dry air. I become hyperconscious of my own presence.

I step through a breach in the wall of the ruin. I notice the indentations in the sand left by dozens of feet. Nike, Adidas, and Teva have all left their trademarks. I pick up a piece of shaggy juniper bark and begin to sweep the prints clean. I sweep the floor of the ruin, working toward the exit so that all that remain are the striations of juniper bark. I want to obliterate all signs of profanity in this space. I wish to wipe clean my culture's impact. I want to erase the past; sweep away Wounded Knee, Sand Creek; obliterate poverty, reservations, alcoholism, diabetes, and depression. I want to place the stones back in the wall and seal this one ruin up from the poking and prodding of the curious. I want to sweep the whole alcove clean. I want to glue the pieces of broken pottery back together. I stand outside the ruin with my juniper bark broom and look at the hundreds of footprints in the alcove and sigh at the enormity of the task. I get down on my hands and knees and slowly begin sweeping.

~

Visiting Cliff Dwellings

Bill and Beth Sagstetter

In the words of archaeologist Peter Pilles, it is impossible for people to respect something they know nothing about. We heartily agree, and believe that knowledge comes first and respect follows. Education, therefore, is the key to respect. By providing readers with information, we hope to inspire love and respect for these fascinating places and the people who inhabited them. That is, in fact, how it happened for us.

But with this information comes responsibility. When we visit a back-country site, for that moment in time we are its caretaker or guardian. We become temporary unofficial stewards of the site, protecting it for future generations of backcountry visitors. It is up to *us* to make sure it is not damaged in any way during our visit there. If we are to visit these sites as they are in the wild—without locked gates and guards—we must know the proper protocol for visiting a cliff dwelling.

However, each national park, state park, tribal park, national monument, Bureau of Land Management and Forest Service land, has its own rules for visitors, which sometimes evolve and change. For example, in tribal parks you will need a guide to accompany you in the backcountry. At some sites, you are allowed to enter a ruin, look around it, and take photographs. At others, such as Canyon de Chelly, the ruins are fenced and you are not allowed to enter them. Therefore, the only way to make sure you are aware of the rules of the places you visit is to stop by the nearest ranger station or visitor center and inquire. Obtain the needed permits and/or arrange for a guide, if necessary. Familiarize yourself with the rules for that particular place before embarking on your adventure. But some basic commonsense guidelines can serve as a starting point for properly visiting cliff dwellings, with the understanding that they will be elaborated upon at each site.

The Hopi people of northeastern Arizona are among the modern descendants of the ancient Pueblo people. They have a word, *qahopi* (sometimes spelled *kahopi* and pronounced *kuh-HOPE-ee)*. It basically means the wrong way to do something—not the Hopi way of doing things. Using their words, it is *qahopi*—wrong—to harm a ruin in any way, even inadvertently. This includes actions such as leaning against or climbing on those old stone walls, which might cause them to collapse. Refrain from touching rock art panels, particularly tracing or outlining in chalk vague rock art for better photographs.

More obscure actions are also *qahopi*. Don't eat your lunch in the ruin, as the crumbs you drop can attract rodents, whose burrowing can undermine walls and cause them to topple. For the same reasons, it is *qahopi* to camp or sleep in a ruin. Instead, camp nearby, safely away from the delicate structure. Keep children under close supervision for their own safety and also so they cause no accidental harm.

Digging at a site is more than *qahopi*; it is illegal to dig on state or federal government land. In tribal park lands this law is also strictly enforced. Even archaeologists must submit reams of forms for permits to excavate. Digging without a permit is punishable by stiff fines and/or imprisonment, and vehicles and equipment will be confiscated.

It is also illegal to remove anything from a site, including arrowheads, potsherds, and even items that seem insignificant, such as rock chips, for example. First of all, removing objects destroys the archaeological record and limits future research. Each artifact at a site is like a book—full of information and stories—that archaeologists attempt to decipher. Digging at a site destroys information. So to preservationists, removing or rearranging anything at a site is akin to burning a book or destroying a library.

Then, from the modern Puebloan point of view, each object the ancients made was created with songs and prayers and thus is imbued with a spirit of its own. So when you find an artifact, leave it and its spirit where you found it. Don't remove it and its spirit from their places; they sing the same song and should remain together.

Some well-intentioned people move artifacts from their original place to a *museum rock*. A museum rock could be a boulder the size of a table or a windowsill or the top of a wall on which people place artifacts they have found at the site in order to display them. Apparently, some folks think that it doesn't count as removing artifacts. But in fact it does destroy the story the artifact has to tell. Artifacts must be left *exactly* where they are encountered.

There are even special ways to walk in a cliff dwelling. It is *qahopi* to walk on the fragile midden (the soft discard area where inhabitants disposed of their refuse). The midden is often found in the front of a cliff dwelling, sometimes downhill or off the face of the cliff.

Also, attempting to retrace the steps of the ancient ones on the old hand- and toehold trails is foolhardy. People have been seriously injured or killed trying to climb the hand- and toeholds etched by the ancients on the cliff walls. These holds have often eroded and are no longer negotiable, and using them hastens their erosion. Also, these hand- and toeholds usually lead in only one direction; if you should become stranded halfway, there is no way down. Other hand and toe trails must be started with one particular foot—if you should begin up the trail with the "wrong" foot, you will not be able to complete the trail and could become stuck there.

If, in your backcountry travels, you should happen upon people vandalizing a ruin, do not confront them. Just observe them discreetly from a distance, make notes, and take photographs of their actions if you have a camera handy. If possible, write down vehicle license plate numbers at the trailhead parking lot if there is one, and report it to the nearest sheriff or ranger or to site personnel at the nearest visitor center. Let us all become an army of unofficial stewards, protecting these very special cliff ruins for future generations of backcountry visitors.

Labyrinth—Southern Utah

Craig Childs

The middle of December, a week away from the frigid solstice. A pot of snow on my stove. I settled over it, reducing it to drinking water liberally dusted with blow-sand and tiny kernels of rock. Two of us had set our camp in the open, unprotected on a sandstone spine arcing above a thicket of canyons. The region surrounding us was an isolated and furious storm, a place where the stone earth has heaved itself upward, opening innumerable crevasses burdened under layers of shadow. We came up to this high point to capture the last prized light of day.

My partner, a tall, early-thirties man named Devin Vaughan, hunted below a cluster of stunted junipers like a mouse preparing for winter, gathering handfuls of dry sticks and old, papery grass stems to burn. Devin is a river outfitter and engine mechanic from Moab, Utah, a frequent companion of mine on long walks. He is an attractive man, his face sharply featured, a small and narrow mouth and a steeply cut jawline. He is one of only four people I know who have enough intimacy with this place to navigate it end to end. He carries a map with him, taped at the rips and folds, worn soft and jotted on

---

"The Labyrinth" from *Soul of Nowhere* by Craig Childs (Boston: Back Bay Books, 2002). Reprinted by permission of the author.

with a pen. He marks every successful route in red. His map's topographic features are as convoluted as a brain, and within them his red lines backtrack and overlap in a way that suggests lunacy.

Little more than ten miles long and five miles wide, this is a confined and arid maze of canyons. Hordes of faults and fractures break through the terrain, dividing the basement rock into thin upright bands. Hundreds of these fins run alongside each other like salmon teeming up a shallow river. Between are plunging unlit banks of boulders and windless glens. The east side is shielded by a twelve-hundred-foot cliff; its northern boundary a nearly impenetrable field of sandstone risers; and to the south and west is a lengthy, straight-walled canyon that cups the region like a hand. Within these protective outer walls is this island of dissected rock where we finally ended our tasks and stood to watch the sun clip beneath the horizon.

Out there, ahead of us in this darkening, perplexing land was our destination. In the center of this labyrinth the fins spread like an opening lotus, wings of stone falling back to reveal the single soul of nowhere. It is a snake carved into the rock, left by the Anasazi maybe nine hundred years ago. Thirty feet long, nearly as wide as a spread hand, this snake sweeps horizontally across the foot of a cliff, its body rippling with motion. Like pilgrims, we had come to this snake numerous times in the past, approaching it along routes from the east, west, and north. This winter we were searching for a new route, starting at the south end of this maze and attempting a northward crossing.

I would have tried this passage with no one other than Devin. His physical movements in rough country are so cultivated and graceful they seem to rhyme. I have seen him fly, sailing into the air, reflecting off a wall to grab a handhold on the other side. He is a fine route finder, perhaps the best I have ever met. The way he sees the landscape's code heartens me, his eyes luring pathways from impossible places. The planet opens to him.

This time of year every night is colder and darker than the last, our bodies a bit slower, more conservative in the chill. We each had a small fire pan. We fed them twigs and pulls of dry grass. As we huddled over our flickers of warmth, we said little, busy adding sticks and rearranging our fires.

"Tomorrow," he said, turning the word up into a question. "Move due north from here?"

I poked the fire around in my pan to keep the smoke down, my face held directly over the flames. "North," I agreed.

~

In the morning north sent us a little west and east, then south again. We kept our gear light. Neither of us carried a tent. Too heavy. We melted snow when needed, keeping the weight off of our backs. Climbing into crossword puzzles of fissures, we removed our packs from time to time, hoisting them to each other. The rock formations passing around us were as elegant as ear bones, great overhead arches and fine lips of handholds.

We climbed into a sandstone cleft, a place where water once ran. Ahead it dropped into darkness, out of sight. A juniper tree had fallen and was jammed, its pewter-colored wood old and splintered. It had been here for some time. We left our packs on a ledge, heading down to explore this space, seeing if it was a way of travel or not.

Devin tied a length of climbing webbing to his waist while I tied the other end to mine. If he fell, my body would catch behind him like the wedged tree. Professional climbers might scoff at our quick and rudimentary techniques, but this is the way to move here, throwing a bowline around our bodies several times a day as a quick backup. We both wore gloves with the fingertips cut off. Day gloves. The fleece had worn so thin in places that the lines in our knuckles were visible. He ventured farther into the crack, using his shoulders and back to hold himself, sending a hand flat against the wall as a brace. Dislodging a rock with his boot, he kicked it free to test the depth of the passage below him.

It clacked and rattled as if dropped down a well. We leaned over to listen. It fell at least a hundred feet. What we could not see below us suddenly became huge, like the throat of an unimaginable beast.

"No, no, no," Devin said, turning around quickly. "This isn't the way."

I agreed, reeling him back on the webbing.

Devin had been studying this region for ten years, poking his way through a place not much larger than the town in which he lived, and had still not deciphered even half of its routes. This hugeness inside smallness creates a matrix of intersections, precious and incalculable channels one after the next. It is a fractal landscape like the surface of a leaf, veins within veins, or the arborescent feathers of ice forming barbs inside of barbs across the surface of a pond.

I had to find a way of keeping track, looking behind me to consider the terrain I had just come through, ledges slick with ice skirting a small plunge above where Devin and I had retreated with our webbing, then beyond that a stone-walled avenue where juniper trees grow along the bottom. It was not an option for me to memorize all of this in order to find my way back in case this route did not go. There were too many turns and decisions. I had to instead remember by allowing myself to remain in each passageway after I had gone. I made a ceaseless inquiry of the place, not asking questions as I walked, but rather presenting myself openly, taking in the environment without governing the incoming information. I did not deal in unnecessary thoughts, concerns about tonight's meal or tiredness in my legs. I walked slowly, brushing my gloved hands on walls, pausing atop high fins, my head filled with imagery and no words.

I left a skein of my presence throughout this maze, strands of sensations that might lead me back, that would be with me days from now, likely decades from now, because they were not sensations restricted to my eyes or my tongue. Everything I came across entered me like a dream. I was turning my life into twine, stretching myself through these corridors until my body was only a mark along the way. Otherwise, I would find myself suddenly lost, turning quickly, not knowing the direction to or from.

But always the snake lay in my mind like a compass point. I was aware as I turned how it was now at my back, then to my side, with days of baffling, unknown topography between here and there.

Devin had first brought me to the snake a few years earlier during the height of summer. We had arrived exhausted, heat shimmering off our skin. I held my eyes up to see the single piece of art, tracing its curved outline along the wall. I had swayed slowly in the heat below it. Dredging deep into my body for any word that might fit, I said, *"Snake . . . yes . . . hot . . . shade?"*

Its interior is pointillist, filled with hundreds of small peck marks that are crowded, but not overlapped. The head is eye-shaped, wide at the jaw and pointed at the tip. The body stretches from right to left with supple curves, the crests and troughs forming perfect symmetry. I had thought upon first seeing it that this snake describes how a person must live and travel here: find the sweet and elegant course that lies within this turmoil; understand the patterns concealed in the land; walk unfettered through the maze. This is the reward for knowing the way through, this snake waiting in the center where the earth unfolds.

As we traveled north this winter we crossed numerous broad openings that appeared at the meeting places of canyons and joints within the sandstone. We came on each of these interior regions surprised, clambering through a crease to suddenly arrive at open sunlight. These were gardens hanging in the chaos, juniper trees and tight clumps of blackbrush finding purchase in sand. Everything was cold and silent in these open places. We ran into the basins shouting, kicking through the sand. Our bodies opened like horses let out at full gallop. Fifty seconds across stood the opposite wall, honeycombed with minor canyon mouths and boulders where we had to slow ourselves and concentrate, finding the way out again.

For the sake of knowing where we were or where we had been, we used these basins as reference points, calling them First or Second Land. Fourth

Land, Sixth Land, whichever. In the Seventh Land we stopped to rest. Devin walked slowly, examining the ground.

"What do you see?" I called. He looked up as if puzzled to hear me. He walked over. "I haven't seen any bighorn tracks. No coyotes or mountain lions. No large animals."

I had not seen them either. In this sort of desert we would expect to at least find the lobed pads of coyote tracks, or the praying hands of bighorn prints, but not here. Like listening to the rock tumbling down the crack earlier, this information about animals suddenly revealed a gulping acquaintance. *A place where even animals can't reach,* I thought.

It was like walking in a dungeon down here, the walls cold and half-lit. A faint mist of breath drifted around us, coiling against the rock. The passage rounded out, womblike. The walls above came close enough together that rocks the size of soccer balls were caught over our heads and we passed beneath, cautiously, curiously glancing up.

Devin found water and called me over. In the crotch of a small, declivitous side canyon was a frozen pool. This was good news. No more sand in our water. He picked up a rock and, with a few well-delivered blows, broke through. Slabs of ice buckled and floated. We both removed gloves and submerged our bottles, plunging our already cold hands into the water.

Devin's left hand came out bright pink. Grinning, he looked up and asked, "Does the desert always provide?" I pulled out my own hand, the skin taut and alive with cold.

◡

We camped that night in this hole of a canyon. Theatrical light from our single campfire broke up through the walls, casting eerie shadows two hundred feet over our heads. The view of the stars was through a single opening where the walls spread like bread dough pulled apart, wedged rocks still joining the two sides. When the fire burned down we could see the stars more clearly, a luminescent trail of overhead dust.

"We need a better view of the sky," I said, standing up from the coals.

Devin followed me with his eyes. Then he looked up to see the stars and back to me. He made a grunting sound of approval, lifting his folds of clothing to a standing position.

Our boots crunched through snow as we left. We walked down the canyon to where it fell open, the walls backing apart. The stone beneath us slid a hundred feet into the throat of a canyon, coatings of ice sloping along it. In front of us the western quadrant of stars came into full view. We stood at this edge as if we had both been presented to the sky, held forward in palms of sandstone.

We were quiet for some time. We listened. There was no wind, no sound. The stars were each clear, not so much lights as they were points of contact. It is said that there are only six thousand stars visible to the eye, but tonight there were more. They fell back from nearest and highest of magnitude to those so faint or distant that they turned to powder, and from powder to a thin brume.

The lines I had been laying of myself across the ground reached upward. I found myself oriented by stars, by constellations and gas clouds where swaths of stars were entirely hidden. I had been out for enough nights over the past years that I came to distinguish suggestive patterns among even the dimmer stars. I had recognized to within a number of days when Mars or Jupiter had gone into retrograde motion and begun slowly backtracking across the sky. There were routes among the stars that were as effective and methodical as those I found on the ground. In the map Devin and I were attempting to create here, the sky held weight equal to the earth, especially in winter.

"Good stars," I finally said.

"Good stars," he replied softly. "This is why we come to the ass end of nowhere. Stars like this."

There is a sameness between Devin and me. We see this same horrible violence, cliffs collapsing and frozen, these stars held as if about to burst. We see this hugeness, leaving the electric lights behind, the vibrancy of human-ity, to enter the dark turns of rock, looking for only these things: process, comprehension, stone, a rope dangling for a way out. The stars were what we looked for tonight. We both saw the sky spreading into paths of insoluble order. The stars moved, winking out one by one as the horizon lifted against them. . . .

~

On the seventh day we had our camp in the high eastern region. Below and to all sides were hundreds of stone temples standing shoulder to shoulder. Snow graced each northern flank. We gathered twigs at the end of the day and once again pulled on our warmest clothing. Wind trafficked through the spaces below us, sending up hissing tones of conversations.

The sun touched the southwest horizon. We stopped whatever we were doing and faced it.

"Every night we go through this," Devin said without breaking eye contact with the sunset. "Everything's going to be different here. In thirty seconds."

I nodded and said nothing. My face was strangely warm in this final, brassy glow. The very surface was nipped cold, but I felt the heat underneath, at my bones.

As the sun shrank, the light turned tepid. Devin pointed straight at the bright, sinking knob, saying, "Watch it. It doesn't even pause. This whole thing is wound around us, some kind of great machine that's about to close us out. There it goes. There . . . there . . ." He inhaled when it happened. The light flashed out.

"Done," he said. He turned to me. His voice was softer now, a little crazy. "Now, here we are."

On these winter days, once the sun is gone, the world changes. Whatever we were in the sunlight, we ceased and became something different in the dark, from mobile, animated creatures to cold, huddled rocks.

A deep violet color poured overhead. We got around to our two small fires in their pans, stoking them as we sat near each other. We blew into the mounds of coals, carefully adding twigs and arranging them as if building a ship in a bottle. The fires rose and fell as we kept them fed. The snake was now a short distance away. Neither of us had seen it during the winter solstice. Tomorrow we would go.

In the stranded hours of darkness I thought of a man I know, an astrophysicist named Kim Malville. He would enjoy this artifact that we were about to reach, I thought. I had studied under him as an undergraduate at the University of Colorado, and tonight I remembered how his talk used to be filled with terms that mystified me: *the houses of the sun, symbolic geometry, sacred mandalas.* He saw ceremony everywhere, and it is perhaps from him that I learned to watch for it. Together we sank into hours of conversation, pushing at the edges of science like excitable children. It enchanted me to see an older man weathered and lithe, his eyes alert to every thought. Once in a planetarium he stood at the controls spinning stars over my head as fast as he could move them, changing the positions to take us back thousands of years. He was laughing like a madman the whole time.

Adding to his role as an astrophysicist, he took a strong, professional interest in archaeoastronomy, drawing the stars down to earth, back to the people who had lived here. A few years back he discovered in the Saharan Desert astronomically aligned stone monoliths and a small circle of upright slabs. The alignments consisted of stones, some weighing two tons; most of the stones were buried in the sand. He found six major alignments extending across the sediments of a dry lake for about a third of a mile. Predating Stonehenge by two thousand years, this site became the oldest known megalithic archaeoastronomical site in the world, dating to 5000 B.C. This knowledge of the sky, he taught me, is as old as the human mind. He had found lifted stone monoliths near the Utah–Colorado border, placed, he imagined, to cast shadows marking certain celestial events. That site, around which thirty thousand Anasazi once lived, may well have been thought of as the center of the universe, considering the way events in the sky are lined up with dominant local landmarks.

He fed my curiosity when I studied with him. He told me of excavations where he had worked, finding astronomical alignments with artifacts that were accurate down to halves of degrees, using transect equipment just to make sure of it. I imagined him in the field the same way he was manning the planetarium, his eyes dazzled with whirling patterns.

At the top of the fins tonight I worked my fire down to coals thinking of Kim Malville and his ravishing universe. It was above my head right now, the dark, consuming hand of the sky. Sitting cross-legged in front of my coals, I kept my face close, blowing into them, my skin warming at each bright pulse. Devin did the same, shoving coals around with his last stick. Finally it was over. The coals were no longer worth it. I had kept my attention on the ground for a couple of hours, never allowing myself a long upward stare. The pleasures of the night needed to be judiciously divided; otherwise the cold would become insufferable.

I sat with my back straight, my head turning up to see the stars. We had the full view from here, stars down to every horizon. Devin and I sat as quietly as possible, the glow reducing beneath us as the world turned from the real into the unreal. Infinite space extended over us. I felt the curve of the planet, how it faced into this celestial landscape, a giant orb of rock suspended among stars, floating because it could not fall. There was no place to fall to. It left a queer sensation, bolts of panic and ecstasy. The threads of my life spread across a landscape of light years, from this desert through the stars and back. My body was too small to possibly contain this.

How long, indeed, until we were pummeled? The sunlight hours gave us the earth—the fins, canyons, and lopsided boulders. These long nights were nothing but sky, a radiant and deep color that could not possibly have a name, the earth gone from us. Tomorrow it would return, tearing like an animal at our clothes. Tomorrow we would go to the snake and step into the winter alignment between this earth and this sky.

~

I left in the morning long before the sun. Stars bathed my movements. Devin was still in his bag. He would catch up later. I walked west, aiming toward the red-eyed star of Orion. It began setting over the far cliffs as I dropped through the first leading canyons.

The land came visible under a thin, watery light. I could barely see fins rising ahead of me, sequential outlines that were the secret to knowing how to navigate this place. I walked a memory of benches and small backtracks from years of travel to the snake, a cut between walls that dropped one after the next, a huge staircase leading through a notch into a basin. A falling star streaked into the southern sky, breaking into a shower of pieces before dissolving, flushing into a green line, never allowed to touch ground. The eastern sky held the final cut of a crescent moon, almost a new moon. In every object around me, in the sky and on the earth, I saw this calendar. The universe seemed poised, each item in perfect place.

The moon was the most glaring of these items for the moment. Clear as a Cheshire grin, it hovered low in the sky, sickle thin. Every day and night the moon rises in a different place at a different time, then every month it is somewhere else again. Among the idyllic cycles of the sun and seasons, the moon is an alluring nemesis. It crosses at unorthodox angles, swinging drunkenly over the horizons.

Fancifully, I thought of the nearby snake as a solar and lunar balance. It has the sun's bearing, but with the moon's data. The length of its body bears six troughs and seven crests, adding up to thirteen, the number of new moons in the year. Within the confines of a solar year, the moon gets abridged, allowed to complete only twelve and a half of its own cycles, which causes a disparity between moon time and sun time. At the snake, lunar phases could be counted starting at the summer solstice arrowhead. Working down the snake's body, every trough and crest would be marked by each month of the moon. The last moon of the lunar cycle would land in the final trough of the snake's tail, exactly one solar year after the moon-counting began, the moment that the next arrowhead of sunlight touches the head of the snake, the moment to begin counting again. Calendars for the moon and the sun would balance out across this snake.

As I walked, twilight met the moon above the horizon and began washing it away. I dropped from view of both Orion and the fading moon, winding toward a broad opening between fins. Crossing this clearing, I heard a raven coming through, its wings flapping hard against the cold. I stopped to watch it pass. Up the other side, I scrambled through house-sized boulders that formed a steep three-hundred-foot apron below a cliff. As I came to the foot of the cliff I saw the snake within arm's reach of the ground. I stopped there, letting my heart slow from the climb. My eyes moved across the entire plane of the cliff, and I could not bring them back to the snake for at least another minute, taking in the angles of rock and the distances around me.

The snake is always a startling find, even knowing it is here, like coming across a Picasso painting lying on its side in an alley. It is literally in the middle of nowhere, boulders unfolded randomly beneath it. The horizontal body carries a sensuous tension flexing thirty feet from head to tail. It had been chiseled into the flesh of deep red sandstone, revealing the much paler rock within. When I came closer I stopped again and lifted my gloved hand in the air, tracing its ophidian crests and troughs. Curves spent themselves across the wall like water.

If you sat in the desert for a year with a clock and a Gregorian calendar, you would find that your time does not match what you see in the world around you. The snake, the stars, the sun, and the moon belong to an interlocking design. We fool ourselves with our inventions. The gears of true time are not round like those of the clock. The earth travels at different speeds during different times of the year, slinging faster and slower around the sun, making European winters eight days shorter than those in Australia. Lunar and solar cycles set up a complex rhythm obeying doublets and triplets, not the singular boxes of weekdays and months. We are made to look like simpletons the way we spoon-feed ourselves with our artless time of minutes, hours, and days, leap years thrown in to jury-rig our twelve months so that they don't fall into disrepair. We add and subtract sixty minutes of daylight saving time to our seasons to make our workdays more efficient, our heads buried in business while around us these flawless patterns pass like the hand of God.

I kept still in the cold, waiting in this place where true time shows itself. Soon the sun arrived. Light soaked each high point of stone hundreds of feet above. Shadows slid back into their crevices. Breezes came up as the cold sink of morning lazily rolled over itself. When the sun touched the head of the snake, it was nothing like summer solstice. Summer light had been pure white. This was the molten color of red curry. Instead of a discrete arrowhead, now came a two-hundred-foot wave of light. Absolutely vertical, it spanned the height of the cliff like an opening theater curtain.

Every tie that I had to the night sky came to me. This was the convergence of unimaginably expansive spheres—the inviolable sky, and the forged land. The snake had been slipped into place, a knot binding the two. I stood at the meeting point as these forces silently crossed each other like galaxies sliding together, and then apart.

When the sun finally moved beyond the snake's tail, warming the rock face until I felt it on my skin, I heard a peculiar, metallic sound. It twanged musically far in the distance, barely audible. I turned from the snake and looked out. The thing, whatever it was, plucked rhythmically. Perplexed, I traced the sound to a high notch I had come through earlier. There, Devin sat against a boulder playing a Jew's harp, snapping the metal tong against his open mouth. He was at my eye level a mile away. How long had he been there? Had he watched the light come across the snake?

I found a place to sit in the boulders, resting in the warmth of my clothes and the new sun. I listened to Devin's performance. With all of this fantastic consequence swirling around me, holy alignments striking down everywhere, Devin was a strange Puck in the rocks. Humans, I thought, what fantastic creatures we are, spinning like dervishes in these forever domains of star paths and canyons, grasping the extent of this landscape in one moment, forgetting in another. We lay out maps for ourselves as if we cannot see clearly enough with our own eyes. At the same time we expand beyond the farthest edges of our girded maps. We are perfect for this place. Never still and never simple.

The Maze and Aura—Canyonlands

Jack Turner

I

Just before dawn sometime in April 1964, I shoved my Kelty behind the seat of a small Piper Cub, climbed into the passenger seat, and fastened my safety belt as we motored onto the airport runway at Moab, Utah. Since it was empty, we kept going into the take-off without stopping and then climbed slowly, the little plane grinding for altitude. Soon we banked west, and as we cleared the cliffs bordering the Spanish Valley, a vast array of mesas spread before us, glowing faintly in the morning light.

We turned again, southwest, and set a course for Junction Butte, a landmark tower at the confluence of the Green and Colorado Rivers. Beyond the confluence was the Maze, a terra incognita some people wanted preserved as part of the newly proposed Canyonlands National Park. *National Geographic* magazine believed the Maze might harbor something to persuade Congress to include it in the new park. My friend Huntley Ingalls and I were to explore the area for three days and photograph what we found. The plane would drop

From *The Abstract Wild* by Jack Turner. © John S. Turner. Reprinted by permission of the University of Arizona Press.

us as close to the Maze as possible. In the darkness of the runway we had flipped a coin to see who would go in first, and I won.

The pilot—Bud—was silent. Since he knew the country below from landing at remote sites for uranium and oil companies, I tried to question him about features in the landscape. But the noise of the motor made conversation difficult so we lapsed into silence and flew on, bouncing like a boat in rapids off the thermals coming up from the canyons. Below, the Colorado River meandered through swells of slickrock muted by purple shadow, while to the north, miles of fluted red walls led to Grand View Point. By the time we crossed the Green River, the first light had illuminated the grass covering the sandbars, and pools of water in the slickrock gleamed like tiny silver mirrors. There was not a cloud in the sky—a perfect day.

At Junction Butte we had turned west toward Ekker Butte. Beneath it, to the south, was Horse Canyon, an open valley that receded into a labyrinth of slots—the Maze. On a bench between Ekker Butte and the canyon was an airfield that looked like a matchstick. Bud dropped the nose of the Piper Cub and we made a pass several hundred feet above the dirt strip. It had not been used in years, Bud said, and I believed him. It was covered with small plants and netted with arroyos. Worse, the south fork of Horse Canyon was far away, and since it led into the heart of the Maze, I feared that if we landed here, we'd never reach our main objective. So I began to search for options.

Beyond the nearest fork of Horse Canyon—the north fork—a two-track struck south to the edge of the south fork, a point now called the Maze Overlook. It was a perfect place to start from and I wanted to land there. Bud turned south. The road turned out to be old Caterpillar scrape, one blade wide—probably cut by a seismographic survey crew when oil companies explored this basin in the fifties. I asked Bud if he could land on the scrape. He wasn't sure. I wanted him to try. He was silent.

We dropped down for a closer look and banked slightly left above the narrow dirt path, Bud's face pressed against the window. Then we gained altitude and headed back, still in silence. Bud nipped switches and studied the instrument panel. Soon we were sinking toward the road, then slowly we settled in. Several feet above the ground, a gust of wind blew us to the right and we landed hard in the blackbush flats. The right wheel hit first, and when the wheel strut punctured the floor between my feet, I pitched forward, striking my head against the instrument panel and spewing blood over the cockpit. The plane bounced gracefully into the air and Bud worked the stick, murmuring softly, "Whoa baby, whoa baby." We lost control in slow motion, but were without panic, a space I've encountered many times. Then the plane hit again, the wheels snagged a shallow arroyo, and we flipped upside down, sliding across the desert with a sickening screech.

When we stopped, we were hanging upside down from our seat belts. The pressure of our body weight made it difficult to release them, so we hung there kicking, trying to brace ourselves against the windshield. I smelled my own blood—that strange metallic tang. I tried to smell gas, and all the while I'm thinking, "We're gonna get roasted." Finally Bud released his buckle and crashed into the windshield. He helped me release mine, and we sat together on the roof of the cockpit, trying to open the doors. Unfortunately, the wings were bent up just enough to prevent the doors from opening, so we both kicked hard on one door until something gave. Then we crawled out into the warm silence of a desert morning.

We were ecstatic—laughing, shaking hands, kicking our heels, and praising each other as though we had by sheer intelligence and talent achieved a magnificent goal. I licked the blood off my hands and congratulated myself for surviving my first airplane wreck. I was twenty-two years old.

While Bud searched for the first-aid kit, I got some water from the Kelty. I had six quarts, the standard rock climber's ration: two quarts per person per day, anywhere, under any conditions. We patched the gash in my head. Then, the adrenaline wearing off, we considered our plight. Bud felt he should walk to Anderson Bottom, a grassy stretch along the Green River with a line shack occupied by one of the local ranchers. I thought we should stay put. We had warm clothes, one sleeping bag, gas from the plane, matches for a brush fire, food, and water. Furthermore, we were highly visible—a light green airplane on a red desert. Within hours, Huntley would organize a rescue flight and easily spot us from above the airfield across the north fork. Bud would not stay, however, and after a few minutes he left, walking north with neither water nor supplies. The next day he was picked up near the Green River.

I examined my Kelty for what, typically, was not there: no compass, no maps, no tent, no stove, no binoculars, no flares, no signal mirror. This probably had something to do with being kicked out of Boy Scouts. There were just two climbing ropes, some rock-climbing gear, a bivouac tarp, a sleeping bag, a Leica M2, the usual climber's food—summer sausage, cheese, gorp—and water.

I walked to the rim of the south fork. It was perhaps a hundred feet to the bottom of Horse Canyon. Across the canyon were spires of shale topped by dollops of White Rim sandstone, a formation now called "the Chocolate Drops." The canyon walls were more eroded than the Navajo and Kayenta sandstone I was familiar with from Glen Canyon, but everywhere were braids of a real labyrinth. The so-called south fork divided into at least three more

canyons and everything kept forking. To my delight I saw marshes and a pool
of water. It was utterly still. I sat on the rim and asked a question that came up
often during the next thirty years: Why, exactly, am I here?

I was there because of Huntley. During the fifties he worked in southern
Utah for the Coast and Geodetic Survey, traveling by Jeep and foot throughout
the canyonlands conducting magnetic surveys. During those years he photographed spires he thought would make interesting rock climbs and showed
his slides to other climbers living in Boulder, Colorado. He had photographs
of the Fisher Towers, Totem Pole, Spider Rock, Standing Rock, Castleton
Tower, and the Six-Shooter Peaks. By 1964 these spires had been climbed,
some by Yosemite climbers, but many by Huntley and Layton Kor. Huntley
had published articles on the first ascents of the Fisher Tower and Standing
Rock in *National Geographic,* and now they thought he might use his climbing expertise to explore the Maze. Since I had climbed a lot with Kor and
Huntley, was interested in wild places and was Huntley's friend, here I was
staring at the labyrinth.

The Utah desert was relatively unknown in the early sixties. In 1960 the
road south of Blanding was dirt most of the way to Tuba City; the bridges were
often one lane and made of wood. Eliot Porter's *Glen Canyon: The Place No
One Knew* was not published until 1963, and Edward Abbey's *Desert Solitaire*
did not come out until 1968. There were no guidebooks to these wildlands.
Many of the parks and monuments and wilderness areas that now cover the
area did not exist, and the country was vast and wild and easy to get lost in;
there were no restrictions, and little management. We wandered the desert as
we wished, lounged in the pools at Havasu, waded the Zion Narrows, climbed
the desert towers, drifted down Glen Canyon, and explored the Escalante enjoying virtually no contact with other people. The Maze was simply another
place on Huntley's long list of wild places to see.

Although the Maze was de facto wilderness, I did not then think of wilderness as a separate place needing preservation. The Wilderness Act was not
passed until 1964. To the degree I even thought about preservation, I pre-
sumed it was conducted by nice old ladies in big cities. It certainly had nothing to do with me. I simply liked climbing big walls and spires and exploring
remote places, preferably before anyone else did. Like most rock climbers I
didn't even like to hike. I didn't know the name of a single wildflower, and
Huntley had to tell me, "These are cottonwoods" or "These are Utah juniper."
My knowledge of animals derived mainly from hunting and killing them.
(Years later, when I read Schopenhauer, I recognized myself in those days:
"in the mind of a man who is filled with his own aims, the world appears as a
beautiful landscape appears on the plan of a battlefield.")

I walked back to the plane and wrote a message on the road with the heel of my boot: "All OK," "Bud"—then an arrow—and "Anderson Bottom." I drank a quart of water, pulled out my foam pad, and settled into the shade beside the fuselage. I had no books, no paints or nature guides. I wasn't worried, I was bored.

Around eleven in the morning I heard a plane and soon Huntley flew over in a Cessna 180 piloted by George Hubler, the owner of the Moab airport. After several passes to make sure I was ambulatory, they dropped a message saying they would land Huntley on the old airstrip. He would then cross the north fork and meet me at the wreck.

I settled back into the shade, even more bored. I could not get over the silence; it ate at me and I couldn't sit still. I wandered around looking for something interesting to do and found nothing. So I sat in the shade, oblivious to the glory that engulfed my every moment.

The day passed slowly with no sign of Huntley. In the evening I walked to the rim of the north fork of Horse Canyon and searched for him, but to no avail. That night I consumed more of my water supply. I slept fitfully.

The next morning, when there was still no sign of Huntley, I went back and walked the rim searching for him. Finally, in the late afternoon, I found him placing an expansion bolt several feet below the White Rim sandstone cap. He had already done some wild unroped climbing, but the cap was featureless, and that meant bolting. Soon he was up. We shook hands and greeted each other formally by last name, in the best British mountaineering tradition.

Huntley had left most of his gear at the bottom of the canyon while searching for a way through the cliffs. Since Hubler would return to the airfield the following day at noon, we had less than twenty-four hours to explore the Maze. We decided to leave Huntley's gear where it was and go on into the south fork. The plan was simple: we would walk into the Maze until dark, hike back through the night to the north fork, collect Huntley's things, and climb to the airfield to meet Hubler in the morning.

We returned to the wreck, gathered my gear, and after some scrambling and several rappels, reached the bottom of the canyon. After filling the water bottles at the algae-filled pool (we never treated water in those days), we hiked to the main canyon and up the middle of the three forks.

Soon Huntley began moving slowly and muttering about new boots. (Eventually he would lose all his toenails, which for years he kept in a small jar as a reminder.) After awhile he urged me to go on so I could cover as much ground as possible before dark. We dropped our packs in an obvious spot and I hurried up the canyon in fading light, moving rapidly, my eyes sweeping the landscape like radar. I missed the soaring walls and alcoves of the Escalante, the water, the seeps. I was still bored. But mostly from a sense of obligation, I walked on doggedly through the extraordinary silence.

Then, in the last light of day, I was startled by a line of dark torsos and a strange hand on a wall just above the canyon floor. I froze, rigid with fear. My usual mental categories of alive and not-alive became permeable. The painted figures stared at me, transmuted from mere stone as if by magic, and I stared back in terror.

After a few seconds, my body intervened with my mind, pulling it away from a gaze that engulfed me. The torsos became *just* pictures. My mind discovered a comfortable category for the original perception and the confusion passed. But strangely, seeing them as representations did not reduce the emotion I felt. I was chilled, shivering, though the air was warm. I could not override the feeling that the figures were looking at me, and that I was seeing what I wasn't supposed to see.

I can say now this fear resulted from confusion: perhaps from the exhaustion of the past two days, perhaps because of my anxiety for Huntley's situation and the increasing extremity of our position. But in retrospect, I believe it was the inherent power of the figures.

They were pictographs, but not the usual stick figures and crude animals I'd seen before. There were fifteen of them, painted a dark, almost indigo blue. Some were life-size, some smaller. Some were abstract, like mummies with big buggy eyes and horns. Others had feet and hands. One particularly beautiful figure I assumed was female. Among the figures were small animals, insects, snakes, and birds, all painted in remarkable detail. The most unusual figure displayed an enlarged hand with clearly articulated fingers; springing from the end of the middle finger was a fountain of what looked like blood—a spurting wound. Farther left along the wall were more figures. One did not appear abstract at all. It was dressed and masked, had feet, perhaps even moccasins, and held what looked like a spear.

I yelled for Huntley, hoping he would hear me and be able to see the figures before dark. In a few minutes he came hobbling up the canyon. Although he'd seen many examples of rock art throughout the canyon country, he had never seen anything like these figures, and he too was captured by their powerful presence. While photographing them with long time-exposures, we stared in silence. Although spooky and unsettling, they absorbed us, and we did not want to leave.

Reluctantly, we walked downcanyon and collected my gear. By the time we headed for the north fork, it was dark, and Huntley kept walking into things and stubbing his painful toes. After a mile or so, we bivouacked, dividing up my clothes and sleeping bag and adopting fetal positions on a sandstone slab in the middle of the wash. Such nights pass slowly, like time in a hospital, where disturbed sleep confuses what is dream and what is real. I dreamed of traps and spears. Huntley talked in his sleep and screamed at nightmares.

At first light we were up and moving, eating gorp and summer sausage as we walked. By now Huntley was beyond cursing. We walked slowly, reaching his equipment by mid-morning. Then we climbed to the rim by way of a chimney that pierced the White Rim sandstone just below the airfield. Hubler arrived on time, hopping his Cessna over the arroyos, and soon we were back at Moab. We tried to drive home to Boulder, but after several hours we stopped to sleep on the bare ground under a cottonwood, my head resting on my folded hands. Then we drove on into the night, talking about the figures and making plans to return. I did not know then that when I returned—and I knew I would—it would be in another context, with expectations and knowledge that would erode their power.

The contrast between that long weekend and my job appalled me. I knew I wanted to have more experiences like that, even if I couldn't explain what "like that" meant. There was the adventure and the wilderness, of course, but what interested me was something more. Two months later we went back.

II

By May it was clear that the Maze would be left out of the new park, so *National Geographic* was no longer interested in our photographs. We were on our own. Huntley and I had been talking up the Maze, showing pictures, and researching rock art, so numerous people were now interested in seeing the pictographs. There would be five of us on this trip. Besides Huntley and me, there was my wife Anne and our friends Judith and David. Since we wanted to stay for a week, the main problem was getting supplies into the Maze. None of us had four-wheel drive, so we decided on an airdrop.

By June we were back at the Moab airport. Hubler was piloting the Cessna. We removed the passenger door and seat, and I sat on the floor tied in with a climbing sling. It was going to be an airy ride. Huntley was in the back with a pile of army duffel bags stuffed with camping supplies and canned food packed in crushed newspapers—there was not much freeze-dried food in those days.

The idea, again, was simple. We would drop into the south fork and sort of stall the plane while Huntley handed me duffels, and I would toss them out. Hubler said we would be close to the ground and moving so slowly they'd survive the fall. Having been a fighter pilot in Korea, he had the right spirit for such an enterprise.

An hour later we were above the Maze Overlook. The Piper Cub was gone, disassembled and hauled out to the old Colorado River crossing at Hite—no mean feat. As we dropped into the south fork, Hubler cut the engine back and we soared between the canyon walls, carving turns with the streambed as we lost altitude. When we were about forty feet above the ground, I shoved a duffel out the doorway and Hubler gunned the plane into what seemed like a ninety-degree turn, straight up the rock walls. From my choice view at the door I could almost pick plants as we cleared the cliffs. Hubler was smiling and allowed that this was better than working for the oil companies. We came around and dropped in again, and this time I got several bags out. A third pass finished the task, and after dropping Huntley and me at the Ekker Butte landing strip, Hubler returned to Moab for the others. By midafternoon, we were all hiking into the south fork. Most periods of bliss in life are forgotten, but our week in that wild canyon is an exception. The weather was flawless, with days of blue skies following one another like waves out of the sea. We explored all the south fork canyons, and David and Huntley descended the steep and isolated Jasper Canyon, which led directly to the Colorado River. Huntley found a perfect arrowhead. We sat in the sun, bathed in slickrock pools, dreamed of other explorations—and studied the pictographs.

The pictographs were still wonderful, but now they were just things we were visiting. I had become a tourist to my own experience. I tried unsuccessfully to recapture the magic of those first moments. I took notes, but they exceeded my power of description. I kept photographing, first in 35 mm, then with my 2 ¼ x 3 ¼ Zeiss. But what I sought could not be captured with photography or language. Indeed, the more we talked, described, and photographed, the more common they seemed. Everyone was appreciative, impressed, but the unmediated, the raw, and the unique was history.

I tried sitting with them alone in the dark, but they neither gazed at nor engulfed me now. The pictographs remained as they had for centuries, preserved by their isolation and the dry desert air, but what I would later learn to call their "aura" seemed to be gone.

When we returned to Boulder, Anne wrote a paper on the pictographs for an anthropology class and used my photographs as illustrations. That fall, Huntley returned with other friends for still another exploration, but then the Maze passed from our lives. I did not return for thirty-one years. . . .

III

In May of 1995 I returned to the Maze. Things had changed. The Maze is now part of Canyonlands National Park, and the pictographs that so moved me are no longer unknown. They have a name—the Harvest Site (or Bird Site)—and they are marked on topographic maps. A small library of books and articles describes, displays, compares, and analyzes each mark and figure, and various theories pigeonhole the paintings into categories created by these theories themselves. This doesn't mean we know much about them, however. Castleton, in the second volume of his encyclopedic *Petroglyphs and Pictographs of Utah,* concludes his discussion of the Barrier Canyon style, which includes the Harvest Site, with admirable candor: "The dearth of extensive archeological study of them makes it impossible to suggest the cultural affiliation or chronology of the style with any certainty." Nonetheless, it is widely assumed that the paintings are the work of an archaic desert people, hunters and gatherers who occupied the Colorado Plateau from approximately 5500 B.C. until the time of Christ. It was their home in a sense we can no longer imagine.

The Maze itself is laced with trails all clearly marked on maps available at the ranger station, and the roads in and around it are described in detail by a series of books. Indeed, there is a hiking guide to virtually every canyon on the Colorado Plateau, a guide to every dirt road, another for every stretch of the Green and Colorado Rivers, and yet another to every river, creek, and stream in the state of Utah. Not to mention, of course, the rock-climbing guides or mountain-biking guides, or slot-canyon guides, or . . . And this is why southern Utah is no longer wild. Maps and guides destroy the wildness of a place just as surely as photography and mass tourism destroy the aura of art and nature. Indeed, the three together—knowledge (speaking generally), photography, and mass tourism—are the unholy trinity that destroys the mysteries of both art and nature.

The Maze is, however, by modern standards, still remote and difficult to reach—the standard approach is an eighty-mile excursion from the nearest paved road. The park describes it as "a rugged and wild area with remoteness and self-reliance the principal elements of the visitor experience." A visit requires a four-wheel-drive vehicle or a mountain bike, and a hard walk. The scrape where we crashed the plane is now the road to the Maze Overlook. At the end are two designated campsites and a parking lot. There's also a trail now, a difficult one that drops into the canyon and requires a bit of climbing.

To the degree that can be expected, the Maze is preserved and protected. In 1995 the park passed a tough backcountry management plan that limits both four-wheel-drive camping and hiking, and the rangers stationed there clearly love the place and guard it with a fierce devotion all too rare in the National Park Service. The pictographs remain unmarred.

I am thankful for all these things.

Enough history of the Maze is now known to place our little adventure in a historical context. We were not the first modern people to see the pictographs. Dean Brimhall, a journalist from Salt Lake City, photographed the Harvest Site in 1954 and later explored the intricacies of the south fork for other pictographs and petroglyphs. Local ranchers also knew about the site. Fortunately, I did not know any of this. Had I known the location of the paintings and seen Brimhall's photographs, there would have been less adventure, no exploration, and no aura—the "quality of its presence" would have been diminished if not erased. I can only wonder how many other gifts from the gods have been obscured by knowledge.

The man who visited the Maze in the spring of 1995 had also changed. I drove a 4x4 and played old Dylan and Emmylou tapes until I reached the infamous drop named the Flint Trail—a lovely so-called road requiring four-wheel drive, compound low, first gear, and lots of attention. For that I switched to Bach and Yo-Yo Ma. Spring had brought unusually heavy rains, and the desert was alive with lupine, globe mallow, evening primrose, and little ruby clusters of Indian paintbrush. When I stopped and turned off the tape player, the silence was still there, but I was no longer bored.

I parked my truck and hiked into the south fork. From my pack hung a tag—my camping permit. I had reserved a spot by phone, paying for it with my Visa card and verifying my existence with lots of numbers. When I arrived at the Harvest Site, a couple was sitting in the shade of a cottonwood across from the pictographs. After we talked a few minutes, they asked if the paintings were the same as they were thirty-one years ago. When I said they were, the woman said she was glad to hear that. And I was glad to say so. To explain otherwise would have been too dark and sad.

After they left, I painted a small watercolor of the wall and figures, ate summer sausage, cheese, and gorp, and waited for dusk. Then I meditated with the figures for an hour, occasionally raising my eyes to study their mysterious visages. In the silence of the evening light, some of their presence returned. I saw the figures as a work of art, a group portrait—the shaman, the goddess, the hunter, the gatherers, an extended family including the birds and snakes and rabbits and insects. Perhaps the little band returned each year to this place and, as animals do, marked their territory. Whoever they were, they knew how to express and present something we have lost. At the end of my meditation I thanked them and bowed to them.

I am pleased the Harvest Site is preserved in the Maze District of Canyonlands National Park. I am happier still that the pictographs remain difficult to visit. I am delighted they remain in such good condition. I support the tough new backcountry management plan. I praise the rangers for their courage, their vision, and their devotion to a place I love.

But I wish we were wise enough to preserve something more. I wish that children seven generations from now could wander into an unknown canyon and receive at dusk the energy captured by a now-forgotten but empowered people. I wish these children could endure their gaze and, if only for a moment, bask in the aura of their gift.

Study Questions

1. How would you explain to a participant/student on a trip you're leading that it's not okay to take an arrowhead or other artifact? Why is it important?
2. Countless cultures have left their marks on today's "wildlands." It seems to be a natural human instinct to want to somehow say "I was here." How do you say this while maintaining "Leave No Trace" hiking and camping ethics? How do you want to be known in history?
3. Jack Turner describes "knowledge, photography and mass tourism" as the unholy trinity that destroys the mysteries of both art and nature. In your opinion, what could be a "holy trinity" that would help preserve the mysteries of both art and nature?
4. How have you, in your adventures, learned to "read the landscape"? How have these stories affected you and what have you learned? What new "languages" or landscapes would you like to learn how to read? What intrigues you about them?

CHAPTER 3

Mountain Hiking and Climbing

Getting to the top is optional. Getting down is mandatory.
—Ed Viesturs

In all the category of outdoor vocations and outdoor sports there is not one, save only the tilling of the soil, that blends and molds the human character like wilderness travel.
—Aldo Leopold

Most people would rather die than think. Many do.
—Bertrand Russell

Hiking and mountain climbing are some of my favorite pastimes, especially here in southwest Colorado with our abundance of twelve- to fourteen-thousand foot peaks. But I'm not interested in heads-down hiking and lengthy, grueling traverses. I'd rather discover old and well-used trails, know my limits, skip the peer pressure, and hike at a comfortable pace. There are plenty of "walk-up" twelve-thousand-foot peaks in the San Juans that provide a variety of thrills. I'm always delighted to pant my way to the top and see that the U.S. Geological Survey got there first in the 1930s with their little brass plaques. I believe in backcountry versus frontcountry use because I want to be far enough out there that I'm alone most of the time or in a small group. But bagging peaks to say I've bagged 'em is not important to me.

John Fayhee, in an issue of *Mountain Gazette,* explained that more than five hundred thousand people a year attempt Colorado's fifty-five Fourteen-ers. While personal goals are laudatory, I'll skip the crowds. Fayhee comments, "But, what the hell? There are worse ways for people to spend time than tromping up the side of a mountain solely because it has made its way onto some list." In typical laidback fashion he adds, "You'll find me and my drinking/hiking chums a couple of ridges over, making our lame way towards . . . a mountain whose summit hovers somewhere about maybe 13,500 feet

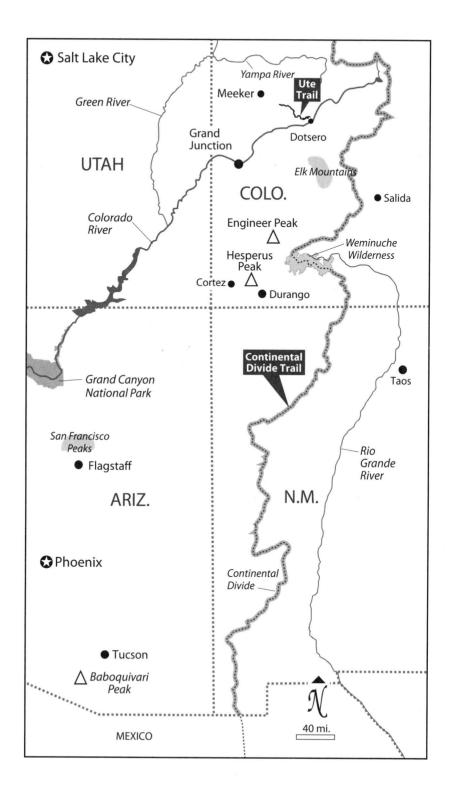

above the sea from which we all long ago slithered, and not giving a rat's ass if we make it to the top or not."[1] So much for goal setting and teamwork! But Fayhee's got a point. You don't need to climb a Fourteener to say you've climbed a mountain.

For too many climbers these days it's plenty of gusto and ambition but not quite enough planning and preparation. Thank you, no. I'll have a good time, hike my own hike, and skip the search and rescue call.[2] I also know better than to think I'm "conquering" a mountain when what I really want to do is get to know the rock and a little more about myself.[3] I know my limits, and fast-packing and going light don't make me comfortable when it's time to settle into camp with a warm meal, a snug tent, and my dog at my side.

In the high country I'm sensitive to not sleeping under dead tree limbs known as widowmakers, and I've heard plenty of stories about the risks of hypothermia. I've been on the Flat Tops in northwest Colorado when a storm front blew in within a few minutes, rain came down sideways, and with the lightning it felt like all hell really had broken loose. Shivering, shaking, wishing I'd brought better rain gear, dodging hail in between stands of tall spruce, those high-altitude summer thunderstorms will make a believer out of anyone. So now I climb early and get down before mid-afternoon.

I climb peaks, but I'm more of a hiker than an alpinist. Still, I know exactly what John Muir meant when he wrote, "In climbing where the danger is great, all attention has to be given step by step, leaving nothing for beauty by the way. But this care, so keenly and narrowly concentrated, is not without advantages. One is thoroughly aroused." He added, "Compared with the alertness of the senses and corresponding precision and power of the muscles on such occasions, one may be said to sleep all the rest of the year. The mind and body remain awake for some time after the dangerous ground is past, so that arriving on the summit with the grand outlook—all the world spread below—one is able to see it better."[4]

Mountain climbing needs to be more about humility and mindfulness and less about summiting and summit fever. Better packs, sleeping bags, clothing, and climbing equipment have created more high-altitude opportunities and hence more dangerous conditions for eager climbers. The National Outdoor Leadership School's risk management guidebook states, "Wilderness and weather are unpredictable. Summit fever occurs when the group is focused on the summit or goal, and they lose sight of clues that this may not be their day." NOLS recommends, "Have the flexibility to turn back from a peak ascent without reaching the top if threatening clouds move in or your group is hiking slower than expected. . . . What we've seen again and again in incident accounts is people continuing when circumstances argued for retreating."[5]

Students from the Fort Lewis College adventure education degree program make a human bridge atop a wooden bridge in the Weminuche Wilderness. Across the nation enrollment is skyrocketing for adventure education, outdoor leadership, and outdoor recreation programs based upon experiential education and learning by doing. Photo by Tim Thomas, courtesy of Fort Lewis College Adventure Education Program.

With bumper stickers on beat-up Toyota pickups, climbers proclaim, "There are no rules above 10,000 feet," but gravity remains inescapable. Steep slopes, dehydration, altitude sickness, sleep deprivation, the potential for snowslides in winter—all require constant risk assessment. Camping below timberline is a sound decision, but also getting out of the wind is always a good idea.[6]

Muir was correct when he wrote, "But we little know until tried how much of the uncontrollable there is in us, urging us across glaciers and torrents, and up dangerous heights, let the judgment forbid as it may."[7] Yet John Muir reached a comfortable old age because he knew when to descend. He knew that down climbing is hardest, and takes more faith, because your head is in the wrong place. Muir understood that a hard move with less exposure is always better than an easy move with more exposure, and that the people who back off, who rethink situations and pace themselves, will continue to have equal measures of stamina and endurance throughout their lives.[8]

I've made a mistake or two sliding uncontrollably down a rocky couloir unable to self-arrest until almost at the edge. The scar on my arm is almost gone, but hopefully the wisdom is still with me. John Muir, our first true environmentalist, loved mountain peaks. He explained, "In that zone below the ice and snow and above the darkling woods, where the sunshine sleeps on alpine gardens and young rivers flow rejoicing from the glacial caves . . . perfect quietude is there and freedom from every curable care."[9]

I like peaks, but I treasure trails. Native American sites may include lines of stone and small stone walls used as game drives in high-altitude settings as well as U-shaped vision quest sites high on promontory points on mountain peaks or passes.[10] Historic native peoples also left their marks where they traveled ridgetops centuries ago.

The Ute Trail on Colorado's Western Slope

Finding intact Indian trails in western Colorado is a major historical discovery, but thanks to dedicated volunteers, archaeologists, and Ute Indian spiritual leaders, one of the last pristine Indian trails left in America has been located. At fifty-seven miles long, the Ute Trail across the Flat Tops Mountains has remained largely untouched because of its remote location on the White River Plateau between the Colorado and White Rivers.

In 1891 President Benjamin Harrison set aside this land, originally the domain of Ute Indians who fiercely defended their "Shining Mountains," as the White River Forest Reserve, the second oldest forest reserve in the nation after the Yellowstone Reserve. The forest floor rises abruptly from irrigated river valleys into steep canyons rimmed by dark stands of Colorado blue spruce and Douglas fir. Higher still are aspen groves. Though perhaps three-fourths of the main Ute Trail corridor has been discovered, its exact location will always remain a mystery.

Understanding the trail and migratory patterns of Ute Indians requires stepping back in time half a millennium. The Utes, who traveled in family bands with older relatives and small children, followed the landscape and terrain contours in a way that four-wheel-drive vehicles cannot. Walking the trail today represents a unique wilderness experience, because in some places the trail widens to almost three miles. But it then funnels down to narrow thirty-yard passageways between ecotones where open meadows and small aspen groves give way to thick, dark spruce. Unlike some trails within federally designated national wilderness areas, the Ute Trail is not overused.

The trail accesses excellent summer range for small bands of Ute families who walked and later rode to the Flat Tops from the south up the Roaring Fork River Valley, and from Utah to the west from the Uintah and Piceance Creek Basins. These close-knit family bands came to hunt, fish, gather berries and seeds, collect eagle feathers, and worship among the tall stands of Englemann spruce and high mountain meadows.[11]

Ute use of the forest was part of an age-old rhythmic cycle that began in the spring about the middle of May and ended around the first of November, or when early snows began to close off the high country. The Utes used the lush mountain meadows in the summer and then descended in the winter from ten thousand feet to the warmer basin and plateau country of five thousand feet in elevation.

The trail is still intact because of the historic remoteness of western Colorado and the Utes' successful attempts to deter Anglo settlement and live in peace with whites. Under the skilled leadership of Chief Ouray, who spoke Ute, Spanish, and English, the Utes managed to keep white settlement out of western Colorado through a series of treaties and through friendships with whites.

But white settlers continued to encroach on Ute lands, and the discovery of gold in the rugged San Juan Mountains of southwest Colorado led to the loss of large areas of land in 1874. In the aftermath of the massacre of Indian agent Nathan Meeker and his ten employees in 1879, near present-day Meeker, Utes were forced to leave their beloved homeland and relocate to eastern Utah in the early 1880s. Cattlemen rushed in from Texas and New Mexico to run huge herds of bony longhorn and Hereford cattle on the public domain land. Mormon sheepmen and Mexican and Greek immigrant herders knew that safety and valuable grass could be found in the high mountain meadows of the White River Plateau, but how to get there without arousing the wrath of the cattlemen? How could a few herders move thousands of sheep almost sixty miles and not be seen? The answer to the prejudice of the day, and the reason the Old Ute Indian Trail can now be located a century after the Utes were banished, is because on the west side of the White River National Forest, the sheepherders found the historic Indian trail and quickly, quietly adopted it.

Existing archaeological features near the trail include a high-altitude mountain bison hunting blind of piled stones from which aboriginal hunters stalked herds of a buffalo species now extinct. Over the decades mountain bison skulls have been found on the Flat Tops, but this is the first time a hunting blind has been identified from which prehistoric hunters would have hunted with spears and, later on, bows.

Near a high-altitude lake the research team also identified distinct patterns in the rock where stones had been moved to either side of the trail to permit easier travel with horse-pulled travois. As Ernest Ingersoll explained in his 1882 book *Knocking around the Rockies*, "a trail is not a road; it is not even a path sometimes. As the word indicates, it is the mark left on the ground by something dragged, as lodge-poles, which the Indians fasten to the saddles of horses."[12]

But perhaps the most interesting find on the Flat Tops, in addition to rock arrangements for sacred vision quest sites, has been a series of lichen-covered stone cairns as tall as a man. Four of these cairns stand as silent sentinels on a windswept plain at ten thousand feet in elevation. They possibly mark an intersection of trails, and though within the last hundred years sheepherders have also piled up stone cairns in different parts of the forest and added stones to older archaeological features, these cairns near Bison Lake seem ancient.

On national forests throughout the Southwest, pioneer packers, bushwhackers, and settlers carved trails through the woods out of a desire to cover distance between two points. But Indians traveled differently. They moved slowly, always hunting, and on established trails each day's ride went from a spring or water source to another water source. To hike or ride the Ute Trail is to experience the forest through the eyes of its first inhabitants.

Hiking in the Sangre de Cristo Mountains of northern New Mexico, William deBuys writes, "All of the trails in the high country have a story to tell, and collectively they reveal much of the mountains' natural and human history. Each trail is like a sentence, a line of encoded intelligence stretching through the landscape and punctuated by the contours of the land." He adds, "To read these trails is to learn something of the complexity and reciprocity that characterize the workings of the mountain environment."[13]

In the Southwest, because of the long presence of Native American tribes, some mountains and mountainous areas are considered sacred. Climbers and hikers should take native perspectives into consideration when visiting areas and leave these places alone. Out of respect and to stay out of tribal courts, avoid climbing Shiprock on the Navajo Reservation in New Mexico or hiking to Blue Lake in New Mexico, which belongs to Taos Pueblo.[14]

Sacred Mountains

Mountains are a special landform sacred to native peoples. They have important meanings because they represent diverse ecological niches where a variety of plants and animals can be found depending upon the elevation. Desert peoples understood that mountain snows and summer storms created their main source of water, and spirits reside in mountain springs, adjacent canyons, crystal blue lakes, and on the tops of peaks.[15]

San Francisco Peaks: Home of the Kachinas

The highest peaks in Arizona rise to the west of the Colorado Plateau and stand as silent sentinels catching the morning sun and reflecting the last light of day near Flagstaff. Sacred to the Hopi and the Zuni, the San Francisco Peaks are also revered by the Navajo, whose traditional homeland is bounded by four mountains, including the San Francisco Peaks to the west. Solitary volcanic mountains, the peaks can be seen eighty miles away by the Hopi, who live on high mesas and for centuries have made annual pilgrimages back to the peaks to leave offerings for the Kachinas or Katsinas who dwell there. Former Hopi chairman Vernon Masayesva writes that the peaks are "the shrine we look to because it is the home of ancient Katsina spirits, emissaries of life. Sometimes we felt we could touch the mountain near Flagstaff."

The Hopis filed suit against the U.S. Forest Service to prevent an expansion of the Snow Bowl ski resort, which would physically affect ancient shrines, religious ceremonial sites, and gathering areas held sacred by Hopi clans. The tribe lost in court. Hopi cultural officer Leigh Kuwanwisiwma explained that his people "once used to go to the mountains unhindered," but now they need a special use permit to gather the sacred plants they have collected for centuries. The permit is required because under U.S. Forest Service rules, plant gathering is subject to federal jurisdiction. Kuwanwisiwma states, "It bothers me because I have been assigned by my clan to lead pilgrimages to the peaks. The last time I led a pilgrimage we were supposed to get a permit, but a Hopi goes where his heart tells him to—not where he is told to gather spruce branches." He adds that there are numerous trails from Hopi villages to the San Francisco Peaks. Though some trails are no longer used, "Ceremonial activities deified the trails that then came into disuse with better maintained roads into Flagstaff. Now when pilgrimages are made we think of the trails and offer special prayers so that the trails do not lose their significance." Pilgrims originally came to the mountains on foot and then by burro, horse, and horse-drawn wagon. Now the clans come in pickup trucks, but their purpose is the same as it has been for centuries.

Kuwanwisiwma argues, "Regardless of its use or not, in our prayers and ceremonies the trails still have integrity because you always have a spiritual element. Clans have living memories and hold specific place-names for ancestral sites." Offering areas are associated with the sacred peaks, and on the ancient trail from Oraibi to Wupatki National Monument, formal shrines mark the route for Hopi travelers. Because of the prominent San Francisco Peaks, a sacred landscape exists across the Colorado Plateau.

Colorado's Hesperus Peak or Dibé Nitsaa

Hesperus Peak in the La Plata Mountains is one of the four sacred mountains in Navajo cosmology. According to legend, the sacred mountains were the pillars that held up the sky, and Hesperus represents the northwest boundary of the Navajo cultural area. In 1868, when the Navajos were incarcerated at Bosque Redondo, Chief Barboncito said they would do anything if only they could go home and not be sent to Oklahoma. He described the boundary areas including Hesperus Peak as one of the four sacred mountains.

Hesperus Peak, 13,232 feet high, figures in Navajo myth and legend. One of the most important of all Navajo ceremonies, the Ye'ii Bi Cheii or Nightway Ceremony, is one of two major healing ceremonies held only during the winter months, when the snakes are hibernating and there is no danger of lightning. This ceremony is performed for eight days and nine nights. By midafternoon of the second day of the ceremony, sand is used to make figures of the four sacred mountains, and the sand is placed in all directions beginning with the east, south, west, and finally the north.

Navajo medicine men go to the sacred peaks to gather soil and special plants for their medicine bundles, because the heart and soul of the Navajo start with the four sacred mountains. Navajo medicine man George Blueeyes explains, "These mountains and the land between them are the only things that keep us strong. . . . We carry soil from the sacred mountains in a prayer bundle that we call *dah nidiilyeeh*. Because of this bundle, we gain possessions and things of value: turquoise, necklaces, and bracelets. With this we speak, with this we pray. This is where the prayers begin."[16]

So hike those trails and bag those peaks, but be conscious, always, of where you are and who has been there before. Slower steps will still get you up and down the mountain. Within the darkness of the forest lies the understanding of the earth. High in the hills is where one is truly free. As my student Kevin Frazier explains, "Mystery lies over every ridge line, adventure lies on every peak." He builds trails for the U.S. Forest Service in the Maroon Bells Wilderness near Aspen. Another trail still being constructed is the Continental Divide Trail.

~

Imagine slimming your backpack, trekking poles, boots, clothes, and socks to fifteen pounds and then hiking 3,200 miles. That's without food or water, but such minimalist extremes are common among hikers who tackle "the king of trails." The most adventurous backpackers contemplate hiking the Continental Divide Trail—the longest, most remote, and most challenging of routes.

At Ghost Ranch, New Mexico, I met Louis Maurer, 30, from Beaverton, Oregon, and his wife Jasmine, 29, from Homer, Alaska. With a tight economy and jobless after finishing graduate school, they decided to take a hike. At Ghost Ranch they'd hiked seven hundred miles as the last couple intending to walk north all the way to Canada in summer 2010. They had gotten lost a few times because the Continental Divide Trail is only 80 percent complete, with notorious twists and turns that leave even experienced hikers wondering which way to go and which ridge to cross.

Longer than either the Pacific Crest Trail or the Appalachian Trail, the Continental Divide National Scenic Trail embodies wilderness values and American character. Hiking it is a major athletic and personal achievement. Of those who start, only half finish. I'm a section hiker, having done a little bit here and there, primarily in the San Juans. I am in awe of the "through hikers" who take five to six months and walk the spine of the continent.

Through hikers are men and women typically between twenty-five and forty who have embraced ultralight camping. CDT mapmaker Jerry Brown comments, "They sleep without a tent and eat without a stove. They don't really have good shelter. A lot of them don't cook or take anything to cook with."

I've got to have tea at least twice daily, and sleeping in the rain makes me grumpy as a wet owl, but the minimalists cut their toothbrushes in half and then drill holes in the handle that's left. Brown chuckles, "If you see someone on the trail that looks like they're out for a day hike—they're the through hikers. The folks all loaded up are the segment hikers." And then there's the Zen philosophy of mind, body, and spirit that comes with dedication and distance. Brown explains, and other hikers agree, "A cool thing about the monotony of a long trail is that you're completely on your own. All strings are cut." Going solo on a long trail, it takes a while to breathe in the loneliness. Then one afternoon you find it's gone and there's just you and nature's clarity and the rhythms of hiking alone.

Through hikers shed not only extra clothes and extra weight but also their names. At Ghost Ranch I met "Aussie Dave," 64, a retired Australian engineer, brown as a hazelnut with blue eyes. He proclaimed, "The best trail names are given to you." He'd hiked the Appalachian Trail and the Pacific Crest Trail, but he said, "The Continental Divide Trail is the one that takes grit and endurance. It's true isolation and because of terrain and few visitors it's easy to get lost." What the CDT represents is ingenuity and self-reliance. "You set a goal and determine to achieve it," said Aussie Dave. He added, "It's not just a hike. Setting targets and goals and accomplishing them is a simulation of working through life." For Aussie Dave, hiking the CDT is an extended fast where he loses about one pound a day. Familiar with Buddhist thinking, he states, "Hiking the trail lets you know all those things in life you don't really need that you think you have to have. It all changes when you can live thirty-five days out of a backpack."

So hats off to the through hikers. On their long trek they learn important things about themselves and the best of wild, American landscapes. They learn endurance. I'll probably always be a segment hiker, but who knows? Maybe I too can cut my toothbrush in half and drill little holes in it.

⌣

John Muir admonished, "Camp out among the grass and gentians of glacier meadows, in craggy garden nooks full of Nature's darlings. Climb the mountains and gain their good tidings. Nature's peace will flow into you as sunshine flows into trees." He concluded, "The winds will blow their own freshness into you, and the storms their energy, while cares will drop off like autumn leaves."[17]

I admire Muir's prose. Although you may personally want energy from storms as he did, you don't want a bolt of lightning shattering your campsite. Lightning in the high country is a late-afternoon, summertime probability, and the United States averages thirty deaths per year from lightning strikes. If you get caught above ten thousand feet, hopefully with an internal frame pack, sit on it. Keep your feet on the ground, hands covering your neck and ears, and try to make yourself smaller. If you can see lightning, begin counting "one thousand one, one thousand two" and stop after the thunder booms. Divide by five and the answer gives the distance of the storm in miles. If thunder roars within five seconds of a lightning flash, the storm is upon you.[18]

The classic account of being struck by lightning is Gretel Ehrlich's *A Match to the Heart*, in which she recounts a direct hit in a Wyoming field. Ehrlich begins,

> When I started out on foot that August afternoon, the thunderstorm was blowing in fast. On the face of the mountain, a mile ahead, hard westerly gusts and sudden updrafts collided, pulling black clouds apart. Yet the storm looked harmless. . . . [Instead,] I woke in a pool of blood, lying on my stomach some distance from where I had been, flung at an odd angle to one side of the dirt path. The whole sky had grown dark. Was it evening? If so, which one?[19]

Ehrlich's gripping story about her recovery is a powerful narrative that describes the vagaries of rural medicine in remote Wyoming and long sessions with physicians in other states. In the summer hikers and climbers need to be acutely aware of afternoon storms, but with winter and deep white powder comes another threat—avalanches.

Cross-country skiing one day in a narrow canyon, I skied into a treeless area and wondered about the loss of pines. Skiing forward into a tight grove of spruce, I heard a "Whumpf" behind me as an upper snow shelf gave way and settling snow cascaded down slope. The unmistakable sound and rush of air startled me and I fell over—much to my dog's delight, but certainly not the best avalanche avoidance behavior.

About the same number of people die each year from avalanches as from lightning, but the figure is ominously rising. Youthful skiers love remote couloirs for hidden backcountry stashes of untouched white powder.[20]

"Every ski day, then as now, death brushes by when I pause too long at the top of a couloir. Assess the pitch. Thirty-five degrees or more," cautions back country skier Tom Wolf. "A slip and a slide kills—or worse, much worse, it cripples. Make a promise to keep for steeps and deeps: Never ski alone. Never tempt the mountain," he advises.[21] Wolf adds, "It is commonplace that when women and men are together in the backcountry, the women often rely on the men to make chancy, crucial decisions about when and where to ski. Until recently, women have been accustomed to following—until the fear sets in." He explains, "Then they want to be responsible for their own safety and risk-taking, especially when they realize that men often act as if they know more than they do, while women act as if they know less."[22]

One woman who knew more was the renowned deep-powder skier and ecologist Dolores LaChapelle. She survived several avalanches, though one put her in a complete body cast. In her book *Deep Powder Snow*, LaChapelle describes the ecstasy of skiing untouched powder as well as the dangers. She writes philosophically about learning from powder skiing but also the difficulties of falling and getting up. "In powder, what is there to push against? Nothing! Occasionally, you can grab hold of a tree and get out that way. Or you can lay your poles on the snow, making an X and sometimes that provides enough resistance for your hand to push against to try to stand up on your skis." She cautions, "More often, none of this works and that's why one should never ski deep powder alone. . . . Sometimes the lone skier never gets out alive. All the commotion and flailing of arms and legs sometimes starts a small localized avalanche and you are covered. People have died with only six inches of snow over their faces."[23]

Historically, avalanche deaths have been a part of winter in the San Juan Mountains, where miners moving between Ouray, Telluride, and Silverton could be buried by sliding snow and not found until spring. "The white death" claimed so many miners in the Silverton area that the book *Death in the Snow* chronicles their deaths with many bizarre details.[24]

Where miners used long wooden skis and a single pole, gliding through snow to and from work, we backcountry ski for fun. But dangers continue to exist. Avalanche clinics are essential preparation, and backcountry skiers need avalanche beacons, shovels, emergency supplies, and most importantly common sense—as the following stories will explain.

The next excerpts in this section are all about climbing, hiking, and adventuring in the high country. A few epic tales are told, but remember, the best stories have a happy ending. Be careful out there.

Notes

1. M. John Fayhee, "The Great Fourteener Debate," *Mountain Gazette* 156 (June 2009): 34. For the lure of Fourteeners see Walter R. Borneman, *14,000 Feet: A Celebration of Colorado's Highest Mountains* (Pueblo, CO: Skyline Press, 2005).

2. Search and rescue can be expensive. See Carolyn Sackariason, "In Backcountry, Rescues Pricey but Come at No Cost to Taxpayers," *Aspen Times*, July 20, 2009.

3. For a good climbing anthology, see Jeffrey Mathes McCarthy, ed., *Contact: Mountain Climbing and Environmental Thinking* (Reno: University of Nevada Press, 2008). For a historic perspective on climbing attitudes, see Peter L. Bayers, *Imperial Ascent: Mountaineering, Masculinity, and Empire* (Boulder: University Press of Colorado, 2003).

4. Quoted in Joseph Cornell, *Listening to Nature* (Nevada City, CA: Dawn Publications, 1987), 36.

5. Drew Leemon and Tod Schimelpfenig, *Risk Management for Outdoor Leaders* (Lander, WY: National Outdoor Leadership School, 2005), 18.

6. For a handy backpacker's manual, see Allen O'Bannon, *Backpackin' Book: Traveling and Camping Skills for a Wilderness Environment* (Helena, MT: Falcon Guide, 2001). Also see Randy Gerke, *Outdoor Survival Guide* (Champaign, IL: Human Kinetics, 2010).

7. John Muir, *The Mountains of California,* cited in Jon Krakauer, *Into the Wild* (New York: Villard Books, 1996), 145.

8. To look at women and mountain climbing in Colorado history, see Janet Robertson, *The Magnificent Mountain Women* (Lincoln: University of Nebraska Press, 1990). Since 1970 an average of one person has died each year on Long's Peak. See Paul Nesbit, *Longs Peak* (Halstead, KS: Mills, 1990).

9. John Muir, *The Wilderness World of John Muir,* ed. Edwin Way Teale (Boston: Houghton Mifflin, 1982), 314. Also see Gerry Roach, *Transcendent Summits* (Golden, CO: Fulcrum, 2004).

10. Andrew Gulliford, *Sacred Objects and Sacred Places* (Boulder: University Press of Colorado, 2000). See chapter 3, "Sacred Places and Sacred Landscapes," 81.

11. Andrew Gulliford, "Ute Trail, Colorado," in Jeff Lee, ed., *The Landscape of Home* (Boulder: Johnson Books and the Rocky Mountain Land Library, 2006). For reflections on Ute land and its transformation into national forests, see Andrew Gulliford's introduction to Robert Emmitt, *The Last War Trail* (Boulder: University Press of Colorado, 2000).

12. Ernest Ingersoll, *Knocking around the Rockies* (1882; Norman: University of Oklahoma Press, 1994), 162.

13. William deBuys, *Enchantment and Exploitation: The Life and Hard Times of a New Mexico Mountain Range* (Albuquerque: University of New Mexico Press, 1985), 302.

14. Roach (*Transcendent Summits,* 100–12) describes a scramble to the top of Shiprock, which is exactly what the Navajo Nation deplores. Other climbers had previously attempted it, including Sierra Club member David Brower, but now access is closed.

15. This section was previously published in Andrew Gulliford, "Sacred Sites and Sacred Mountains," in Suzanne J. Crawford and Dennis F. Kelley, eds., *American Indian Religious Traditions: An Encyclopedia* (Santa Barbara, CA: ABC-CLIO, 2005).

16. Robert McPherson, *Sacred Land, Sacred View: Navajo Perceptions of the Four Corners Region* (Provo, UT: Brigham Young University, 1992).

17. Quoted in Doug Scott, *The Enduring Wilderness* (Denver: Fulcrum, 2004), 21.

18. Jeff Renner, *Lightning Strikes: Staying Safe under Stormy Skies* (Seattle: Mountaineers Books, 2002), 85; also see Craig Springer, "Riding the Storm Out: Living Outdoors with Lightning, Wind and Hail," *Inside/Outside Southwest,* July 2009, 8–9, and Allison Pease, "Lightning Survivor Tells Powerful Story," *Durango Herald,* July 10, 2008, 1B. For caution outdoors, see Richard A. Keen, *Sky Watch: The Western Weather Guide* (Golden, CO: Fulcrum, 1987).

19. Gretel Ehrlich, *A Match to the Heart* (New York: Penguin Books, 1994), 5.

20. Amy Maestas, "Corner Posts," *Inside/Outside Southwest,* August/September 2008, 10; Jeff Barnard, "Avalanche Deaths on the Rise," *Durango Herald,* February 10, 2008; and Alan Peterson, "Prepare for Your Southwest Winter Adventures," *Durango Herald,* January 6, 2008. The 2007–2008 winter season resulted in a record thirty-six deaths, including eight in Colorado and Utah.

21. Tom Wolf, *Ice Crusaders* (Boulder, CO: Roberts Rinehart, 1999), 217.

22. Ibid., 188.

23. Dolores LaChapelle, *Deep Powder Snow* (Denver: Kivaki Press, 1993), 31–32. Also see Jill Fredston and Doug Fesler, *Snow Sense: A Guide to Evaluating Snow Avalanche Hazard* (Anchorage: Alaska Mountain Safety Center, 1994).

24. Freda Peterson, *Death in the Snow* (Silverton, CO: Ferrell, 2003).

Southwest Solo Hiking on the Continental Divide Trail

Aussie Dave

> The trail is the thing, not the end of the trail. Travel too fast and
> you miss all you are traveling for.
> —Louis L'Amour, *Ride the Dark Trail*

A shadow passed over me as I hiked. The vultures circled. Were they stalking me or looking for prey disturbed as I made my way through the desert landscape? This is Southern New Mexico in mid-May. With clear deep-blue skies and a temperature of 90 degrees. My solo hike on the Continental Divide Trail would take me northbound from the Mexican border. I will meet very few hikers, only three or four in 41 days. Much of New Mexico is an empty canvas through the midsummer, free of interference from man's activities, a true wilderness.

Modern man seeks the solitude of wilderness. This idea harks back to our days as primitive hunter-gatherers when man lived close to nature and was, by necessity, more in harmony with nature's moods and challenges. Unconsciously we all crave the linkage to nature and its absence is a hollowness that we can't really explain. I think, deep down, we actually feel more at home in the wilderness than we do in civilization, after the initial shock of leaving our comfort zone has passed.

Four and a half million people visit Grand Canyon National Park in Arizona each year. Modern man demonstrates a great need to seek a wilderness experience, but what is the quality of the visitor experience? I would say for many people it is quite superficial. An overnight stay in a motel and a bus tour, perhaps even a short hike and a photo opportunity for the visitor to record this World Heritage landscape. Perhaps a rare glimpse of wildlife.

Edward Abbey described the demise of the unspoiled wilderness of Arches National Park in Utah as it became more famous and popular. In 1968, when he wrote *Desert Solitaire*, there were 135,000 visitors to Arches National

Monument. By 2010 Arches had more than one million visitors. As the park roads were paved, new facilities added, and people queued to get in, the wilderness experience declined. In effect, Abbey predicted (and ironically promoted) the transformation by writing so eloquently about that wilderness in his books.

I advocate extending the wilderness experience into a longer encounter with nature and adding the extra element of solitude, which is increasingly missing from our modern lives. This solitude can be gained in smaller doses in Bryce Canyon, Zion, or Canyonlands National Parks, but I believe it can be fully experienced by hiking alone for about a month or more on one of the long-distance trails that pass through the Southwest.

I have recently ventured into the Southwest wilderness, hiking the Continental Divide Trail in New Mexico, Colorado, and Wyoming. The CDT is a three-thousand-mile trail that traverses the Continental Divide from Mexico to Canada.

My love of hiking and wilderness grew from an Outward Bound course I attended when I was in my twenties. I then began seeking wilderness experience, fitness and mental toughness through hiking (known as bushwalking in Australia), trail running, and orienteering.

In the last ten years most of my hiking adventures have involved long-distance solo hiking for periods of thirty to forty-five days, using the lightweight hiking philosophy advocated by Ray Jardine in *Beyond Backpacking*. I have adopted a food and resupply system that enables me to hike up to ten days between resupply points. This methodology has permitted me to extend my stay in the wilderness and better attune to the environment. The duration of a long-distance hike enables the hiker to settle into a daily routine. My routine involves hiking eighteen to twenty-five miles per day, rising at dawn and hiking until dusk, eating basic trail food, with minimal shelter and suitable clothing, using maps and compass to find the trail.

～

The solitude of the long-distance hike simplifies the day-to-day clutter of your life, and you can seek inner peace while living in a self-reliant "present."

> *Day 29, New Mexico*
> *A pretty good day! I got away from Ojo de los Indios at 6 A.M. I took too much water but soon had a tea/breakfast stop and another drink stop. The new trail over the mesa was really good; I took some photos of a few nice views of the desert below and distant mountains. I wanted to get to Ojo Frio to have lunch and get water then hike into*

the desert. The descent from Chavez Mesa past Bear Mouth was spec-
tacular. As I guessed, Ojo Frio had no shade and by this time the tem-
perature was in the high nineties. So I had my lunch in the sun, the
spring water was under a plywood cover. No cows even at the trough.
Then it started getting cloudy. Good. I set off from Ojo at about 1:30
P.M. I took the wrong road and had to go cross-country to relocate the
trail. I descended into a massive arroyo covered in cacti and quite hot.
A nice wind was blowing, a tail wind! I crossed the worst desert part
and into some really neat sandstone canyons complete with weird rock
sculptures. I felt drops of rain.

After finding a cavelike rock shelter, I had a rest break then de-
cided to keep going. After some more sand I decided to camp at 7 P.M.
by a big rock on a mesa ledge. Storm approaching! I put up the tarp in
a light breeze and got out all my gear. Then it hit! With 60 mph wind
and blobs of rain.

All I could do was to drop the tarp poles and hold the tarp down
flat over the gear to keep it dry. It blew for about ten minutes followed
by ten minutes of heavy rain, then it stopped and I had my dinner
and settled in, happy to have made good progress today. This spot is
fantastic. I can see the storm in the distance, against a remarkable
backdrop of mountain peaks jutting out of the desert. Today's very
beautiful scenery is a real surprise! What a unique hike this has been.
Real grunge and real magnificence could happen at any time. Today's
stats: Mileage: 21.0 m, altitude here: 6497 ft, max. altitude: 8195 ft,
ascent: 1059 ft.

The Southwest provides a wide variety of landscapes with many different environments, away from roads, towns, and cities. While these environments are not entirely devoid of man's influence, there still remain many suitable large tracts of wilderness to explore. The contrast with city life is stark, and it is that contrast that attracts us to wilderness. The magnificent scenery, the unique flora and fauna, and the impression of limitless open spaces inspire us to closer contact with natural landscapes.

Hikers see: in Utah, the sweeping canyons and mesas, with rocky pinnacles and ancient rock structures, wind blasted into arches, slickrock, and magical shapes. In Colorado, dense spruce, lodgepole, and ponderosa forests with river valleys, grassy meadows, and snow-capped "Fourteeners." The Grand Canyon in Arizona, the New Mexico high deserts, canyons and plains. From its source in the San Juan Mountains of Colorado the Rio Grande sweeps through New Mexico to the Mexican border. These are truly amazing places in the Southwest that can provide wilderness ready to explore. If you take the time to look, you will find true wilderness that exists beyond national parks and tourist crowds.

Modern lifestyles have limited the duration of wilderness adventures. Busy schedules mean forays into wilderness are brief. A typical expedition in the Southwest now starts with car travel to a trailhead, then a two-day hiking trip with one overnight camp, then a return to the trailhead for the car journey home. Busy hikers, fishermen, and hunters grab short doses of wilderness.

I see a continuum of wilderness experiences. At one extreme would be adventure racing or a trail-running race. At the other extreme would be a long-distance hiking expedition, an extended peak-bagging trip, a week-long kayaking trip, or a hike to a remote wilderness for fishing or hunting. Extreme adventure activities allow less time for absorption of what nature is all about. For the trail racer the scenery is only a backdrop to the race. Traversing the wilderness at a fast pace does not allow for relaxed observation and contemplation of nature.

As a solo hiker, every hike allows me to strip away unnecessary mental and physical baggage and concentrate on fully experiencing the wilderness. Over the years I have improved my techniques and progressed to using lightweight hiking equipment and supplies that provide for my basic needs. My comfort level is fairly spartan and my needs are simple. I exist on a diet similar to "a bowl of rice a day," and each new hiking trip builds upon my previous wilderness knowledge.

~

Hiking solo enhances this individual experience, but "solo" is not essential, and most hikers start by exploring wilderness with friends and share the experiences as they are encountered. How would you cope with this kind of extended wilderness adventure? You may be outside your "comfort zone" and into the realm where nature calls the tune.

Your awareness of wilderness is also improved if you can avoid distractions from the outside world. I often meet other hikers who attempt to translate their routine "civilized lifestyle" onto the trail. They bring cell phones, satellite phones, iPods, laptops, personal locator devices, SPOT devices to report their location to the outside world (all with the additional paraphernalia of keeping batteries charged) in order to maintain an unbroken link to their social network.

Apart from being heavy to carry on a hike, these gadgets do add a sense of security but detract from wilderness since they impose on privacy and interrupt the solitude and ambiance. I look at these items in my pack as burdens that I do not want to carry, and I try to dispense with as many as I can given the needs of that particular hike. In reality your place in the wilderness does not need many modern conveniences other than some shelter, some clothing, some basic food, and maps. As you remove the distracting gadgets you start to observe around you things you would never notice with your iPod drowning out the sensations. You again become an individual, apart from the electronic group. You will see sights you could never photograph properly. The place for the real experience of wilderness is in your brain and bodily sensations. However, like most hikers, I carried a digital camera, a GPS, and a personal locator beacon on my recent hikes.

A solo hiker deals with some dangers not faced by a group hiker. Hikers were once advised that the minimum party size should be four: in the case of an injury one person to stay with the injured, while two go for help. Now we see increasing numbers of solo hikers.

Daniel (trail name "Goat man") was hiking on the Black Range in southern New Mexico with his pack-carrying goats. He stumbled over a rock face and broke his ankle. He was about three miles from a deserted forest road and could not expect to get help quickly. So he activated his personal locator beacon. The New Mexico SAR [search and rescue] mounted a search and quickly located him. They then decided to call a helicopter to evacuate him. At the time I was hiking one day behind Daniel but following a slightly different trail, so he could not assume I would arrive to help him. There were no other hikers in the area.

Daniel's safety plan for solo hiking included the personal locator beacon, which enabled him to survive a life-threatening injury and facilitated his rapid rescue. Solo hiking requires additional precautions and a more cautious approach in dangerous situations. In the wilderness experience counts, and the self-reliance of the solo hiker adds another layer of difficulty but also adds extra satisfaction to the hike.

~

Man is an intruder into wilderness; he is a visitor, tolerated but not really the highest of the food chain here. Man is an observer in transit; one who will return soon to the twenty-first century after experiencing the "ebb and flow" of nature that has not changed in thousands of years. We enter the places where our ancestors had to carve out an existence. Our ancestors depended upon primitive methods, rudimentary technology, and hunting for basic survival.

One afternoon in southern Colorado I came upon a herd of around fifty elk. I reached for my camera (not my gun). Three of the magnificent male elk came towards me, while the others, females and youngsters, galloped away. The three were attracting my attention and leading me away from the herd elk who were heading for safety.

I marvel at the resilience of elk, forced to endure a daily cycle of threats from predators and challenges from weather: heat, cold, rain, ice, snow, thunderstorms, and blizzards. In winter up to fourteen hours of darkness combines with shuddering cold. To survive each day elk need to locate and eat sufficient suitable food to keep the body furnace going. They also need to be alert for threats and remain constantly prepared to outpace predators.

Later that day I met a hunter in a full camouflage outfit. He was from California and had flown in that day to scout out likely places where he could shoot elk later when the hunting season started. He was struggling a bit with the rapid change in altitude from sea level in California to 12,600 feet at Montezuma Peak in Colorado and with his heavy backpack. He asked me whether I had seen any elk.

I said, "Yes, I have."

He said, "Where did you see them?"

I said, "You wouldn't hurt them, would you?"

He said, "Oh no, I wouldn't hurt them. Where did you see them?"

I said, "Generally if a hunter can hike for two days from the trailhead, then the place I usually see the most elk is three days from the trailhead."

He could see my point. Here was a person prepared to fly all the way from California to find a good place to hunt, but he probably wasn't willing to hike an extra day to get the elk. He was thinking more about the trophy on the wall than gaining an experience and understanding of nature. How different to the trout fisherman or bow hunter who has to become part of the landscape and stalk his (or her) prey, giving the animal a better than even chance.

Getting into the wilderness is best done with humility and respect for your prey (if you hunt or fish) and surroundings. Ask any wilderness fishing or hunting guide.

∿

In the Southwest the weather adds another layer of difficulty.

> *My near-death encounters with lightning have been fearsome and un-*
> *pleasant. To lie under a flimsy tarp in the midst of a Rocky Mountain*
> *thunderstorm at 11,500 feet and only 120 feet below the summit on a*
> *bare hillside while the thunder and lightning nailed me with flashes*
> *that appeared to be inside the tarp. Trying to "will" the strikes away for*
> *about fifteen minutes, each strike being closer to the thunder blast until*
> *they were simultaneous. While the storm raged and the noise roared*
> *like a jet next to the tarp, I was in my sleeping bag nervously writing*
> *in my journal, "These could be the last words I ever write!" Being hit*
> *with stinging hailstorms twice in one day added to the drama of that*
> *Colorado hike.*

On a long hike I must be prepared to cope with all types of weather. If the worst happens then I take shelter among trees or even drop into a valley. Animals do this, too, and it is a key to their survival. They have an instinct that gives advance warning of impending storms. They also understand what they can ignore and what they must not ignore. Many hikers don't have this awareness (or we ignore it and press on) and can often be caught at the wrong place as I did when a storm arrived.

> *Being pelted with hail in a full-scale Colorado thunderstorm for one*
> *hour while I crouched under trees I saw lightning hit some rocks and*
> *for a few minutes steam billowed from the rocks. The awesome power*
> *of the storm humbles the observer and threatens your very existence.*
> *A reminder that you should respect the "mountain gods" and you are*
> *in this place only under their sufferance.*

Just as there is an abundance of water in some places, in many parts of the Southwest finding enough water can also be a problem. Water is scarce in New Mexico. Animals need water to survive, and water is also essential for me so I can continue my cross-country hike. On the trail it seemed almost every source was shared with cows. So you get used to the idea that these wallowing, foul-smelling animals that spit grass into water troughs, coughing and sputtering, must be useful for something. Well, they are useful for making hamburgers and also useful for hikers. Many water sources are windmills, solar wells, piped springs, water troughs, and stock tanks, put there by ranchers for the sole pleasure of cows. Sharing this water with cows enabled me to cross deserts, often carrying as much as one gallon (four liters) of precious water. Of course, we hikers treat the water and somehow stay healthy.

> *South of Cuba, New Mexico, I passed a windmill at 7 A.M. and could see from the trail that it was not turning (there was no wind). So I decided to hike to the next water source some two miles ahead. On arriving at a big steel tank I found it to be empty and there was a polluted disgusting trough for cattle. So I hiked back to the windmill (now turning) and shared the clean piped water with a fox and an antelope at the windmill trough. While I think the cows should be removed from wilderness, this view is not shared by ranchers who are the latest members of a long tradition of cowboys scraping a living from the desert rangelands. Thanks for the windmill, boys.*

⌒

A long-distance hike requires regular replenishment of food. Every five to twelve days hikers seek a town or a highway crossing to resupply. My strategy is to try to stay in wilderness as long as possible and to minimize the town stays. So I send parcels of food and supplies to post offices in towns along the way. When I arrive I pick up my parcel, get a nice meal, a shower, and a real bed, do some laundry, then get back onto the trail. A "zero day" is a day with zero hiking, and hikers generally try to minimize the number of zero days.

You can imagine the hitchhiker who has not showered for five days, is dirty from trail dust, sweat, and grime, may be dressed in ragged clothes, carrying a backpack and holding sharp hiking poles. Would you pick up such a person? A few times people were happy to give me a hitch but told me to sit in the SUV bed with their dogs.

⌒

Hikers are supported by "trail angels." These angels are helpful people who provide transportation to and from towns for resupply, detailed trail information, caches of water or sodas on the trail, and sometimes accommodation. They make hiking the long-distance trails easier and are much appreciated.

> *Pie Town is a small town in New Mexico that boasts only three shops—a post office and two pie shops (not even a gas station). On arriving in Pie Town I found the residents were very hiker friendly. I learned how pies are made and Kathy, the owner of the Pie-O-Neer pie shop,*

let me use her phone (the public phone was broken) and I stayed at the "Toaster House," a hostel for hikers and bike riders. The pies were excellent but the genuine Pie Town hospitality was better. In the visitors' book at the hostel I saw the names of people trekking through the New Mexico desert and mountain wilderness. Names and stories included hikers from all over the USA and many (like me) from around the world. Pie Town provides a glimpse of real small-town America and its human values.

Hiking can be a form of meditation. As you remove the trappings of city life and travel longer into the wilderness you become aware of the present. By living totally in the present, as I do after some time in the wilderness, it is possible to temporarily suspend past and future thoughts. Constant tasks include navigating the trail, dealing with weather and terrain, confronting dangers (like river crossings, wild animals, or exposure on steep slopes and cliffs), finding suitable campsites and setting up camp, searching for water, cooking meals, and remaining alert to the surrounding environment. I find that these ever-present tasks require my full concentration.

Day 37, Colorado

Perfect weather, no rain today, nothing but sun and later some clouds. Ice on the ground but the tarp remained dry under the trees. I left Berthoud Pass determined to take the more difficult direct route across the peaks. At Flora Mountain you get a route choice, so after a break I chose the tough way, but when I came to an exposed section I decided to turn back (cowardly). My reasoning was that despite the tough route being shorter, I would later reach a more difficult pass and if I couldn't cross the pass I would have to retrace my steps and take the alternative. So down I went on the official CDT, three thousand feet down and then another three thousand feet back up, plus about seven miles extra. It took me from 2:30 P.M. to 6 P.M. to climb back up onto James Peak (13,228 ft). I climbed James Peak the hard way, from the valley on the "official CDT route." Today's stats: Mileage: 18.5 m, altitude here: 11,440 ft, max. altitude: 13,228 ft, ascent: 4,828 ft.

I have found interesting linkages between my observations as a hiker and Buddhist teachings that describe the benefits of meditative states reached by walking. I know I sometimes enter a trancelike state while hiking often counting paces unconsciously. Perhaps it is just fatigue or the monotony of one step after another? You clear your mind of trash and open yourself toward nature.

A focus on the present can also deliver small miracles. Several times I have created a "thought picture" that has resulted in an event actually taking place. Like the pole-vaulter who mentally rehearses a perfect jump, then carries it out.

> *One day in Bonita Canyon near Grants, New Mexico, I had longed for a cool drink on a long hot day. I had seen no traffic on the remote dirt road all day. Soon after I had this thought, a small truck came over the horizon. The Hispanic driver and his girlfriend stopped next to me and said, "You look thirsty. Would you like a beer or a soda?"*
>
> *"Yes, thank you, that would be great." They gave me two cans of Coca-Cola before driving away.*
>
> *Truly remarkable things often happen on the trail. Like needing a phone in Pie Town and Kathy immediately arriving to offer me her phone and some tasty pie. Hikers call this "trail magic." Meeting other hikers and sharing trail experiences also provides a magical reinforcement of trail culture.*

Buddhists say that peace and happiness are available here in the present moment. Your goal becomes the hike itself rather than the end destination. The Southwest offers a real chance to see nature and to find out more about yourself.

> I am home,
> In the here and now,
> I am solid,
> I am free,
> In the ultimate,
> I dwell.
>
> Thich Nhat Hanh, *The Long Road Turns to Joy*

Fear Falls Away—Arizona's Baboquivari Peak

Janice Emily Bowers

Throughout the wet November night I have been aware of the hard knot of fear that has been lodged in my throat for ten days now, ever since Renée invited me to accompany her and three others in climbing Baboquivari Peak.

"I'd love to," I said, whereupon my throat tied itself into a knot. The other major peaks in southeastern Arizona are accessible by trails, and anyone with strong legs and lungs can hike to the summits. Only Baboquivari requires more: ropes, harness, and carabiners if you have them, or better-than-average climbing skills and plenty of confidence if you do not. I have a harness, a cara-biner, and not much else except Renée's assurance that I can make the climb. The route we will use is rated class four, so it is not a technical climb—the holds being large enough that ropes are not absolutely necessary. On the other hand, a class four rating also indicates enough exposure to kill or maim you if you fall. Renée promised that she and Gordon, her husband, would bring their climbing equipment. This would have set my mind at ease if she had not emphasized *bring,* leaving me with the impression that she would prefer not to use the equipment at all. For a whole week, I have been promising myself that if I just do this one climb, I will never have to climb again. I've lost track of the number of times I have asked Renée if she is absolutely positive that I can do it. Am I secretly hoping she will change her mind?

Of the five of us, only Kirk has no experience with rocks and ropes. Gordon has been climbing since he was a boy and could manipulate the equipment in his sleep. Renée is also a good and fearless climber. Gordon and Renée have ascended Baboquivari Peak several times by the Forbes route, the one we will use today. Laurie, strong and graceful on rocks, has enough confidence to climb anything. Knowing that I could hardly be in better hands brings no comfort. People have died on this route. People have also started and been turned back by incapacity or fear. I knew two women twenty years ago who began the climb with their husbands in expectation of an easy scramble. When the women became terrified and wanted to turn back, the men refused. My friends survived, no mean accomplishment, but what remained in their minds was the fear, not the triumph.

Even if I had never heard that particular story, I would still be scared. My fear of heights is exceeded in my experience only by my husband's fear: I am decidedly nervous when I am less than two feet away from a precipice; standing another two feet behind me, Steve will be outspokenly anxious on both our behalves, and only when we retreat to a safer distance will he relax. Like my friends of twenty years ago, I have experienced uncontrollable fear in the midst of a climb; like them, I have been unable to move and certain of death. I too survived, but it felt like failure.

Despite these and other truly excellent reasons for staying at home with a good book, or even a bad one, here I am. Years ago, when I half believed in astral travel and other occult nonsense, I read somewhere that not only is Baboquivari Peak sacred to the Tohono O'odham, it is also a "power point" such as Carlos Castaneda describes in his Don Juan books. Castaneda's work has been exposed as fictional, if not fraudulent, but the idea that Baboquivari Peak is a sacred and powerful place transcends scholarly criteria for verifiable truths. The desire to be on Baboquivari Peak, born at the moment I read those words, has never left me and is one reason I am here. Unlike other sacred peaks in our area, Baboquivari looks like a holy mountain. A 1,500-foot-tall granite dome rising from an otherwise unremarkable ridgeline, Baboquivari Peak resembles a bishop's miter tossed on a rumpled robe. It can be identified from a hundred miles away, and when I am high in the mountains, I never fail to look for it. Always I have looked, then shifted my glance, all too willing to accept Baboquivari Peak as my Impossible Dream. Now the prospect of moving away, combined with Renée's fortuitous invitation, makes it clear that if I do not tilt at that windmill today, I never will.

Apparently no one slept very well last night. To call us *subdued* this morning would be to greatly overestimate the average level of cheeriness. The ground is still wet from rain, and the log where we sat at suppertime is sodden. Breakfast is a dismal meal eaten under dreary skies. Gordon and Renée talk quietly together in one part of camp, Laurie and Kirk in another. I sit on an uncomfortable rock by myself and sip coffee from a plastic mug. My free hand, shoved into a jacket pocket, fingers a metal bottle cap that I have brought on purpose. Long ago someone told me that if you throw a bottle cap off the peak, the cap falls up instead of down because wind currents snatch it away. Dubious but hopeful, I am prepared. Maybe that is the real reason I have come—to fling a bottle cap from Baboquivari Peak.

Eventually, a spattering of rain stirs us to pack our belongings. There is some laconic talk of what to do in case it really rains. Wait out the storm in a rock shelter? Cancel the climb? In my head I am shouting, "Cancel! Cancel!" but I suspect that only a hurricane could allow me to back out at this point without losing face. Immersed in my own pitiful misery, I nearly miss Gordon's quiet statement that everyone will use ropes for the entire climb. My heart lifts. I might fall, but at least I will not die, probably will not even be maimed. Bless the man. I will love him forever.

~

We camped last night within easy striking distance of the peak, so we have only a short hike this morning. This side of the Baboquivari Mountains—the west side—belongs to the Tohono O'odham Nation. Renée and Gordon obtained permission for our climb ahead of time; most people use the eastern approach to save themselves the bother of getting a permit. As we walk, a blue umbrella unfurls overhead, rolling the clouds to the perimeter of the sky. We talk of this and that, including how the Forbes route was established. Georgie Scott, the young woman who eventually became Mrs. Forbes, had so many suitors that she could not decide among them. ("Oh, poor thing," Renée interjects.) Like a princess in a fairy tale, Georgie set a challenge: the first suitor to climb to the top of Baboquivari Peak, something no Anglo had ever done, would be the one she married. Robert Forbes made three attempts before he finally discovered a feasible route in 1898. It required creeping up the Great Ramp, a vast granite slab, then scaling an eighty-foot vertical pitch that had decent holds unless you strayed off line. Above that pitch, you had an easy scramble to the top. It was nightfall by the time Forbes completed his first successful ascent. Elated, he lit a bonfire that could be seen as far away as Tucson. Georgie might have been the only person to know the fire for what it was. Everyone else thought that Baboquivari Peak was erupting.

Our trail parallels the crest of the range, ducking under small, gnarled oaks and skirting boldly colored outcrops shaped like prehistoric beasts. These rocks are not the smooth, hard granite of the peak itself but a crumbly volcanic tuff in hues of tan, rusty orange, and maroon. Gray twists of coyote scat are plentiful on the trail, crumbled bear dung not uncommon. The abundance of wild animal sign suggests a place not much used by humans or, better still, one used in ways that create little disruption.

Much sooner than I like, we arrive at the Great Ramp. It tilts upward at just enough of an angle to make my palms sweat. We step into our climbing harnesses, which basically comprise two adjustable thigh loops connected front and back to an adjustable waist loop. My harness, garishly striped with pink and yellow, elicits the usual comments—"if the rope breaks, at least you'll be easy to see at the bottom of the cliff," and so forth. Gordon and Renée snake out the ropes, feeding them length by length from neat coils into loose, lazy loops on the ground. I pick up a rope and, about three feet from the end, tie a knot that looks like the number eight. I thread the end of the rope through my harness, leaving the knot dangling, then loop the end back to the knot. Next, by coaxing the end of the rope through the knot, following every twist and turn, I create an identical figure eight that hangs the original knot. This ingenious two-phase device links my harness (and therefore me) to the climbing system so securely that it will be hard to untie when the climb is over. Finally, I secure the loose end with half a double fisherman, which is a double fisherman tied once. Don't ask me why it is not simply called *a fisherman*.

I check to make sure that my knots are properly tied. Renée checks my knots, and I check hers. Gordon checks my knots and double-checks his own. Laurie checks my knots and Kirk's. Kirk and Renée check one another's knots, then I check Kirk's, and he checks mine. All of them look fine. Clearly, none of our lives will be jeopardized by a badly tied knot today.

At last we are ready to ascend the Great Ramp. Gordon and Renée go first, then Gordon belays me, and Renée belays Kirk. Laurie is gloriously on her own. After a minute or two of scrambling apelike with hands and feet, I realize that I could actually walk up the slab, so I do, legs a little rubbery at first, then fully in control. Midway, 1 look back down the slab. The base appears to drop into infinity, an unnerving illusion; I am glad for the rope even though I do not really need it.

Above the Great Ramp, we follow a well-worn path to the vertical pitch I have been dreading. Gordon climbs first. I probably should watch every move, trying to memorize exactly where he places his hands and feet, but getting the route by rote never works for me—climbers differ greatly in strength, flexibility, and height, not to mention skill and confidence, and the holds one person uses could well be irrelevant to another's build and mind; moreover, the topography of a cliff to which you are clinging seems very different from what you saw when standing on the ground. Others climb in sequence as Gordon belays, then my turn comes. I am unpleasantly nervous until I make my first two moves, after which fear falls away, replaced by a deep interest in what I am doing. Holds arise as I need them, almost as if evoked by my need. The thick encrustations of lichen on the rock look like green snow or cucumber soup. Gray liverworts, shingled among the lichens, crunch faintly underfoot like the slender bones of birds. Aside from one tricky place where the holds become what climbers call *thin*, that is, virtually imaginary, I climb quickly and well, I feel. Renée agrees. At the top of the pitch she tells me, "You climbed that like a pro."

As advertised, the rest of the route is an easy scramble and walk. Gaining the summit is almost anticlimactic. I had expected the five of us to be crowded together like angels dancing on a pinhead; instead, the summit is flat, and broad enough for a two-bedroom house. The air is still, the sun almost hot. Renée and Laurie, having located the Tucson Mountains to the northeast, puzzle over which summit is Safford Peak. I stroll from edge to edge, grinning foolishly. I can't believe that I'm actually here. How can an Impossible Dream yield so readily to a Possible Reality? When I thank Renée for including me in the group, she says simply, "Now that you know the way, you can come back again."

Now I can remove Baboquivari Peak from my mental list of places I yearn to see at least once in my life—West Clear Creek, Aravaipa Canyon, Desolation Canyon, Mount Whitney, Keet Seel, and on and on. The list shows such a strong inclination to grow that I suspect I will never reach the end. Why it exists in the first place is not easy to explain, even to myself: it has something to do with seeing the sights that others guarantee as worthwhile, maybe, or with wanting to discover for myself the lasting appeal of some particular place.

Someone finds the trail register in a jar inside an ammo can under a small cairn. The jar holds a sheaf of paper scraps and several extremely blunt pencils. Laurie writes, "If Georgie Scott had known it would be like this, she would have climbed the peak herself." My mind goes blank, the same as it does when I must inscribe an appropriate sentiment on someone's birthday card at the office. All the time I spent fretting and worrying about the climb I could have more usefully employed in thinking up trenchant reflections for the trail register. I thumb through its pages. Many entries include praise of God and His creation. Some climbers write that they feel closer to God up here. A surprising variety of people have made the ascent: a woman five months pregnant, a group of nuns who thankfully note the assistance of "Señor Julio and his rope," a party who climbed by moonlight, reaching the summit at 2:30 A.M. Suddenly my presence here seems not such a remarkable achievement after all.

Across the Altar Valley, the Tucson and Santa Catalina mountains look like waves on a choppy sea. From past experience, I know that within a week, I will have forgotten how they look today. Within a year, I will have forgotten how it feels to be here looking at them. If I seek out new places only for the sake of accumulating sights and experiences, I might as well stop now. Yet I won't, nor would anyone else with such a list. My persistence, I suspect, has less to do with assembling a collection than it does with attempting a minor miracle: I harbor a noble but futile hope that the next climb or journey will change me for the better, or if not the next, then the one after it.

Psychological case studies demonstrate just how futile my hope is. People clutch their concepts of self as tightly as a starfish clings to a rock. A man who pictures himself as a failure is blind to whatever small successes he does achieve. A woman who has convinced herself that she is unattractive requires more than a look in the mirror to change her mind. Yet, despite our propensity to stick with the familiar, as painful as it may be, moments come when we are capable of assimilating new experience, of adapting our concepts of self to fit experience, rather than the other way around. Could it be that such moments arise most often when we let down our guard? And are we not less guarded than usual when immersed in the sights and sensations of an unfamiliar place?

Even though our favorite places offer a comfort and intimacy not to be found anywhere else, other needs lure us to unknown landscapes. Over time, the details of my climb today might slip away or even become altered in memory, but I dare to hope that being here now—and the courage it took to get here—will forever shape my attitudes and expectations. Whether I find my way back here or not, I hope that Baboquivari Peak will always be part of who I am.

Electrified: Struck by Lightning . . . A Survivor's Story— Weminuche Wilderness

Dean Cox

Massive cumulous clouds had been building since noon. At around 2 P.M., a sprinkle started and my hiking partner, Bill Price, and I helped each other slip ponchos over our packs.

Our trail climbed steadily along the west side of a steep ridge that rose to the nearly thirteen-thousand-foot summit of Mount Hope, just two miles away. From there, an eight-hundred-foot descent separated us from the last camp of our trip, a ten-day backpack trek in early July of the Weminuche Wilderness in Colorado's San Juan Mountains.

As we eased up the trail, flashes and booms of lightning and thunder talked to us in the distance. We pushed on, undaunted by the drizzle and its bright, noisy companions. Flash—pause—boom!

I began counting the decreasing intervals between lightning and thunder to determine how far from us the lightning was striking. The last strike was about four seconds between boom and strike—less than a mile away. Bill stopped in his tracks and said, "Looks like we'd better wait awhile." I nodded. "The trail hits ridgetop in a few hundred yards," I said. "We're better off here."

Crowded against alpine spruce on our windward side, we continued to gauge the lightning's proximity. I waited for the static that I had experienced

Originally published as "Electrified: Struck by Lightning . . . A Survivor's Story" in *Inside/Outside Southwest,* August/September 2008. Reprinted by permission of the author.

several times with Saint Elmo's fire in storms at high altitude. Hair stands on end. Sparks follow fingertips. Nylon clothing crackles and eyebrows tingle. I knew that these indicators could precede a close and dangerous lightning strike. They didn't come.

In spite of being wet and cold, I stood in stillness, watching a cow elk graze near the saddle in the ridge, below and across the basin from us. Peace reigned.

The storm passed. A light drizzle continued as thunder rumbled in the distance with no visible lightning.

The trail curved to the left around the shoulder of the ridge into a pass. Several hundred feet below, the headwaters of Hope Creek came into view. We stopped momentarily and drank in the view.

I noticed a small storm in Beaver Meadows, four miles to the west and a few thousand feet below. It appeared as a narrow, white column tilted at a thirty-degree angle, approaching us. Sun filtered through the clouds onto the beautiful column. "Must be hail," I thought, the rain increasing.

Without warning, a blinding white flash and simultaneous deafening explosion enveloped me. Every muscle in my body contracted violently, dropping me into a fetal ball. In the flash, I knew that I had been struck by lightning. Having lost total control over my body, I fell, feeling as if I were floating down in slow motion. I never felt myself hit the ground.

When I opened my eyes, I noticed my rain- and mud-splattered left leg angled above me. Lying in boulders, groggy, I heard myself say, "That's my leg, I must still be alive." I could sense misty rain peppering my eyes and face.

Looking for Bill, I noticed that my pack had twisted crossways across my back but with shoulder and waist straps still in place. I was twisted into it like a pretzel. Slowly, I painstakingly unbuckled the waist strap and pulled an arm free. My legs flopped like dead meat onto the rocks as I struggled with the pack. I felt no feeling in them, nothing. I moaned. Bill said later that he thought I had died.

"Dean, are you all right?" The tone in Bill's voice revealed that he was really asking, "Are you alive?"

"I'm OK," I answered. "You?"

"I can't get up," he said, "but I think I'm all right."

"She nailed us, didn't she?"

"She sure as hell did," he replied.

I lay on my pack among the boulders, head downhill and face up. I was gasping, my heart pounding as if I'd sprinted up the mountain.

The rain on my face was refreshing—the first sensation I felt since the violent contractions. With no recollection of tumbling in the rocks, I must have been out for a few seconds.

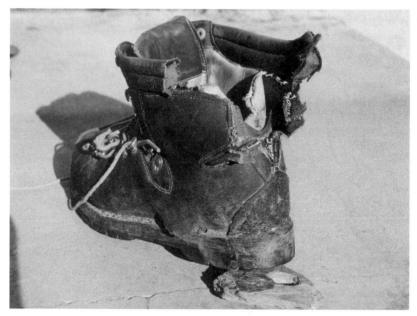

While they were backpacking in the Weminuche Wilderness in the San Juan Mountains of southwestern Colorado, Dean Cox and a friend were hit by lightning. Cox's body acted like a lightning rod as the voltage ran down his external-frame pack, across his hips, down his legs, and destroyed his hiking books. Photo courtesy of Dean Cox.

As my heaving chest subsided, I assessed my body. My arms, head, and neck moved freely and seemed normal. From the waist down, though, I felt nothing. My legs couldn't move. Hard as I tried, they wouldn't respond to anything I asked them to do. My hiking shorts and underwear were in shreds, and my socks and boots were nearly demolished.

The rain continued to pelt my face, and my mind began to clear. Realizing there would be no one to help us, the seriousness of the situation began to sink in, as did the rain. Knowing that hypothermia was our biggest danger, I forced myself into action. I squirmed over the boulders, reaching the trail just as Bill pulled himself up and sat on his pack. Puffing like a steam engine, exhausted from the effort of getting to the trail, I laid back against the cut of the trail. Bill crawled on hands and knees up the trail to me. Spreading his poncho to cover us both, we huddled together as lightning hammered the ridge above us.

"Do your legs feel like they're asleep?" asked Bill.

I took stock. "My thighs do," I responded.

"Mine feel like pincushions from the knees down," he said.

Within moments, I knew exactly what he was saying. Accompanied by an extreme sensation of heat, I felt as if an infinite number of needles were being forced into my legs from all directions. My stomach began to roll as I writhed in agony on the muddy trail. BOOM! Another close strike. Nearly bare from the hips down, I began shivering convulsively as my body heat drained. BOOM! Closer yet.

"Don't hit me again," I heard myself say out loud. "I can handle this, but please don't give me any more."

The rain drummed hard on our shelter, Bill's poncho, as lightning struck just a quarter mile above us.

Over the thunder, we hollered our ideas of what we should do next. Beaver Creek was the nearest refuge from the storm, Hope Creek the shortest route out of the mountains. Neither option would put us anywhere near our vehicle.

The storm began to ease but the leg needles and body convulsions persisted. For the first time, I noticed the heavy smell of lightning—a concoction of ozone and pulverized rock. I had never experienced it in the near nauseating concentrations that hung over us like a cloud.

"I can't feel anything yet, but I can move my ankles," Bill said. "I'm going to try to stand up." Shakily, he made it to his feet. As he picked his way over the boulders to my pack, I noticed that the needles had moved to below my knees and that my hips could move. In an agonizing progression, relief was creeping back into my body.

Bill tossed my sleep pad, sleeping bag, and tent up to me. While I crawled into the bag, which I had slipped into the unsupported tent, Bill put on warm clothes. The rain slowed to a drizzle.

We massaged our legs, gritting teeth against the pain. We rehashed our frightful ordeal. Gradually, mobility returned to my legs, starting at my hips and moving toward my feet. Sensation followed close behind. Bill had been paralyzed from the knees down, his pants and boots still intact. A few feet higher on the trail, I had taken the brunt of the charge. Cup-shaped holes about the diameter of small dinner plates remained where each of us had stood.

The drizzle gave way to hail. Thunder became louder and nearer. Before full sensation and mobility returned to my legs, I attempted to stand with the hope of moving out to safer ground before the next wave of the storm hit. Stand I could. Feel the ground under my feet, I could not. But I could walk, gingerly taking steps, so we decided to go for Archuleta Lake and on to Wolf Creek Pass where we knew we would find help.

We packed quickly. Walking without feeling the ground required intense concentration. Each step was calculated to avoid rocks and slick spots—no easy matter with a half inch of hail underfoot.

On the shoulder of Mount Hope, I looked back for Bill. Thirty yards behind, he came steaming and puffing up the trail. In spite of the extra effort required to plant my feet, I was charged with adrenaline, moving quickly. I even breathed easily.

After a long descent and an arduous creek crossing, two tents came into view at Archuleta Lake. Amorous sounds coming from within one tent told that tale. The larger tent, however, appeared empty. Pushed on by persistent rain and hail, we looked into the four-man tent. It was uninhabited. We claimed it for the night.

With water heating on the stove, we again took stock. Luckily, Bill found only bruises. There was no obvious point of entry on himself or his pack. But a top corner of my backpack was charred and melted. Had the charge gone through me, into the ground, then back up into Bill's legs? It was evident that my external aluminum pack frame had carried tens of thousands of volts around my upper body. Had my lungs and heart been paralyzed for as long as my legs, that would have been my end. My aluminum pack frame had saved me and perhaps both of us.

My hips sustained first-degree burns where the lower frame of my pack crossed my back. My ankles and feet had second- and third-degree burns where gaping holes were burned in my boots and socks. We theorized that because steam has twenty times the volume of water, the intense heat of the lightning strike hit my wet feet with a force that literally blew apart my heavy climbing boots and scalded my feet.

In spite of the hits we'd taken, first-aid cream and a Valium took us into a leisurely supper and a comfortable night's rest.

The next day dawned cool and clear. With eight miles between us and our vehicle, the plan was to move out early and get to Lobo Overlook before afternoon storms moved in. With my climbing boots out of commission, I was thankful for the running shoes I had along for use in camp. But my feet were so swollen I couldn't get the shoes on, even without laces. Cutting slits down the sides and along the soles expanded the shoes enough for me to slip in my feet.

Soon after packing up and moving down the trail, it became painfully obvious that my burned feet would present more challenges.

As blood rushed to attend to the burns, the swelling increased. Within a half mile, my shoes were again overstuffed and additional modifications to them became necessary. Again and again, I stopped to modify the shoes to relieve the pain, until the shoes more closely resembled thongs. After a while, the shoes fit so loosely to my feet that I was back to calculating each step to keep my feet from slipping out of their rigging. We progressed slowly, as did the swelling. Even though stepping lightly, every step produced a sharp, hammering pain on the top of my arches. As a countermeasure to the swelling, I frequently stopped to prop my feet up on a tree. When the swelling subsided, we pressed on, whittling away slowly at the eight miles to the car.

Finally, the microwave tower and the car appeared. The car loaded, Bill turned the key, anxious to drive us to medical help and safety. The car had other ideas. It didn't start, producing neither a moan nor a click from the starter. Another try and the same result. Lifting the hood revealed the problem—the car's battery had been stolen, leaving us with no means of starting the car. With no choice but to get back on our feet, I ignored my swollen and throbbing feet and trudged with Bill the three miles of access road to the Wolf Creek Ski Area, where we "borrowed" a ski-area vehicle—the keys were left on the seat.

The doctor smiled and shook his head. "You guys and your lightning," he exclaimed. While dressing my burned feet, he described a local farmer who was smart enough to get out of the field when a storm passed through but managed to get zapped while sitting on his couch in his living room. Lightning had traveled through his antenna, wiring, and TV set.

Another case featured a man who having previously been struck twice by lightning got hit yet a third time when he stopped his car to watch a storm several miles away over the Sangre de Cristo Range. Lightning never strikes the same place twice?

All we can do in the presence of lightning is to use good judgment and common sense, knowing that even if we stay home the powers of nature are so extreme and unpredictable that our best efforts are not a guarantee of safety. Maybe coming away unscathed six out of seven times wasn't bad at all. That holds as well for the three Saint Elmo's events I've experienced since getting struck by lightning. Now I am more careful, but nothing will keep me from my beloved San Juan Mountains.

Pinned by a Boulder: A Contest with Quartzite— The Elk Range

Jane Koerner

Elk Range, mid-July: I am alone today. My camping companions left before dawn for Pyramid Peak, a pyramid of rotten rock zippered with vertical couloirs, frequented by unpredictable thunderstorms. A peak I already climbed in my impetuous, immortal youth. I have no desire to repeat the experience.

I finished my Fourteener list first, knocking off fifty-four of them in a couple of summers.

Before we parted this morning, Joe and Sam asked for a route description, and I mustered the best advice I could offer at five-thirty in the morning. Something about cairns, sudden shifts in wind direction and speed, and sensible judgment. Follow the cairns; they mark the safest route up. The wind, if you pay enough attention to it, will serve as a reasonably reliable barometer. If it picks up, changes direction, and blows in from the northwest, count on a lightning storm. I worry most about Joe, an affable Mormon from Grand Junction, the first to sign up for my Colorado Mountain Club trip. He married young, and he's got a sedentary wife and two toddlers at home. This is his second Fourteener in the Colorado Rockies. If he bags this one without mishap, the remaining peaks on his list may seem like romps through the tundra. In a tight spot, would his speed and enthusiasm overrule common sense? At least he's wearing a red jacket.

When I was his age, I was chomping at the bit myself. In May, the skis in the trunk of my Honda were replaced with my camping gear in anticipation of fulfilling the promise of all those topo maps in my file cabinet. Six hundred thirty-eight mountains in the Colorado Rockies over thirteen thousand feet high, each one a monument to someone's version of history. It would take several lifetimes to do them all. I would do them all in this lifetime, if my joints could tolerate the punishment. I want to leave my mark, scrawl my signature on a scrap of paper and add it to the collection inside the glass jars. I want to possess these mountains as they possess me. I want to know everything about them—the density and condition of their forests, the scent and variety of their flowers; the angle, age and condition of their rock, the size of their summits. I rank them by altitude—the highest ones first. One hundred and fifty highest. Two hundred highest. The tricentennials. I will conquer them all in that order. I was the first woman to climb the hundred highest peaks of Colorado; mathematical precision reduces the enormity of the rest of the task. I group the mountains on my lists in logical, achievable categories, recording each triumph, like a bird-watcher, in my notebook with the date and initials of my companions. The solos with my dog are signified with his nickname spelled backwards: God.

After nearly a decade of mountaineering alone or with friends, I lose track of details, unable to distinguish one conquest from another, and to revive my memory I classify my trophies by name: San Luis, Tijeras, Blanca, Pico Asilado, hidden away in a back valley, like the name implies, with enough exposure to skip my customary self-portrait on the summit. Cyclone, Cirrus, and Oso, where a member of the Hayden survey of 1874 encountered a grizzly and lived to write about it. Heisspitz, Heisshorn, and Little Matterhorn, as if the Colorado Rockies were an extension of the Swiss Alps. Engineer, Galena, Eureka, Gold Dust, Crystal, Treasurevault; and Lucky Strike, which isn't how I felt about it a century after the bust as I detoured around one collapsed mine shaft after another, dragging my mutt by the collar to keep him out of the arsenic-tainted water. The Ts, the Vs, the Ss, the numbered and nameless peaks. My preference. A name transfers ownership.

I hike for the exercise, burning off excess energy like Christmas calories, transforming greed into muscle. "What's the rush? Are you training for an ultramarathon or something?" my friend asks when I return to camp an hour after he does. He turned back at timberline, defeated by the pace I set.

I hike for the thrill of it, scaring myself semiconscious on more than one occasion. But my body is up to it—legs of granite, heart and lungs a two-hundred-horsepower engine that propels me upward at 1,800 vertical feet per hour. Sixty-five heartbeats per second, 360,000 per hour. On the trail my body has a weight to it. My footsteps land lightly but my feet feel rooted. Every step a declaration of independence born of intimacy with the turf, the rock, the soil. The tapping of my hiking poles synchronizing with each inhalation and exhalation. My breath distilled into the clarity of light. And then the reward on top: millions of years' worth of architectural treasures at my feet, the handiwork of a bygone Ice Age and a stressed continental plate.

Mummy Mountain, Rocky Mountain National Park: as I scramble up the last two hundred feet of the summit block, I glance back at the dilating, bruised clouds and pick up the pace, beating the lightning-charged monsoon to the summit by ten minutes. The ridge I pick out as a logical shortcut to camp proves correct, and I outrun the storm's southward progression in my direction. Back at camp, I am welcomed by a Boy Scout troop leader who covets my spot for his party of ten. I am happy to comply, confident I can beat nightfall too and make it out in time for a sanitary dining experience. I don't want to break my date with my parents, who rented a condo in Estes Park for the week. I told them I was hiking with a friend. Even though I often hike alone in the mountains, I am not as alone as they might assume.

Ophir Pass, San Juans, early August: a coyote shows me the truest of seven false summits. Head cocked back, nose sniffing for a meal, he eyes me warily and lopes off the other side of the ridge, exposing the summit cairn next to where he sat.

Pole Creek Mountain, San Juans, late August: Eight miles up Lost Creek, I find a reasonable place to cross, where the elk have flattened and narrowed the bank with their habitual crossings. Their hoofprints in the mud provide stirrups for the leap to the other side. I land without a splash. Several hundred feet below the summit, another set of elk prints guides me safely through a cliff band. I will reach the top before the hailstorm and return to camp by lunchtime.

Uncompahgre Wilderness, mid-September: The *whoosh* of a low-flying hawk awakens me from a late-afternoon nap in a basin beneath Mount Silver. It is three hours back to camp and the sun will set in two. The persistent bark of a coyote encourages me to keep moving. She is safeguarding her pups, leading me away from her den, toward my car.

Culebra Range, early October: A trail of fresh bear scat through the forest issues a warning. I hustle along at warp speed even though I know it is not a grizzly. The last grizzly in Colorado was slain in 1979.

∼

Reassured by the color of Joe's jacket, I zip up my jacket in preparation for a chilly ascent and hoist my pack to its customary position. We wave good-bye as we head off in opposite directions.

As expected, neither the cramp in my right calf nor the fog in my sleep-deprived brain dissipate until I'm high above our camp and squinting into the first rays of sun to touch the shoulders of Pyramid Peak. I must cross two passes today. Part way up the first one, I scare up three bull elk. They bolt into the basin where I am headed. Marshes of recent snowmelt are decorated in the dehydrated spots with carpets of bluebells, dusty rose paintbrush, and red King's crown. One sloppy footstep and I'll be wading knee-high into frostbite. Good for my misshapen calf. Not so good for my cold feet.

My destination is a peak with no name. I've climbed lots of those over the years. This journey, though not particularly long or treacherous in comparison to previous outings, requires the same degree of commitment. For a reasonable shot at the summit, I must cross the basin and scramble to the top of yet another pass. The peak's alternating layers of white and maroon sandstone keep me going, whetting my appetite with their resemblance to a wedding cake that has sat out in the sun too long. After several hours of nonstop hiking, I'm feeling half-baked myself.

The basin conforms to the contours on my topo map, rising and falling in gentle, surmountable undulations, the high points jammed with boulders teetering above aquamarine pools. A fleet of cumulus sails across the sky, momentarily darkening the basin, and then the ridge between me and the one where Joe and Sam are probably making their way up Pyramid Peak. Will the storm arrive in thirty minutes, or three hours? I have less to worry about than they do; I can bail without a rope.

The next pass should deposit me on the summit ridge, provided my interpretation of the topo map is correct. I don't have a route description; this mountain is not mentioned in any of the guidebooks. The scree looks tedious and I am thankful for the switchbacks of migrating elk and the backpackers who have followed in their wake.

The clouds have bloated into an armada of warrior ships. I have to get to the top of the pass before the storm does. From there, the summit will be feasible, a mere sprint. My destination is farther than I think. It usually is. The closer I get, the more elusive the trophy—the distance distorted by optical delusion. I forget about the darkening clouds, my advice to Joe and Sam before we went our separate ways this morning, and concentrate on route finding.

I forget until I'm sitting on the summit forty-five minutes later and gulping the contents of my second canteen. If it takes me as long to return to the saddle as it did to reach the summit, I may be the loser in a neck-and-neck race with a lightning storm, and Joe and Sam will never trust me again, the woman in charge. Maybe I'm the one who should follow my advice of this morning.

Seventy feet back along the ridge, an opening appears in the cliffs. It drops me into a steep couloir, steeper than I like. The thundershower that kept me awake half the night struck here as well, softening the gravel so the heels of my boots can dig in and apply the brakes, stabilizing my rocking body for the bumpy descent. I listen for the discharge of loose rock, the makings of a landslide.

Two years ago I wouldn't have thought twice about such a descent. An encounter with a boulder last summer has made me more cautious. The boulder was the tallest obelisk in a field of tabletops, seemingly undisturbed by the passage of centuries. It had the stature to bear witness to a solstice ceremony at Stonehenge, a human sacrifice at Teotihuacan. I must have brushed the boulder with my elbow when I looked back to check on Drew. Somewhere in the maze of gullies that gouged the summit block, he was making his way down, in running shoes with no ankle support, testing each handhold and foothold for reliability. It wouldn't take much to start a blitzkrieg. Drew didn't have enough experience to visualize the consequences. I forgot to tell him about the cliffs below.

One second the boulder stood upright, testifying to the migration of glaciers; the next second it tipped over, pinning my right leg to an adjacent boulder. The shock of the blow threw me on my back, and the weight of the toppled boulder registered instantly in a tsunami of pain. My right leg was caught below the knee in a tightening vice. Stifling a scream, I sat up and pushed. The boulder did not budge. I pushed again and felt a slight tremor that suggested a lessening of resistance. Encouraged, I pressed my buttocks into the boulder beneath me to maximize my leverage and so I could ram the boulder on top with a hip and shoulder butt. The rebound knocked me flat and the boulder bore down with even more weight.

I could hear Drew's curses as I scrambled up the chimney to the summit ridge. Could he hear my shrieks now? Barb had long since disappeared over the next rise, clocking her pace with her watch probably as she raced for the car. Would my shrieks reach her? I hadn't shrieked this loud, this long since my mother gave birth to me.

Barb arrived first and knelt by my side, watching helplessly as I flopped on my back, exhausted by the pain and futility of a one-sided wrestling match. The slightest movement on my part increased the pressure on my leg. Barb barely weighed a hundred pounds. A featherweight in a contest with a ton of quartzite. I heard the click-click-click of advancing hiking poles as Drew approached, panting. He tossed the poles and shoved with all his might. The boulder wobbled and tilted farther in my direction. I cursed in three languages and wailed from the pain, the fear. We were three and a half miles from the car, 2,700 vertical feet. It would be dusk by the time my friends hit the road, tomorrow afternoon before the search and rescue team could assist me. The steep, rocky terrain ruled out a helicopter landing. Unlike the trapped solo hiker who cut his arm off in Bluejohn Canyon, I had no knife, not that I could bear the thought of using one.

Drew studied the position of the boulder from every conceivable angle. Then he squatted as if he were competing again in a collegiate wrestling match. Relying on the laws of physics rather than brunt force, he braced himself with his muscular thighs, hugged the boulder tight and pushed with his arms and his chest. The boulder gave slightly, shifting in the right direction until there was enough space to pull my leg out. I rolled up my bloody pant leg, expecting to see exposed fibula. The skin was torn in several places, the calf double its normal size, but no bone protruded. I swallowed a pill from Barb's supply of Percocet and another from Drew's, and they got me up on my left leg. Using their shoulders as crutches, I hobbled a hundred feet down the talus, to a snowfield. They packed some snow in my rain jacket and wrapped the jacket around my calf, now the size of a watermelon. Three hours later they bundled me into the back of Drew's pickup for the one-hour drive to Lake City, Colorado, and the only medical clinic within a hundred miles.

Next morning the orthopedist in Gunnison examined the X-rays. "You're a lucky woman. No broken bones. One inch higher and I'd be scheduling a knee replacement. One inch lower and I'd be reconstructing your ankle joint with plates, screws, and a bone graft."

"How long could my leg have withstood that much weight?" I asked.

"An hour at most. Then we'd be amputating—not that there'd be much to amputate at that point."

He showed me how to check for impaired circulation, a dangerous side effect of massive swelling that could cost me my leg. I followed his advice religiously. Two weeks' confinement in a wheelchair with my leg frequently wrapped in ice followed by another two weeks on a walker seemed inconsequential, a mere inconvenience to be borne with a sense of humor. A year later, whenever I hike in shorts, strangers on the trail sometimes ask about the crater in my calf. If they're from Texas, I tell them I was kicked by a moose. If they're hiking alone, I recount the real story as a cautionary tale.

~

Atop the pass overlooking our campsite, I take a break, stretching out my right leg on the uppermost step of a talused terrace. The clouds have departed. The restoration of summer or an intermission? Sun-kissed and sleepy, I recline on my back and listen to the sermon of wind on rock, Pyramid Peak, the tallest stained glass window in the cathedral. Beyond Pyramid, a ring of spires and buttes equally humbling and familiar. I tick off their names: Thunder, Point 13,722, Belleview, North and South Maroon, Sleeping Sexton, Buckskin. Only two unclaimed trophies. Next summer, perhaps? The orthopedist said the crushed nerves might grow back. Then I remember a Tibetan Buddhist saying, "Surrender completely. If you try to conquer or possess a place, it will always elude you. You can't seduce a place. It seduces you."

I could sit here all afternoon contemplating the absurdity of peak-bagging lists, but I've got Joe and Sam to consider; they might appreciate a cup of hot tea after their climb, and a warm sleeping bag awaits me in a dry tent. If the storm materializes, that's where I should take refuge—in a snug, tree-sheltered tent.

I apply more sunscreen to my chapped face, tighten my boot laces, shoulder my pack, and rise. Cupping my hands to my eyes, I scan the upper couloirs of Pyramid Peak for a glint of red. I finally spot him on the ridge, then look again through squinting eyes to make certain the figure is not a mirage, a trick of the bright light at this altitude. The spot remains motionless and congeals into a column of maroon rock. Wherever I look, I see no flickers of red to indicate movement. I turn my gaze toward the summit. Just below it, a speck of red descends.

When I arrive at our campsite, I run into a member of another party attempting Pyramid Peak. He says he turned back. He didn't like the look of the weather. "No mountain is worth dying for."

He offers me a sip of wine from his Sierra cup. "I watched you limp down those switchbacks. Long day?"

"No, my last solo."

Backcountry Travel and the Darwin Effect—San Juan Mountains

*Oral History Interview with Leo Lloyd, Emergency Medical
Service Captain with the Durango Fire and Rescue Department*

I've been involved with La Plata Search and Rescue since 1985. I've been an active member with that volunteer organization, and I got involved when I was in college, before I graduated. Things can go wrong in the mountains. 'Cause they did for me. Early on, I was involved in an avalanche on the west face of Snowden Peak, on Halloween day, 1982, myself and another climber. We were climbing the peak and triggered an avalanche on the northwest face of the peak that took us both about two hundred meters straight down a couloir that we were in. We were both injured, my partner significantly, but we did self-rescue.

At that time I was nineteen and had tremendous amounts of ambition and knowing what I wanted to do, but very little judgment. A fair amount of technical expertise, as well, but no real experience to make judgment calls, certainly as it pertained to avalanche conditions that particular day.

Slight snowfall had occurred on the passes, but there was enough . . . there had been one storm, I believe, that had put probably three to four inches of snow on the pass. However, there was wind associated with that. Of course, I wasn't following any of that at the time, but snow had filled up the couloir that we climbed . . . it's amazing that we didn't trigger an avalanche because we were post-holing up to our waist in wind-drifted snow in this gully.

We summited late in the afternoon and decided to go down a different route and traversed over to another couloir and then started descending that, and just as we got into that couloir, the snow was, maybe, a half a meter deep and we could feel rock underneath our boots. We had ice axes, no crampons. We weren't skiing. We were climbing and the whole thing let loose when we were probably fifty meters into the couloir and took us all the way to the bottom. And we both hit rocks and debris throughout the ride and that's what caused our injuries.

Neither of us were completely buried, but we had lost our gloves. My friend had lost a pack, and, of course, right when we would need to start making some decisions it started snowing.

There was nobody around and fortunately we were able to literally crawl out on our own. It took us four hours to get back to the highway from the base of Snowden Peak, mostly in the dark. And because of the lack of snow cover, it was quite treacherous trying to get over all the deadfall in the rocks. But we were fortunate. We made it to the highway and a couple of college students gave us a ride back into Durango and the hospital.

My injuries were mostly soft tissue. I had a deep, deep laceration to my left knee, right to the bone. In a couple spots, I had a real nasty contusion on my right thigh. I twisted my ankle and that was pretty much it for me. The bleeding associated with the laceration was minimal. My ankle was the most difficult. Fortunately, I could actually put weight on it.

Now, my partner, he hit a lot more of the rocks on the way down than I did, and he just got pummeled. I was buried up to my waist, standing up. I could barely move. That's how consolidated the debris was, the avalanche debris. We'd gone almost six hundred feet, as far as our distance. He was probably about twenty meters above me, and on top of the snow, and he was moving, and once I could get a visual on him, I could see that his gaiters were gone. His wind pants were just shredded, and he was literally covered with blood.

He had multiple scalp lacerations that looked much worse than they actually were, but he looked a mess, and he was quite a bit older than I was, and he was able to slowly start sliding his way down to me. By this time, I'm getting myself out. We had no avalanche beacons. We had no shovels. We had nothing. I did have a little first-aid kit in my pack, which had actually stayed on me.

So he gets down to me. His name was Jack and very nonchalantly, he says, "You know, Leo, I think my intestines are coming out my back end."

"What?" I said. And so he starts to take off his wind pants and his underwear and he had a pair of long underwear, saturated with blood.

"Oh, my gosh!" and sure enough, he had a puncture wound about the size of a quarter, about a half inch from his rectum, that was bleeding profusely, and probably from a rock or something. I was not, at that time, a paramedic or a nurse, but I did know that we needed to try to stop this bleeding. So I went ahead and started filling this hole with dressing and got it to where it did stop, and, again, we were getting colder by the minute. He had no gloves. It's starting to snow and I didn't think he could walk, and I told him that I guess I'm going to go for help. And he said, "No, we're both going to go."

I said, "All right." It was better that we went together. He could walk better than me, at first, but by the time we got closer to the highway, he got worse and worse . . . He went slower and slower, and because of shock he started saying that he just didn't feel like continuing. He was giving up. He just wanted to sit down and be done with it. "I'm just going to hang out here." And I wouldn't let him.

We stayed together and by the time we got near the highway, I was pretty much supporting him to the road. We had driven his car and I just put him on the hood. He's still awake, but he's losing it. And it's ten o'clock at night. Out of the blue, a car pulled over. This other car just stopped. So they guessed that we were in trouble. I hadn't even had time to flag anybody down, really. I don't remember doing that, but we put Jack in the back seat and then we went to Durango. He ended up going into emergency surgery that night; he spent a week in the hospital. I was discharged with eighty-five stitches in my knee that night. That was one of the first epics that I had.

After that accident, I definitely focused on upping my avalanche education and really took to heart the lessons learned from our slide, as far as being prepared, and also being able to make good decisions and not assume that things were going to be fine.

It takes more than technical skill. And it takes more than fitness level. It takes more than ambition. It takes more than enthusiasm. It takes a concerted effort at taking the time to learn why you're doing what you're doing, and whether it's technical rock climbing, ice climbing, or backcountry skiing, there's a tremendous responsibility that we all have, as backcountry travelers, I feel, to be prepared.

Have the proper tools and education. Go with people that can assist you as well, in the learning curve progression that you may be in. And know when to back off, and read the signs that are sometimes screaming at you in those situations, certainly as it pertains to avalanche awareness and terrain recognition and route finding, and all those things that go into making a judgment call.

Ask, "Are we good to go with this?" And don't be afraid to say, "No. I don't feel good about this and this is why, and . . ." Be a leader. Learn how to make decisions.

Having the proper equipment certainly plays into this. And also, we had a weather event on the pass. There is only this much snow on the ground at this elevation, but what's going on up high, on the peak? What about those couloirs? And certainly when we got to the base of Snowden Peak we knew that we were going to be in deeper snow. And all of a sudden, we're post-holing up to our knees, then our thighs, and we're going up steeper and steeper terrain. It was fun climbing but, again, we didn't even think about an avalanche. And as we approached the summit and the top of the ridge, we fortunately made it that far without getting buried, 'cause it could've easily happened there, too. It was probably the time of day that helped us. We were much earlier in the day, and then as it tended to warm up toward the afternoon, around four o'clock, we ran into problems on the descent.

I am glad that we didn't try to descend the same route, but it was still probably 50 degrees, as far as that gully goes, and it barely held snow. The substrate below the snow was nothing but loose, nasty scree, so its ability to hold snow was marginal at best, especially early season. When I look back on that, knowing what I know now, early-season snow can be incredibly dangerous, not only because of the lack of depth, but also it really hasn't had a chance to bond yet to any substrate.

Nowadays tools and equipment make access sometimes too easy, and the personal learning curve does not equal the desire to practice extreme sports. In kayaking the boats are now such that they're able to do steep creek boating that only a select few would train for years to get psyched to do in spring runoff. Now you really haven't done much unless you've done some of these descents around here.

We've definitely seen it with climbing. I've been a part of that over the years, in the tools, whether it's rock or ice climbing. In ice climbing especially, the technology in crampons and ice tools is such that it allows relatively new climbers to progress very quickly in difficulty. Younger folks, college age, that have a decent fitness level progress quickly as far as their technical skills, but they still don't have the experience to make the judgment calls that are required. It is all about who you're with.

You need some of the lessons learned that other climbers have already gone through, so you're not having to reinvent the wheel. A lot of people don't understand that. They want to see how quickly and how fast they can do something.

In backcountry skiing the lines that are getting descended right now, whether it is on skis or snowboards, are unbelievable. I'm doing stuff that I wouldn't have thought of doing twenty years ago unless it was spring conditions. But there are still things that I wouldn't do that I see getting done routinely, and I think if you talk to any avalanche professional, they'll say the same thing. The tools, the technology in skis and boots has allowed greater flotation, maybe less impact force on a given snowpack or slope. Still, I am surprised that we don't see more avalanche-related incidents in the San Juan Mountains as unstable a snowpack as we have. Around here an increasing volume of skiers are pushing the limits on some of these descents and lines on big peaks that you just wouldn't think of doing in midwinter. In spring, maybe, when it's a different snowpack.

We get more accidents occurring because of high skill levels, but you add the peer pressure and you combine all of the human factors, especially with backcountry skiing, trying to make a decision . . . is this slope good to go or not? It's very difficult, and there is no good answer. There are a lot of important tools that can help you make a decision, but it ultimately comes down to your experience level, and your ability to make informed decisions and a judgment call. If you are the team leader, the group that you are with is expecting you to make that decision.

Peer pressure is real. After hours in a truck traveling to a departure point, friends say, "By God, we've come all this way, and we're not going to ski this slope?" Yes, right. We've been climbing for three hours. We're going to ski something. We're not going to ski the approach path back down. No.

I see it happening all the time. And I have to admit that I have to fight it as well. I also look at it as personal responsibility, and whether it's climbing or backcountry skiing, it is all about who you are with, and in an avalanche burial, a search and rescue team isn't going to save anybody. It's going to be the group that's there and their ability to make relatively rapid-fire decisions and try to control that situation in a way that hopefully saves lives, if someone has been buried.

If they are fortunate enough to have the right equipment and know how to use it, and they have the ability to save a life, once they do find that person, now the real work begins, if they are injured and in a remote setting. Do you have enough gear between the group to take care of this person if you have to leave them or go for help? What if you have to move them on your own? It just sets up an incredible array of variables that most people don't think about addressing in a crisis.

It is interesting that the cell phone phenomenon has created an almost "drive-by" mentality call. We get them all the time. It's almost like it's a crutch, because backcountry hikers and skiers inherently will rely on cell phones and otherwise don't communicate enough with each other. They don't make a pre-plan. They don't have all these other layers of backups that we used to do. We still have backup plans, those of us that realize that we don't want a search and rescue team to come after us till we get a chance to get out on our own. The cell phone is a crutch; people assume there will be a response. It allows people to get complacent because they think that they can always call for help. And they don't really take the time and the effort to have a preplan.

A lot of people will call with no clue where they are. Who knows what cell tower their call is going to hit? It would be so nice if people knew what county they're in, and what peak they're on, or whatever drainage they're in—it's amazing. You'd be amazed at the apparent incompetence that we're there to serve.

Do you know the Darwin effect? Survival of the fittest? Sometimes those of us in search and rescue wonder if we should continue to interfere with natural selection. I don't know . . . are we doing the right thing or not?

Falling Nine Hundred Feet Off Colorado's Engineer Peak

A combined oral history interview with mountain climber Fred Hutt and helicopter flight care nurse Leo Lloyd

Climber Fred Hutt begins: I was born and raised in upstate New York, and like many folks, it was mountain biking that initially drew me to Durango, Colorado. I started mountain bike racing when I was in late high school, early college years, around 1989 or so, and read a fair amount of mountain bike magazines referring to Durango. After culinary school I wanted to travel around the country and play the journeyman chef and thought the Southwest would be an interesting place to come visit for a while.

I had a fairly broad athletic background besides cycling, and I was fortunate enough when I was a kid to be able to travel to Europe with my family several times. I had done some fantastic hikes in the Alps and that planted the seed, very early on, and when I got here, it was the first time I had seen the American Rockies. It was the first time I saw anything that reminded me of the Alps, versus the Catskill Mountains where I grew up. The sous chef that I was working the lunch shift with, he and I became close friends. He was an avid cyclist and also an avid mountaineer. So he would talk about his trips after coming back from a weekend, and it started to spur my interest. The next thing I know, I was starting to venture out to explore some of the local peaks with him.

My first winter ascent was North Twilight Peak at 12,400 feet. I'd grown up alpine skiing, and I was comfortable on snow, and to me, that was truly mountaineering. There wasn't any thought of why not to. But we spent a fair amount of time getting back in there from Andrew's Lake. It was an overnighter trip, and we had done some overnighters before that just to go out and do some winter camping, but this was the first trip that we had done with a peak ascent in mind.

We got close to Crater Lake by nightfall and we were experimenting with a sled, an alpine glacier sled that you would haul a fair amount of gear in with, and that was a lot of work, especially in the conditions of the day. We were doing some post-holing, even with snowshoes.

Things got serious when we were ascending the ridge, and at one point we got kind of closed out a little bit. Mike stepped out onto this fairly precarious edge, and he started skirting along on hard ice under a thin layer of snow. He looked back at me and explained, "All right, man, this is your first test." He said, "This is some pretty serious shit here. You don't want to fall here. Move carefully and just be deliberate with your steps." And at that point, I looked down and, yes, this is serious. So that was my first initiation into an exposed environment like that.

Engineer Peak I had attempted solo once before I'd gone up, and wanted to get my eyes on it, and this was before I had some decent boots or crampons, and it was earlier in the year. It was in October, I believe, and I got fairly high up on the ridge, to that critical point, and there were maybe four or five inches of snow up there, but I had no idea about the terrain, because I hadn't been up there in the summer. I had no idea what the terrain was like underneath that layer of snow and it turned me back. I got to that point, the crux area on Engineer, and I realized, "I don't really know what I'm doing here."

The crux area is about halfway up on the ridge where it flattens out for a little bit and then all of a sudden it closes out. You have to step out onto the left, onto the southern face, and you sort of skirt the ridge. During the summer, the handholds on the ridge are really good, and once you're comfortable you can be out on that face fairly safely. It's probably a forty-five- or fifty-degree pitch or so. But when you're new to it and when you take somebody up there, it doesn't matter, summer or winter, that's where a lot of people turn around. It's where they have to step out on that face. That's where it cliffs out and it drops about 180, maybe 220 feet or so. You become aware of the fact that, "Wow, if I were to slip here and slide and fall, I'm going over the edge. I'm going over a cliff." So it's more mentally challenging than physically, once you know the terrain.

In April 1995 we were three guys and a dog going for a mountain climb. Our group included Michael Seaberg, David Ganley, and his dog, Ancho. We decided that we finally had gotten to a point where we felt like, "Hey, our dining concept has caught on. We've got a bit of a following. The restaurant's doing well and we decided that it was time to get out and take in a peak."

We were up until about two o'clock the night before. We agreed to meet at 6 A.M., so we went home, got about three hours of sleep, and woke up. I think David was maybe half an hour, forty-five minutes late. We kind of knew going up that he was a little bit behind, but he was going to meet us up there and Mike and I rode up together.

We left the cars at the top of Coal Bank Pass at predawn, and we got on the trail and took the short-cut trail, straight up. We didn't take the traditional trail. We took the telemark traverse trail up the headwall, in order to get to the base of the peak. We made fairly good time and got to the base of the peak in about an hour and fifteen minutes. I had stopped to take some pictures as the sun was coming up. I got some good sunrise shots.

We stopped at the base, got rid of our snowshoes. We put on our crampons and got out our axes and had a little quick snack and then just continued right on up the ridge. There was a lot of snow. It was a big snow year on the ridge, for sure. On the way up, I remember thinking that the dog was a little bit of a distraction for me. I didn't really know how much to trust him in that environment. And this was before I had ever had any avalanche training, and I still really didn't have a concept coming from the East Coast of just how volatile the snow conditions were in this area. But I did feel better about the fact that both Mike and David had been on the peak many times, and quite a few of those times were in the winter. So I felt much better about that, as my second trip back there.

We got to the crux area and it was definitely deep snow at that point. It was a combination of post-holing and packing our steps down to get through that area, and Ancho, the dog, was doing great. He was just running around and he didn't really have much trouble, but he was in deep. He was post-holing himself, and it did make me feel better, at least at that area, to see him going up and down without triggering a slide. So, in a way, he was helping us gauge conditions.

And so I had stopped, at that point, and I took a picture of David and his dog and Mike was in the lead. David went up second and I followed them. Things were easier for me, especially because the steps had already been packed down a fair amount. We got through that section and continued up on the ridge. Michael stopped and stated that he wanted to take a little journey out onto the north face, to scout any potential routes.

That was sort of the initial breakup of the team, and it made me a little nervous. I looked over there and I thought, "Man, that's really steep." I thought if what we're on is 50 degrees, that's more like 70 or 75 degrees. But he felt confident that he was not going too far away from us and that he was going to be fine in that environment.

David said something to the effect of, "I don't want to spoil the virgin summit for you, so why don't you take it from here? He was a little tired at that point, as well. He was laboring and I was definitely, from the cycling that I had done, more aerobically fit than Dave.

I didn't mind going around; we were still within 30 or 40 feet of each other and it was only another 150 feet to the top. I got to the summit and looked around real quick and still had my camera around my neck, so I took a few more shots. I took some shots of Dave as he was coming up the ridge, and I was kind of preoccupied with watching Michael, to see that he was still doing all right on that face, and he wasn't triggering a slide and heading down the north face himself. To be honest, my number one concern was keeping an eye on him.

So David topped out and got to me, and I took a few summit shots of him and his dog and then David said something to the effect of, "I'm going to head over to the western summit and sit down and start working on a little lunch."

I said, "All right, sounds good. That's fine." I looked over at the western summit and I had two thoughts in mind. One was I wanted to keep an eye on Mike. My other thought as I was looking across toward the western summit was that I wasn't really sure . . . I could tell that there was a bit of a cornice built up and I wasn't really sure where the mountain was and where it ended and it was definitely a conscious thought of mine.

But I was comfortable with the fact that David did know where he was going, because he had been up there before. So I took one or two shots of him walking in that direction and then turned my attention back to Michael and took a few photos of him as he worked his way up to the summit on a direct route up from the face. As he got to the top, I joined up with him and he asked me where David went. I said, "Well, he went back there . . . said he was going to go over and work on lunch on the western summit." And Mike had a response sort of like "Huh! . . . That doesn't really make sense, but all right . . ."

So we proceeded in that direction. We were walking along and Michael was to the left of me and I was basically staying close to him. At the same time, I was conscious of the fact that we were fairly close to Dave's tracks and that Ancho was walking to the right of me. He had been walking farther out onto that cornice than I was, so I felt like, "Well, all right. Must be on some fairly stable ground." All of a sudden, Michael stopped. I got about half a step in front of him and I immediately stopped and turned to look at him like "Why are you stopping?"

And as I was doing that, Mike had this look on his face and was starting to say something to David, like "Hey, David, don't . . ." and at that instant the cornice broke directly between Mike and myself, and I went down.

Mike was left at the top, literally right at the edge of the fracture line. He recognized that David was sitting quite far out on a cornice, and Michael was stopping because he wasn't sure where we were at that point. As he started to signal to tell David not to move and to get off of there, as he started to say that, I realized what was happening. It broke at that instant.

Michael had his eyes fixed on David and watched him fall. He didn't even recognize the fact that all of a sudden, a split second later, I was gone. All of a sudden there was just a void.

～

Helicopter nurse Leo Lloyd explains—April 2, 1995: It was a relatively normal snow year for the San Juans, but three climbers from Durango decided to climb Engineer Mountain via the northeast ridge route, the standard route on the peak, on a Sunday morning. Their names were Fred, Michael, and David, and they also had a dog with them, David's dog, Ancho. They took off from the top of Coal Bank Pass that morning on snowshoes. That particular year, when you look at this peak, the prevailing winds are typically out of the southwest. The crux of this route forms a cornice along the ridgeline, and the cornices typically hang over the north side of the peak. That particular year, the cornices were huge near the summit. It was probably, as far as mass, many tons of snow overhanging the north face of the peak near the summit. The cornices were sticking out as much as thirty feet in some places. So the objective, obviously, is to stay on the windward side of the ridge, staying off those cornices, as you climb the peak.

The north face of Engineer is actually quite steep. It's almost like Half Dome in Yosemite. It's not that vertical, but the relatively benign south face compared to the north face is a significant difference, and there's quite a demarcation line along the ridge here.

These cornices that year were overhanging the north face of this peak by about thirty feet. The real ridge on this thing is way over here [he gestures]. Again, there is air underneath this entire mass. Now these cornices have been sitting there all winter long. It's now April. A tremendous amount of mass is hanging over the north side of that peak.

This is Fred's first time to the top of Engineer in these conditions. He was relatively new to the area at that time, as well. So he's just pretty much following David. Michael, who was probably the most experienced of the three, is behind these two taking photos of the north side of the peak as they come off. Well, as Michael gets up, he stays farther toward the actual ridgeline, but I don't think it really dawned on him how exposed they were. Fred pretty much walked along the tracks to where David was sitting. And, typical summit, they're happy to be there. I don't think there was any communication between the three, but as Fred got to within fifteen feet of David, he stops and turns around and actually makes eye contact with Michael, and Fred then turns around to go toward David, and a thirty-by-thirty-foot section of the ridge fails—the cornice. And it fractured right in front of Michael. Unfortunately, Fred was in the middle of it, and so was David. The whole thing dropped off the north face of the peak with those two and the dog on it.

Michael does not remember any screams for help or anything. It was just this rush of air as it filled the void of where that cornice had been. Imagine seeing your best friends . . . [the three of them had recently opened a

In a dramatic mountain-climbing accident, Fred Hutt fell nine hundred feet off the north face of Engineer Peak in the San Juan Mountains and was rescued by helicopter nurse Leo Lloyd. Today they work together on the La Plata County Search-and-Rescue Team. Pictured is the north face of Engineer Peak. Photo by author.

restaurant together] . . . drop off this peak. So Michael keeps his wits about him. He starts cruising back along the ridge and running back, just in time to see a plume of snow as this cornice mass hits the base of the peak. At that time, it starts an avalanche at the base of the peak and goes another three hundred feet or so. Michael is literally running down the ridge, and he gets about three-quarters of the way down and is able to traverse out onto the north face.

Michael makes his way down onto the face and starts traversing over to where the avalanche debris is. As he gets closer to the debris, he realizes the dog is limping and bleeding but going around in a circle on the debris, just going around and around this one spot. As he gets there he can see blood in the snow, then notices a bloody face in the snow. The dog appeared to have licked it clean of snow, and the face was breathing. That was Fred, completely buried except for his exposed face. So Michael quickly starts digging him out with his hands. They had no avalanche gear with them.

Fred is actually awake and talking. He cannot see, though. The whole left side of his cheekbone and the left forehead area was injured. He had many, many fractures in his face, and he had quite a deformity on that side of his face from an impact of some kind. But he was conscious—and he was already getting very, very cold.

It was around 12:30 in the afternoon when the accident occurred. But to Michael, Fred was already getting cold. This is what I think was significant. Michael had an extra big puffball jacket in his pack, and he also had a bivi sack with him. First of all, he had to deal with the big bleeding gash on Fred's forehead. Michael was able to control the bleeding with some direct pressure and, I think, using a shirt or something to deal with that, and then he got Fred into this down jacket and then into a bivi sack. Fred has multiple trauma injuries. It does appear that his belly, his chest, his pelvis are intact. I think he ended up having some shoulder issues. I think it was his left or right shoulder, but other than that he's doing pretty good, except that he can't see, and he's cold.

Michael kind of gets him propped up in the snow and starts looking for David. Fortunately, he was able to find David relatively quickly. I believe there was some type of debris or a hand sticking out of the snow, and he went up and quickly started digging David out. Unfortunately, David's condition was kind of what you'd expect from a nine-hundred-foot fall. He had major traumatic injuries including the head and chest, and it was obvious that David was dead.

And this really shows the character of Michael, because he was able to just completely focus, refocus, 100 percent, right onto Fred and again ensuring he was protected from the environment as best he could. He had stopped the bleeding in his head, and then he told Fred he was going for help.

∽

Fred Hutt remembers: As I started to fall, I basically felt like I fell directly, vertically, about twenty feet at most, in a free-fall state, and then all of a sudden, I met back up with the terrain and immediately started to swing my axe. . . . My axe was still in my hand, and I tried to swing my axe into the snow to my left. I tried to plant my pick into the left and it was moving. I was trying to plant an axe into the sliding snow and it wasn't going anywhere. I immediately rolled over on my back doing a little bit of a backstroke and thought to myself, this is serious shit. I said, "You're probably gonna die here!" And I told myself, "Well, hang on, because you never know what's going to happen."

I remembered something that Michael had told me. If I was ever in a slide it would probably be a good idea to try to get rid of my pack. So the last thing that I did was try to free my arms . . . tuck my arms through the shoulder straps, and then at the same time, I covered up my face. I don't remember anything else on the way down other than a brief glimpse of a memory as we were being deposited down at the bottom.

I remember the force and I remember going in feet first and I remember that sound, that omnipresent thunderous roar of the snow coming down all around me. I was thrust, very violently, forward, down where my head met my knees, and I gave out a quick "UUUOOONNN" type of grunt, because I was trying to fight that force.

Then things were blank for about the next fifty to fifty-five minutes. Until the point when Michael got to me. I have a few memories of him . . . hearing him in the area . . . knowing I was in trouble and recognizing that I was having vision problems, and I couldn't see him. I could see some light, but I couldn't focus in on him or anything around me. I knew I was in a semiconscious state. When Michael got to me, he started to assess me and I asked him, . . . my biggest concern was my vision. I knew there was blood around me and I thought that perhaps I had either punctured my eye or my eye was out of its socket. And I asked him, "Mike, how's my eye? I can't see anything. What's going on? What's the story with my eye?"

I had an open skull fracture. Michael said to me, "I'm not going to lie to you, Fred, because you're in bad shape, here, man." He said, "You're gonna have to do everything that you can to save your own life here. I'm going to have to go and get help." And I said, "Yes, yes, okay, no problem."

I have very little understanding of time at this point, but he got everything out of his pack that he could. He had an extra down jacket, extra hat, extra layers; he took a shirt and he basically took the left half of my face and flapped it back over, tied a T-shirt around my head to keep things intact, and propped me up. The last thing he said was, "All right, man, I'm going now. You cannot fall asleep. Whatever you do, you cannot fall asleep."

And I said, "Yes, yes, okay," . . . because I was concerned with resting. Sleeping or falling in and out of consciousness was not something I was trying to fight. But he tried to drill that into my head.

∼

Leo Lloyd recounts: So Michael traversed over to where his snowshoes were, grabbed those, and then started running down to the top of Coal Bank Pass. Now, when Michael did reach their vehicle, he realized David, the fatality, had the car keys in his pack. They did not have a plan on leaving keys somewhere on that vehicle in case something would happen, so Mike had to start hitchhiking. He got a ride down to Cascade Village where he was able to call 911. Because this was San Juan County, it went through their dispatch and they went ahead and started looking for a helicopter right away. That's how I got involved. I happened to be working that day in Farmington, New Mexico, on the helicopter.

Fortunately I had gear with me. I was able to change clothes completely. Unfortunately, my partner flight nurse that I was working with that day was not familiar with mountains. And so we land, but I'm thinking that there's already a rescue in progress. We land at Cascade Village on the highway and as we are landing, I look over and I can see the San Juan County sheriff and then I saw Michael Seaberg, who was a friend of mine. Michael, who was with Fred . . . Michael was on our search and rescue team! And I'm going, "Oh!" My heart sank because we knew there was a fatality.

Michael's pretty adamant that we need to get back up there, that Fred's critically injured. So I asked the sheriff, "Can Michael go back up with me, and we'll go back in?" And I did that for couple of reasons. First of all, I knew Michael and I knew that he'd be a tremendous asset because it was just going to be the two of us going in. Plus, he knew exactly where Fred was located. Plus, the weather was deteriorating by the minute. And thank goodness Michael was there, because it was very difficult to see. The light was so flat.

We had to jump off the helicopter, and we took a skid litter with us and a couple of wool blankets. I had my pack with me. We took some oxygen. We took a very rudimentary wound management kit and a little bit of rope, and a KED, which is a spinal immobilization device, and that was it. And that was plenty for two of us to try to slog through. And it was post-holing, too, until we got to the snowshoes. So Michael says, "We got snowshoes. They're right up here . . ." and so we cruised up and grabbed the snowshoes.

We made our way over toward the accident location. As Michael and I got close, we could see the dog was still there, and Fred is not responding. I could see him but he was slipped over in the snow. Closer, I could actually hear him just kind of gurgling, snowy respirations. And the reason he was doing that was because he was unconscious and had slumped over in the snow. The first thing I did was open his airway, which helped, and Michael and I started digging a platform to package him in. It was obvious that he was profoundly hypothermic and had deteriorated significantly since Michael had left him. By now, it's about two o'clock.

Michael and I get him into this roll-up skid litter. We get him packaged with as much insulation as we had, and we got him connected with this rope. Michael and I started traversing across the bottom of the ridge and it's hard to do. It's very difficult. We'd been pulling him across this slope and now we're trying to get to the landing zone. The only thing I did for Fred was open his airway and put him on some oxygen. We were just eking the oxygen out because it was a small bottle, and I focused on getting him to the landing zone. It was obvious to me that what was going to save Fred was getting him out of this environment. This was no time to start IVs. Any delay was probably going to kill him. He was breathing on his own and he was maintaining, barely, but it was really scary to see how critical he was. And trying to minimize any jostling that we were doing with him . . . it was very difficult. I knew that he was hypothermic. I just didn't know how bad at that point.

Another thing we were dealing with when we were with Fred was the rock fall from the peak. There were still rocks whizzing down from up there. There was hangfire like you wouldn't believe from those cornices. A tremendous amount of energy was released when that cornice broke. When you're looking back up there, you can see how big these cornices are, and if another one of these falls off, we are going to get buried. But I didn't even think much about that.

During this time, a second helicopter came into play. It was from Tall Timbers Resort, a much smaller helicopter, better suited for this kind of environment. And then we were running low on fuel and we still had to get him to the hospital, so we were going to transfer him to the newer helicopter, the smaller one, and just do a short jump, put him on our helicopter, and then fly him to Durango. And that's what we ended up doing. We had to take the doors off to put him in the back seat, keeping him supine.

Right now I am very concerned whether he is even going to make it. I'm not holding out a whole lot of hope. He was barely breathing. The only thing that was going to save him was getting him out of here. He arrived at Mercy Medical Center with a core body temperature of 82 degrees.

⁓

Fred Hutt recalls: I had no comprehension of time. I didn't know what passed. I still don't know whether I fell in and out of consciousness, if I didn't fall asleep or if I did. I have very little memory of any of the interactions with the helicopter or the medical team. I remember them saying they were going to have to take the doors off the helicopter. I don't really remember them having to drag me across the slope. I have a brief memory of understanding that Leo was there. I did not know Leo beforehand, but I kind of thought to myself, "Well, this is like the movies and this is the mountain medic right here."

And I have a brief memory of being in the helicopter when I was transported from the NewAir helicopter to Air Care at the Cascade location. I have a glimpse of the memory of that, of flying down the valley in the Air Care helicopter. I have a glimpse of a memory of being in the emergency room for the first time. So there are bits and pieces along the way.

I remember them saying something about being careful not to jostle me too much. But I really don't have much memory of that. There are just a few split second things of . . . Whoa! There's a lot of light in here, and there's a bunch of people, and hearing something about fluids in the stomach and not really understanding what kind of treatment was happening and not knowing the hospital chaplain had called my parents and told them I was not expected to live.

I don't really know what the chaplain said. From what my mother tells me, and my sister, it was one of those phone calls that is the worst phone call they ever got. He conveyed to them that my chances of survival were probably not that good, and the condition was serious and that they may want to come out from New York.

Because I had a head injury, the first time I woke up, I was combative. I remember seeing my sister and they had my sister hold my feet, because I was kicking, and I was thrashing my arms. I think I was trying to get the IV out, that type of thing. I think my sister said something to me and I was mad at her for saying it, so I looked at her, straight in the eye, and I basically yelled at her really quickly, and that was the first time that she thought, "Wow! That's Fred back there. He might make it." And what they would do, I guess, for the next several days, was bring me in and out of consciousness.

When I woke up, for good, I guess you could say, when they brought me to for the first time, and I wasn't combative . . . it was a series of three or four times, I believe, where I would come to and I was agitated and they would put me back under and they would just confirm that I was still there. The first time they brought me to and I thought, there's my mom, there's my sister. There's my dad, and I could talk. I could put a sentence or a thought together. At that point, I recognized or realized that, I think, Dave went, too. And I asked, and I think it was Michael who told me that Dave didn't make it.

And I just kind of went, "Yes, that's what I thought." And I just thought to myself, "Well, it's amazing that you're here. You really shouldn't be here, either."

⁓

Lloyd, the flight nurse, explains that for Hutt: The next day he started a series of surgeries on his face and dealing with some of his other orthopedic injuries. He ended up spending a couple of weeks in the ICU. He did have an epidural bleed in his head, but it was small enough that they didn't have to surgically deal with it. He did have a significant shoulder injury. He had a multiple lower-back compression fracture and facial fractures. All that healed up. He's lost vision in one eye, but it did come back a little bit. His eye injury came from the camera hitting his head as he fell just after he took the last photo of his friend David Ganley.

On the next flight off the mountain we retrieved the body. Ganley's dog ended up with a paw injury and a broken tooth and that was it. Fred Hutt's arms were buried in the snow and yet he was able to breathe somewhat. Perhaps the dog had licked the snow off around his face. We'll never know.

Lessons Learned and Giving Back

Fred Hutt explains: I lost a tremendous amount of weight. I wasn't a heavy guy at the time. I was six feet one, and at that time maybe 145 pounds, and I went down to about 122, 123. So a large part of my recovery and the things that they needed to watch were (1) my lungs, and (2) my kidneys. They were concerned about renal shutdown, essentially, because I had lost a fair amount of muscle tissue. A lot of muscle tissue died off, and my system had to purge that out. So I lost a lot of weight and I recognized the fact that, wow, I'm a skeleton. When I first came in, they were more concerned about saving my life, and they took a quick set of X-rays, but they didn't find my vertebrae cracked.

They weren't aware that I had back problems. They weren't aware that I had any complications from the head injury. They knew I had some swelling in the brain, so I went through a series of CT scans and MRIs. They sent me back for another set of X-rays after I complained and they realized that I had some compression fractures of some vertebrae. Wow! I broke my back here, and somehow I'm not paralyzed. So that was just another, "Whew! Dodged bullet."

But I was in the hospital without my contact lenses and I'm blind as it is, relatively speaking, and it took me a day or two to realize that the vision in my right eye was impaired beyond just my normal vision loss. They brought in another doctor for that, since they thought that this could end up being a complication from the head injury. I could have suffered damage to the optic nerve, or it could just be pressure on the optic nerve. They weren't really sure. But whatever it is, it's permanent, so it seems like it's probably damage to the optic nerve at this point, and that is the biggest handicap from it all. I wasn't sure what was going to last the longest. I thought maybe I'd have back problems for the rest of my life, but fortunately, I haven't had any complications with that.

The paralysis in my hand and my arm went away after six months of physical therapy. I did have to have some facial reconstruction done before I even left the hospital.

I was very conscious of the risks of getting involved. I didn't embark on a mountaineering adventure not knowing or thinking about the risks. I knew what I was getting myself into, but I didn't really have a whole lot of commitments at that point, and I didn't have a wife or kid. And I was also quite confident in my partners. Mistakes were made in terms of recognizing terrain and not understanding completely the snow conditions. But accidents . . . mistakes are made in all accidents, whether it's a car accident or not. I'm not going to beat myself up over it for life.

I know that Michael has had his own issues to deal with in terms of where responsibility lies and things like that. So everybody has to process an event like this in a different way, and everyone has a different set of issues, but I guess, if I were to do one thing differently, I would probably have assured that maybe we did this on a more complete night of sleep. I know that breaking up the team dynamic that day was probably the single most critical factor that led to this. We were all responsible for that. I don't blame any one particular individual.

Meeting Leo Lloyd was sort of an introduction to search and rescue. I think I was invited to a search and rescue meeting after the incident; basically folks just wanted to meet me, and Leo wanted to introduce me to folks and Michael as well, so I didn't jump into it right away.

After the accident, right from the beginning, I didn't really want to capitalize on it. It wasn't something that I was looking to go hawking books and magazine articles about. I got back to work. I got back on the bicycle and about six months later, I climbed Engineer again—six months to the day, actually. It was in October. I went up there by myself and that was an important trip for me. Sort of to get back on the horse. I was definitely breathing heavy at that one, but it broke the ice, and after that I kept in touch consistently with Leo.

Michael and I went down, and it was more important for me to meet and greet and thank the folks from Air Care, the flight crew there, because they were more instrumental than, say, La Plata County or San Juan Search and Rescue. I just wanted to meet the individuals who were involved and talk to them. I think it was eight or ten months later that I went to the first search and rescue meeting and I said, "Yes, I can get involved in this organization."

I just started showing up to meetings. A part of my motivation was to give back as much as I could. I know that the county took on some financial obligations for the helicopter fees. To a certain extent, my thought process was, "Well, if I do this long enough to be involved with a couple of missions, that will help pay back the funds that they spent on me. That's the least I could do." That's how I saw it.

And I had been involved with or around the fire and rescue community all my life. My father was an EMT. I was a lifeguard through college at a state park, and my father was always on the fire department, so that was ingrained in my blood. It just seemed like a fairly low-impact, easy way to get involved with the EMS community here in Durango.

I did finally join Durango Fire and Rescue a little over a year ago. Search and rescue, I'm still active with them. It's going on sixteen years. I've pursued that heavily because it makes me feel good about still going out in the mountains. That sort of training helps me feel like I can justify going out and staying in shape and being in a mountainous environment without being irresponsible about it.

It would be a lie to say that the incident didn't change my perspective on how I pursue my climbing or my mountaineering adventures. I think there's always this reluctant climber side of me. I'm a reluctant climber in that I've got this reservation about my pursuits. It keeps me from truly excelling at it, and it keeps me from doing it as frequently or as often as I could. I guess, to a certain extent, I have more natural skills than I do natural ambition for it at this point. And I don't know how much of that is a result of the accident, but I try not to overanalyze it, either. I just accept it.

I value the spirit of youth very much, and to a certain extent the innocence, I guess, and the ignorance of youth. It's a good time when you're somewhat invincible. Anytime I see somebody who moves here, especially from the East Coast or from "out of the area," I'm constantly keeping my ears out for people that move here and want to start venturing out in the snow, but they don't have the first idea of what they're getting involved in. And I'm probably more active in recruiting and trying to educate people in private on the proper steps to take to pursue those hobbies.

They don't understand that it only takes a hundred-foot slope with a half a foot of snow to slide and bury you and your dog. So understanding just how easy it is and how volatile the snow conditions are here and things of that nature is critical.

I was fortunate enough to have health insurance when this happened, and David didn't. It's partly ironic that he was killed. We had just had a conversation not three or four days prior to this incident about how he was hanging out to dry because he didn't have health insurance. He knew it and he knew that he needed to get on that when he could afford it, but David was scraping by to make his business.

I had just left a place of employment that had given me health insurance. All of a sudden I didn't have health insurance, so I took out my own private policy and I just made that transition. I was in the first month or two of my new policy when this happened. My total bills were in excess of $120,000. I still had close to $10,000 worth of personal commitments that I had to make and pay for over the next couple of years, but that's nothing compared to $120,000. So that's something I keep my ears peeled for and try to convey to folks.

I had not given any thought toward taking an avalanche class before this incident, before I joined search and rescue. I hadn't really been warned about the volatility of the snow conditions around here.

I tell folks they need to be stewards of the craft. It's more than just going out and having fun and getting big air or climbing a 5/11 pitch today and climbing 5/12 tomorrow, working up to your personal skills. It's about pursuing your craft in a professional manner and truly knowing . . . doing it professionally, I guess. It's about doing it well and knowing your rope management skills.

One of the things that keeps me from climbing a whole lot is the fact that I am so picky about partners. If somebody doesn't have the right frame of mind, I don't want to go out and get on a top rope. They have to have the right frame of mind to actually want to learn what they're doing. I don't know anybody who truly sticks around and makes it through year in, year out, who doesn't approach it from that frame of mind.

Be prepared.

The helicopter bills are $25,000 or $30,000 these days. Health insurance won't cover that. Have your search and rescue card.

When you get up on the top of a pitch and you're tying in your anchors and you know what you're doing, because you do it in the same manner and you scramble and you manage the rope in a similar manner and you know that you're not going to get into trouble and be stuck up there for twenty minutes untangling a rope because your partner's rope management skills are poor . . . Those are the things that lead to the downfall of any outing, and those create epics. They create problems when you have little issues that start to compound on each other. You need to micromanage the little issues so that they don't become big issues, all along the way.

Somebody has to recognize that; everybody needs to understand, as things are happening, that you take care of this. It's similar to a car accident or a rescue scene. The search and rescue crew manages the call in a similar frame of mind, same sort of situational awareness, to not become a victim within the incident or become an incident within the incident.

There are so many climbers, sport climbers, who can climb 5/11 and 5/12, but if their partner is leading and got knocked on the head and was hanging out two pitches up, they wouldn't know how to get themselves down. They wouldn't know how to execute a self-rescue. It's about spending time learning those skills as much as it is about working on your absolute ability, your ascending ability. So you take on a responsibility of not only doing it but of also promoting it and looking out for where the folks around you are pursuing it, and helping them be safe.

⌒

Leo Lloyd adds: Extra keys down by the truck would have helped, and having enough insulation, and weather protection, to be able to deal with a delayed scenario in an accident context, where you are not able to get out . . . or you have to leave somebody. I don't know if they had headlamps with them, but that's another thing that I always carry. I carry several space blankets. I carry a puffball down jacket. I carry a tarp. I carry cord, extra synthetics, as far as insulation goes, and that just stays in my pack, and I think if you look in Fred's pack, it'd be exactly the same.

And you know, what's really neat about the type of person Fred is, that here's a guy who went through an absolute epic and he's had to endure people talking about it and it still garners the same reaction. People just cannot believe how somebody could survive that. And I think that it is a testament to the kind of person Fred is, but it's also such a good example of how a companion that's prepared can make decisions in a crisis and truly save a life.

Fred was very, very fortunate to have someone like Michael there. I think they would've made a lot of different decisions that day to prevent that scenario from happening, but it happened, and things do happen. It doesn't matter how skilled you are. If you do anything long enough outdoors, you're going to face a crisis. It may not be in your own group, but it may be someone you come across, and early decisions will dictate a lot of times the outcome of a backcountry accident.

Training is important because if it happens to you, you would hope that your buddies do not succumb to the pressure of panic and ill-conceived decisions. You know, it's amazing. Some people that you'd never think can perform rise to the occasion when they're put under emergency pressure, but it's not the ones you think.

Yes, it is all about whom you're with, that's for sure. But backcountry survival skills can be taught. People can learn to do that. It's a concerted effort that you have to make. I want to know enough to make a difference if we have a medical problem. And that takes jumping through hoops a lot of times, and it costs money and it takes time for skilled training. And it takes keeping your expectations at a reasonable level. That is why you get experience, so you can hopefully have the right skills at the right time.

Fred's with us now. He's joined the La Plata County Search and Rescue, and he's a volunteer with Durango Fire Rescue. And he's becoming a firefighter, too, and I think, eventually, this may be a career change for him. He's already gone through his EMT training, and he's really been working hard the last several years to see if this is something he might enjoy doing, but you know, I think, for him, especially, it's about giving something back to the community. His spirit of volunteerism is excellent.

On search and rescue we don't get a lot of calls, compared to what we get with the fire department, but when it does happen there's just something about a volunteer team, too, that comes together, day or night, to have a competent response, a safe response, and spends just countless hours training for one or two calls a year where we might use those skills. All it takes is one emergency response call to make it completely worthwhile, and this is why we do it. We give something back when it happens.

Study Questions

1. Leo Lloyd talks about people becoming complacent in the backcountry with lots of newfangled gear. What gear do people rely on today that might not really be that "essential" and could even cause more harm than good?

2. If you could create your own "dream team" for a month-long backpacking/trekking adventure, who would you take? What characteristics/personalities would you want on your team?

3. Lightweight backpackers are all about stripping it down to the bare minimum. However, we are taught to always be prepared for a worst-case scenario. So what heavier items would you take (if any) in case of an emergency that might push your pack out of the "lightweight" range?

4. This chapter contains a lot of scary stories. What is the point of sharing fearsome and even gruesome stories with other outdoor enthusiasts? Do you have a scary story to share?

5. As seen in the different articles, we always have twenty-twenty vision after an incident/experience. Reflect on your outdoor adventure experiences. If you've had any close-call "epics," what would you do differently now?

6. Describe your ideal solo experience. How long would it be? Where would it be? How would you spend your time? What food/gear would you want, if any?

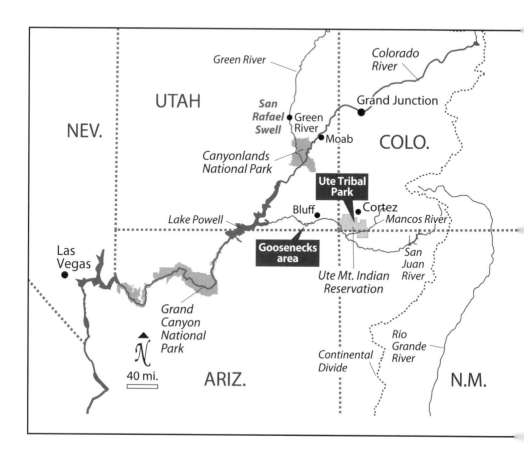

CHAPTER 4

Canyons and Deserts

The canyon country does not always inspire love. To many it appears barren, hostile, repellent—a fearsome mostly waterless land of rock and heat, sand dunes and quicksand, cactus, thornbush, scorpion, rattlesnake, and agoraphobic distances. To those who see our land in that manner, the best reply is yes, you are right, it is a dangerous and terrible place. Enter at your own risk. Carry water. Avoid the noonday sun. Try to ignore the vultures. Pray frequently.

—Edward Abbey, *The Journey Home*

Early mornings in the canyon have a distinct quality; they are a time I cherish. Out here there is time to watch the day begin, hear the small secret sounds that no one else is awake to hear, time to watch the light change, to anticipate the coming day, all the good hours stacked ahead. Cool dawn, in these dry canyons, is a time of rare perfection, fresh beginnings, infinite peace, total awareness.

—Ann Zwinger, *Wind in the Rock*

To the deserts go prophets and hermits; through deserts go pilgrims and exiles. Here the leaders of the great religions have sought the therapeutic and spiritual values of retreat, not to escape but to find reality.

—Paul Shepard, *Man in the Landscape*

The one-armed Civil War veteran Major John Wesley Powell left Green River, Wyoming, in May 1869 with a party of men to explore a blank spot on the map: the Colorado Plateau and the deep canyons of the Colorado River. Their wooden boats, designed for the Great Lakes, were little more than large and cumbersome walnut shells, hard to navigate and control. With leather boots and uncomfortable woolen clothing, the crew chafed in the desert heat. Powell would often explore side canyons with barometers to measure elevation; once, on an exposed ledge, he became rimrocked and could not go sideways, up, or down. But he was saved by quick thinking and long underwear.

Desert and canyon hiking is like that. One moment you're safe in the sun and the next you're out of water or falling off a cliff. You're in a perfectly dry desert wash, and then out of a clear, blue sky comes the sound of a freight train. You run for high ground before the frothy, twisting mass of boulders and tree trunks boils past in the flash flood that began up canyon miles away.

Time shifts and changes in the desert. Canyon light can lazily stretch a day into forever, but slipping on rimrock, or losing footing on a ledge, can focus everything into split-second survival. As Utah writer Chip Ward notes, "Sometimes Mother Nature does a pop quiz and you fail." A female canyoneer entered Quandary Canyon when it was raining, and between two minor fifteen-foot drops, she drowned in a flash flood. At Chop Rock Canyon two hikers died in a pothole having pulled their only rope toward them and thus eliminating any way out. At Knotted Rope a woman rappelled a fifteen-foot drop into a pothole, broke her arm, and eventually drowned because her husband, above her, did not know how to save her.

As for Major Powell rimrocked on a cliff, he had been climbing with one of his crew members, who had forgotten to bring rope. So the boatman took off his clothes, including his long underwear, and dangled his drawers down to Powell. The major had to lean back off his precarious ledge and with his only hand tightly grab the legs of the long johns to be pulled up to safety.

"The moment is critical," Powell wrote. "Standing on my toes, my muscles began to tremble. It is sixty or eighty feet to the foot of the precipice. If I lose my hold I shall fall to the bottom and then perhaps roll over the bench and tumble still farther down the cliff." His crew member George Bradley thinks quickly. "At this instant it occurs to Bradley to take off his drawers, which he does, and swings them down to me," Powell explains. "I hug close to the rock, let go with my hand, seize the dangling legs, and with his assistance am enabled to gain the top."[1]

I make mistakes, too, but I've never been saved by underwear.

Once, a friend and I drove to Island in the Sky in Canyonlands National Park. We locked the VW camper bus and decided to backpack down to the Colorado River, just the two of us and a Border collie. As canyon hiking novices we soon lost the trail and began to edge along the slickrock, which fascinated me. I'd never walked on a cross-bedded surface before. Slickrock hiking requires standing straight, putting solid weight on hiking boots, and leaning slightly forward to push your feet into the rock. Katie Lee explains, "I've called the business of mastering slickrock hiking 'getting in touch with the stone': paying attention to balance and pressure, reading and navigating the land like a boatman does rivers."[2] I had yet to learn that. Slowly, carefully, we made our way down, and as the spring day got hotter we sought shade under a large overhang. We weren't the first ones to do it, either.

In the back, slightly buried in sand, we found thirty-year-old artifacts from a uranium prospector. We found 1950s magazines, a lantern, a few odd tools, and a pair of shriveled, leather boots, dried and desiccated. We put everything back on the sandy shelf, shouldered our packs, and headed down canyon toward the river.

Soon there were narrow side canyons, large boulders, wet mud with wave-like patterns, and broken rocks everywhere in the harsh early afternoon light. We found a sandy flat area, set up our tents and camp, and with hours of day-light left thought we'd mosey on down to the river. Relieved to have left our packs, we didn't take anything. Not even a water bottle. No map. Just cameras and light cotton flannel shirts over T-shirts and shorts. We had a lot to learn, and several hours later the lessons began.

On the way down to the river we found iridescent green maidenhair ferns dripping water like a smooth natural sponge. Water squeezed from sand-stone! Amazing! Finally, with an hour's light left in the day, we walked past stately cottonwood trees to arrive at the tamarisk-choked Colorado River. After the canyon hike, the sparse overgrazed river bottom was uninspiring, so we started back up. Twilight blended into night. The stars popped out one by one from their dark velvet background, then the moon rose full and bright, creating smooth shadows in side canyons.

Tired, hungry, and thirsty despite handfuls of water from the maidenhair ferns, we longed for a quick dinner and the comfort of our down sleeping bags. We followed our own tracks up the canyon, but where was camp? The moon rose higher, temperatures dropped, and quiet concern became mutual desperation. Where were our side canyon and all our gear? Hour after hour we walked up, down, back, and forth, but because of the moon's shadows all the canyons and rocks seemed to be going in the wrong direction. Exhausted, eventually we gave up, dug a shallow pit in the sand, and lay down, shivering, to hug our warm, furry Border collie.

At dawn we woke to find how close we'd been. Sixty yards away camp was exactly as we'd left it. Midmorning found us still snoozing, but valuable lessons had been learned about being prepared, taking adequate gear, paying attention to time, and not getting lost. Terry and Renny Russell wrote, "Well, have we guys learned our lesson? You bet we have. Have we learned to eschew irresponsible outdoorsmanship, to ask advice, to take care and to plan fastidiously and to stay on the trail and to camp only in designated campgrounds? You bet we haven't. Unfastidious outdoorsmanship is the best kind."[3]

Since that experience I've come to love the beauty of high sandstone walls with desert tapestry varnish and dark streaks where water has poured off for centuries. I seek the distinctive cascading arpeggio of canyon wrens, a desert sound that opens your heart. But mistakes? I've made plenty of them. How else do you learn in the backcountry?

~

Recently I made a mistake by guiding an eighty-year-old man who'd had a triple heart bypass six months before into Chesler Park in Canyonlands in ninety-five-degree heat. On the tour he'd been a troublemaker, so the other guide took the whole group and left me with Mr. Grumpy, who was convinced he wanted to hike ten miles that day. We'd done two and a half miles when his skin tone went from bright pink to crimson red. We found some shade and I said, "That's it. No more. Drink up. Rest up. Then it's back to the van."

He spluttered, cussed, demanded we go on. Said he'd paid all his guide fees and by God he wanted to hike. I let him spout off for awhile and then I said quietly but firmly, "No. You've walked in this far and you'll walk out. You're not going farther only to have me carry you out." Finally he calmed down and we had a leisurely walk back as the afternoon grew even warmer. While I'm admitting mistakes, I've lost people, too.

I'll never forget losing two clients in the 164,000-acre Canyons of the Ancients National Monument in southwest Colorado. It was a glorious May morning, cool along the East Rock Creek Trail. Just off the plane from Chicago after a restful night at Durango's historic Strater Hotel, two friends walked too fast ahead of the group and disappeared. The other members of our tour began to worry.

They asked me, "Will you find them? How long will it take?"

"Sure," I said, "Look up."

Above four turkey vultures circled slowly. "Yes, we'll find your friends. But I can't say when . . ." Ten minutes later we had reigned in the speedy hikers, and the group stayed close to me for the rest of the tour. But Canyons of the Ancients is like that. It's a stunning setting for anyone with its red rocks, multicolored sandstone layers, hidden small cliff dwellings, and the past presence of Ancestral Puebloans everywhere.

~

One of the many unique aspects of canyon and desert hiking in the Southwest is the ability to visit tribal parks and native peoples, such as at Navajo Tribal Park in Monument Valley on the Arizona-Utah border. Or consider the people who live in Havasu Canyon, on the west rim of Grand Canyon. Imagine an American community so remote that all groceries and mail are delivered by horse and mule pack train because no roads and vehicles access the village. Now imagine that on a trail two miles below this desert community, three sets of waterfalls cascade, each taller than the one above it. This southwestern Shangri-la is Supai Village, home to the Havasupai people on the western edge of Grand Canyon, two thousand feet and eight miles below the rim at Hualapai Hilltop.

The Havasupai are "people of the blue-green water," which is exactly the color of Havasu Creek as it descends through narrow, polished travertine channels carved from Grand Canyon's limestone layer. Since the 1890s they have lived at their village on 518 acres along Havasu Creek safe in Grand Canyon, where they settled to avoid cowboys and miners encroaching ever closer in northern Arizona. But though the Havasupai lived in Grand Canyon, about halfway between the top and the Colorado River, they always accessed tribal lands high on the rim.

That land was taken away, returned, and taken away again. Relations with the federal government have been cool at best, but legal boundaries are now secure. In the village live 330 tribal members and 20 nontribal members. Beginning in early spring, a steady stream of thirteen thousand annual visitors hike into the village and walk two miles beyond it to camp near the spectacular waterfalls. In the village you'll find a lodge, two churches, a Bureau of Indian Affairs school, and a café with a helicopter pad beside it, where wealthy Europeans land as they try to "do" the Southwest and see Grand Canyon between business meetings in Phoenix and Las Vegas.

At twilight, Supai Village can be a cacophony of braying donkeys, barking dogs, and reggae music. High above the village are two natural stone pillars named Wigleeva, part of Supai oral tradition. The Supai have electricity and a central water system but no streetlights and no streets, just narrow lanes between prefabricated houses and cinder-block community structures. In the spring, white apricot trees blossom against the canyon's red rocks.

Havasu Falls is a magnificent cascade of moving, sparkling water dropping a hundred feet into a pool that reflects turquoise blue. The first birds of spring flash green against white rocks and the sound of perpetually falling water. In the heart of the canyon Havasu Creek runs aquamarine through a creek bed polished white and scoured by flash floods as Grand Canyon's red cliffs step farther and farther back.

Below Havasu Falls is Mooney Falls, which is twice as tall and dangerous to descend. Havasu Falls has a wide trail beside it to walk to the lush oasis and pool below the falls. To descend to the bottom of Mooney Falls, tourists crawl through a steep rock passage grasping slippery chains and worrying about other climbers, because there's no room for two people side by side in the narrow cavelike passageway. With exotic plant life, watercress, and sandy beaches at the bottom, visitors feel like they are pirates entering a secret grotto on a Caribbean island, when in fact they're in Grand Canyon. Legend has it that in the nineteenth century Irishman James Mooney tried to descend the 200-foot cliff with a 150-foot rope. Because of the waterfall's roar his friends on top couldn't hear him, and he dangled for a day before falling to his death.

For the Supai people there's poverty with too many unclaimed dogs and boarded-up windows, yet Havasu Falls is one of the rarest riparian habitats in the Southwest and worth the ten-mile hike. The Supai have endured searing desert heat and deadly flash floods. Daily, skilled Supai horsemen ride quickly up the trail with "mule train mail" in plastic U.S. Post Office bins to return in a few hours with groceries, tourist luggage, and horse feed. They are masters of the fading art of horse packing and the intricacies of the Diamond Hitch knot. The riders on their small, sturdy ponies symbolize survival and cultural persistence.

At Prescott College in Prescott, Arizona, horses are part of outdoor leadership programs. There are courses that emphasize equine-assisted mental health (EAMH), because folk wisdom states "the outside of a horse is good for the inside of a man."[4] Prescott College offers Centaur Leadership Services as well as undergraduate courses in Relational Horsemanship weekend retreats. These fall within a workshop series titled "Equine Assisted Explorations: Confronting Issues That Affect Women."

So imagine combining outdoor leadership, a multiday group expedition, horses, horse packing, and a tribal park. I did that with a select group of southwestern aficionados for a memorable experience. The trip became more of an adventure than we had bargained for.

Flash Floods and Cliff Dwellings in Ute Mountain Tribal Park

The basic idea was simple: gather some family and friends, find the best local guide and outfitter, and ride into the backcountry of Ute Mountain Tribal Park to visit eight-hundred-year-old cliff dwellings. In the 1890s, from their Alamo Ranch near Mancos, the Wetherill brothers had taken tourists in by horseback to visit remote ruins before the establishment of Mesa Verde National Park in 1906. We wanted to follow their old cowboy trails, ride in their horses' hoofprints, and come into the country the way the pioneers did—upright in the saddle, boots in stirrups, eyes peeled for the dark shapes of tiny windows high under the ledges of sandstone cliffs. We wanted that sense of discovery, that thrill of seeing remote rooms hundreds of feet above the valley floor—then we'd tie up our horses and begin to climb.

We wanted to explore the old way, on the backs of roans, buckskins, and bays, with tents, a camp cook, a few wranglers, and even a small buckboard wagon to haul in our packs, sleeping bags, and assorted gear. We'd stay off the main graveled road in Ute Mountain Tribal Park and instead follow ancient travel routes down Mancos Canyon along the Mancos River. We had it all planned with our Ute Mountain Tribal Park permit and our Ute Mountain guides lined up. No pavement, no assigned campsites, no electricity, and no cell phone reception. We'd sleep among the sagebrush and have campfires. We'd count the stars in Orion's belt and have cowboy coffee served in graniteware pots blackened by years of breakfast fires.

We expected a few saddle sores and stiff muscles. We expected to see carefully constructed cliff dwellings deep set in south-facing alcoves, and we did. We found prehistoric corncobs, hundreds of broken pottery or sherds, and collapsed kiva roofs. We found historic, hand-carved signatures with nineteenth-century dates etched into room blocks. We found 1930s Ute rock art of cattle, horses, and cowboys.

One day we even followed our intrepid Ute guide Marshall Deer straight down "Moki steps" or hand-carved Anasazi toeholds. First he disappeared over a cliff, without ropes, and then one of our party descended. Just when my friend shouted, "I can't do this," the guide placed my buddy's feet in toeholds that he couldn't see and he was quickly down to terra firma. With trepidation, we followed. As we quietly entered Hoot Owl House, with amber afternoon light streaming through a rare grove of aspen trees, our guide explained, "The Utes just leave these things alone. These were ceremonial people and we leave their homes alone. It's the pothunters and archaeologists who take everything."

So we had adventure aplenty. We expected a good time on our educational expedition and we earned one.

～

What we didn't expect was driving rain, rising creeks, and flash floods. We should have known the weather would get bad when on the first night a gust of wind completely toppled the cook tent. A big storm was coming. Getting into Mancos Canyon was easy, but leaving on the expedition's fourth day proved to be a true nineteenth-century western experience when the wagon slid and tipped over on a dangerous corner of the old access road. In pouring rain we unhitched the team of Belgian horses.

~

In June 1874 photographer William Henry Jackson, journalist Ernest Ingersoll, and guide John Moss didn't worry about torrential rain. The weather was fine and they had plenty of grass for their horses. They were chasing rumors, tall tales, preposterous stories of ancient cities hidden in cliffs somewhere in southwest Colorado. According to legend, Jackson had become irritable over not finding any cliff houses. They camped along the river and toward sunset, as he complained again about not finding any ruins, one of the party, perhaps John Moss, looked up at the nearby cliff and said, "You mean a ruin like the one right there, high on the cliff face?"

Yes, there in the last light of day shone Two-Story House, one of the first southwestern cliff dwellings ever photographed. Jackson was elated. At dawn they started the climb up to the site with his heavy camera and tripod. Jackson would photograph and publish the first images of a Colorado cliff dwelling, though he missed the larger sites found deeper in the side canyons now part of Mesa Verde National Park. On the second day out our group, on horseback, rode toward Two-Story House, dismounted, tied our horses, and with our Ute guide began our own morning ascent.

In the century since 1906, when President Theodore Roosevelt signed legislation creating Mesa Verde National Park as the world's first cultural park, other groups and organizations have worked to preserve Ancestral Puebloan sites beyond the boundaries of Mesa Verde. One of those groups is the Ute Mountain Ute Tribe.

Ute Mountain Utes come from the Weminuche band. Their last traditional chief, Jack House, lived in the old way spending summers on the mesa and winters in Mancos Canyon. Recognized as the hereditary chief of the tribe, Chief Jack House wielded firm political power until his death. Because he knew it to be sacred ground where spirits dwell, he began plans to set aside 125,000 acres in Mancos Canyon as Ute Mountain Tribal Park. Author Jean Akens writes, "It was his desire to preserve the ruins for the future, and to share them with others," but "his was an idea opposed by many in the tribe, especially those of his own generation. There still remained a strong belief that no good could come from disturbing the spirits of the Ancient Ones. But the chief was not to be dissuaded."[5]

Ute Mountain Tribal Park, surrounded by the golden circle of national parks and national monuments in the Southwest, is a one-of-a-kind visitor experience. Tourism is small scale and very low impact with vigorous hiking and climbing, including the ascent of ladders thirty-two feet high. What makes the tribal park special is its isolation and the intimacy that develops when twelve to eighteen people spend an entire day with an authorized Ute guide learning to identify Ute and Ancestral Puebloan rock art.

～

As the rain poured down we knew we could become trapped in the canyons. The only way out was the way we came in—riding horseback across the Mancos River.

Everything we had with us was tied into the wagon, now on its side. Swollen creek waters continued to rise. One of our party who had been on the wagon seat fell hard and now had a painful hip. The skies poured. Thunder boomed. The horses skittered sideways across wet rocks and soft caliche soil. We weren't sure we could lift the wagon, much less get across the next creek.

As I slogged around in the brown mud trying to untie ropes that secured the wagon's load, I realized the creek was rising an inch every five minutes. Soon the bottoms of my boots were under water. Our cowboy outing had taken an unexpected twist. What had been a lark was now all too serious.

～

The solitude in Mancos Canyon is punctuated by wind soughing through the tops of aging ponderosas. Eagles and red-tailed hawks soar upward on thermals. The personal discovery of remote cliff dwellings arrived at by hiking original Anasazi trails becomes all the more surreal as afternoon thunderclouds rise high against a dark blue sky. Sheer sandstone cliffs give way to hidden villages shaded by pines and fir that grow tall at the heads of canyons. Because the cliff dwellings are approached on foot, guests feel they are among the first nonnatives to see the ruins, as indeed they are. Unlike Mesa Verde National Park, these ruins have no asphalt walkways or metal access steps.

Visitors stoop low to enter ancient Anasazi T-shaped doorways and touch rocks and boulders etched with long grooves where Pueblo people straightened their arrow shafts. Onlookers marvel at small rooms where smoke from old fires blackened ceilings. Tourists touch prehistoric fire pits with distinctive stone heat shields that both trapped and reflected the wood's warmth. This is tribal tourism at its best—close up, quiet, one with the earth and sky.

Along every trail are scattered pottery sherds. In the middle of the park a huge kiva lies collapsed and surrounded by sherds of all sizes and descriptions.

At Lion House, the largest village on the Main Ruins Tour, lie the remains of a sunken D-shaped kiva. Anasazi fingerprints are visible in dried mortar between hand-dressed stones. Door lintels made of wood tied together with yucca leaf fiber still have the original Ancestral Puebloan knot. Items found in Mancos Canyon include spools of handwoven thread, turkey feather cordage, yucca fiber pot rests, pieces of woven mats, stone tools, black-on-gray bowls, hammer stones, and small corncobs from early southwestern agriculture.

⌒

The trip started on a Thursday morning with clear skies, fresh horses, dry clothes, and endless enthusiasm to retrace the trails of southwest Colorado's earliest Anglo explorers. But on that September Sunday, soaked and cold despite our rain gear, our historic reenactment had become an authentic adventure. Our ride out of the tribal park raced the rain. Water ran off the brims of our hats and down our backs. Could we get the wagon upright and moving? How badly hurt was our companion with her injured hip? Could we make it across the raging Mancos River before it rose even higher? Were we at risk of getting hypothermia?

Our outfitter and horseback hero Anne Rapp, with a lean cowgirl figure and silver hair in twin braids, had found an orange flicker feather and placed it in her hatband. Hopi Indians believe that finding flicker feathers along a trail is a sign of good luck. With the wagon overturned, creek waters rising, and nine cold, wet, unseasoned riders on horseback, Rapp knew we'd need all the luck we could get.

⌒

Chief Jack House risked the ire of his people by not letting them settle in Mancos Canyon and by not permitting any changes to the canyon floor or rim. Today Ute guides lead all-day tours into an unspoiled canyon. Visitors sense the rhythms of Anasazi life and walk single file beside remote clusters of stone rooms. These rooms are tucked deep into canyon alcoves to utilize southern exposure in winter and maximize water runoff during spring and summer rains.

Home to a shaman who guided his people, Eagle's Nest ruin towers above Mancos Canyon with full southern exposure and a square of white ochre painted on the shaman's house indicating his power and prestige to travelers. Grappling with an overwhelming sense of vertigo, visitors ascend a steep ladder to walk along the sandstone ledge of Eagle's Nest, where a granary still stands with its original small stone door hand-tapered for a perfect fit.

Juniper poles jut out from walls. From the top of Eagle's Nest, Mancos Canyon opens to the east and west. A millennium ago anyone on foot could easily have been detected.

Standing on the narrow ledge at Eagle's Nest, gazing into those dusty rooms, our modern preoccupation with time has no apparent purpose. In Mancos Canyon centuries have passed and will pass again with little disturbance of the landscape. The view the Anasazis beheld remains complete and unaltered, and a hand on aged wooden beams touches what the Ancestral Puebloans touched. All is silence and sunlight.[6]

~

We had toured Two-Story House, lunched on Moccasin Mesa, carefully crept down Moki steps to the deep quiet of Hoot Owl House, and on the third day explored Hemenway House.

On one of the narrowest ledges I've ever walked, the sky opened, the canyon fell below, and in between short breaths I knew I was on top of the world standing where few people had been in the last thousand years. Carefully I looked over the edge and with binoculars found our horses tied in the distance. To the north was the boundary of Mesa Verde National Park. Far from Mesa Verde's paved tour stops and away from the tribal park's graveled road, our little group was in one of the most remote and inaccessible places in the Four Corners. I took a deeper breath, exulting in our isolation.

When it was time to go, I slipped—not on the narrow ledge but in descending the twenty-five-foot rock chimney I had climbed up. I began to fall down the inside of the rock chimney. Instantly, Ute guide Roger Wing reached out and caught me in the climber's clasp, forearm to forearm. I left some blood on the rocks, but that was a small price to pay for such a magnificent view. On that ledge, time had stopped.

~

We searched out other small ruins. There were no trails. We scrambled through oak brush, under and around juniper trees; we slid off smooth rocks and finally approached three unnamed ruins, all in alcoves. All made by Ancestral Puebloans. All different. Some with stacked stone. Some with dressed stones with careful chinking and mortar. One two-room ruin even had vertical grooves carved into the cliff face to steady an ancient ladder, but the most interesting ruin must have been a shaman's home. It contained a miniature altar and a smooth, rounded fire pit, but there was no ceiling soot.

Fascinated, we spoke in soft tones, studying the ancient workmanship, lost in our own thoughts, aware of our own mortality, yet keenly, vividly alive as we turned and twisted and climbed to explore what we could. The sky darkened. Rain was coming and we had to get out of the cliff dwellings and quickly down to our horses. We scrambled and slid on decades of dry ponderosa pine needles, laughing now, exhilarated, hungry for dinner and the comfort of camp chairs.

We saw the curtain of rain coming up Mancos Canyon. Luckily it held off until we were almost in our saddles. The sweet scent of wet sage permeated the air. Tired, bruised, dusty, and now wet, we had wanted an adventure and we had had one. Everyone slept well that night. The rain did not stop.

⁓

Now it was our last day. We were headed out of the canyon and our supply wagon had tipped over. Working as a team, we righted the wagon, got back on our horses, lowered our hat brims, and trotted toward the swollen Mancos River. Outfitter Anne Rapp knew we were as wet as drowned ducks. Out of her saddlebag she produced two pine knots rich with resin. Under old piñon trees wranglers found dry wood, and soon we had a warm fire to ward off hypothermia. We passed around a bottle of rum and finished off a spice cake. Back in the saddle, we rode two abreast, dreading what we'd find where Weber Canyon met the Mancos River.

Ever the consummate guide, Rapp slowly, carefully, walked her horse across first. From her saddle, she warily studied the currents, wave trains, and a deceptively dangerous sandbar. Then she slowly rode back, rushing water breaking against her stirrups. Without saying a word, just by her actions, her coolness, and her confidence, we knew we could do it. The wagon went next. We held our breath. As it moved into the fast-flowing water, it stayed steady, and as Willie Richardson, the wagon master, slapped the reins and the two big Belgians pulled the wagon up the muddy bank on the other side, we let out a cowboy yell. Then one at a time we crossed.

Turns out that was a record rainfall. In canyon country averaging 7 inches of precipitation a year, we had 1.73 inches of rain in 24 hours. That's why the creeks flooded and the wagon slid and tipped. We were lucky to get out.

⁓

Our horse pack trip had too much rain, but in desert and canyon hiking there are often high winds to contend with and sand in your soup, clothes, sleeping bag, and hair. In the spring of 1892 explorers in the Four Corners region experienced quite a sandstorm. Archeologist Warren Moorehead wrote, "A fearful wind-storm arose in the north, and, sweeping down upon our little caravan, raged with such fury that we were scarcely able to make head-way." He explained, "Mile after mile we trudged through the howling storm, our eyes and ears filled with dust, our faces stung with the force of the flying sand, our limbs aching and tired." He added, "Every step was made with difficulty. Even where the sand was not deep the wind would be so powerful as to almost blow one from the trail."[7] Yes, high winds can be "a real turtle-flipper," in local parlance.

In a dust storm have a bandanna to cover your nose and mouth, and always drink before you're thirsty. Make every effort to stay hydrated. "Dehydration is the main cause of death in the desert," stated Paul Rimer, a park ranger at Death Valley National Monument, on National Public Radio. "Many people can die out here in one hour after leaving their cars unprepared. They leave the air-conditioning, finish their can of Coke, and go on a ten-mile hike. There are some people we still haven't found." Wear water on your belt, don't just keep it deep within your backpack, and be aware of your surroundings.

Some of the most outstanding desert and canyon country is in southern Utah in the Escalante region, where the bare bones of the earth protrude from ancient ocean beds. Wallace Stegner wrote, "Utah. It is a lovely and terrible wilderness, such a wilderness as Christ and the prophets went into; harshly and beautifully colored, broken and worn until its bones are exposed, its great sky without a smudge of taint from technocracy, and in hidden corners and pockets under its cliffs, the sudden poetry of springs." He added, "Save a piece of country like that intact, and it does not matter in the slightest that only a few people will go into it. That is precisely its value."[8]

In slot canyon hiking there's a reason sticks, logs, and mud piles can be several feet above you. Imagine the immense volumes of water during flash floods.[9] Look at the height of the debris and be aware of the limited time available to climb to safety. While looking up and around, also look down. Watch your step. Stay on trails and avoid cryptobiotic soils, which can make up 70 percent of the living ground cover and take decades to rebuild. So "tiptoe through the crypto."

In desert regions the cyanobacteria are some of the oldest life forms; the dark soil crusts include lichens, mosses, bacteria, green algae, and microfungi.[10] Grand Canyon river guides have found the spot in the 1890s where the Robert Brewster Stanton expedition placed tripods as they photographed the canyon. After a century the tripod marks can still be seen where photographers trampled the desert crust.

Enjoy desert and canyon hikes. They're some of my favorites. And enjoy the following essays about traversing the land of little rain.

Notes

1. John Wesley Powell, *The Exploration of the Colorado River and Its Canyons* (1875; reprint, New York: Dover Books, 1961), 169. Also see John Wesley Powell, *Down the Colorado: Diary of the First Trip through the Grand Canyon, 1869,* ed. Don D. Fowler and Eliot Porter (New York: Dutton, 1969), and Edward Dolnick, *Down the Great Unknown* (New York: Harper Collins, 2001). For a different perspective on Powell, see Robert Brewster Stanton, *Colorado River Controversies* (1932; reprint, Boulder City, NV: Westwater Books, 1982). The classic biography on Powell is Wallace Stegner's *Beyond the Hundredth Meridian* (1953; Lincoln: University of Nebraska Press, 1982). The standard reference for Powell's thoughts and writing is now William deBuys's edition of *Seeing Things Whole: The Essential John Wesley Powell* (Washington, D.C.: Island Press, 2001).

2. Katie Lee, *Sandstone Seduction* (Boulder, CO: Johnson Books, 2004), 230.

3. Terry and Renny Russell, *On the Loose* (Salt Lake City: Peregrine Smith, 2001), 83.

4. See Neda DeMayo, "Horses, Humans, and Healing," in Linda Buzzell and Craig Chalquist, eds., *Ecotherapy: Healing with Nature in Mind* (San Francisco: Sierra Club Books, 2009).

5. Jean Akens, *Ute Mountain Tribal Park: The Other Mesa Verde* (Moab, UT: Four Corners Publications, 1995), 15.

6. See Andrew Gulliford, *Sacred Objects and Sacred Places: Preserving Tribal Traditions* (Boulder: University Press of Colorado, 2000), 170–76, and "On Horseback in Search of the Ancient Ones: Following Cowboy Trails in Ute Mountain Ute Tribal Park," *Inside/Outside Southwest,* January/February 2008.

7. Quoted in James H. Knipmeyer, *In Search of a Lost Race* (New York: Xlibris, 2006), 28. Also see Andrew Gulliford, "Four Corners Odyssey: The Ill-fated 1892 Illustrated American Exploring Expedition," in *Inside/Outside Southwest,* April 2009.

8. Wallace Stegner, "Wilderness Letter," December 3, 1960, reprinted in *Marking the Sparrow's Fall: The Making of the American West,* ed. Page Stegner (New York: Henry Holt, 1998), 116.

9. Some of the best slot canyons on public land in the West are in the Grand Staircase Escalante National Monument. See Steve Allen, *Canyoneering 2: Technical Loop Hikes in Southern Utah* (Salt Lake City: University of Utah Press, 1995), and *Canyoneering 3: Loops Hikes in Utah's Escalante* (Salt Lake City: University of Utah Press, 1997). For an overview of the area, read Greer K. Chesher, *Heart of the Desert Wild: Grand Staircase–Escalante National Monument* (Bryce Canyon, UT: Bryce Canyon Natural History Association, 2000).

10. "Biological Soil Crusts: Webs of Life in the Desert," handout, USGS Forest and Rangeland Ecosystem Science Center, Canyonlands Field Station, "Don't Bust the Crust," n.d.

The Honaker Trail—San Juan River

Ann Zwinger

I have wanted to make one last trip back to these canyons by myself, but in this drought year it is not wise to go alone. However, there's plenty of water at the foot of the Honaker Trail—the whole San Juan River—and the trail itself is just around the corner and upstream from the mouth of Johns Canyon. While I've walked the Honaker Trail several times during other explorations of the canyons, from plateau to river and river to plateau, this is the first time I've gone it alone to camp down by the river.

I've looked forward to this time, and yet, as I sit here at the top, I know a tinge of apprehension. I'm not quite sure what I expect, and now that my ride is long gone and it's too late and I'm committed, I'm not sure even why I wanted to do this. But here I am, quite alone, and I should start down before the sun bathes the whole slope and I have to cope with heat along with everything else. Yet I sit a moment longer because the view is so glorious.

Sitting at the top of the Honaker Trail is to be suspended in the middle of a rocky, sandy, sagebrushed nowhere. Cedar Mesa rises a thousand feet above me at my back; a thousand feet below me the San Juan River silts its way downstream. To the west, hidden in the turning of the earth, are the five canyons that I have walked. To the south, across the river, lies Monument Valley, looking just the way geologist J. S. Newbury described it in 1859:

> The distance between the mesa walls on the north and south is perhaps ten miles, and scattered over the interval are many castle-like buttes and slender towers, none of which can be less than 1,000 feet in height, their sides absolutely perpendicular, their forms wonderful imitations of the structures of human art. Illuminated by the setting sun, the outlines of these singular objects came out sharp and distinct, with such exact similitude of art, and contrast with nature as usually displayed, that we could hardly resist the conviction that we beheld the walls and towers of some Cyclopean city hitherto undiscovered in this far-off region.

The Honaker Trail runs down the north cliff of the San Juan; the two inches' worth of river that I can glimpse from here are just about the proportion of

---

Originally published as "The Honaker Trail" from *Wind in the Rock* (Tucson: University of Arizona Press, 1997). Reprinted by permission of the author.

water to land in this country. Across the river are tiered cliffs, mirror images of what I shall be walking down. Passage looks absolutely impossible. In 1904 Henry Honaker bossed the building of this trail down to the river; he had gotten a permit from San Juan County to do so some eleven years previous, in 1893. Prior to that he and his brothers had run a daily stage between Cortez, Colorado, and Bluff, Utah, and before that he lived in the Mancos area and helped the Wetherills run their cattle. Gold fever was in full swing on the San Juan when Honaker envisioned an access road from river to canyon rim that would aid in transporting all that heavy placer gold that was going to be found.

The first horse taken down the trail fell off the narrow path, and after that supplies were lowered over impassable cliffs by rope. The anticipated gold boom came to naught; only some $3,000 was ever recovered, the flour gold that was more trouble to sift out than it was worth. The trail is a formidable piece of rough engineering and cuts through strata that are the "type section" for the Honaker Trail Formation, surely a kind of immortality undreamed-of by a hard-working businessman with his eye on the dollar.

The predominantly gray Honaker Trail Formation underlies the red Halgaito Shale. The Honaker Trail strata were laid down some 280 to 300 million years ago when a tropical sea flowed and ebbed here, leaving thin deposits of marine limestones, sandstones, and shales, some of which are oil producing in the Four Corners area. These strata have been eroded into a tiered, multi-layered cliff some 1,500 feet thick.

For the most part, in building the trail Honaker traversed the friable shale and siltstone talus slopes until he found a break in a wall of sandstone or limestone through which he could descend to the next step down, building dugways in only a couple of places to get through the thicker layers. In all, Honaker blazed a tortuous three-mile trail in order to make a quarter-mile descent.

～

I check my gear one last time, a useless gesture since what I don't have I don't have. And one thing I've forgotten is halazone tablets, so I'll need to boil drinking water, but at least the river will provide plenty of that. I have full water bottles for going down, and I plan to eat lunch halfway down at Horn Point, a sharp promontory that juts out thirty or so feet toward the river with a precipitous drop on either side. The view there is unparalleled, the next best thing to hang-gliding, without the worry of landing. I have enough food to last a week if need be and the usual gear of sleeping bag, mattress, etc.—it strikes me as grossly unfair that no matter what *my* size I still have the same amount of basic gear as someone a foot taller and sixty pounds heavier.

I get out my note cards from various sources that give the layer-by-layer description of the Honaker Trail Formation to read as I go down. I take my glasses off. Since I am nearsighted, the bottom half of the lens is plain glass, and the bifocal line between makes a slight blur just where I'm about to put my foot. I've found I'm better off without them when navigating treacherous or littered slopes.

The trail is visible for only a few yards, then disappears behind boulders and a turn of slope. It's always a surprise that, in this vast and open country, one can be totally out of visual contact with familiar landmarks in a matter of minutes. I recheck all the fastenings on my pack. I retie my bootlaces. And finding nothing else that needs to be done I stop procrastinating and take the first steps down with combined eagerness and reluctance.

I'm down the trail ten minutes and I'm lost. The trail has simply ended, and having been here before I know that it doesn't *do* that. Not much of a path, true, but a path nevertheless. I turn around and look back. Nothing seems right. I can't even see where I went astray. At this moment the cliff above me appears undifferentiated talus and impassable ledges. I couldn't even get back up from here!

I sit down, ease off my pack, and a grasshopper, as rusty red as the soil, jumps onto it. I flick him off before he crawls inside. I put on my glasses and look around. I spot the trail threading down and stopping behind a pile of boulders. I've gone straight when I should have made a hairpin turn. I stow my glasses, pick the cheatgrass seeds off my jeans, struggle my pack on, and put a cairn of four stones on top of the boulder at the turning. And I continue placing one at every uncertain turn the rest of the way down. I will topple them off when I come back up. A beetle takes off with a soft burr that sounds like a rattler. My heart still stops at such a sound.

I continue slowly downhill, holding back my weight on the steep parts, trying to keep my toes from jamming against the boot toes. Having no one I have to keep up with, I pick up rocks to my heart's content—a tube of limestone with a black chert center, chunks of red jasper that gleam in the hand— all the while trying to keep track of the separate strata through which I walk. My note cards are becoming increasingly smeared with shuffling and being held so tightly because the wind is kicking up. No matter what direction I turn the wind catches me, from the front, the back, the side.

There are handsome fossils in the rock, a fat brachiopod just weathering out, another on the ground. I pick it up and it fits closely into my palm, convolutions of its shell shape matching pad and hollow. I close my fingers tightly over it and the perceptible pulse seems to belong to the shell rather than to me.

~

I reach Horn Point, where I intended to have lunch sitting out on the exposed promontory, but the wind is gusting so fiercely that I think perhaps wisdom is the better part of valor. I am suddenly *extremely* conservative about reaching the end of the promontory—to get there I must leap over a three-foot-wide crevice that looks as if it goes clear through to China. So instead, I move to the dugway on the north face of Horn Point, a formidable job of road building. Honaker constructed a ramp a precipitous hundred yards long by blasting out rock above and using it as fill material below. Near the top of the dugway, I sit on a limestone step near the top and without taking my pack off fish in the side pocket for a can of vegetable juice. Somehow I'm more thirsty than hungry but the warm juice isn't very good. Thinking to be protected here, I find it unpleasant to have the wind still whirling dust and sand, which unerringly stings me in the face. The wind seems to attack the very rock itself, pushing and shoving with intent to maim the cliffs, the slopes, to reduce them to particles small enough to be spun away to another continent.

A Shell Oil Company geological trip left large yellow letters marking the tops of various zones in the Honaker Trail Formation, along with yellow numbers of various stops and points of interest. I find it helpful to know I'm sitting on the top of the Ismay Cycle of the Honaker Trail Formation, a highly oil-productive unit in the Four Corners area. Within a shallow niche I pass below are unusual rounded shapes that look like stone heads of lettuce with the outer leaves peeling off, fossilized beds of calcareous algae. In the shallow edges of the Pennsylvanian-time seas, these algal reefs formed and the porous beds have proved to be excellent reservoirs for oil. Still the big yellow letters are graffiti and highly visible pollution. Fie on rock painters.

Below Horn Point is a near-mile-long traverse going due north, along a narrow, narrow ledge that drops off sharply, rimmed by a sheer cliff fifty feet below. I keep my eye on the path and ignore the drop to my left. Suddenly a wave of nausea makes me stop, jolted. I turn to face the wall, press my hands firmly on the rock, and close my eyes until the nausea subsides.

When I open my eyes I get another shock: I can't believe *those* are *my* hands in front of my nose, splayed out, clawed into the rock, tendons rigid, fingernails broken to the quick, scraped, a fresh scratch beaded with tiny drops of blood, swollen from cutoff circulation from the pack straps. I recognize the hand shape, but not the dirt under the nails and packed into the cuticle. I read them not from the palms, pressed so close against the rock upon which my life seems to depend at the moment, observing heart and life lines and stars of fate, but from the scruffy backs. Abraded, unladylike, rough as the rock they cling to, sunburned, callused, and in them I recognize a different reality. I can go home, clean up, buff the nails, repair the damage, put on lotion, make them look better. But these ill-used hands clutched into the abrasive wall belong to another place I live, where I am also at home, another way of life whose isolation and quiet have become a necessity. I lean here until I feel steadier.

I start out again with a sense of uneasiness. This is *not* the place to be nauseated. As soon as I walk on again, another wave hits, and another. Ridiculous, I tell myself, as the path blurs again. Ridiculous, I say, and discipline myself to continue walking carefully and slowly. I feel a wave of total despair: why did I come? I worked so hard to get here and now I'm ready to cry. Like a little kid, all I want to do is go home! I stop to look at no note cards, no rock formations, no interesting plants. I just want to get off this shelf. The nausea and dizziness do subside but my shoulders ache with tension. A sharp switchback finally brings me off the ledge and starts another traverse. I rest on a ledge labeled "Barker Creek Cycle," identifying another oil-bearing layer. I really don't much care.

∿

When I get to the river beach at last, the wind blasts down the canyon. Great swirling gusts broadcast their arrival in a cloud of sand. I try to find some kind of windbreak; the best I can do is a cluster of willows and they're not much good. When the wind really gusts, the sand stings right through the leaves. Ordinarily the first priority of business would be to find a campsite, but right now it's more important to find shelter from the wind and get myself together.

I wonder if part of my uneasiness is that I remember all too well a raft trip on the San Juan in a windstorm one April; if I thought I would have to endure that again I'd walk back up right now. It had been windy that spring morning, just the usual river wind, when far downstream the water changed sheen and a peculiar crinkled surface proceeded upstream. I watched, totally unprepared for the flat gust that caught me full face with a blast of sand. As the wind intensified, it pumped up the canyon with a locomotive roar, amplified against the walls, a great hurtling heavy sound as if it would uproot the cliffs themselves. Although there were no clouds, the light was so dimmed by blowing sand and silt that it looked dark enough to storm, the light an odd rosy tan. The canyon ahead was fogged in, the rimrock obscured, all outlines blurred. I felt in the middle of a cauldron of wind. Even though everyone on the raft paddled to exhaustion, time and again we had to pull ashore, time and again we were beaten back, exhausted, until the wind quit at darkness.

I hope that with the setting of the sun today's wind will diminish, but that's a long time off, and until then there's no sense in trying to set up camp. I might as well stash my backpack, ignore the wind, and go walking. I remember a cobble beach upstream. To get there I cross a beach well used by boating parties, and although not dirty, certainly not pristine—chunks of burned logs, a few branches broken, rocks left in rectangular patterns where ground cloths were anchored.

At the cobble beach the variety of colors is fascinating, all stones smoothed to a size that just fits comfortably in the hand, rocks carried all the way down from the San Juan Mountains to the northeast. The beach is on the inside of a meander, a broad hard beach that's usually covered with water partway up. Now it's open and would be a great place to camp; the hard sand doesn't pick up and blow all over, but it's much too exposed and gets the full brunt of the wind charging around the corner, so I discard the idea. I also remember the description, written by Hugh Miser, the geologist who made the first geological reconnaissance of the San Juan River in 1921, of a flood in August at the foot of the Honaker Trail. The flood stage was six feet higher than normal and carried so much silt that Miser says it was brick-red in color, and hundreds of fish that could not get oxygen swam to the surface, exhausted.

I stoop down to examine the rocks, which are rendered jewel-like by a thin laving of water. Quartzite, agate, conglomerate, chalcedony, they all derive from mountains nearly three hundred miles away. Overhead two ravens patrol the canyon and make a second pass just over me, calling; doubtless they know that humans leave tidbits and are just checking.

On the underside of many of the cobbles caddis fly cases are cemented. On the tops of many of the dry ones spiders sun like eight-legged starfish, hurrying away at the sign of any crossing shadow. While I'm hunkered down a half dozen chukar partridge fly low across the river; I just catch a glimpse of them out of the corner of my eye. The white faces outlined with a dark stripe, the stripes on the wing, their direct and sure flight, and their size are unmistakable. They thrive on the cheatgrass that grows all over the slopes. They would have made marvelous Anasazi food but are only a recent introduction to the United States.

I walk on until my equilibrium is restored, until I feel at peace with the river and myself, and then sit quietly facing the river: "The rush of the river soothes the mind," Richard Jeffries, an English naturalist, wrote a century ago. With my eyes closed I listen to the soothing peaceful murmuring. . . .

Flash Flood: Driven by Thirst into the Path of Danger— San Rafael Swell

Chip Ward

We were driven by thirst across a landscape that could not quench it. The hike into the remote canyons of the San Rafael Swell over heat-reflecting ledges of bare stone was long and hard. We started while the morning sun was still pushing its bright yellow fingers into canyon recesses. By noon, the temperature hit 100 degrees Fahrenheit on the desert floor. Precious shade was intermittent, so we made the most of what shade there was, hugging the slim shadows that pooled along the cliff walls and aiming ourselves under the green and glassy hands of the occasional cottonwood tree along the route. By the time we reached the little oasis at the mouth of Chimney Canyon and its rare spring, we were eager to fill our depleted water bottles.

The San Rafael is a vast uplift in south-central Utah. If you want to know why we war over water in the West, the San Rafael is a good place to start—as dry as a bone, as they say. But awesome, too. Wilderness advocates argue that "the Swell" is the geological twin of Utah's Capitol Reef National Park and its uplifted universe of sandstone nooks and crannies, the Waterpocket Fold. As such, they argue, it deserves full wilderness protection, if not national park status.

Those who place a greater priority on resource extraction and off-road vehicle recreation than scenic beauty and habitat integrity have held off the conservationists for decades. In the 1960s when Capitol Reef and Arches got national park status, the Swell was originally part of the package, but it was pulled out because it was thought to hold reserves of uranium useful for making nuclear fuel and weapons of mass destruction. Now the threats to the Swell come from all-terrain vehicle, Jeep, and dirt bike riders, who want to turn the place into a theme park for off-road vehicles.

My hiking companion, Bill Hauze, and I were out to exercise our legs, find some solitude, and explore the maze of red-rock canyons, untouched by cows or gearheads, that lay right behind the small oasis we were fast approaching. "Let's pump water so we can guzzle some right away," I suggested as we reached the first cottonwood tree. "Iodine is too slow." In even the most remote canyons of the Southwest, naturally occurring water must be filtered through a pump or treated with iodine tablets to avoid a case of giardia, a

From *Hope's Horizon* by Chip Ward. Copyright © 2004 Chip Ward. Reprinted by permission of Island Press, Washington, D.C.

dysentery-like affliction caused by a ubiquitous bacteria that is the legacy of the correspondingly ubiquitous presence of its host and carrier, cow crap, on Southwest public lands.

I was eager to show Bill the hidden splendors of the canyons that I had first visited with another hiking buddy, Steve Allen, who is legendary for his knowledge of Utah's red-rock wilderness and his standing-room-only slide-show fund-raisers for the Southern Utah Wilderness Alliance. The Chimney Rock complex of canyons is a gallery of stone art brimming with life, its diverse plants, birds, insects, and reptiles animating a sensuous realm of flesh tones and smooth shapes. The name is not unique—the West is covered with "chimney rocks"—and naming a canyon after its typical, though beautiful, sandstone spires while ignoring its uniquely stained and exquisitely sculptured walls misses the mark. It's like calling a goddess Dick.

As we kicked through the scattered debris of an abandoned prospector's camp that also shared the little oasis, my suppressed thirst moved up my throat and curled like a hairy beast in my parched mouth, where it waited impatiently behind lips as dry as lizard skin. Moments later, I knew something was wrong—the cattails that should have been plump and dark brown were faded and wispy. Where the ground should have turned spongy and wet, we found nothing but powdery soil and dry rushes. Adrenaline flooded into my limbs.

"Damn!" I said to Bill. "This is not good." The understatement was a thin veil over my heart-pumping panic. The dry spring was not just disappointing, it was life-threatening. An agonizing death involving thirst-induced fever, shock, and delirium is not a top-ten way to leave this life—not that any way is great, but falling off a cliff is certainly more thrilling and sudden. The view is better, too.

We could not go on without water. In fact, the risk from dehydration was real. We were a full day's hike away from the truck, which we had left at the trailhead at Tomsich Butte. We had no cell phones to call for help, and we were way out of range anyway. It would be a long night without water and a torturous walk out the next day. But we had no choice. Unlike my desert-savvy friend Steve Allen, I had not found and marked on topo maps every water-bearing pothole hidden in the deep folds and thin crevices of the sandstone landscape.

I remembered to breathe deeply and think. There were other springs tucked up in the canyon behind the gnarled cottonwood tree that leaned over the dusty ex-oasis where we stood. During a previous trip to the Chimney Rock canyons, we had reached them by climbing through a narrow break in a canyon wall that was just a few yards away.

We dropped our packs, gathered empty water bottles in our shirts, and started climbing. In a few minutes we reached two shaded pools by a mossy seep, deep enough to dip the bottles under the surface without disturbing the easily aroused bottoms, plenty deep for pumping. We spread wet bandanas on our baked foreheads and let our fears evaporate. It felt good to be free of the backpacks we had left on the floor of the dry wash below.

In the desert, the water we might take for granted almost anywhere else can become a sweet and sensual joy—even when it is amber-tinged and warm. On backpacking trips I have been thankful for green water and returned to civilization with a newfound appreciation for the tinkling music ice makes against a glass and the way it startles the tongue. "How can something so simple and elemental be so delightful, so exquisite?" Bill didn't answer, but smiled and sighed. He finished filling his bottles and headed for an overhang laced with pink columbines and pastel wisps of green grass. I followed, then rested with him. We napped briefly in the silence, awakened only by the high-pitched whistle of hummingbirds and the soft thrum of a dragonfly. The clap of thunder, however, brought us to our feet.

Just over the canyon edge, the sky went from deep blue to an ominous dark, bruised color in an instant. Summer is flood season in canyon country. Ocean mist is sucked up off the coast of Mexico and pushed inland. It rises with the afternoon desert heat and banks up against island mountain ranges and escarpments, where it billows into brilliant white thunderheads that eventually darken and collapse. We looked up to see a jagged bolt of electricity crackle as it arced across the cliff tops. Moments later, booming thunder shook the canyon walls so hard that rocks broke loose and clattered down. Then fat drops of rain splattered all around us like little water balloons. The rain polka-dotted the pale surfaces of stone, puffed the dust, and nodded the broad leaves of the cottonwoods. Ropes of rain followed, then sheets.

There is precious little soil to absorb the rain in "standing-up country," the high deserts of the Colorado Plateau that are known throughout the world for their rocky buttes, bluffs, and towers. There are few plants to shield the ground from driving rain, and only sporadic webs of roots to hold scant soil in place. The face of slickrock has been carved into channels, basins, and rills that gather rain and spill it to the canyon floor. Ribbons of running water are braided into reddish cascades that run over cliff walls onto desert floors until the canyons become galleries of waterfalls that are as varied as the sleek dips and lips that the water pours over. On the bottom, dry washes become torrents that churn colors of chocolate and blood, sand and ash. The silence and stillness of deep-cut rock masks the potential for periodic catastrophe. It can take a river in the incrementally shaped landscapes of the East several days

Environmentalists call Lake Powell "Lake Foul" because the dam at Page, Arizona, flooded ninety-six canyons within Glen Canyon. But for serious explorers, the beauty and mystery of Glen Canyon can still be found by hiking beyond the water's edge. An ongoing drought reveals more of Glen Canyon as Lake Powell's waters dramatically recede. Teacher Tiffany Mapel enjoys water run-off in Glen Canyon National Recreation Area. Photo by author.

to reach a flood stage that can be merely twice the river's normal flow. In the dry canyons of the more dynamic West, a stream or river can reach a hundred times its volume in a matter of hours. And it is not just the river bottoms and floodplains that fill with runoff. In the West, a storm can break out of view and send a wall of water down a canyon drainage several miles away with no more warning than the faint rumble of distant thunder.

Just as backcountry skiers have to learn the language of avalanches and sailors must be attuned to squalls, Southwest hikers must listen for floods. In places like Muddy Creek in the San Rafael, or Buckskin Gulch on the Utah-Arizona border, I have seen thick logs and shrubby debris jammed between canyon walls thirty feet above the merely wet ground. These serve as powerful warnings that slot canyons can fill up fast where there is no way to run. Even wider canyons can be impossible to exit during floods.

Like the one we were in. All that spilling water had to go somewhere, and the crevice we had climbed through was where it was headed. As that simple realization sank in, we looked at each other's faces and read each other's thoughts: we could be stranded up this canyon overnight with no packs and no gear. We broke away from the storm's thrall and bounded down the banks from our overhang shelter. The anxiety we had dismissed only an hour earlier returned with a vengeance.

We bolted across a growing torrent of muddy water just moments before it became too swift to enter. Too late. We reached the notch in the canyon wall just in time to see it fill up with latte-colored froth. Worse, we could see our packs below and realized they could easily be swept away by the water that was now swelling in the wash below us. Damn! Why hadn't we left them on higher ground, away from the bottom of the wash? The prospect of no food was not much pleasanter to face than dehydration had been. The desert seemed to be toying with us. It was big and we were small. We desperately scoped the ledge we were on for another way down. One route we tried didn't go down, but luckily the next one we tried did, and we snatched up our packs in the nick of time.

Once we had our packs on, we started climbing as high along the canyon wall as we could, eventually dropping under a long alcove, where we spent an uneasy night listening to one flood after another pulse through the narrow canyon below. As the rumbling chorus of floodwaters grew louder and closer in the pitch-black night, Bill and I wondered if we were high enough to escape the reach of the muddy monster we could hear below us. We plotted how we could climb up higher and cling to thin ledges if we had to. In the forest, you might be treed by a bear. Here in the dry desert of the San Rafael Swell we were treed, ironically enough, by water.

The thought of being swept up and away in the dark was strong enough that we ignored the risk of sleeping in rodent dung possibly saturated with deadly hantavirus and pushed ourselves farther up into the crevices of our stone-cove shelter. Getting a lung-clenching case of hantavirus seemed an acceptable risk compared to the more immediate danger of being soaked, rolled, dashed, and drowned in the dead of night.

There is something about a cave that invites a story. As we waited for the parade of storms to pass us and subside, we told each other about our "first" floods. I will never forget mine. It happened on a summer day in Capitol Reef, along the lush banks of Pleasant Creek just below the Sleeping Rainbow Ranch, where we were living. We watched a storm break over the face of Boulder Mountain, several miles away, and suspected a flood was coming, although the sun-drenched stillness offered no hint or clue. We watched and waited for so long that we decided nothing was coming our way after all.

Just as we turned back toward the ranch house, we heard an utterly unique and ominous *shush* of gravel and the knocking percussion of stones rolling and clapping against one another underwater. The weird sound grew louder, followed by the oddest sight I'd ever seen. The advancing tongue of the flood was like a rolling wall of grass, sticks, tumbleweeds, and leaves. It looked dry and seemed to be migrating slowly. Its speed, however, was deceptive. Once the debris pile it was pushing with its nose had passed, the flood revealed a full-throttle power that was humbling. Anything swept up in that rushing current would be as helpless as a rag in a hurricane. The roar of boulders bouncing along beneath the swollen water was so loud that we had to shout at each other to be heard. When the banks of the creek started to cave in and wash away, we walked a safe distance from the boiling stew of earth and rain. A couple of hours later the waters ebbed, and by the next morning Pleasant Creek was reduced to fresh puddles threaded by a thin, meandering banner of chalky water. Weeks later, a carpet of fresh grass embroidered by wildflowers pushed up through the drying mud. Bees and butterflies danced to a chorus of birdsong across the flood's green wake. Frogs plopped into fresh water that was covered with tasty bugs skating on gossamer legs. Potholes teemed and swarmed. Buds poked up along the edges of stranded and stagnant pools. The flood's hammer blow was followed by a delicate caress, and in a million nooks and crannies life was nurtured and renewed.

Our stories over, we rolled up like burritos in our blue ponchos, slept fitfully, and were occasionally awakened by strobes of distant lightning as a procession of thunderstorms spent themselves over the desert swell. By morning they were gone, and we awoke to a quiet world washed clean and brimming with bright light. The desert air had been scoured clean. The overwhelming rumble of the night was reduced to a subtle music of trickling and dripping. We climbed down from our uneven perch to sparkling washes with swollen pools rimmed with silken mud and smooth quicksand. The air soon filled with chirping birds, the thrum of busy insects, and the celebrating chant of frogs. By midmorning there was no hint that the canyon could be anything but still and benign.

~

Life evolves according to the circumstances. One size does not fit all. Although the grammar and syntax of life may be common, ecosystems speak the vernacular of whatever landscape generates them. Just as we have learned that forest ecosystems can accommodate, incorporate, and express fire, we now know that in canyon country, floods are an expression of canyon geology. Canyon plants, animals, and insects have evolved around that unavoidable fact of life.

Just as wildfires clear debris, release nutrients into the soil, and reset the successional clock for renewed growth in forests and prairies, floods build beaches and make niches for canyon life, especially in the spring, when runoff is high. Wildfires and floods are natural disturbances that play key functions in their ecosystems despite their unpredictable timing. Just as a forest fire can break seeds in its wake, thus renewing growth, flash floods in canyon landscapes pulse moisture and nutrients into dry reaches where life has evolved to bloom, breed, and recede quickly.

Canyon country is scattered with hidden pockets of water called potholes, which can hold anywhere from a couple of quarts to thousands of gallons of precious water. Because floods replenish the water and nutrients in potholes, they bloom with sudden activity after it rains. Floods fire the starting gun in a procreative race that evolution has fine-tuned to fit the circumstances. Two days after a big flood, the typical desert floor becomes the scene of a bug and toad orgy.

Desert mammals rely on potholes for drinking water. Floodwaters also reload precious seeps and springs, create quicksand reservoirs, and are pumped up into the fleshy architecture of succulent plants. Floods carve the land into niches, and a persistent, creative life force loads those niches with microbial critters, insects, birds, plants, fish, and animals that fit together to become communities, tuned into and dependent upon one another.

As our biosphere unfolds, it makes loops, links, and cycles even in the challenging heat of a desert, where evolution's touch has been fine and particular. Like fearsome wildfires, slickrock floods are so dramatic, deadly, and unforgiving that we may miss the necessary and beneficial role they play in the dynamic of the ecosystems they shape. Stop that pulsing flow with a dam, and you stint the desert's life-giving artery.

Canyon Country Epic: Stuck in Chambers Slot Canyon, Robbers Roost

Steve Susswein and Sue Agranoff

Account by Steve Susswein

We headed for southern Utah for a few days of canyons. We did the Middle Fork of Upper Maidenwater and had a good time with no difficulties. I'd probably rate my skills as intermediate and Sue's as novice (but not beginner). After Maidenwater we headed for the Roost, where we planned to do White Roost and the North Fork of Robbers Roost. We were both interested in doing Chambers, but I thought it was a bit too difficult to do with just the two of us. On the drive through Hanksville, Utah, I got a call from a friend inviting me on a river trip, and as a result, we changed our plans and decided to do Chambers and then drive home. We had Tom's write-up of Chambers with us.

Neither of us is a morning person and, since the canyon was reported to be only three to four hours, we didn't start until a little after 11 A.M. on Wednesday. We had no problem finding our way into the canyon and had a great time squeezing and downclimbing our way down what Tom calls the first section of narrows. We got to the rockfall area around 12:30 P.M., had a quick snack break, and headed on down the elevator shaft to the second (last) section of narrows.

Fifty to a hundred feet into this section, we came to the first really narrow spot. I think this is the section that's usually called the crux of the canyon. The canyon was quite narrow for about thirty feet, with water in the bottom and almost vertical walls above. It looked to me like chimneying over would be doable but difficult. But I thought we could squeeze through at the bottom— I'm five feet seven, 145 pounds, Sue is a little smaller. I took off my pack and headed into the slot. A few feet in, I got stuck.

At first, I didn't think it was too big of a deal, but as we tried different techniques to get me unstuck, I found myself wedged in tighter and tighter. At this point I was wedged in on my ribcage at sternum level, looking upcanyon, unable to turn my head, and just able to touch bottom with my toes. It was probably around 1:00 P.M. when I first got stuck, and we tried for about an hour to get me unstuck. One of the things we tried was having Sue chimney above me and drop an étrier so I could try to pull myself up using my arms; but even while exhaling, the effort of trying to pull myself up expanded my chest, and I wasn't able to move upward at all. I was able to get a piece of webbing around my waist, which I passed back to Sue so she could try to pull me out that way; but while she could get my hips to move a bit, my chest was still firmly stuck.

I couldn't think of anything else to try and decided that the best course was to send Sue out to call for a rescue. I had Sue place my pack next to me in the slot so that I had access to food and water. Then she chimneyed over me and headed downcanyon. It was about 2:00 P.M. I knew that we had cell phone service where the van was parked at the trailhead, so I figured that there was a good chance that search and rescue would be able to reach me by nightfall. I listened as Sue made her way downcanyon, feeling reasonably confident about the situation and how embarrassing it would be to get rescued. I opened my pack and got out my wool hat since I was getting a little chilly (my feet were in the water about ankle deep). I also opened my first-aid kit and popped a couple of muscle relaxants; I was starting to get cramps in my back and legs after being stuck in the same uncomfortable position for a couple of hours.

Shortly afterward, Sue called out to me that she had reached a section she couldn't climb up and was heading back to me to try to exit upcanyon. At this point my heart really sank. I knew what we had climbed down and didn't think there was much chance that Sue would be able to upclimb it by herself. The seriousness of the situation really started to sink in—the realization that I might end up dying where I was, stuck in the slot, over the course of a few agonizing days.

Sue chimneyed back over me and headed upcanyon. As she headed up, I told her that if I didn't make it out, I wanted all my possessions donated to SUWA (the Southern Utah Wilderness Alliance).

The first obstacle, the elevator shaft down from the boulders, was only about fifty feet upcanyon of where I was stuck, and I could hear when Sue started climbing it and then fell. When she came back and said that the up-climb wasn't doable, I figured that our only way of getting out of there alive was if someone happened to come through and rescue us.

I'm guessing it was around four or five o'clock by this point. When I was going through my pack, getting out the wool hat and first-aid kit, I had come across my pocketknife and tried to chip out some of the rock around my chest, but the angle and the fact that I only had one hand available meant that I wasn't getting anywhere. Once Sue came back to where I was stuck, I had her find a hammer rock and try to chip out the rock around my chest. She could barely reach me. So I held the knife while she pounded on it with one

Slot canyons, so narrow that canyoneers cannot even extend their elbows, may become dangerous deathtraps during summer storms. But slots have a powerful allure and offer breathtaking group and solo experiences for properly equipped canyon hikers. Photo © Chad Neufeld.

hand. We managed to chip out a little rock, but it soon became apparent that it wasn't going to work.

I'm not exactly sure which one of us thought of it first, but I asked Sue to find small rocks that I could drop down under my feet. I wasn't really thinking that this would get me out, but I was hoping to get into a slightly less uncomfortable position. Sue started bringing rocks.

I had to stretch out my left arm to grab them, then hand them over my head to my right arm, and drop them blind near my right foot. I'm guessing that only about one in three or four actually landed in a helpful place, but I was soon able to stand with my right foot flat and even push up a little to release some of the tension on my chest. Sue kept digging up rocks, I kept dropping them under my feet, and I slowly worked my way up and out of the constriction. I'm guessing that we probably collected and dropped more than fifty rocks over the course of a couple of hours until I was free.

I was pretty shaken up and probably a little shocky. I felt totally drained, physically and emotionally, and was shaking uncontrollably and not thinking real clearly. It was after 8:00 P.M. and I'd been stuck for more than seven hours.

Sue was also exhausted after all her work, both trying to rescue me and climb out, and made the (very good) decision that we should spend the night and climb out the next day. When I was getting the muscle relaxants out of my first-aid kit, I was only able to use one hand and ended up dropping the remainder of the kit. I hadn't thought much about this at the time but now realized that the kit, along with the emergency space blanket inside it, was just out of reach. Sue tried unsuccessfully to snag it with a talon hook on the end of a piece of webbing. We bedded down for the night in a small sand-filled pothole.

We each had a wool hat and windshirt and put our feet into our packs. I was wearing long pants but Sue was in shorts, so she wrapped our dry bag around her upper legs. We snuggled up together and tried to sleep. I think I actually got a few hours' sleep (maybe from the muscle relaxants?), but Sue couldn't stop shivering and hardly slept at all.

The next morning we got up at first light, had a little bit to eat and drank a bit of our remaining water, and tried to head out. We were both weak and exhausted, and neither of us could make the crux moves into the chimney above where I'd been stuck. Sue had easily done the moves three or four times the day before but couldn't do them now. I was terrified of falling back into the slot and backed off every time a foot slipped a little. After three or four attempts each, we realized we weren't getting anywhere and headed back to where we'd slept to rest up. I realized that even though I was no longer stuck, there was still a chance we might not make it out of the canyon; but I was comforted by the thought that at least I could move around and wouldn't die wedged in.

As the morning wore on, the sun eventually made its way to where we were resting, and we both napped and warmed up in the small patch of sunlight. After a few hours we both woke up feeling much more rested and stronger. I think we both realized at this point that we had one more good shot left in us and that, if we were going to get out, it was now or never. We each tied a long piece of webbing to our packs so that we wouldn't have to bunny strap them through the slot, and we headed back for one last try. Sue made it easily up, into, and through the slot and pulled her pack through after her. I also made it up and through the slot, but my pack got wedged when I tried to pull it through.

For about two seconds I thought about going back for it but knew that there was no way in hell that I was going to go back in there. Sue had a spare car key in her pack, so even though we would lose my valuable water, we decided to leave my pack behind and go into survival mode. We made it through the rest of the canyon, staying high to avoid the upclimb that Sue wasn't able to do the previous day. The sight of sunlight at the end of the slot was overwhelming, but I was so drained that I didn't even have the energy to feel excited.

Sue's GPS case had leaked, and the directions for the exit were back in my pack. But we managed to slowly find our way out, up, and back to the trailhead, stopping every fifty feet to rest. I'm guessing it took us more than two hours to do what should have been an easy forty-five-minute walk.

We ate, drank, and drove out to Green River, Utah, for the night. I'm home now, mostly none the worse for wear. I have scrapes on my nose, cheek, and chest, and my ribs still hurt when I breath or cough (probably bruised but not broken). My right arm/shoulder is weak (possibly from a pinched nerve) but seems to be getting better.

~

Account by Sue Agranoff

Steve and I managed to turn a three- to four-hour adventure in Chambers into a twenty-nine-hour epic. Before we left home Steve said he didn't think it was wise for us to do such a tight slot with just the two of us. But then, when we got to the White Roost area on Tuesday after doing Maidenwater, it just sounded too interesting to pass up. I was a little concerned about my abilities on the "spicy/5.9ish" upclimbs; little did I know that I'd end up doing what we think was the canyon crux about five times.

We drove to the end of the road and headed out for Chambers about 11:15 A.M. We enjoyed the squeezing and downclimbing in the Chambers section, then we went thru the subwaylike section and took a break to bask in the sun and enjoy a snack. We then enjoyed the nice elevator downclimb; I noted at that point that up until there, we could possibly have climbed back upcanyon, but this last one looked too tough for me.

Steve was in front. Soon he entered a tight section and said, "I'm not sure if I should be going high here."

Two seconds later I hear, "F***! I'm stuck."

He tried as hard as he could and couldn't get himself out of there. I was able to get within about an arm's length of him, but we were very cautious about me going any closer and getting stuck also. I tried pushing on his hips with my leg; I got him some webbing, which he was able to wrap around his waist for me to pull on; I tried chimneying up and over him several times to different spots and dropping étriers for him to pull himself up with. Nothing was working. It probably was shortly after one o'clock when he had gotten stuck; at this point it was now two-ish. He told me it was time for me to try to get out and go for help.

I filled my pack with webbing, a pot shot, several hooks, and a few other assorted things. I brought Steve his pack so he could get water, etc., with his free hand and once again chimneyed up and over him (this time with my pack hanging on a bunny strap) and headed downcanyon. I made it out of that narrow section (maybe twenty feet long). I went through a few more narrow sections where I could stay low, then one where I went up high, and came to a silo and dropped down. Then came another climb that I just couldn't make. I realized that I probably should have remained high through that silo, but I was exhausted and the adrenaline was probably running out and I just didn't think I could make it. So I headed back upcanyon to Steve.

I was having difficulty with the climb back to him, and he suggested that I attach webbing to my pack and just leave it down in the bottom of the canyon (which was wet) and pull it along occasionally. That worked. I told him about my difficulties getting downcanyon and that I was going to go upcanyon to see how that looked. I got up to what had been the nice elevator coming down and gave one quick attempt at climbing up it directly (useless). Then I thought that if I got up high down below it, I might be able to climb around, staying up high. I got up and where it widened out I found a few good footholds and thought I might have a chance.

Oops, a foot slipped and thud, I was down in the sand seven to eight feet below. Luckily, I didn't hit anything on the way down and was basically okay. I made one more attempt at going up even higher a little farther downcanyon, which I quickly aborted because I realized that what had looked doable from down below was just likely to result in another fall. I went back to Steve to report that I wasn't getting out that way. Meanwhile, he had dropped his pack and first-aid kit. I was able to recover the pack but not the first-aid kit. GOTTA TRY MORE WAYS TO GET STEVE OUT!

He had a small knife in his pack, which he took out. He held it in his upcanyon hand against the wall, and I leaned over with a rock and tried to chip away at the wall just beside his chest. It soon became clear that method was not going to save us. He suggested that I bring him rocks to try dropping under his feet. Luckily I found a good pothole about fifty feet upcanyon that had a bunch of good rocks. I went back and forth: excavating and gathering rocks; carrying them to my "holding area"; then bringing them to Steve a few at a time (I had to carry them through narrows with both hands outstretched to my sides). Maybe one rock out of three that he dropped did any good. He couldn't turn his head to see what he was doing. Slowly he was able to get his feet up enough to be able to pivot his body and crawl up onto the chokestone between us. HOORAY!

He had escaped the chokehold of the canyon. Finally he emerged back out of the narrows. It was sometime after 8 P.M.; he was probably stuck for more than seven hours. A LONG, COLD NIGHT . . . BRRR!

Steve, not thinking particularly straight and not quite comprehending the 8:00 P.M. part, wanted us to try to get out of there that night. I convinced him that that wouldn't be the smart thing to do with darkness not far away (those canyons would have been very, very dark) and both of us totally exhausted. He said, if we were spending the night we ought to try to recover his first-aid kit, which contained a few potentially helpful items: a space blanket and a balaclava. I tried retrieving it with a hook attached to some webbing, but there was nothing for the hook to grab onto and it just wasn't working.

It was a long, cold night and Steve actually slept a bunch—three or four hours, he says. I think I did well if I got an hour total. Most of the night I sat up because I found that I shivered less that way. Dawn came; we discussed our plans around 5:00 A.M. I wanted to wait a little while until it lightened up a little more. About six-ish we both decided that we had to get moving and should give it a try. Downcanyon we went through the fifty feet that I now knew so intimately. Who should try the climb first?

Steve started up but began to slip. Fearful of dropping back into the narrows he knew so well, he came back down. I gave it a try, made it a little farther, slipping, trying to keep going, just gotta come back. Over the next couple of hours we each gave it several more tries, but we just had no energy; the adrenaline's gone; the mind's not right; just doesn't happen. GOTTA REGROUP.

We figured we had one shot left at it; we had to wait to get in the right frame of mind and go for it. We noticed the sun was just starting to peek into our "bedroom" and felt that the warmth of the sun was what we needed to energize us. We huddled in the rays as they moved along the wall and napped a little. And sometime, shortly after noon, we both decided that the time was right.

I go first. My pack is down below connected to webbing. Up and across I go, hopping my pack along over a few obstacles, and I get to the end of that narrows section. I tell Steve not to worry too much about his pack; it'll pull along fairly well. Up he goes. He makes it across. But he hasn't done anything with his pack. We pull on the webbing and the pack gets stuck. Not moving. He says he's not wasting his energy going back for it. Having done it the previous day, I knew that climb heading back was harder and decided it wasn't worth expending any of my energy on it, either.

So he lost a few things: more than half of our much-depleted water supply, pot shot, harness, hooks, watch, car key (of which I had another in my pack), baseball cap, etc. The good news (for Steve) was that he didn't have to carry a pack through the rest of the narrows or on the hike out. We were feeling pretty good at this point, but we knew we weren't totally out of the woods yet. On we went through a few more sets of not-too-difficult narrows.

Then we got to the stretch where I had downclimbed too soon. Steve stayed up high across the silo and had no problems continuing up high. A few more fun sections and we saw the wide open sky!!! WOW! WE'RE OUT!

We just went over to the shade and plopped down in exhaustion. We knew we still needed to find some energy for the hike out; but we knew now we would both get out. We pulled out the GPS from my pack, figuring it would help us find the canyon exit and Steve's van. The dry case around it wasn't dry; a hook had probably poked a hole in it. The GPS didn't power on. Oh well, we shouldn't have any problem.

Once we exited the canyon the hike out seemed interminable. One foot in front of the other; as long as we were making forward progress, we were doing well. We stopped to rest a lot and managed to each get a sip of water every twenty minutes or so. Steve picked a fairly good route; I don't think we did too much excessive climbing and dropping.

Then Steve spotted his van—still way in the distance—but it was there. Finally, it's a hundred yards ahead. Can I get there? Yes, it's finally in front of both of us. HALLELUJAH! Open the van and gulp down some water. We've made it, both "relatively" unscathed.

Afterword from Sue Agranoff

Chambers is a beautiful and fun canyon. I will definitely go back to enjoy its magic (after all, I was not the one stuck for seven hours). I just hope that Steve can also one day go back and enjoy its splendor.

Afterword from Steve Susswein

No negative long-term effects (nightmares, PTSD, etc.) but I've made some changes in my life/recreation. First off, I now think about the rescue consequences if *I'm* the one who gets hurt. In the past I was often the most experienced person on a trip and would think about rescue scenarios that involved me rescuing others in the group, but I never really considered the ability of the rest of the group if something happened to me. More nebulously, the incident has resulted in my spending a whole lot of time thinking about my life—who I am, goals, plans, relationships, etc. No "Aha!" life-changing revelations, just more time thinking about things . . .

Grand Canyon Trail Guide: A Job Worth Living For

Wayne Ranney

I have the best job in the world. That's not my appraisal of its many and varied privileges; it's simply what I'm told all the time from people who hear what I do for a living. Think about it. My boss is many miles away every day that I'm at work and has absolutely no way to bark orders at me—no phone, no fax, not even e-mail can reach me when I'm hard at work. In most respects, I don't even consider that I have a boss, since *I'm the one* who ultimately decides exactly how my workday evolves and the pace that suits me.

Those who are around me hang on every word I say and consider me to be a knowledgeable authority who is also caring, comforting, and intimately invested in promoting their own success (my job runs smoother when they perform their best). The walls of my "office" are painted in the brightest, most interesting colors, and the ceiling is the widest dome of blue sky you've ever seen. These walls hardly ever feel confining, but in those rare, sought-after instances when they are, it's a good thing! I often shake my head in disbelief that I have the good fortune of being a trail guide deep within Grand Canyon.

My journey into this unique "job" began with one simple creed: "Do what you love and the money will follow." Not a lot of money, mind you—nobody gets rich in a material sense being a trail guide. But the intangible rewards— heaps of fresh air, significant exercise, healthful sunshine, beauty beyond description, and a satisfying intellectual freedom while working on the job— may be the perfect antidote to the many detractions found in an increasingly unrewarding work environment. I wouldn't trade my job for all the money of a lawyer, a politician, or a weapons manufacturer.

How did I get here? In a sentence, I just followed my heart. In high school and even college, I never enrolled in courses with the primary interest of defining a career path. I remember feeling incredibly lost as my friends identified their life choices at eighteen or twenty years of age. Heck, I didn't even know what the possibilities were at that age. So I just took classes in the things I was interested in and worked at jobs that were satisfying and not just a paycheck. I did what pleased me and identified the things that I definitely *could not do* (subjects whose textbooks had no pictures). This had the unintended but fortunate effect of leaving me dozens of choices for the things that I *could do*. And in those wilder and freer times of the early 1970s, I discovered and wandered into Grand Canyon.

Instead of a career path, I got a footpath. Who would have thought that a rather spontaneous four-day hike that I undertook as a twenty-one-year-old kid would turn into a career? I sure didn't, but because I was able to let my young life "flow" wherever it wanted to go, I found satisfaction far beyond a fat bank account and fancy car. No. If a person wants to live an extraordinary life, they should make extraordinary choices, rooted in the heart and without regard to status, wealth, or fame.

So what's it like being a trail guide in paradise? Many times each year I enter an orientation room and see nine or ten strange faces staring back at me wondering what the hell they've just signed up for. Some of them are there because they've backpacked the Appalachian Trail and want to try their luck out west. Others are unwilling spouses, sisters, or dads who've signed on reluctantly at their companions' urging. And occasionally, a few of them are in denial about their advancing age and figure that if they can drop one vertical mile in just seven miles of trail, then maybe they still "have it." You see all types of people in this business. If I've had one unexpected and pleasant surprise in this line of work, it's that I couldn't have known that I'd be so damn interested in working with and learning about people. This job definitely brings out the best in people, along with a few of their limitations.

The first day of a typical trek to the bottom of Grand Canyon is devoted to getting to know one another in a classroom setting. I look at their gear and make sure they do not bring too much stuff. (Stuff is heavy, and the lighter you go down, the happier you are.) It's a great exercise to pare down your needs to a bare minimum, but at the same time it's a fine line between sneaking through the canyon without that hardcover edition of *War and Peace* (camp reading) and leaving behind your boots (it happened once).

In the course of looking at all that trail mix and underwear, I'm slowly getting a picture of who these people are. Sometimes it makes you worry when you realize that the last time this person was on a trail was when the Boy Scouts still thought hatchets were useful for cutting down firewood. Most of the time, it gets you really excited to know that you're about to take people on the trip of a lifetime, one that they will accomplish on their own two feet. I love it.

After a day in class, it's time to head down the trail. Invariably, someone is late to meet at the appointed time; more often than not, it's a married couple with one of them moving a whole lot slower than the other. Or if there was anyone you might have had some concerns about the day before, they're late, too. I've noticed that folks who fail to show up on time for this little deadline are also the ones who were likely conflicted in deciding whether to attempt the trip or not. No matter, that's a concern to deal with later on down the trail. It's time to start the fun!

At the trailhead, people are keen to take a picture of themselves and the group while they're still clean (and the cleanest they'll ever be until the trip is over). I usually do the honors, but oftentimes there are rim-bound individuals nearby who are recruited for the job. This is a great opportunity for me to have a little fun with everyone. If the chubby visitor with nine cameras dangling down from their wrist doesn't ask, I always throw out a baited comment, "We're going down for four days!" This usually yields the intended result: "Four days? And you have everything you'll need in those packs?"

I don't have to say another word because by now I've got this group really pumped up—about the canyon, camping under the stars, seeing Bright Angel Creek, and enjoying a cold beer at the bottom of Grand Canyon. Suddenly the person who volunteered to take our picture is getting an earful about our itinerary. It has the intended effect of crystallizing in the participants' minds just how unusual this venture is going to be and how lucky they are to experience it (in fact, fewer than one out of a hundred people who visit Grand Canyon sleep on the ground inside of it).

Thoroughly imbued with confidence, we begin our descent. The South Kaibab Trail was constructed in the 1920s in response to an übercapitalist who insisted that he owned the rights to the Bright Angel Trail and could charge a one-dollar fee to anyone who walked on it. So the National Park Service built a trail of their own that, unlike most other canyon trails, does not follow a fault and thus was constructed on a protruding ridge of rock. The effect is that it is one of the steepest, most straightforward descents found in all of Grand Canyon.

The trail starts out steep and never lets up. Occasionally, I'll look up after descending through the Chimney and see that someone is already inordinately behind. Uh-oh, what could that be about? (All sections of the Kaibab and Bright Angel Trails have colorful names for reference, and the Chimney is the very first portion of the South Kaibab Trail that leads to Phantom Ranch.)

So I stop at Oh-Ah Point and wait. I show the others what's visible from here—besides all of creation, it seems. We look east toward the Desert View Watchtower and in those twenty-five miles of unfathomable space, numerous side canyons slash their way down to the Colorado River in deep but regular intervals. Between each of these drainages, jagged rows of rock project up from the recesses, with their familiar lineup of weird-looking but spectacular buttes, spires, mesas, knobs, and temples. Yes, even temples. Zoroaster. Vishnu. Brahma. Deva. Isis. Shiva. The list goes on.

Many times in these instances I wish I wasn't a guide. I wish I could be out here on my own, with my own schedule and not constantly having to tell people to tie their laces or keep drinking water. I wish I could just stop here at Oh-Ah Point with my hands crossed and look in perfect reverence at a landscape I have become intimate with. In this imaginary solo journey, I am a prayerful and silent worshiper paying homage to bare, naked rock—the most essential of all earthly gifts, providing soil for our crops, foundations for our homes, and silt for our rivers (well, once upon a time).

Nowhere else is rock exposed in such a grand and sublime fashion as here in Grand Canyon. But then I come to my senses and realize that were I not a guide, I most likely would not be privileged to know the canyon as deeply as I do. It's a small price to pay to experience this joyful intimacy in a great rock cathedral. I bring others into the temple, and while they experience its magnificent beauty and many charms, I become intimate with it in the process. Circular perfection. How cool is that?

Wait a minute—what about "Susie"? I forgot all about her way back up on the trail. She's missed out on all of these subtle musings as she fussed with her hiking poles or emptied the red dirt out of her boots. I'm beginning to worry that with the slow pace we've started with, we might not make it to the cantina at Phantom Ranch before it closes at four o'clock. Wanting to speed things up, I ask her, "Hey, Susie. How's it going?" She looks at the group and wonders if maybe she should apologize for holding us up. "Come on over here, Susie, and check out this view," one of her companions exhorts to her. Sure enough, Susie is impressed with the view. But I'm far more impressed at the lessons my groups repeatedly teach me on each and every trip—camaraderie on the trail is more important than speed, and togetherness is better than aloneness. I smile. It's going to be a good trip.

After a pee stop at the Cedar Ridge toilet we descend through the Supai Group of rock layers. My ticket into this breathtaking world of sculpted rock was that I became fascinated with earth history while working as a backcountry ranger for the National Park Service. There were many things of interest to me in those early days of my career, but I always gravitated more toward the geology stories that I heard from those who lived here. I always paid a little more attention to them and just had a knack for easily remembering the rock names and the ancient stories they whispered to me as I walked the trails. Shinumo. Tapeats. Muav. Hakatai. Coconino. These words may sound foreign to visitors, but to those deeply connected with Grand Canyon, they are cherished sounds. The rock layers are like old friends you can count on every trip down. Even in side canyons that I've never visited, I know with geologic certainty what colors will be around the corner, and what textures the rock walls will contain. Such is the magic of being in love with stratified terrain.

One of these layers, the Redwall Limestone, stands as a great barrier to foot travel in Grand Canyon. The ravens, of course, don't even notice the Redwall as they dive-bomb into the canyon at 60 mph with their black wings swept back and their sharp beaks pointed downward with poise and confidence—those cheaters! The Redwall is more than five hundred feet thick, composed of pure limestone that rises up like a skyscraper into the dry desert air. In a more humid climate, this cliff face would be chemically decayed into a gently sloped ruin, but here on the Colorado Plateau you can barely break it with a large rock hammer.

Thus, the legendary Reds and Whites, switchbacks of dynamited torture almost a mile in length that twist and turn through the sun-drenched Redwall cliff. Invariably, someone will get a blister here and we'll need to stop and tend to it. But inside my head I'm always trying to get the group to go just a little bit farther down the trail. I'm way too invested in a strategy of delayed gratification, I think. Slow down. Slow down.

This time it's Mike. He's the one who came to the trip reluctantly with his wife, losing out to her desire to go with a group and a guide. I can hear the words in his mind now: "Only sissies need a guide. We just wasted four hundred bucks each going down with this group of Girl Scouts." Beating back my inner feelings of glee that the blister belongs to Mike, I point out an arch in the rocks high above the trail. "I actually walked up there once," I tell the group, and stare in disbelief at my own exuberant youthfulness back then.

They can't even imagine such a side trek, since by now the question of "How much farther?" easily spills from the recesses of their minds to the forefront of their lips. I look down to the trail below us and point out the toilet at the Tip Off. "Let's all rendezvous down there," I say. "Once we get there it's only about two miles to Phantom Ranch." I'm always framing our endeavors in the most positive light, lifting their spirits with every opportunity they give me.

Although it might seem logical to eat lunch here at the Tip Off (I mean, really, it's a toilet in the heart of Grand Canyon!), I have a special place just two hundred meters farther on that I'd like to take them to. It has a view of the Colorado River, but more than that, I know of a little geologic secret I want to share with them. For sure, 99.9 percent of all the people who walk by there will miss this little gem entirely and I don't want my group to be part of that crowd. So if we are lucky enough and strong enough to have lunch this far down the trail (5.5 miles), it's where I like to stop.

The view is fantastic and we can now pick out our campground in the trees below us next to the creek. After everyone finishes their sandwich, I draw their attention to a small cliff of purple quartzite that has provided us with some welcome shade. I show them where pieces of this dense, purple rock had fallen from the same cliff a very long time ago. The fallen boulders then became engulfed in a swash of brown sand that was being deposited along the shoreline of an ancient beach. Like the chocolate chips found in cookie dough, there are dozens of purple quartzite boulders that stick up in relief here from within the brown sandstone.

And I tell them that on a single day, 525 million years ago, storm waves lashed this same cliff face and battered it, causing the purple boulders to become dislodged and fall into the soft sand below. After burial, the brown sand became lithified (turned to stone), and the entire event was preserved for 524.5 million years or so, only to become reexposed by the relatively recent incision of the Colorado River. Some of them will understand this story; some of them won't. Their feet are talking to them, and it's probably time to move on.

The day before, I told the group that the trip down would be the hardest of the whole trip. They weren't expecting to hear that and probably wondered if I was telling the truth. But I assured them that the relentless drop for seven miles took its toll and that if they were to get a blister, or a sprained ankle, or a bum knee, it would be on the way down into the canyon and not on the way out. At Panorama Point I remind them of this, and now they get it. Down is hard—at least as hard as the up. They're already learning about life down here, and they've only just arrived.

I've always liked that about Grand Canyon. It chews you up and spits you out, scrapes your skin and gives only a rocky place to lay your bed. It's steep, it's rocky, it's hot, and most of the plants have spines that never seem to need water. But by doing this, the canyon teaches you what it is like to be a very small being in a very large place. I suppose that if everyone could come down here, most of them wouldn't like it. Yet, of all the people who do, just about every one of them can't wait to come back. How can a place be so cruel and so welcoming at the same time? I wonder.

Finally. The bridge. The Colorado River has taken six million years to carve its path through the rocks we just walked down in six hours. We are a fast species, I remind my tired hikers. They laugh at me again as we walk across the bridge, entering another world of babbling streams and cold beer. First we visit our campsite and set up the tents. I only bring one if it's going to rain, and it hardly ever does. In more than thirty years, I've been caught without shelter only a couple of times, and at four pounds per hike, I figure that I've saved well over a ton of weight by not carrying one.

One of the times that I should have brought a tent was with a girlfriend who left me afterward—the most expensive four pounds I ever left behind. (I'll bet she still brags about it, though . . . nah.)

After the boots come off I encourage everyone to go down to the creek and place their tired, sweaty "dogs" in the cool spring water. It has the magical effect of washing away a lot of the pain inflicted by the trail. A breeze rattles the leaves in the cottonwood trees overhead and I have to remind myself that I'm at work. This is work!

Wandering up to the cantina at Phantom Ranch is like going back in time when small human villages were set discreetly upon the much larger landscape (and you actually had to look hard for them from the heights). Some people bristle at the notion of a commercial "lemonade stand" in the bottom of Grand Canyon, but I never harbored such feelings. It seems the place was home to me before I even arrived. When I worked here in the 1970s, I was a very young soul, and the character of my life had not yet formed. This place in a sense created and shaped me as a person, and for that, Phantom will never be just a lemonade stand to me.

Now comes the fun part. We'll be inside Grand Canyon without having our packs or boots on for almost forty-eight hours. There's so much to do! We can explore other nearby trails (unbelievably, many of these are somewhat flat), visit a secret waterfall, rest by Bright Angel Creek or the banks of the mighty Colorado River, discover nine-hundred-year-old Indian ruins, write

For decades artists, photographers, and writers have sought to capture the essence of Grand Canyon, but to truly know the Canyon, each person must experience it on his or her own, preferably below the rim. Grand Canyon drawing by John Heyer, author's collection.

postcards, enjoy a glass of wine or beer, or just do *nothing*. How long has it been since any of us just did nothing?

In this modern world, we move too fast. Of all the things that I could possibly teach those on this trip, it would be this: life is fast; slow down. I have just four days to be with them, and I would hate to see them spend all of their time down here in a hurry, which is how most of them live at home. So I lay out all of the possibilities and within minutes we're headed up to the cantina for postcards and beer.

We'll eventually get around to the trails, the ruins, and the Colorado River, but there is never enough time. This place has everything I need—blue sky, salubrious air, a running stream, loads of happy folks stumbling around drunk on bliss. Every time I come down here I say to myself that I will return, to volunteer at the ranch, living day to day as a compassionate sage offering encouragement to weary hikers, while I pull weeds along the side of the path leading to the cantina. When it's time to pack up and go, I always vow to return, and so far that's held true. In fact, there will only be one time in my life that this won't happen.

No matter how much I tell the group that the hike out will be much easier than they think, they never believe me, and they fret when they see that one-mile vertical wall looming ahead. The easiest way to get people out of Grand Canyon is to break the nine-and-a-half-mile hike into little parts, and the Bright Angel Trail lends itself well to this kind of beneficial division. In slow deliberate words, I tell them: one and a half miles along the River Trail (easy, scenic); one and a half miles along gurgling Pipe Creek (easy again); one mile up the Devil's Corkscrew (nine brutal switchbacks but over in only forty minutes); and another easy mile along Garden Creek (waterfalls, ruins, chirping birds!). That brings us to Indian Garden, more than halfway to the top—five miles completed, and most of them did it in just two hours. When I tell them that they are more than halfway out at this point, they actually start believing that they're going to make it out. Smiles all around.

Until Mike reminds us all that even though we've accomplished more than half the distance, we still have three-quarters of the climb to go. Upon hearing this, Susie slumps back against her pack and just glares at the last four and a half miles and the three thousand vertical feet. Thanks, Mike.

"Ah, yes," I remind them. "Mike is right. But we'll break this part up into three bite-sized pieces as well." This has the effect of making the hike out pure joy if you let it feel that way. Okay, I exaggerate. But they *will* feel joy when they actually do "top out." I remind them, "Remember to always look down at what you've done already, rather than up toward what you still have to do." It's a tried-and-true trick of the trail, one that has a magical way of making

Grand Canyon River Guide Questions

We asked some Grand Canyon river guides, "What's the craziest question you've ever been asked about the canyon/river?" Here are some responses.

Ariel Neill, guide for Wilderness River Adventures: "What time do they let the animals out of their cages so we can take pictures?"

Ann-Marie Dale Bringhurst, guide for Grand Canyon Expeditions: "So did people build these ruins or was it the Indians?"

Matt Claman, guide for Oars/Grand Canyon Dories: "Do you ever get bored in Grand Canyon?"

Nikki Cooley, guide for Arizona Raft Adventures: "Why do we have to sit on sand all the time and where did it come from?" and "I love your color! How long have you been working on your tan?" (Nikki is a member of the Navajo tribe.)

Kristin Huisinga, guide for Arizona Raft Adventures: "How often do they have to come down and paint these layers?"

Steve Lonie, guide for Arizona Raft Adventures, Prescott College, and other entities: "How much does the canyon weigh?"

---

the ominous walls gradually recede into the postcard view of the canyon that we all grew up with. "I've never had to leave anyone down here before, and I don't think any of you will be the first. You're doing too well." Mike frowns, but everyone else is smiling again.

Of course, as the guide I have to stay with the slowest hikers, so I'm only too happy to tell Mike to "go on ahead and lead the way for us." He's happy to oblige, although I notice just a bit of apprehension when he realizes he has to walk alone with only his own wits now. The rest of us (including his wife) are happy to let him go, to have a moment when he can stretch it out and just be alone with the canyon. Throughout the trip I have encouraged everyone to have some "alone time" in the canyon—just them and their thoughts and the big, beautiful gorge. These moments are where they too begin their own intimate relationship with Grand Canyon.

And when we finally do reach the top, there are hugs all around from everyone. We assemble near the wooden sign at the Bright Angel trailhead, and this time I do not need to do the asking—they all run right up to the nearest overperfumed visitor and ask them to take their picture with their knotty hair and scraped knees. Everyone's laughing and feels good about the experience. I point out a couple of nonguided hikers who invariably walked too fast to start out their day and too slow to end it. They look haggard from the experience, nothing at all like the festive group we've become.

True, not everyone needs a guide to complete this trip successfully, but having one creates a much different experience that cannot be easily duplicated. Pacing is everything in Grand Canyon, and the proper tempo is only learned from repeated experiences and an intimate knowledge of the trail.

Invariably, it is the "Susies" of the group who end up being the most touched by the whole journey. They don't even try to fight back the tears. Walking back to the classroom, I see a raven fly toward the lip of the canyon, ready for another dive. I do have the best job in the world.

Study Questions

1. In the introduction, Gulliford describes a story where he, a friend, and a dog get lost in Canyonlands National Park. What could they have done differently to prevent their night of sleeping in the sand?
2. As this chapter describes, why is it that humans have a "modern preoccupation" with time? Why are we drawn to sites such as Mesa Verde or Ute Mountain Tribal Park?
3. What is the main cause of death in a desert environment?
4. How must one go about truly experiencing Grand Canyon without taking it for granted?
5. Name three major considerations that one must take when entering a canyon or desert environment.
6. Despite the obvious dangers of flash floods, what are three positive contributions that flash floods make?

CHAPTER 5

Running Western Rivers

For thousands of days my life has been ruled by a river, by its flow and the distance it takes us each day, by its speed and volume, its ever-changing light. After twenty days a month with oars in the fists, the river's muscle shows itself in our arms and backs and in calluses so thick, winter's respite won't be long enough to soften them. Our hands will be ready to take the oars next spring without blistering. Sun, papery dry air, and swims have mapped themselves on our hides. Tenderness lives in the lines at the corners of my husband's eyes. When I stand against the sandstone, he says there is no difference between me and the red-gold canyon. I have turned the color of Desolation (Canyon).

—Ellen Meloy, *Raven's Exile*

There is nothing—absolutely nothing—half so much worth doing as simply messing about in boats.

—Kenneth Grahame, *Wind in the Willows*

How do you know when a river guide is lying? When his mouth is open. That bit of truism speaks volumes about river guides who interpret river history, culture, and lore to visitors going down the Colorado, the Green, the Yampa, the Dolores, the Animas, and the Salt. River runners run white water on inflatable rafts and self-baling kayaks or duckies; they use canoes on relatively calm, flat-water stretches of the White River, the Green, and the lower Gunnison. Rivers offer movement, changing scenery, new vistas daily.

But because we live in the arid West, many of our rivers are both dammed and damned along the Colorado River system with accompanying impacts on endangered fish species. The proliferation of invasive fish and plants, such as tamarisk, can suck up to 150 gallons a day out of local ecosystems.[1] In the

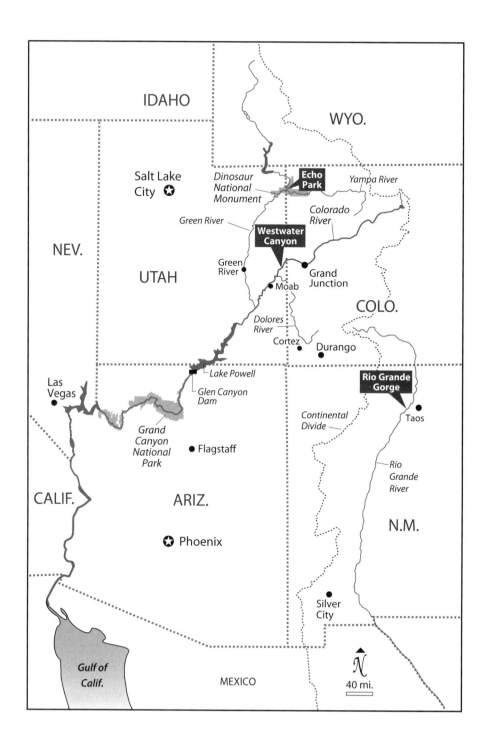

twentieth century we made numerous environmental mistakes based on our own hubris or pride and the belief that we could alter nature. Now we know better. Some of those hard-earned lessons have come from the river community and the constant observations of boatmen (both men and women) whose lives and livelihood are controlled by river flows and releases from upstream dams.

The first explorers into the West used river systems for transportation, including the French fur trapper Denis Julien, who paddled upstream on the Green River in the 1830s and left his inscription in at least five places. He wrote "16 mai 1836" just south of Labyrinth Canyon and also in Whirlpool Canyon below the Gates of Lodore.[2] Surely he knew that the market had collapsed for beaver pelts, and yet he bravely paddled on.

River legends circulate in the quiet currents and eddies of all major southwestern rivers. On the Colorado through Grand Canyon, there's the tale of honeymooners Glen and Bessie Hyde, who in a unique wooden boat, an Idaho sweep scow, vanished below Phantom Ranch. Searchers found everything intact on their craft, but their bodies were never found.[3] One intriguing story tells of three French kayakers in the late 1930s who decided to paddle from Green River, Wyoming, all the way down through Grand Canyon. The kayakers included two male friends and a young woman, recently married to one of the paddlers. They never made it through Grand Canyon but instead returned to France to join the Underground during World War II.

Originally, explorers feared rapids in rivers and for good reason, but as equipment and paddling techniques evolved, river running became a passion and a calling as well as a commercial endeavor. Norman Nevills, a pioneer of western river running, made boats of ¾ inch marine plywood, admonished his customers that "Danger can be fun," and urged his guides and clients to "face your danger."[4]

In 1938 Nevills took the first two women through Cataract and Grand Canyon. These women, Elzada Clover and Lois Jotter, were botanists who came complete with a plant press. After World War II Nevills had a full-fledged commercial river-running business, but in 1949 he and his wife died in a plane crash at Mexican Hat, Utah. Three years later friends erected a bronze plaque at Navajo Bridge. The memorial reads, "They run the rivers of eternity . . . by the river they loved so well, in the desert that was their Home. This record is placed by The Grand Canyoneers."

Running western rivers has become so popular that federal permits are required on almost all white-water stretches. Only a few short segments of flat water remain unpermitted and open to canoeists. The goal of Bureau of Land Management and National Park Service managers is to control river corridors for wilderness values, to limit group size and social contact to try to maintain a sense of solitude, and to "leave no trace." Fire pans are required. So are "groovers" or special Porta Potties, named because the original river runners' toilets, which were U.S. Army surplus ammo cans, left a groove on your butt when you used them. "Pack it in and pack it out" is the mantra. Even tiny pieces of potato chips or slices of cheese are considered microtrash that should be picked up to avoid ants and small animals scurrying into camp. Yet once upon a time river runners were not so thoughtful. Many of the early runners down the San Juan and the Colorado simply put their garbage in bags, weighted it down with stones, and dropped it into the main current. Veteran river runners regret that now.[5] The goal is to paddle—rafts, kayaks, duckies, canoes—and leave no trace.

The other goal for private and commercial trips alike is safety. Most accidents occur within ten feet of shore. River runners know to leave their PFDs (personal flotation devices, the new euphemism for life jackets) on when at river's edge. Serious lessons are taught about assuming the river flotation position on your back, arms outstretched, sandals forward, to avoid deadly foot entrapment. River runners learn what goes in the groover and what goes in the river, because "the solution to pollution is dilution." On the riverbank it's "skirts up and pants down," indicating where women and men pee in the water relative to the river's flow.

Most of us are only on western rivers for a few days or weeks a year. River guides are on much longer, for entire seasons, with commercial trips, private trips, and even scientific trips to monitor fish species or sedimentation. In Grand Canyon if you're sleeping in a tent, you're stealing from yourself because the star show at night is spectacular. Grand Canyon river guides are some of the best, and once a year they meet for an annual rendezvous.

～

It was a warm March afternoon at the Hatch Warehouse just behind Cliff Dwellers Lodge above Marble Canyon. I'd come to the legendary annual Grand Canyon River Guides Training Seminar, which I'd heard was a wild river rendezvous, preseason information session, guide get-together, and beer keg blowout. I was not disappointed.[6]

River guides shuffled in from Flagstaff, Dolores, Anchorage, Merced, Bend, and remote rivers in Maine—young, old, wannabes and veterans. Some remembered the raging Colorado in the summer of 1983 when it blew through the canyon at 93,000 cubic feet per second and it seemed Glen Canyon Dam might wash out. Others had guided on the Snake and the River of No Return and were itching for a chance to row through the Grand. They knew that even to think about being a Colorado River guide they would have to row baggage boats for hundreds of miles, six full trips, at no pay. But they wanted a chance so here they were—nylon shorts, Chaco sandals, tousled hair, the remnants of deep tans, muscles rippling beneath faded T-shirts. They wore river hats that had been smashed, dunked, crumpled, and dried out just like the guides themselves had been.

Of all the great river trips in the American West, none compares to the Colorado River through Grand Canyon. On a sixteen-day rowing trip from Lees Ferry and Marble Canyon to Diamond Creek, passengers learn to respect and admire their river guides, proudly called boatmen regardless of gender. So here they were, beer in hand, the elite of the elite, smiling, laughing, telling stories, catching up.

Grand Canyon river guides believe in protecting the canyon. The group's mission includes setting the highest standards for the river profession, celebrating the unique spirit of the river community, and providing the best possible river experience. Steve Martin, former superintendent at Grand Canyon National Park and a boatman himself, explained, "Special places like Grand Canyon are going to be even more important for Americans in the next century." Overcrowding, urban pollution, and clogged freeways will see to that. He praised the river guides and said, "More than any other collective group you have an opportunity to teach people."

Of the annual 4.4 million visitors to Grand Canyon, only a fortunate few, about 26,000, have the time and money to float the river. The success of their vacation adventure is in the hands of about 350 boatmen each season. As Ethan Johnson quipped, "Storytelling is the butter on our bread for Grand Canyon river guides." So guides need to tell the truth, or at least a version of it; know safety procedures; keep the beer cool; cook with a dutch oven; and not only satisfy customers but also push them beyond their limits, stretch them out on day hikes and paddling, so that the pristine riverine environment and unmatched scenery changes them just as it has each and every guide. Grand Canyon, and the sense of deep geologic time, opens people's lives.

Sam Jansen, Grand Canyon River Guides president, noted, "Our voices really do matter. We know these places and people want to know what we know. We all love Grand Canyon. We may not agree on oars or motors, or even on drinking whiskey, but we all love the Canyon." He added, "It's a lot of work and a lot of fun. We get to go down in the canyon with people and leave the rest of the world behind. Being on the river is an intense experience. There's nothing quite like it."

At the training session, the reality of a deep and abiding river community, from the rowers to the baggage handlers, from the shuttle drivers to the nurses working with the Whale Foundation to monitor and assist with guides' physical and mental health, was heartfelt. Sessions included information on the National Park Service's River Patrol Program, operations at Glen Canyon Dam, Native American perspectives, Grand Canyon National Park issues, and a hands-on ropes clinic. We learned about unique dragonflies on the Colorado Plateau, and about prearranged pulses or floods and what they're doing, and not doing, to reestablish Grand Canyon beaches and warm-water habitat for endangered fish such as the pikeminnow and humpback chub.

If clients pay a high price, so do boatmen. Guides have to leave spouses, families, and pets behind for days and weeks, often on short notice. At trip's end, reentry into a world of fast food, small apartments, and monthly expenses can be jarring after the canyon's quiet. Guides ache to return to share the river with visitors. End-of-season depression for some boatmen is real. Away from the water, river guides may lose their travel trip omnipotence and sense of self-worth.

From river's edge, the bottom of Grand Canyon is a refuge, a sanctuary, and almost everyone reevaluates their short life and ponders deeper meanings, especially on the longest floats. Boatman Pamela Mathues said, "I guide because of the significant transformation I see in myself and with our passengers. Once they get past the fear, the river strips you to your essentials. There's something very healing about being out in nature. It's a magical thing." But she admits, "When you first get back into town it's surreal, then you can have a significant crash. If I'm not careful I just hole up and don't see people." She explained that river guides always miss the sound of moving water and the canyon because there's "an oldness to it that makes you very small and very large at the same time."

As snows melt from mountain peaks and rush downhill into creeks, then into rivers such as the Animas, the Dolores, the San Juan, the Green, and the Yampa, water works its way into the Colorado. Grand Canyon boatmen are ready.[7] They're loading up at Lees Ferry, packing food, checking straps, counting paddles and life jackets—getting ready to give their passengers, soon to become their friends, the ride of a lifetime.

~

Those of us who love rivers respect obstacles such as major boulders in white-water rapids, or on canoeable stretches, strainers or tree limbs with the current going through them. Then there are canoe grabbers such as sweepers—upside-down cottonwood trees with exposed roots. There are very real dangers increased by peer pressure, inadequate skills, and false courage, but white water is all about getting wet and cooling off in summer's heat. It doesn't

Canoeing western rivers, and camping along the way, provides excellent exercise and a great appreciation for plant and animal life along riparian corridors. Paddlers practice "Leave-No-Trace" ethics for clean campsites. White water canoeing in Colorado. Photo courtesy of Centennial Canoe Outfitters.

matter how many gallons slosh over a self-baling rubber raft or a duckie, but don't try that in a canoe.

Imagine wrapping a canoe around a rock and having it quickly fill with hundreds of pounds of rushing river water, which is why it's important to keep the canoe upright. However, if you hit rapids too fast and water rushes over the bow and your wife, grabbing onto the gunnels, tips the canoe into the Dolores River, fall out and join her. In ninety-plus-degree heat it doesn't really matter. Just hang on to your paddle, point your feet downstream, and enjoy the ride as your butt bounces off unseen river rocks.

Other lessons learned from a three-day, two-night Dolores River canoe trip include not waiting until dark to set up your tent; not setting it up two feet from a large anthill; and learning that scorpions may or may not be harmless. Cacti are always ankle height when you're wearing river sandals, and happy hour on the river is also a happy time for gnats and mosquitoes who consider bug spray an appetizer.

We put in at the confluence of the San Miguel and the Dolores Rivers below stunning views of the old wooden gold mining flume known as "The Hanging Flume" because it dangles off tall sandstone cliffs. One construction technique suspended carpenters in bosun's chairs. The ten-mile flume moved eighty million gallons of water daily to blast gold from a sandstone placer deposit. Built between 1888 and 1891, it closed in 1894 having lost millions for investors. The flume is on the National Register of Historic Places and has been extensively studied as one of the last major hydraulic mining operations in the American West. To paddle beneath it in canoes is to understand the daring and determination of workers who built the flume using two million board feet of locally cut planking.

Our guides served dinner on two upside-down canoes, and we cleaned our plates in four tubs of bleach and rinse water. We became adept at using the "groover" or portable toilet. Such opportunities exist on the 170-mile-long Dolores River, which descends through remote forests and canyons, including 250,000 acres of potential wilderness areas. At twilight the sharp relief of canyon walls became silhouetted against night skies so clear you could see the shadow behind the crescent moon. Mellifluous birds woke us at dawn.

Canoeing canyons is a great way to see the West, meet new friends, share stories, practice teamwork lining canoes around gnarly rapids, and enjoy the rhythms of the river. River time is not about watches; it's about sunrises, sunsets, hot afternoons, and cold beer in the evenings. We endured water fights and multiple shots from "soaker" pistols, and it's not whether you'll flip your canoe or go down the river backward—it's only a matter of when. Historian Dan Shosky explained, "We all went down the river. It's just that some of us stayed in canoes."

∼

River runners love "river time" when we embrace our body's natural rhythms. Boatmen sleep on their rafts. On dry land they wake up at night missing the sound of moving water. We love getting up with first light and heading to bed as the stars pop out. We put our watches and our wallets deep into dry bags and forget where the car keys are. In the Southwest, the land of dry deserts and canyons, rivers are indeed a blessing.[8]

∼

At river's edge the college community hummed with excitement: airing the rafts, checking the kayaks, packing provisions, counting the PFDs, and checking on helmets and paddles. Mid-September and my first trip on the Green River, my first multiday raft trip, and we laughed and joked, and swapped river stories, and when everything was ready we walked to a large cottonwood tree, stood in a circle, and listened to the safety talk.

Not much water or CFS (cubic feet per second) on the Green in fall, but still enough volume for a nice trip if only the Indian summer weather would hold and the cold front would move in after we'd taken out at Split Mountain. But as we stood around the ancient cottonwood looking west toward the red-rock ramparts of the Canyon of Lodore, we knew that it would be a four-day, three-night trip regardless of the weather. Everyone had rain gear, or so they thought.

We were on the edge of the Colorado Plateau, the northeast corner, where the Green River drains out of the Wind River Mountains in Wyoming, through Dinosaur National Monument in Colorado and Utah, and down to the confluence with the Colorado River in Cataract Canyon.[9] The trip leader explained that we would scout all rapids by walking beside them to learn the way of the water and path of the currents. On our trip we would study the largest rapids eloquently named by river runner John Wesley Powell. On the Green he christened Winnies Rapid, Upper and Lower Disaster Falls, Triplet, and Hell's Half Mile.[10]

It seemed simple enough. The college students were eager to hit the river and the deep red walls of Lodore beckoned us forward. A tiny white cloud appeared above the canyon walls, but the sky was blue, the river a deep pine tree–green color verging on brown. Sun shone on the rafts. We cast off and became a curving thread of boats finding the current and moving between two thousand feet of vertical canyon walls. Soon the campground was gone and dark red walls towered above us. We drifted with no way up or out except to stay on the water and float the river's course.

I thought of the final phrase from Norman Maclean's book *A River Runs through It*. Though he was writing about Montana, on this overcast day he could easily have been with me on the Green when he wrote, "Eventually all things merge into one and a river runs through it. The river was cut by the world's great flood and runs over rocks from the basement of time. On some of the rocks are timeless raindrops. Under the rocks are the words, and some of the words are theirs. I am haunted by waters."[11]

No wonder one of Powell's men on his first trip in May 1869 abandoned the group after the Gates of Lodore. No thanks, he said. I've had enough. Indeed, Powell had been warned that somewhere in the canyon was "a big suck" that no party of men had ever survived. But in covered wooden boats, better suited for lake travel than western rivers, Powell had come through this very canyon. Soon we would be at the rapids that had claimed one of his boats and smashed it on the rocks, resulting in lost supplies and a decline in the expedition's morale, but that was the nineteenth century.

We had new inflatable rafts for our gear, duckies or self-baling inflatable kayaks for one to two persons, and hard-shell kayaks for experienced paddlers who wanted to dance around the rocks and rest in eddies behind boulders. We had Gortex clothing, neoprene wetsuits and river booties, special life vests, lanterns, river sandals, and enough food for two trips. We had cotton clothing in river bags to keep it dry, and we wore polyester shirts and shorts that would dry quickly in the sun, if there was any. That little cloud had grown.

The dark red walls loomed even higher, and a light rain began to fall. There were no shadows, only small rivulets of silver rain rolling down the cliffs. It was much too early to camp, so down the river we went, a more subdued group, huddled on the rafts in our rain gear, feeling the wind pick up. Absorbed in our own thoughts amidst black boulders, we rode the river deeper into the ancient canyon.

I thought about the movable community we had become, the young kayakers like dolphins on our flanks, gliding beside the rafts, and I knew that as timeless as this river seemed, it had almost been dammed, this canyon flooded and forsaken. Where we now floated would have been hundreds of feet under water. As a historian and college professor, part of the reason I came on the trip was to tell stories about river travelers who had preceded us—Native Americans, prehistoric Fremont and historic Ute Indians, beaver trappers in the early 1800s, cattlemen and cattle rustlers, and early river runners in wooden boats.

My job wasn't to paddle or to cook but to explain the environmental history of the river and how the magnificent canyons of the Green and the Yampa were almost lost to large concrete dams, giant wedges of power and pride to be placed within these million-year-old rocks in the 1950s by a federal agency run amok. I had several historic tales to tell, but it was raining, and we had miles to go, and as the oars slipped quietly through the dark gray-black water I realized my rain gear was already soaked.

~

There are plenty of dangers on the river, but the story I wanted to explain was a different kind of danger, the threat of industrial-scale development in these remote canyons. The conservation groups who had rallied to save the canyons changed the course of American environmental history. It takes courage to go through rapids, but it also takes courage to fight for nature. The dark walls in the Gates of Lodore may be ancient beyond memory, but sometimes in the American West canyons need a human voice.

∽

When Progress Is No Progress: Echo Park and the Modern Environmental Movement

This is a story about wisdom and courage half a century ago, when there was no rafting industry in the West and the U.S. Bureau of Reclamation could put their damn dams any place they wanted. It's a story about two rivers, the Green and the Yampa, that no one had ever heard of, much less rafted, and it's a story about environmental principles and the need to stand by them in the face of intense political opposition. Sound familiar? How do people actually thwart industrial development in the Rocky Mountain West? In the early 1950s, conservation associations found out.[12]

In 1950 the word "environment" was not in the American vocabulary. The Sierra Club had never dealt with any issues outside of California, and groups such as the Audubon Society and the Isaak Walton League had members who watched birds and fished. Green was the color of grass, and it had nothing to do with politics. We had just finished World War II, the Cold War was upon us, and it was time to ratchet up development. Everyone needed water for agriculture, and smooth, flat reservoirs for speedboats so that pretty water-skiers could wear those dangerous new swimming suits called bikinis. The baby boom had begun and it seemed logical, even patriotic, to continue damming every free-flowing river in the American West. Yet what if progress means leaving things alone?

∽

Dinosaur National Monument on the edge of the Colorado Plateau in northwest Colorado and northeast Utah contains two ancient rivers. Over millions of years waters of the Green River have met waters of the Yampa to carve canyons at the confluence. The Yampa meets the Green beside a huge sandstone cliff named Steamboat Rock. Where the rivers merge was christened Echo Park by one-armed Major John Wesley Powell, who descended the Green in 1869 through the Gates of Lodore. He affectionately named the rapids Disaster Falls, Hell's Half Mile, and Triplet. Though Powell went down the Green to the Colorado River and all the way through Grand Canyon, it was on the

Green, soon after entering the Canyon of Lodore, that he lost the only boat on his trip.

Eager beaver dam builders from the Bureau of Reclamation sought to destroy the rapids that had terrorized Powell's men in the spring runoff of May 1869. The bureau's boys sought to submerge some of the finest white water, and biggest drops, of any western river. In 1938 President Franklin Roosevelt expanded the eighty-acre dinosaur quarry site at Dinosaur National Monument to include 259,000 acres and both of the spectacular river canyons. The next year, the bureau showed up, maps in hand.

The Bureau of Reclamation took the first action toward erecting Echo Dam by building a road. In *A Symbol of Wilderness: Echo Park and the American Conservation Movement,* Mark Harvey writes, "In 1939, along with its surveys, the Bureau of Reclamation constructed a primitive road thirteen miles long which ran from the Iron Springs bench—the high plateau far above the rivers—down into Echo Park, and managed to do so without obtaining clearance from the National Park Service."[13]

~

In the 1930s we had also begun massive projects to dam the Columbia River. No one worried about salmon or Native American fishing rights. Even the left-leaning Okie folksinger Woody Guthrie wrote about hydroelectricity and "turning our darkness into dawn." Dams were proof of American technological know-how. Electricity generated along the Columbia had won World War II by providing the juice that created aluminum to build the ships and planes essential for the war effort.

So why not put a dam on the Green River in the far northwest corner of Colorado in a place no one had ever heard of? Why not put a dam in Echo Park? Why not pour a concrete wedge between five-hundred-million-year old walls of red Uinta quartzite, which would back up water into both the Green and Yampa River canyons?

Why not? Because Echo Park was in the middle of Dinosaur National Monument, a unit of the National Park System, and symbolically it was in the geographical center of the West. National parks and national monuments were supposed to be inviolate and protected from modern intrusions, but the busy beavers of the U.S. Bureau of Reclamation and all their dam-building buddies had other ideas.

Yes, Americans wanted plenty of water for irrigation and recreation. The baby boom was in full swing, and by 1957 an American baby would be born every seven seconds. The Colorado River Storage Project was smoothly moving through congressional committees under the stewardship of Colorado congressman Wayne Aspinall from Grand Junction, who never met a dam he didn't like. Aspinall was from the old school, the multiple-use, use it or lose it, conservation-at-any-cost philosophy. Rivers were for irrigation, not for running white water.[14]

So you can imagine the surprise in the halls of Congress and in the offices of Brown and Root and other major construction companies when opposition began to swell against a dam in Echo Park, Colorado, only a stone's throw from the Utah state line. The tiny Sierra Club and the even tinier Wilderness Society decided that this was a big deal. Conservation groups (remember, the word "environment" was not yet in the lexicon) had lost a bitter fight in Yosemite National Park in 1913 to prevent building the Hetch Hetchy dam to provide water for San Francisco, which was still recovering from the 1906 earthquake and fire. The dam went in. In 1916 the National Park Service had been officially created with the mantra to leave its lands "unimpaired for future generations." Conservationists took that phrase seriously. Contractors and Congress thought they were nuts.

Thus began one of the pivotal flashpoints in the twentieth century that created the modern environmental movement. Another turning point was Rachel Carson's 1962 book *Silent Spring*, which revealed the deadly effects of the pesticide DDT.[15] But ten years earlier no one knew enough to care about dying songbirds. The public did know, however, that developers planned a major dam in a minor unit of the National Park System. And the public responded.

~

World War II veterans returned home to their wives and began the baby boom, and they also returned with new technologies that would change the West forever, such as Jeeps. Surplus rubber rafts made Class IV rapids such as Warm Springs on the Yampa and all the Class III rapids on the Green runnable. Over the years a variety of intrepid white-water fans had made their way down the Green after Major Powell. Some of the finest wooden river boats had been built by Nathaniel Galloway in Vernal, Utah, and the enigmatic Buzz Holmstrom had come down the Green on his solo voyage through Grand Canyon in a wooden boat of his own design.[16] But rubber rafts reduced dangers, could accommodate friends, and, as Bus Hatch learned, could be enjoyed by paying customers.[17] After World War II a new industry was slowly born: river running. Combine Americans' love for camping and the outdoors with the thrills, spills, and chills of white water, and a new industry was bobbing and bouncing its way into the future.

The Hatch family of Utah understood that, but their neighbors did not. The Hatches opposed the dam, so they were shunned, shut out, and ostracized in Vernal, the closest town to the dam site. They wanted free-flowing, sparkling rivers and they paid a painful, personal price. It was the age of Cold War conformity, and in Mormon Utah no one was to stand out—except the Hatches. They believed in wild rivers, and they believed that no damn dam should go in a place as stunningly beautiful as Echo Park.

~

In the 1950s there was no environmental movement and no National Environmental Policy Act (NEPA). No public meetings, no local hearings, just Washington bureaucrat fat cats going about their business with the blessings of pro-growth, pro-business politicians, but then for the first time local legislators met their constituents—river runners. And it was a collision of cultures, a clash between the past and the future. Despite the enormous odds, river runners did what they could. They took on the establishment. They argued that the Green and Yampa Rivers needed to flow free past Steamboat Rock and other locations first named by Major Powell. Bus Hatch took tourists down the Green in surplus rafts including members of the Sierra Club. For the first time Sierra Club mountain enthusiasts came to see a new kind of wilderness; they came to see and appreciate western rivers, and they realized that damming the Green would destroy the Canyon of Lodore.

Not since 1913 and the fight over a dam in Hetch Hetchy Valley in Yosemite National Park had the Sierra Club and other organizations taken on such a massive project to stop a federally endorsed dam in a national monument. Never before had the Sierra Club attempted a vast campaign outside of California, and never had the legal question of building a dam in a national monument come up. Under the leadership of their new director, David Brower, this crusade would rocket the Sierra Club into national prominence.

~

Thousands rallied to the cause, including many Americans who had never been to Dinosaur. The dean of western writers, Wallace Stegner, wrote *This Is Dinosaur,* and Bernard de Voto railed against the dam in major magazines. For the first time super 8 movie film helped convince Congress to leave Dinosaur National Monument's rivers alone. Stopping the dam at Echo Park began a sea change to create the twentieth-century environmental movement out of the older nineteenth-century conservation movement.

David Brower of the Sierra Club, Howard Zahniser of the Wilderness Society, and other conservationists tried to save the breathtaking river canyons, where the Green and Yampa Rivers merge, from destruction. Brower worked side by side with groups such as the Izaak Walton League, the National Parks Conservation Association, and the Wilderness Society to stop the Bureau of Reclamation. Letter writers appealed to Congress to protect the spirit of the national park system. After a hard battle between the American citizens and the entrenched bureau, the dam was defeated. That was nationally, but locally . . .

Hatch family members in Vernal were the only ones opposed to the dam. Everyone else basked in potential economic development because "a playground for millions" was promised. The Hatch family became avid river runners and the first commercial permittees on the Green. The Hatches took magazine writers and filmmakers through rapids to show what would be flooded. As a result, letters flowed in to congressmen and senators. Finally, in April 1956 the dam was deleted from the Colorado River Storage Project, though few Americans had yet to visit Dinosaur National Monument or float the Green and Yampa Rivers.

The Echo Park controversy sparked the biggest conservation crusade to date in the twentieth century. It shifted arguments from conservation and multiple use to the environmental movement. Howard Zahniser stated, "We're not fighting progress, we're making it."

～

The beautiful canyons of the Green and Yampa had been preserved because of concerned citizens, many of whom had never rafted a western river. Half a century ago the canyons were saved by the slimmest of margins. Echo Park remains, but at a cost: Flaming Gorge dam was built upstream, forever changing the Green River while leaving the Yampa the last free-flowing river on the Upper Colorado River System.

Though Congress deleted dam projects at Echo Park and Whirlpool Canyon, Congress authorized Glen Canyon Dam in Arizona. The new town of Page was built, and hundreds of archaeological sites were flooded under the waters of Lake Powell. Glen Canyon Dam became David Brower's cross to bear and Ed Abbey's perpetual nemesis. Someday the dam will silt up and become a magnificent waterfall, but for now houseboats skim blue waters, and an ugly white bathtub ring along the canyon walls goes up and down depending upon drought years.

So, yes, river runners should mourn the loss of Glen Canyon, but let's not forget our upstream victory on the Colorado-Utah border. The fight continues against two competitive visions of the West. We can leave it alone and adjust ourselves and our society to a land of limited water and irreplaceable riparian

To raft the Yampa River through Dinosaur National Monument is to experience the last undammed river on the entire Colorado Plateau. Trips usually last five days and four nights, with impressive canyon scenery on the Yampa, which merges with the Green River in Echo Park, where stopping a dam in 1956 helped create the modern environmental movement. Photo by author.

habitat, or we can dam every river, creek, and stream for water projects that will in the end fail. The human perspective is always the short view. Canyons know river time, geologic time, and swirling white water dancing between dark stones.

~

We ran the Green in the rain for a day or two. We ran Triplet Rapids and avoided the wall and the Birth Canal. At Hell's Half Mile we played through the fall rock garden and tried not to tag the boulders, especially the rock Lucifer in the middle, so we ran river right. Camping at Rippling Brook, we climbed up to the microclimate and ecosystem of the seventy-five-foot Rippling Brook

Waterfall. Indian summer returned for our final glorious day through rapids in Split Mountain Canyon. I was hooked.

I now have favorite campsites and memories of camping over the years. In addition to the river's human history, I have learned about endangered warm-water fish species such as the pikeminnow and the humpbacked chub. I learned how a remote site on Steamboat Rock in Dinosaur National Monument helped save the peregrine falcon population in the American West because one of the last breeding pairs of falcons lived there. I learned how Rocky Mountain bighorns, once gone from the canyons, have been reintroduced.

Being on river trips with movable communities where friendships are formed and stories shared, I learned about "river time" and letting one's cares and concerns flow on down the canyon. I learned about being present, engaged, and focused on reading rapids. Sure, I've dumped a time or two. Who hasn't? But I've learned that to be outdoors in the Southwest on a river is to understand the West, and one's self, in a new and vital way. We need rivers and streamside riparian habitat for the ecology it represents, but also for the human ecology, the friendships made, the time alone in nature.

And for me there's nothing like a Class IV rapid, late in the afternoon in a sun-drenched canyon, to clench your stomach, to focus your senses on rocks and obstacles, to question your competence, and to bring that taste of fear into your mouth as adrenaline courses through your blood. Warm Springs Rapid on the Yampa sounds like a rolling freight train in the distance, and once you're there, scouting on river right, it's easy to see the proper path either river right or down the main tongue through the center. Then it's time to cast off. PFD tightened, paddle firmly gripped. Off into the bright white waves, boulders on either side, water flowing over, under, and around the duckie. A few intense moments of Zenlike focus and then you're done, out the other side, laughing, yelling, still upright.

Writing about rapids in Grand Canyon, naturalist Ann Zwinger explained:

> To someone who has not run a rapid before and questions the need to do so at all, the lure of this charging volume of water pointing towards your very own vulnerable, frangible body is difficult to explain. For some it is the challenge to "beat the river." Those who row have the intellectual and physical challenge of coordinating head and hand and doing something difficult well, very well, even with grace and precision. For others rapids give an edge to living, a baptism that blesses with a reminder of mortality. Still others need the willingness to risk, to push the limits one more time, to cherish the sense of monumental natural power into which one must fit in

order to survive. Once is enough for many, and forever not enough for some.[18]

That's what wild rivers can do. They can let you relax for hours at a time, as you drift under tall canyon walls. Then abruptly rivers require total concentration. They waken all your senses to focus just a few feet in front of you as the river's roar calls you forward.

Let the river essays in this section give you focus, too. River stories, told and retold, are some of the best tales in the West.

Notes

1. For endangered fish see the brochure "Swimming: The Endangered Fish of the Colorado River" and the newsletter "Swimming Upstream for the San Juan River Basin Recovery Implementation Program and the Upper Colorado River Endangered Fish Recovery Program," November 2008, and Gerald W. Roehm, "Draft Management Plan for Endangered Fishes in the Yampa River Basin" (Denver: U.S. Fish and Wildlife Service, July 2003). For tamarisk, see various issues of *High Country News*.

2. Bill and Buzz Belknap and Lois Belknap Evans, *Belknap's Waterproof Canyonlands River Guide* (Evergreen, CO: Westwater Books, 2008), 26, and Wallace Stegner, ed., *This Is Dinosaur: Echo Park Country and Its Magic Rivers* (New York: Alfred A. Knopf, 1955; Boulder, CO: Roberts Rinehart, 1985). Also see Hal Crimmel and Steve Gaffney, *Dinosaur: Four Seasons on the Green and Yampa Rivers* (Tucson: University of Arizona Press, 2007).

3. Brad Dimock, *Sunk without a Sound: The Tragic Colorado River Honeymoon of Glen and Bessie Hyde* (Flagstaff, AZ: Fretwater Press, 2001). For extended discussions about running the Colorado River and its ecosystem health, see Colin Fletcher, *River: One Man's Journey Down the Colorado, Source to Sea* (New York: Alfred A. Knopf, 1997), and Jonathan Waterman, *Running Dry: A Journey from Source to Sea Down the Colorado River* (Washington, D.C.: National Geographic Society, 2010).

4. For a short biography on the Nevills family, see Nancy Nelson, *Any Time, Any Place, Any River: The Nevills of Mexican Hat* (Flagstaff, AZ: Red Lake Books, 1991).

5. See Katie Lee's books *All My Rivers Are Gone: A Journey of Discovery through Glen Canyon* (Boulder, CO: Johnson Books, 1998), and *Sandstone Seduction: Rivers and Lovers, Canyons and Friends* (Boulder, CO: Johnson Books, 2004).

6. Andrew Gulliford, "'We All Love the Grand Canyon': Colorado River Guides," Gulliford's Travels, *Durango Herald*, May 11, 2008. Also see Brad Dimock, "The Secret Lives of River Guides," *High Country News*, May 10, 2010, and David Sievert Lavender, *River Runners of the Grand Canyon* (Tucson: Grand Canyon Natural History Association, 1985).

7. To learn more about the San Juan River, see Robert McPherson, *River Rising from the Sun* (Logan: Utah State University Press, 2000). For a poetic interpretation, see Ann Weiler Walka, *Waterlines: Journeys on a Desert River* (Flagstaff, AZ: Red Lake Books, 2000).

8. Two great sets of river-running stories are Christa Sadler, ed., *There's This River: Grand Canyon Boatman Stories* (Flagstaff, AZ: This Earth Press, 2006), and Michael Engelhard, *Hell's Half Mile: River Runners' Tales of Hilarity and Misadventure* (Halcottsville, NY: Breakaway Books, 2004).

9. See Lito Tejada-Flores, *Wildwater: The Sierra Club Guide to Kayaking and Whitewater Boating* (San Francisco: Sierra Club Books, 1978), and Les Bechdel and Slim Ray, *River Rescue* (Boston: Appalachian Mountain Club Books / Globe Pequot Press, 1985).

10. Read Powell's own account of these rapids in his book that combined both the 1869 and 1871 accounts. See John Wesley Powell, *The Exploration of the Colorado River and Its Canyons* (1875; reprint, New York: Dover Books, 1961), 169. Also see John Wesley Powell, *Down the Colorado: Diary of the First Trip through the Grand Canyon, 1869,* ed. Don D. Fowler and Eliot Porter (New York: Dutton, 1969), and Edward Dolnick, *Down the Great Unknown* (New York: Harper Collins, 2001).

11. Norman Maclean, *A River Runs through It, and Other Stories* (Chicago: University of Chicago Press, 1976), 104.

12. See Andrew Gulliford, "When Progress Is No Progress: Echo Park and the Environmental Movement," *Inside/Outside Southwest*, September/October 2006, for an earlier version of this essay.

13. Mark Harvey, *A Symbol of Wilderness: Echo Park and the American Conservation Movement* (Seattle: University of Washington Press, 1994). For a shorter history, see Jon Cosco, *Echo Park: Struggle for Preservation* (Boulder, CO: Johnson Books, 1995).

14. Steven C. Schulte wrote about Aspinall's opposition to the Wilderness Act in "Where Man Is a Visitor: The Wilderness Act as a Case Study in Western Public History," in Andrew Gulliford, ed., *Preserving Western History* (Albuquerque: University of New Mexico Press, 2005).

15. Rachel Carson, *Silent Spring* (New York: Houghton Mifflin, 1962).

16. Vince Welch, Cort Conley, and Brad Dimock, *The Doing of the Thing: The Brilliant Whitewater Career of Buzz Holmstrom* (Flagstaff, AZ: Fretwater Press, 1998).

17. Roy Webb, *Riverman: The Story of Bus Hatch* (Flagstaff, AZ: Fretwater Press, 2008).

18. Ann Zwinger, *Down Canyon* (Tucson: University of Arizona Press, 1995), 121.

River Guide Jokes

How many river guides does it take to screw in a light bulb?

Answer: Ten. It takes one to screw in the bulb and nine to describe how big the hole was.

What's the difference between a river guide and a large pizza?

Answer: A large pizza can feed a family of four.

How do you starve a river guide?

Answer: Hide their tip under a bar of soap.

What do you call a river guide who just broke up with his girlfriend?

Answer: Homeless.

What's the difference between a river guide and a catfish?

Answer: One is smelly and has whiskers and the other is just a fish.

How do you fit seven river guides in a closet?

Answer: Tell them they can live there for free.

How do you know a river guide has been sleeping on your couch?
Answer: He's still there.

What's the difference between a female river guide and Sasquatch?
Answer: One's big and hairy and the other is a myth.

What's the difference between a river guide and God?
Answer: God doesn't think he's a river guide!

What's the difference between a river guide and a savings bond?
Answer: One eventually matures and earns money.

River Ranger: Beer and Dinner—Westwater Canyon

Chad Niehaus

The season had grown into an extension of my body. This reflection of me had become paramount to my existence. I wanted everyone to know that this was how I lived, that these things were what I considered important. I wanted a common passerby to see the sparkle of the river in my quick glance and instill in them a desire to experience a place like I do. My hands had roughened, my skin had grown dark, and the confidence that resided deep within me surfaced each morning before I opened my eyes and stayed with me until I laid my head down again. I had developed friendships with people who shared stories to make you weep, guffaw, and admire. I had learned from these characters that above all you must possess a deep sense of respect for special places and everything that depends upon them.

A plan made prior to accepting the job of Westwater river ranger was now taking shape. Summer was coming to an end and the steady traffic of class registration, health insurance, and other mailings connected to graduate school reminded me that I was obligated to another place, another life. I suddenly questioned this shift in lifestyle vehemently. It felt reassuring to have such a complete plan when I was making it, but now that I was in the middle of its execution, I was seriously considering a bailout. My current job and residence created a smile that hadn't been there for a long time. I was

Originally published as "Beer and Dinner" by Chad Niehaus, from *Hell's Half Mile: River Runners' Tales of Hilarity and Misadventure*, ed. Michael Engelhard (Halcottsville, NY: Breakaway Books, 2003). Reprinted by permission of the author.

earning money, I was working, I was doing good things, and *I was really enjoying myself.* If it was contentment I was chasing after, well, I had found it. I knew this job would change my perspective of "work" forever. The next time I considered employment that would be a "good career move," my hopes would race back to the time when I was earning enough to live and living enough to be fully satisfied. This experience was going to make it painfully difficult to enter Cubicle Land, a dreadful place that seemed to be eagerly awaiting my inevitable arrival.

My fate was essentially sealed. I had gone through the steps to make all of this happen, and would presumably give myself a black eye if I pulled out now. But the pain of detachment started to pulsate as I wrapped my mind around the idea of taping the box shut that contained my beaten river shorts, my sun-bleached cowboy hat, bug-stained and water-warped paperbacks, and a voluminous collection of memories created on and off the river. I couldn't do it, not yet, anyway. I extracted the shorts and hat from their place of safety. One more run through the canyon was in order to feel right about this. I needed to say farewell and absorb another dose of the place's mystical elements that would monopolize my thoughts while I was away. It would give me a chance to say thanks.

I donned my sweat-stained and faded polyester button-up ranger shirt for a final patrol of Westwater Canyon. I was still not entirely comfortable with the concept and statement of a collared short-sleeved shirt tucked into shorts, but this was the image the Bureau of Land Management was aiming for. This was the look that conveyed bureaucratic competence and demanded public respect and adherence. Besides, who was I to question the fashion sense of the United States Government? My irrepressible quest for personal expression was pushing it as it was, with shorts depicting an aquarium scene and flip-flops conspicuously revealing my big toenail painted a low-key cosmic blue.

Routine duties had consumed the bulk of yet another beautiful day in the desert. I had spent it dusting, mopping, and polishing the trailer for the next damned lucky resident. It also took time to put the last touches of paint on a personalized oar blade that would be added to the ranger station alumni wall. Since the shadows were growing long I loaded dinner, breakfast, and my ammo can full of river life's necessities into the ranger raft. I shouted a word of appreciation to Alvin, a longtime ranger station resident, for giving me a hand with the shuttle and sympathizing with my likely-futile-but-worth-it-anyway attempt at closure. I kicked the river's edge and floated into a heavy world of reflection, determined to come to grips with my situation along the way.

The current was strong enough to let me stay off the oars, so I sat cross-legged, sipped a cup of milk tea, and slipped past what were now intimate features of the canyon. I watched cliff swallows depart their mud nests to graciously consume swarms of busy gnats along the river's glistening surface. I drifted past the spot where not too long ago four mule deer had ferried across the river a hundred yards in front of me. I took a head count at the great blue heron rookery. I marveled at the cottonwood and willow gallery highlighted by the soft, late afternoon glow.

As the boat spun slowly around, I spotted a dot of a woman running frantically up and down the beach at the campsite known as "Fault." Upon seeing me, she waved her arms wildly and leaped into the air. The arm wave was close enough to textbook to signal that my presence was needed at camp. I pulled on the oars and headed in the direction of the distress signal. Words were cast my way, but the moan of the oarlocks and the distance between us made it impossible to understand any meaning. I shook my head, pointed to my ear, and yelled, "*Louder!*" At this, the woman reared back and let out with everything she had. Two of my favorite words made their way to the ranger boat, words that always sound sweetest spoken in a female voice: "*Beer*" and "*Dinner.*" What a treat, I thought, to be invited over for a warm meal and alcohol served by an enthusiastic and striking river goddess.

I moved the boat swiftly and surely, smiling at the luck of it all. I looked over my shoulder once more and noticed that the woman was still pacing back and forth, running from one collection of gear to the next. It pained me slightly to see that she was making such a fuss over little old me. I drove the boat high onto shore and performed a daring but graceful "tube bounce" exit, landing solidly on the beach with bare feet and a grin to make even the most ardent Ani DiFranco devotee go soft with yearning.

No words were offered to me, neither from the woman nor the family huddled by the commercial raft. But several trembling fingers of various sizes pointed toward the dinner table. Having nothing to refer to but my gut, I walked toward the roll-a-table in eager anticipation, rubbing my hands of any river dirt that might get in the way of enjoying a freshly cooked meal. Upon arrival at the dinner table, though, I was dismayed to find nothing but crumbs, not even enough for a light snack. Bowls were turned over, scraps of tortilla were strewn about, and I couldn't find a cold beer anywhere. I turned around and flashed a look of confusion at the raft guide. I watched her eyes grow large. She tilted her head to the side and motioned with her chin a little beyond me and just to the right. Must be more on the stove. I turned to prepare a plate and suddenly locked eyes with another dinner guest. He was roughly my size but seemed to be much more assertive and stronger. As he headed toward the table for another helping I reacted the only way I knew how: I stood way up high on the tips of my toes, puffed up my chest to its full capacity, waved my arms, and let out a booming blabber of gibberish.

As he continued his approach, absolutely unimpressed with my display of machismo, I had to smile. It was now quite clear that I had not in fact been invited over for beer and dinner. Instead, a bear was eating these poor people's *comida Mexicana*. I ballooned and shouted once more, this time louder and fiercer. I reached down and grabbed a skillet that had been licked clean of *frijoles* and pounded on it with a wooden spoon.

Behind me, an uncertain moan grew to a ferocious shrill howl. I looked back and saw the crazy-eyed guide gaining speed toward the bear and me, kicking up plumes of sand with each lunge. Impressed and intrigued, I joined her as she passed and contributed a wavering growl indicating, I hoped, power and immensity, not puberty. The bear looked at us, we looked at each other, and just like that the guide and I were digging our heels into the sand in true cartoon-braking fashion. We skidded to a stop within smelling distance of the beast, which hadn't moved so much as one of its enormous muscles as a result of our storming. We stood our ground and profanely described all of the various places the bear could go besides right next to us.

Being a sensible bear, the seventh F-bomb was one too many. He huffily turned his shoulder to retreat to the few scraps of fajitas that remained in a tuft of tamarisk. We needed this bear to run away much farther, though, so he wouldn't develop a habit eventually leading to his demise. This was my cue. I brought back my shaking hand and held it high in the dusky air. Then I belted out a yodeling battle cry and delivered my big old hand squarely on the visitor's rump. It remained there long enough to feel his substantial body heat and coarse wiry hair. This bright idea triggered a unique amalgam of surprised gasps from the still-subdued and concerned family, a soft "whoah" from the guide, an "uhhhhh" from me, and a primeval grunt of disapproval from our hairy friend. The noise, however, was more impressive than the results. After three more ass-slaps and nothing to show for them but louder bear grunts, it felt like time to switch tacks.

The guide suggested we remove the temptation of food and humans altogether and pack up camp. Hearing this, the family showed obvious relief and was suddenly more than happy to do anything that would speed up their departure from this different and definitely-not-in-the-brochure experience. The kids hefted their little matching dry bags back to the raft, the parents broke down the tent, and the guide disassembled the kitchen. I remained on bear duty, shadowing his movements and engaging him in a soft discussion about why he really needed to head back to his home on the Uncompaghre

Plateau to pick up where he left off. Once the raft was rigged and ready to go, I raised my hand one last time. Blackie had gotten the picture, though. I didn't need to follow through this time. As he sauntered away, I wished him good luck and returned to the ranger boat.

Once we arrived at Miner's Camp, and the family's anxieties had mellowed to a tolerable level, I thanked everyone for a memorable evening. I lingered after making my closing statement, assuming an engraved invitation to the "we survived the bear scare" dinner party was on its way. Once all backs were turned, though, and the group began speaking about me in the third person (and about my outfit in particular), I took the hint and headed downriver to warmed-over soup and a solitary perch.

⁓

I rose the next morning as the walls were glowing red with the coming sun. From the honeymoon suite high atop Hades Bar, I stared for a long time into the desert ether that always felt so pure, so right, so real. I gazed too long, though, and burned something bold into my brain. Closing my eyes and looking at what was there I found desert varnish, an impossibly blue sky, water reflected on black rock. I found contrasts of deep harmony. I saw a river home. This image—I knew—would be my memory of place, and I made a quiet pact with myself not to let it fade while I was away.

I realized the only thing crazy about our run-in with the bear was that it represented just another day in the canyon. I tucked the "beer and dinner" story onto the tightly packed Westwater shelf of memories, wondering how long I would be able to last in my new place between readings. As I walked down the path toward the boat, the commercial party drifted past. "You ready to go?" shouted the guide in an easily distinguishable voice. "Yeah," I replied, "I guess I am."

Running High Water on the Yampa River

Dinosaur National Monument, Colorado

It was just luck that we launched our rafts on the Yampa River the day before one of the highest recorded river flows in its history. It was just luck that we slammed through Class IV Warm Springs Rapid at 25,000 cubic feet per second on the last undammed river in the Colorado River system. High water can be cold, fast, dangerous, and fun.

I rode those rapids twice in two weeks for History Colorado and Rocky Mountain Public Broadcasting System (PBS). I raise money for nonprofit organizations by putting together clients and rivers, and I go along as a historian/interpreter/storyteller, donating my services. The trips with Adrift Adventures in Jensen, Utah, had been planned months in advance, long before we knew the Colorado Rockies would have a mammoth snowpack 247 percent of normal. Six of us floated with guides on the first trip and twenty-one with guides on the second trip, paddling through Warm Springs with adrenaline-soaked anticipation.

Forty-five-degree water on a cloudy day leaves no room for mistakes, because if you fall out of a raft you've only got about 4½ minutes before hypothermia sets in and you can't easily move your arms and legs because they've gone numb.

Then there's foot entrapment. If you're out of a boat trying to get to shore and catch your foot between river rocks, the weight and speed of a river will prevent you from standing up to breathe. In high flows with a stuck foot, you can drown in three feet of water. And the rapids in high water? Some wash out, but others get bigger, much bigger. We were headed for one of the legendary Big Drops.

Those concerns weighed on me after the news release from the Utah Bureau of Land Management: "Above average amounts of precipitation and unpredictable snowmelts are creating some of the highest river flows and most unpredictable flash floods in decades. The BLM recommends that public land visitors reconsider any plans to undertake these outdoor activities if your group does not maintain the expertise to respond to these types of conditions." My two groups would all be novices, including an eighty-year-old and a seventy-year-old who'd never been on a river before. As passenger Hugh Bingham noted in his journal, "We're apprehensive, but the guides are stoked."

So did we consider canceling the trips? Not really. Instead, we increased the number of rafts and the number of guides when we knew we'd hit the peak of high water with our June 8 launch. We carried full wetsuits. At Deer Lodge we couldn't find the put-in because it was under water. The Yampa River where it entered the canyons had become a wide lake and a mosquito heaven. Before we could find the river's current, we paddled through a grove of cottonwood trees that was normally high and dry.

In a few days' time we'd hit Warm Springs Rapid, normally a Class IV with a huge hole in the center. What would the hydraulics be at 25,000 ft³/sec? No one knew because they changed daily. In that constricted canyon so much water volume creates new wave patterns, lateral waves bouncing off boulders, pushing rafts exactly where they don't want to go—into the hole named Maytag that can clutch a twenty-six-foot raft, stand it straight up, and spill all the occupants. I know because we saw the aftermath of such a flip.

But while I worried about our guests, real river rats were in white-water ecstasy.

Because of the warnings some private groups canceled, but others jumped on the open permits. High water brings out true white-water aficionados, eco-crazies who lie awake at night dreaming of big water and rowing west into tumbling waves and foaming holes. When the water's high they break out old boats and lucky charms—the river hat they found drifting in an eddy on the Colorado, the REI mug left at the scout for Big Joe Rapid, the extra paddle found below Snaggletooth on the Dolores. While we squirmed into our too-tight wetsuits, here came the Amazon rowers with firm biceps, dreadlocks, nose rings, nylon shorts, sports bras, and deep tans to die for.

At our camp in Harding Hole the guides couldn't park the boats where they wanted to because of the speed of the water. One raft landed on a sharp limestone rock, and with constant wave agitation, by morning we had a blown-out tube. Hugh Bingham wrote about our camp that night, "The river roars without stop. Accustomed to camping as close to lapping waters as we can, we find ourselves surprised and frightened by its force, and pitch our tents on higher—much higher—ground. What is that sound? Midnight I awake, and get it: it's the sound of the Pacific surf crashing—but without the intervals between waves."

We had large roller waves like ocean swells, rare on a river. Whole trees on the banks vibrated in the froth, and driftwood logs rolled and tumbled. Our Adrift guides kept us away from dangerous undercut walls—and then we got to Warm Springs.

Calm and placid on top, there was no way to know the white maelstrom below. The guides climbed a cliff to do their scout. We sat quietly in the rafts tightening our life jackets. Then it was time to shove off. To stay out of the gaping hole in the center, we ran river right but had to perform a complicated ferry angle to stay off the boulders at river's edge because the Yampa was folding in on itself. Bingham wrote, "We go over the lip, come round the corner, and hit the first giant wave, spin sideways and tip hard starboard. A 55-gallon drum's worth of water pours up my nose and into my mouth and my blue seat cushion flops over my head—so I don't see our guide go over the side. He later says he found himself instantly under water, popped up, grabbed the rope and hoisted himself back in, all in the space of four or five seconds."

I was in the next raft, and though I didn't view the guide exiting, in between sheets of cold water smacking my face, I thought it was odd to see a raft with no one at the oars. Later I asked trip leader Tappan Brown how big the hole was. His eyes widened and he said, "I could have parked a school bus in there, easily."

And that was the Yampa River's flow before it met the Green River in Echo Park and added another 7,000 ft³/sec for a total of 32,000 ft³/sec through the rollicking roller-coaster of Split Mountain with ten-foot swells and rapids affectionately named Moonshine, SOB, Schoolboy, and Inglesby. PBS passenger Bill Daniel exclaimed, "Plenty of thrills! Plenty of fun! Plenty of good friends! Great trip!"

It's hard to be off the river now. Adrenaline adds spice to life and compresses time. I miss that white-water roar, and I agree with Ed Abbey, who pleaded, "One more river . . . may there always be one more . . ."

White Water, Scorpion Stings, and a Steep Hike Out: Welcome to Grand Canyon

Andrew Gulliford

Six months of planning for a Grand Canyon river trip then bam! A scorpion sting the first night! What did I do to deserve that? At 3 A.M. I'm wide awake. My left shin felt seared by a red-hot poker.

Darkness was coming on, and we'd been forced to camp on a narrow beach under a rocky ledge that offered protection from rain but also made a perfect habitat for nocturnal scorpions, *Centruoides sculpturatus*. When it started to sprinkle, one of the straw-colored three-inch Arizona bark scorpions must not have liked the raindrops. He took it out on my leg, giving me a dose of his thirty nerve toxins. One guidebook labels the sting "often painful but rarely lethal." I can attest to that.

By noon the next day the venom had traveled up my groin and into my hands and head. My fingers felt like five volts arced from fingertip to fingertip. I distinctly sensed each nostril, and the tops of my ears.

Originally published as "Grand Adventure: Rafting the Colorado River through Grand Canyon for PBS," *Grand Junction Daily Sentinel*, October 31, 2012.

Luckily, we had more rain and cool weather. The day after the sting the fifty-degree water splashing onto the paddleboat anesthetized my leg. But trying to sleep the second night was almost impossible as the shin pain rolled back. By day three I was able to enjoy our six-day, ninety-mile Rocky Mountain Public Broadcasting System (PBS) trip with Arizona Raft Adventures (AzRA). Our trip leader, Nate Klema, offered sage advice: "White water is almost the safest part of the trip. Swim. Dip your hat in the water. Keep that bandana wet and eat salty food."

We'd planned on an Upper Canyon hybrid trip, meaning we had rafts and a paddleboat but no motors. We wanted to experience the Colorado River the way the original explorers had, though they certainly didn't have our steak, salmon, and burrito dinners or beer kept cold in wet gunnysacks and a drag bag.

There were deeply colored canyon views at sunrise and sunset, bighorn sheep, California condors circling high above us, ospreys, herons, canyon wrens, and ubiquitous ravens. Klema claimed, "Down here on the river the ravens have a higher IQ than most raft guides, so keep everything zipped up. Ravens will steal anything and they've even carried off daypacks."

As one of the most popular destinations on the planet, Grand Canyon annually receives more than four million visitors, yet only 10 percent of those hike below the rim and only 1 percent make it to the river. We were part of the lucky 26,000 river runners each year who enjoy one of the wildest stretches of rocks, cliffs, canyons, and beaches in the world. There were twenty of us on the trip with five guides and a swamper or helper.

We hiked into ancient Ancestral Puebloan ruins near Stanton's Cave. We drifted past the lush green vegetation at Vasey's Paradise and lunched at the Marble Canyon dam site where in the 1960s the Bureau of Reclamation planned to dam the river to a "scenic trickle." Stopping that dam and another at Bridge Canyon helped galvanize the environmental movement.

At Redwall Cavern I gave a history lecture on the damn dams and we practiced yoga. We learned about saving endangered fish such as the humpback chub. Later we were stunned by dark red runoff from the Little Colorado River flush from summer monsoons. Anyone who had not yet washed their hair or clothes gave up.

The hikes up South Canyon, Saddle Canyon, and Carbon Creek left one in awe because of the geology. The guides enlivened the trip with historical and scientific anecdotes, tales of river runners, and ongoing threats to Grand Canyon's ecosystem. We learned that Bert Loper died at 24½ mile rapid and that the hiker who found Bert's skeleton sixteen years later took a bottle of

In the upper part of the Grand Canon at river mile 4 (downstream from Lees Ferry) the Colorado River is entrenched 400 feet deep in such a short distance. It will continue to deepen its track until it reaches river mile 52 at Nankoweap Canyon, where it is over 6,000 feet deep relative to the North Rim. The depth of the canyon is due not only to incision by the river but also to the way the canyon layers rise upward toward the south.

whiskey, poured half on Loper's bleached bones, and then sat down to drink the rest.

My role was to tell historical stories to put our trip into context and to provide details on famous folks such as John Wesley Powell, Buzz Holmstrom, the missing George and Bessie Hyde, the Kolb Brothers, marathon canyoneer Harvey Butchart, and architect and designer Mary Colter. At Nankoweap we hiked high into the cliffs to photograph Anasazi granaries. At Unkar Delta we explored the largest prehistoric Indian site in the canyon.

We ran the big rapids in the Inner Gorge—Hance, Sockdolager, and Grapevine—and came face to face with the 1.7-billion-year-old Vishnu Schist, ebony rocks so old they are the earth's twisted, ancient roots. At night stars rose over the vivid, jagged silhouette of the Inner Gorge.

Then came morning, without a cloud in the sky, and the daunting 7.6-mile hike from river to rim with a 4,460 ft. elevation gain. We landed at Pipe Creek and, thanks to our boatmen, were on the Bright Angel Trail by 8 A.M. Two hours later the thermometer at Indian Gardens registered 104 degrees. We had six hours and 3,400 ft. to go. Friends had urged us to take long-sleeved cotton shirts in zip lock bags and keep the shirts soaked in cold water. As a shirt dried in the intense heat we switched to the next one and thus walked up the trail literally wearing water and acting like evaporative coolers.

Finally, after eight hours of hiking and numerous whiffs of the sweet-sour scent of mule poop, my wife and I set our 25–35 pound backpacks on the South Rim. Am I going back? Absolutely. There are rapids I have yet to run, hikes to take, slot canyons to explore. To see Grand Canyon is one thing; to float through its heart is another. The canyon calls to me.

Only next time, if we're camped on a rocky ledge, it rains, and scorpions come out, I won't be lying in moist sand. I'll beg the boatmen to move over so I can sleep on a raft.

A Psychiatrist Looks at River Trips and Being a Better Boatman— Grand Canyon

Oral History Interview with Dr. William Karls, Psychiatrist and Twenty-three-year Grand Canyon River Guide

I grew up in Nebraska, a place not known for its outdoor activities, but my brother and I were in Boy Scouts. We canoed on some of the flat rivers in Nebraska, but we worked during the summer for a character that had at one time raced canoes in Canada as a professional canoe racer. I was probably a freshman in high school when we loaded up my brother's van and went to the Boundary Waters Canoe Area with a couple of friends and some aluminum canoes. While we were there the portaging was so tough that we decided to run this little creek that connected two lakes. We were just hooked on white water from that moment on.

We got back to Nebraska and this guy also ran a marina there in Lincoln. So we said, "What canoes should we buy if we want to get into white water?" and he said, "You know, if you want to get into white water, you need a kayak."

So, it turned out, he sold a brand of kayaks through the marina, so my brother and I bought a couple of boats and we threw 'em up on a car and we went out to the Arkansas River in Colorado. We hadn't paddled more than five minutes when I split my head open and I think my brother lost his boat.

I ended up on the wrong side of the river, after hitting my head. I didn't know how to get back to the other side of the river where the cars were, so I remember saying to myself, being a good Catholic boy, I said a little prayer right there. I said, "God, you get me to the other side of the river. I'll never get in this thing again."

And so I got in my kayak and I didn't know how to paddle the ferry angle or do anything like that, but I got in this kayak and I swear it was just like a miracle, that thing just left the eddy at a perfect angle, carried right over to the other side of the river, and I said to myself, "Wow! That was so cool! Maybe I'll get back into this thing again."

So we got some stitches and went back to Nebraska and saved up some money and came back to the Arkansas River again and were camping at the put-in for the Numbers, but we weren't going to do that section. We weren't good enough, but we were camping there and this guy pulled up who ran a kayaking business in Crested Butte. He was shooting a brochure on Pine Creek. It was real high water and it was very impressive, so he had a photographer along and he was going to run the rapid, and he needed somebody to repeatedly carry his kayaks. So my brother and I volunteered to do that, and at the end of the day, he said, "I'll give you guys two free days' worth of lessons for helping me out so much."

In about fifteen minutes he taught both of us to roll our kayaks in a little pool there, and then we did a lower stretch, and then for our graduation on the second day he took us on Brown's Canyon. And it was a gas, and right then, we realized that if we ever were going to be serious about kayaking, we needed to get out of Nebraska. We needed to go to a place that offered instruction. And at that time the only place that we knew of in the United States that offered instruction for white water was the Nantahala Outdoor Center in North Carolina.

It was one of the training grounds for slalom racing, and a lot of the guys that worked as guides were also training for the Olympics and the world championships. And they were so great that at five o'clock when work was over, we'd all throw our kayaks in the back of a pickup and head up to the top of Nantahala. You'd be paddling with five or six Olympic-level kayakers and you were straight from Nebraska, but they were such nice people that by the end of the summer we were Class III boaters and had trained to be guides the next year.

That was *the* most important influence in my life for several reasons. One was just getting the skills of kayaking and guiding rafts, particularly paddle-boats, but the other was just learning a love for water. These people were fish. Every waking moment that we weren't working, we were paddling or doing something outside. The outdoor life for them was not just something that you left when you graduated from high school or college and started working; it was part of their lives.

A lot of these guys were old Outward Bound instructors, too, so they also had that sense of not just enjoying it yourself but teaching it to others. The second part of Outward Bound is using the outdoors not just to teach about the outdoors but to better yourself, improve yourself.

When I started as a Grand Canyon river guide there were around twenty-six companies working there, and they were so different. At Arizona Raft Adventures or AzRA, the owner, Rob Elliott, and his guides used paddleboats where everybody in the boat had to paddle, and then at the bottom of the rapid you shared responsibility for a good run or a flip or whatever happened. You could turn to each other and say, "We did that!" instead of looking at the guide and telling him what a great job he did.

So at AzRA running paddleboats was part of the whole process. And we've had people come back many times with us. And some of them—not all of them—liked the paddleboats, but one thing that a lot of them really enjoy is coming back and feeling like they are part of that whole process rather than just sitting in a ride in Disneyland or something. And I think that's part of that Outward Bound thing, too, sharing it—many early AzRA guides had worked for Outward Bound.

The other thing that AzRA and many Grand Canyon companies were known for was pushing their guests to the point where the people usually walked away thinking, "Wow! Not only did I do things that I've never done before, but now I have skills, after two weeks on the river, that I never had before, and I can actually take these skills with me and do some of this stuff." Maybe not taking a boat down Grand Canyon, but hiking or walking along a ridge or hiking in the desert, whatever. And there were some people that were primarily responsible for that, in AzRA, that were just incredible about getting clients out of their groove and experiencing new things. And I was lucky enough to be exposed to those mentors and it meant a lot to me. AzRA is probably the second biggest influence in my life as far as outdoors go. Some of those guys are lifelong friends and we do private trips together.

I remember my first trip down Grand Canyon with Bob Melville, a good friend, and it was real high water. It was 1984, the first time I did a commercial Grand Canyon trip, and I was rowing a baggage boat. The water was real high and I'd only done the canyon twice before, at a much lower level. We went down the first day . . . I had a heavy baggage boat. . . . The boats in front pulled over to camp that night and I went to pull in and I didn't realize the dynamics of the water. There was a huge boil along the bank and I never made it to camp.

I finally made it over a quarter of a mile downstream or so. I thought to myself, "Well, I've blown that. That's the last trip I'll ever do with AzRA." I was apologizing over and over, and they said, "Just forget it." We went down, and they pulled over and we started camping and, of course, they started making gin and tonics right away and everything. I pulled up and grabbed my gin and tonic and was talking to Bob Melville and I said, "God, Bob, I am so sorry I missed that camp."

He looked at me and he said, "I don't care about that." He said, "Hell, you can even flip your boat. I don't give a damn," he said. "But don't burn the cake!"

And his message was . . . yes, be safe, yes, have good runs, as good as you can, but the whole thing of taking people down the river has more to do with helping them set up their tent, finding their beer wherever it is in the raft, so they can have a beer in camp, telling jokes, cooking good meals, listening to their fears or their stories. Ninety percent of guiding is the human aspect of it. Each year 26,000 people float Grand Canyon, not counting the guides.

Before starting in Grand Canyon I got into medical school, and I remember vividly being in Omaha, Nebraska, on winter days where it was a blizzard. I'd get a postcard from my brother and he was in New Zealand, guiding down there, or these guys would be in Nepal. I really questioned whether I'd made the right choice at that point, 'cause a lot of the people I had worked with were in river guiding as a profession, instead of a summer job. I really thought about dropping out of medical school.

Instead, I got permission to extend medical school a year so I would do four months of rotations in medical school and then work on the river for two months. It was great! Probably didn't do much for my medical education, but it was great for me, and it kept my mind in a good place. I figured when I went to my internship in New Mexico that that was going to be the end of my commercial river running. So I started down in Albuquerque. I did my internship year, which was tough, kind of biting the bullet, but when I got into the psychiatry part of the internship, I did have some weekends off, finally, and I had met a guy down in Santa Fe who had a rafting company there. And he was friends with guys I had known through the grapevine. He said, "Well, if you ever want to guide during the weekends just for the hell of it, come on up."

And so I started doing it and it was great. It was during the high-water years on the box of the Rio Grande. It doesn't get that high anymore, but I just thought that was great. A bunch of us would go up and I could usually bring some friends, and we'd go down. I met a couple of guys there that had worked on Grand Canyon for AzRA. So when summer would roll around, I'd usually take three or four months off and go and guide on Grand Canyon. By then I was in love with Grand Canyon, and I was working down there whenever I could.

I remember coming back one time and I walked into the VA hospital, there in Albuquerque, where all the residents write their notes, and here was an old friend of mine in internal medicine. And he looked like he hadn't seen the sun for three years. He had a two-day growth of beard, just coming off call, and he looked at me. I had just gotten off a raft trip fully tanned and in shape . . . and I walked in and he just looked up at me and said, "Fuck you!" He didn't even say anything else.

So I finished my residency and by then I had decided that I was never going to work full-time again, especially in psychiatry. So ever since I've worked some situation where I had about 50 percent time off. And that's allowed me to pursue rafting. My dad used to say that my profession was whitewater guiding and medicine was a hobby.

Being a Shrink on a Raft

You could always see the head boatman when he's coming at you. They'd start out, "Karls, this one's for you." Now, that happened a lot with simple medical stuff. But when it was a psychological issue, it was always pretty interesting, and you know, you get those on a trip sometimes and it can be a spectrum of things. At one end of the spectrum is a medication question.

A gal I used to date one time had a woman who halfway through the trip started wearing a bucket upside down on her head and never took it off again the rest of the trip. It got to the point where it was scary for people. They're going into a rapid and this woman's got a bucket over her head, a bail bucket. AzRA flew one guy out who was frankly paranoid and thought that this other guy and his son were trying to kill him. And then you get depressed people. I've seen a couple of very significant cases of alcohol withdrawal on the river, where AzRA lets you take, I think, a case of beer on a trip and by the third day this guy was out of beer and was going into withdrawal, and that can be a medical emergency.

And then there are personality disorders where you get some guy that just likes to fight, and he's picking fights with either the passengers or the guides. It can be a real challenge. That's really where the expertise of a good head boatman comes in.

One time I was on a trip where there were two army nurses. They were sisters. They hadn't seen each other for a while, and they had both seen combat and everything, so they were really letting their hair down. They had walked into Phantom Ranch, and we were camped just below a big rapid. They got pretty drunk and decided that they were going to swim across the river at night.

Thank God, they announced that they were going to do it, and they said, "We're going to swim across the river." And I said, "Well, you can't do that!" And the more I said, "You can't," the more they said, "Well, we're going to. We're army nurses and you're not going to tell us what to do."

So I went up to Dave Lowry, the trip leader (TL), and I said, "Dave, there are these two gals that want to swim the river. They're drunk. It's night out. The water is forty-two degrees." Dave just looked at me and he smiled and he said, "Well, I know how to handle this."

He went up to them and he said, "You gals want to swim the river?" And he said, "Well, that's up to you. I just ask one thing." And they said, "What's that?" and they were all psyched because they were going to swim across the river. He said, "Well, it's going to take you about thirty seconds to get to the other side of the river, at least, maybe a minute. And all I ask is that you get into the water right now up to your neck in the eddy and stay there for twenty seconds. If you can do that, you're welcome to swim the river."

Well, of course, they got in there, with their clothes on, up to their necks for twenty seconds—and they were completely freezing. There was no way they were getting back in the river. They got out and he just smiled and walked away, and the case was solved at that point. It sobered them up. Rather than fighting these two gals who were going to push back against any authority, he knew exactly how to handle it.

It seems to me there was a shift in the National Park Service's attitude toward evacuations for psychological reasons about ten years ago or so. A lot of people, they thought psych stuff was not as important as medical stuff . . . and I think there were a couple incidents where psychiatric issues happened and they were very serious. The National Park Service realized that someone that's mixed up for whatever reason on the river, it's just not a good place for them.

It can turn into a medical problem real fast if their judgment's impaired, and I also heard an archaeological site was destroyed. A woman who may have been psychotic destroyed this archaeological site because people had been giving her a lot of latitude. Now if you call the Park Service and you say, "I've got somebody that's out there and they need to get out. They aren't hurt yet, but they might get hurt. Something's going on"—in the most serious cases, they come in immediately.

Some problems arise with the person that is used to being in total control of their corporation or their business, twenty-four hours a day, seven days a week, and now they are in a place where someone else, someone without a college education a lot of times, is telling them where they need to crap, what they can eat, what to wear, and all this. Some people just cannot let go of that responsibility. They can be their own kind of problem.

On the other side the head boatman, for one reason or another, may have a pretty good ego, himself or herself, and those egos face off and that's where the skill comes in. And that was one thing about having a female head boatman. Oftentimes, power-oriented people would have problems with a woman telling them what to do and everything, but when it came to the face-off, it seems to me women almost always knew how to handle it better than men.

Lead Guide Skills

The face-off would be something like, somebody takes off their life jacket because they feel like it's chafing their neck or something and they're lying back on the boat. Maybe it is day eight or something, and they've had enough of somebody telling them what to do, and the boatman says, "Hey, you need to put your jacket back on."

And the guy says, "No. Shit! I paid three thousand bucks for this trip and it's flat water. I'm not going to put my jacket back on!" And at that point, the guide says, "Oh, no, John. You really need to put it back on." And he says, "No, I'm not going to." Well, there it is. There's the face-off.

There were two women who were experienced head boatmen with AzRA that I worked with my first year. And those women were just uncanny at their ability to get people to do things that they didn't want to do—either because of the face-off situation or maybe because the person was too scared or whatever. I remember this gal who was not the typical professional boatman. She could get close to these people. Maybe there is the guy that thinks he needs to be in power out there in Grand Canyon, but subconsciously he realizes he doesn't know what he's doing. Suzanne was so nonthreatening to those kind of people that she could sit down and talk to them and say, "What's going on here?"

She had this southern drawl and she could buy 'em a beer, whatever, and maybe she'd say, "You know what we should do? Let's go throw a bail bucket on that guy over there. He looks hot," or something like that, to break the ice. Pretty soon, she was right there with him and he was doing right what she said, and maybe that person by the end of the trip would make a jump in his personal improvement.

AzRA runs their trips with five boats, five guides, and two assistants, so Maggie, my wife, was often my assistant. The assistants are girlfriends, they're wives, they're husbands, whatever, or maybe somebody from the office. The point is, they're not a guide and they're not a person that wants to be a guide, usually. They're just friends. But if there's ever a problem on the trip, the people often go to the assistants first instead of the guides.

If there's a peer problem, they go to the assistant first. And, again, it's that liaison thing. The assistant's not a boatman, they're not a passenger, but they're somewhere in between. They're not as threatening. The people feel like, and oftentimes they're right, that the assistants understand the problem better. Maybe they've been able to see it more than the guides, 'cause the guides are thinking about so much at once, but that was true almost without an exception.

The assistants would come to us and say, "Hey, Bill, this guy just said . . ." and then you'd go talk to them and you'd talk to the passenger. Your "peers" on a raft trip might be somebody you've never met before, and you're going to go complain about a total stranger to another stranger? Yes, sometimes that was a big problem. Those kinds of problems show up most often in a semicharter.

There are all sorts of different trips, but the normal AzRA trip would be a couple of single guys or women, here's a couple of couples, there's a family over there. Here's four firefighters from Pittsburgh. . . . It's a real mix. There are also trips that started out a charter of eighteen and then at the last minute, two people cancelled and two new guys signed on for the trip. They might be totally different from the rest of the clients.

Personal Transformations and Play on the River

One guy in the beginning of a trip said, "I have horrible acrophobia. Anything over fifteen feet off the ground and I have a panic attack. Been that way all my life and I know it's going to be a bummer because I'm not going to be able to go on a lot of these hikes." We put in at mile zero and at mile fifty we pulled over for a hike. We'd done a couple of hikes that he hadn't been able to go on; finally we were right above Nankoweap at Dinosaur and we were going on this exploratory hike that we knew was going to involve some elevation change. He said, "Can you take me along on this trip? If I have to turn back, I will, but I'd like to try it." He stuck with us. It was very interesting route finding. There was a big chip of Redwall limestone that had fallen off and we had to climb behind it and everything. It was very exposed.

Finally we went out to the edge of the mesa overlooking the river right above Nankoweap. It's a drop of eight hundred feet or more, straight off, and he said, "Will you walk with me to the edge of that?" and I said, "Yes." And the guy's wife was with him. The three of us walked to the edge and he was just petrified. I said, "You know what? Let's just stand here, right here, not move. You're perfectly safe. Let's just stand here until you feel comfortable." We just stood there for about fifteen minutes or so. . . . Finally, he said, "Well, okay, we can go now. I feel okay." So we walked back down and we looked back up to where we had stood. It was about a sixty-foot overhang where we were. He went and got a beer and just looked up there for about two hours. The rest of the trip he did all the hikes. About a month after the trip, I got a postcard from him. It was a picture of him and his wife up on this peak and they said, "This is what we do now!" I thought that was pretty cool.

There was this one guy, Jon Hirsh, who worked down there and knew more routes out of Grand Canyon than anybody I had ever met. He was a climber, an explorer, and everything, but if there were four elderly ladies on the trip or something he would stay behind with them. He'd say, "I'm going to stay here with these gals and you guys go on." The second everybody was out of camp he'd go cut willow twigs and teach these ladies how to make those split-twig figurines. He would go collect clay and they would make pots out of it, and then if we had a dutch oven that night, they would fire their little pots in the thing . . . and those gals went from feeling like outsiders to becoming enthusiastic over the next big hike, 'cause it meant they could play with Jon some more.

And there were certain people who worked for AzRA that specialized in finding those two people who didn't relate to anybody else on the trip. They would focus on them and get them to have a good time, either by bringing them into the group or finding what they were interested in and making sure that they had a good time. And if you're the TL with one guide like that on the trip, it's a tremendous responsibility off your shoulders. If you've got a team of guides and assistants that you're working with, where they all have different skills, it's just a joy to run trips.

Boatmen and Trip Leaders

A characteristic of good lead guides includes breadth of knowledge. It's huge things such as safety, and it's small things such as knowing which camp has shade or which camp has sun. The other characteristic is flexibility. On a fourteen-day trip on Grand Canyon, you can make up a list of things you want to do before you put on the river. We want to visit all these sites. We want to camp at these places. Here's my itinerary for the river, but somebody's going to be in the camp that you wanted to use. An hour before you'd like to be pulling over and starting dinner, another group is in your chosen campsite.

So the good TL says, "Oh! Here's plan B," and if that's taken, here's Plan C, without thinking about it. Those are the good TLs. They understand privacy.

If somebody's hiking at North Canyon, you don't stop and hike with them. You give them North Canyon and you go on downstream a little bit and hike something else by yourself so that your people have an experience by themselves, not with forty other people, and you've just given the other group their solitude.

There are some guides that don't do that. They say, "Here's where we're going, wham, wham, wham. I don't care if somebody's there or not." But the guide that knows all of the alternatives, especially the little secret camps and the secret hikes, they're the good TLs. It's essential for clients to bond with nature and with the canyon.

One characteristic of a good nonhead boatman is to respect the head boatman's decisions, whether they're what you would've done or not. That is a huge thing. AzRA is an experienced enough company that on any trip of five guides, two or three of them will have been previous TLs. They've got their own secret places, and some of them are really good about saying. . . . They'll pull you aside and they'll say, "Have you ever camped at . . . on the left down here about a mile? It's a cool camp and there's actually a hike there we could do."

And if the TL says, "Yes, that's cool, but I think we'll do this other thing," at that point, the guide says, "Oh, cool! I love that place. Let's do it!" There are other boatmen who argue, "Oh, I've done that five times already this summer." You hear that all of the time. The boatman will say, "Oh, let's not hike there. I've done it five times." But the guests haven't. You've got twenty people who have never been down Grand Canyon. None of them have seen it. And the boatman is bitching because he's been up there on a specific hike five times. Well, hey, I go to the same office every fricking day I work. I'm not bitching about that. Well, hopefully not too much!

The maturity of the guides to accept the TL's plans is essential. If the head boatman makes the wrong decision, then when other boatmen hop back in the boat, they may start talking about the head boatman to the passengers. That is really damaging, because the people talk among themselves. So as soon as you get to camp, they'll say, "Well, Bill told me that we really passed up a cool place there. We should've hiked there. And Bill should've stopped." And it's an ego thing.

If the TL's not around, a guide will say to another guide, "God, why didn't we go to Havasu Creek, man? It's so beautiful up there. I can't believe. . . ." And the other will say, "Oh, yes, I can't, either." They are not realizing that the TL has the big picture in his or her mind. The key is communication, open communication with the guides. So, every night, if the TL meets with the guides and says, "Here's what I'd like to do tomorrow. What do you guys think?

Okay?" it gives them a chance to express their ideas, talk about it, maybe follow some of their ideas.

Another thing a good TL will do at the beginning of the trip is say to the guides, "Is there anything any of you would like to do this trip? Particular places you would like to camp, hikes you'd like to do, exploring, or whatever?" and then he writes those down. He keeps those in mind as you go down, and a good TL will come up to you and say, "God, Bill, I know you really wanted to hike Redbud Canyon, but it just didn't seem right today. I'm sorry, man." And just that contact lets you know that he remembered, that he didn't forget, and that's all it takes.

Every morning you have a trip meeting where you say to everybody, "Does anybody have any questions? Does anybody have any thoughts about what they'd like to do, or problems along the way?" Rarely does anyone speak up in that format, but sometimes they do. At least you are giving them the chance. And then you tell them about today, and you emphasize that the schedule has to be very flexible because there are other people on the river. A friend once told me that he learned the Colorado by hitting every rock. I learned to guide and lead trips by making every one of these mistakes . . . repeatedly!

Passengers and Trip Dynamics

Once we got to Diamond Creek and derigged. It was a great trip. It was just high energy. . . . Everybody loved everybody. Everything was perfect and taking out was sort of like the catharsis, after all the work. Everybody was just so high. It was 110 degrees there at Diamond Creek and we sat there with the boats. . . . The shit cans were perfectly in line, symmetrical. . . . There was nothing more to do and we're sitting there and we're waiting for the trucks to come in and something has obviously happened, because they are two hours late. We have no lunch.

So, anyway, we're sitting there and because it's the last day, the guides have totally shot their wad. I mean, they just didn't have any more to give. And at that point, they hadn't dug down in. And you could hear the grumbling. You could hear the guides start saying, "Ah, the office, sometimes . . . the drivers . . . sometimes they do this to us . . ." instead of saying, "We don't know what happened, but we've got good people in the office. We've got good drivers. They're going to be down here for us."

But the guides were just so exhausted from their excellent trip that the interesting thing was, we were going to blow it in the fourth quarter with the last two seconds left. We were going to let people walk away from that trip with a totally negative last experience. And we were so tired that we didn't have the wherewithal to notice it, nor did we know how to deal with it. So we just sat there in our little shade and grumbled and were swearing at the office.

All of a sudden a passenger stood up and he said, "Well, I have a story I could tell. . . ." And everybody said, "Oh, what's that?" And he launched into this incredibly interesting story about Emory Kolb or something, a book he had been reading on the river, and he told this story for an hour, and at the end of it, it was like being hot and jumping into cold water; all of a sudden we came out of the fog. The guides realized that this guy had just saved the trip, probably (and we were going to get twice the tip we would have). We appreciated that.

On Grand Canyon there are several variables on every trip. One is the people, the passengers. The next is the guides. The third one is the weather. And then, maybe you can throw in the water level some, but that's not so much of a factor. But those other three things are big.

So if it's nice weather and you've got jovial people and good socializing guides, by the first night you can say, "Wow! This is going to be a really good trip." Most trips have a family of four here and a family of three there and then some single people and a bunch of couples. If you see one of the guys from one of the couples over there talking with the kids from the family, and then the mom from the family is over there talking to a couple of the single people, you know it's going to be a good trip, because at that point, they realize that a big part of the trip is experiencing the other people on the trip. And that just carries through.

The biggest thing, probably, on Grand Canyon that jells the trip are rapids. And so the gorge on the upper half starts around Unkar and goes all the way to Phantom Ranch. On the lower half, it starts at Phantom Ranch and goes past Crystal Rapid. Those days are justifiably where everyone is nervous. They are checking everybody's life jackets. We are going over safety. If somebody in the boat falls out, you've got to pull them back in, whether they're your wife or a total stranger.

You get people really keyed up, almost like going to battle. Some guides really play it up great. You don't have to play it up very much because it's real, but some guides throw a little extra something in there. It gets people frothing at the mouth. And that night, after the gorge, the trip has always jelled. And then some of the other bigger rapid days can do it, too, or a big hike can do it, like a big all-day hike. Those things put icing on the cake, as far as jelling the group, for sure—something that people have experienced together. And, ironically, if something goes wrong, it can do that, too—a flipped boat; maybe, hopefully, just a minor injury; maybe an evacuation back to camp, where all the passengers help, or whatever. But the sooner it happens, the better, for sure.

Private vs. Commercial Trips

Commercial trips have their problems at times, but I've never seen an actual trip split up into two trips like a private trip. On private trips usually you're going with your friends, so automatically you think that everyone has similar values. But I've never seen trips split up like private trips: I'll take one stove. You take the other. We'll see you later. The homogeneity of passengers on a trip can be good or bad. If people are too alike, any flaws in the group are magnified. You see that in charters with commercial trips. If everybody is a certain way and there are negative aspects to that way, it just becomes a huge issue, whereas if you've got a couple people that aren't that way, it buffers it a little bit.

One of the things that I noticed was that the charters always had the greatest potential to be weird. And they also had the greatest potential to be the best trips. An example of that would be this charter from Alaska. They're still coming every other year. I was on the first trip with them, and everybody there was older but athletic. They were friendly. They were go-getters. They wanted to help in the kitchen. Those were their positive aspects, and since they were all that way, it turned into a special trip, the kind only the most experienced guides get. The Alaskan trip—it's every other year. These same guys come back. It is THE golden trip. And only the people that have been there the longest get to go on it.

But charter trips can be awful or great. There was a group of doctors who had gotten jaded with Western medicine, so they decided that they were going to study herbs. They studied mind waves with chanting and all this other alternative stuff. And they had traveled the world seeing places together. And they had just huge egos. All doctors have huge egos, but this was beyond. And they were upper-echelon financial people, they had been pampered, and also all of them had an agenda. That's one thing to always watch with a charter. Is it just a bunch of friends coming on the river together, or is it some company or somebody with an agenda who wants to bring people down to Grand Canyon to act out that agenda there?

On this doctors' trip, all of them had an attitude and it was all the same attitude. If it had been just one or two people that had that attitude, it would have gotten tossed around, maybe expressed a little bit. But because everybody had the same attitude, it became this huge force that was to be reckoned with, and it was wild! I think there were actually fists thrown on that trip.

I mean, imagine inviting the world's CEOs on a raft trip together. Everybody that was used to telling everyone else what to do. . . . If everybody on the trip had that idea, obviously it can't be played out because not everyone can be the leader, especially when you are not knowledgeable about the activity that's going on. And here's another one. There was a group of guys that got together—I think they were firefighters. They all got together and said, "Let's do a raft trip on Grand Canyon. It'll be so great. We're not going to invite any women. [That was idiotic to begin with!] We're going to smoke cigars every night at the campfire. We're going to drink lots of beer and tell dirty stories. . . ." And they showed up and there was a woman guide on the trip. They refused to go. They said, "Call your office up and get another male guide up here because we're not going on the river with this gal." At the put-in!

The head boatman said, "Well, boys, if you don't want to get on the river, that's fine with us, but we're going. And I'm not taking Ginger off this trip because she's one of our best guides." At that point it was like the head boatman saying, "Fuck you!" and the firefighters were saying, "Well, fuck you!" And they were at the put-in and nobody was moving. Something eventually was worked out, but it was ironic because this female guide could have kicked all their asses, plus she had much better campfire jokes! Anyway, the clients had a preconceived idea of what the river was going to be like, instead of just saying, "Let's do a river trip." And if it hadn't been a charter, that conflict would have been diffused. If there were six guys that wanted to smoke cigars and tell dirty stories, they could have gone and done that, but the rest of the people would have etched away at their beliefs, and they would've been brought into the larger group.

On private trips, if you have three TLs and one of them has an idea that's different from the other two, it's a conflict. My brother went on a private trip this spring where it was a big issue. For instance, one guy wanted to bring wine every meal, and he wanted that to be a trip cost. Well, there were people on the trip who said, "I don't drink wine. I'm not going to pay for somebody else's wine." It became a huge issue. On a normal commercial trip where you've got people that don't know each other, it diffuses the tension.

Letting Go

We had a rule at AzRA that six trips was a full season, and seven trips was a really busy season. If at seven trips you needed to be off the water, you needed to listen to people saying, "God, man, your season's over," That eighth trip could really hurt you.

There's a phenomenon on Grand Canyon called the "belly to belly" or "back to back." On a back-to-back trip you get off the river, go to the trip dinner, go to the Laundromat after the trip dinner to wash your clothes, and you're loading out the next day. A belly to belly is when you can't go to the trip dinner. Somebody's already up at the ferry rigging your boat. You get off the river and hop on a van and sleep while they drive you up to Lees Ferry again. AzRA had a policy where they didn't do bellies to bellies unless somebody got hurt or something. And you could only do one back to back a year, once, which was really rare. If they didn't have a big break after that, it almost ruined the guides for the rest of the season. Isn't that something? It was that exhausting, both physically and mentally.

If the back-to-back guide was the TL, then you really had to help take as much responsibility off their back as possible, because they were still bouncing from the last trip. They needed to concentrate on the schedule of the current trip and the people, not worrying about tying the boats up at night or something. If you get a couple of guides burned out on a trip, sometimes the TL would have to pull them aside and say, "You guys, this is a river trip. It's fourteen days long. I don't care what you did off the river or what you did last trip, but you're here on this river trip, right now. You need to suck it up. We're going to have a good trip." But those kinds of talks, only a good TL can do that. I had a few friends pull me aside a few times . . . I really appreciated that.

There were two guys famous for being great people the first eight days, and then they just died. They barely got off their boat. They stopped talking to people. It's like they went into a clinical depression from day eight to day thirteen. You just can't do that. That was another thing that AzRA management talked about: pace yourself. Don't spend everything you have socially in the first eight days of the trip, where the last five you're not going to be talking to any of the customers or going on any of the hikes. It would be better for you to be middle Joe than the coolest guy on the river for the first eight days and then just die.

Here I am, the old guide, and I did a trip with four guides that were all younger than me, all new-generation guys. I came there after working for twenty-three years for that company, and three of the four guides didn't even know who I was or had never heard of me. I was thinking, Whoa!

We went up Havasu Creek and a young guide named Matt just started doing his play thing in this little miniature rapid, taking these guys through and letting them swim upside down and everything. First I thought, "Oh, that looks kind of dangerous to me. It'd be foolish." Then I tried it, and man, it was fun. I couldn't get enough of it. Well, all of a sudden I realized Matt is an

Bill Mobley, a veteran Arizona Raft Adventures (AzRA) river guide, concentrates on reading the water as he blasts through Kolb Rapid in Grand Canyon. Though over four million visitors come to Grand Canyon each year, only 26,000 people run the river corridor. Trips put in at Lees Ferry and often take out at Diamond Creek, which is 14 days and 226 miles downstream. Photo by author.

incredible guide. He knows how to get these guys having fun and everything. Just because it's something that I haven't always done, doesn't mean that these folks aren't going to have as much fun or more than from my techniques. That was letting go of my ego, too.

I was from Nebraska. I was never a sports star in high school or anything. Guiding in Grand Canyon allowed me to feel confident. It allowed me to do that at a later time in my life, and eventually it allowed me to be a leader, which helped me feel good about myself. It was a huge decision for me to stop guiding on Grand Canyon. My wife Maggie watched me struggling with it, to not have the sticker on the back of your truck that says "Grand Canyon River Guide." That's part of who I am. To let that go, to say that's what I was, was huge, but it feels good.

The later years I was guiding, I was the guy saying, "Oh, it's day ten. We've got four days left." And I found myself doing that on good trips with good guides and good people. If it's not enough fun being in Grand Canyon with good people, something is wrong. You've got to make a change. The older guides always said that. When you're counting the days, it's time to do fewer trips.

Study Questions

1. Early in the chapter it said, "On dry land they (boatmen) wake up at night missing the sound of moving water." Why do you think rivers are so compelling?

2. "Eventually all things merge into one and a river runs through it. The river was cut by the world's great flood and runs over rocks from the basement of time. On some of the rocks are timeless raindrops. Under the rocks are the words, and some of the words are theirs. I am haunted by waters." What is meant by this quote? What "haunts" *you?*

3. Name three major risks that are specific to running white water. Considering the many dangers associated with river running, why do river runners believe the dangers are "worth it"?

4. What can we learn from river trips that we cannot learn anywhere else? How do extended river trips provide for life-changing epiphanies? What are the advantages and disadvantages of river runners joining together in short-lived floating communities? What is "river time"?

5. In the essay "A Psychiatrist Looks at River Trips," Dr. William Karls writes about psychological conditions that can be a detriment to the health of other clients. What mental and psychological dangers can one encounter on long river trips?

6. Consider the idea that progress can be defined as simply "leaving things alone." In today's society, progress is usually defined by production and expansion. How is it that progress could be landscape protection? What would it take for Americans to adopt this concept in a variety of settings?

7. Why is it that despite so much being expected of river guides, they are only paid a little above minimum wage? Could this be a reflection of the importance of nature and rivers to the general public?

8. The United States has three and a half million miles of rivers and streams. Fewer than 2 percent are free-flowing, impeded by more than 5,500 large dams and almost 80,000 small ones. What would we lose as Americans if we were to lose all of our naturally flowing rivers to dams? What do we learn about ourselves and riparian habitats on multiday river trips?

CHAPTER 6

Solo in the Southwest
Going Out and Coming Back

He was alone. He was unheeded, happy and near to the wild
heart of life. He was alone and young and willful and wild-
hearted, alone amidst a waste of wild air and brackish waters.
>   —James Joyce, *A Portrait of the Artist as a Young Man*

I admitted that we—I—had made a big mistake. It's a funny
thing, trouble. It arrives with a smile and leaves with a sneer.
You keep thinking you can *will* yourself out of it. But panic is a
wild card that erases common sense.
>   —Kim Heacox, *The Only Kayak*

A venturesome minority will always be eager to set off on their
own, and no obstacles should be placed in their path: Let them
take risks, for Godsake, let them get lost, sunburnt, stranded,
drowned, eaten by bears, buried alive under avalanches—that
is the right and privilege of any American.
>   —Edward Abbey, *Desert Solitaire*

The core of many outdoor education and wilderness programs is a solo experience. Solos have long been a fundamental part of courses led by Outward
Bound and the National Outdoor Leadership School. Time away from others,
outdoors in solitude, can be frightening, overwhelming, and also deeply satisfying, leaving a lasting sense of confidence and an inner resilience. Clifford
Knapp and Thomas Smith explain in *Exploring the Power of Solo, Silence, and
Solitude*, "What can be found in the purity of the wilderness can be found
nowhere else as readily. It is in such settings, with beauty, harmony, and grandeur, that human beings can best come to know themselves by connecting
through the living earth to a higher presence and purpose."[1]

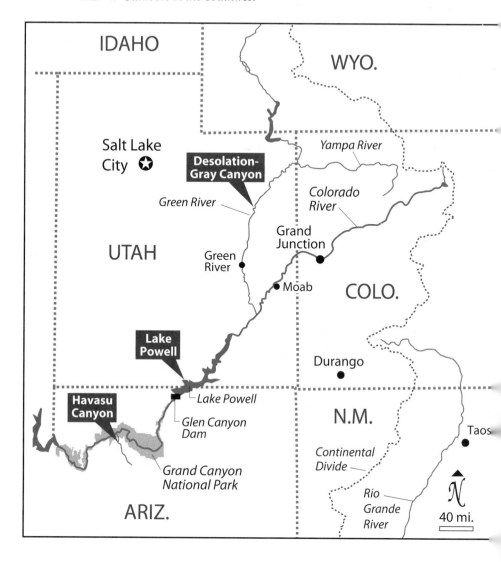

Nineteenth-century conservation leader John Muir understood. He wrote, "I only went out for a walk and finally concluded to stay out, til sundown, for going out, I found, was really going in."[2] For me, my first solo hiking experience was in an unlikely place—the shortgrass prairie, the high plains of southeastern Colorado, and the broken country that borders New Mexico. At sixteen I went in search of Jesus Canyon.

I grew up on a quarter section of land with no live streams and only a few cottonwood and elm trees near an irrigation canal constructed in the late nineteenth century. Above the canal the prairie stretched for miles with songbirds in the spring, and raptors, especially red-tailed hawks, posed on telephone posts and ranch gates. My family had moved to the plains and would not stay there. After I finished high school we all departed. It was a safe place to grow up, but I longed for different landscapes—mountains, canyons, deserts.

I ached for a world without barbed-wire fences and the monotony of farm and ranch life. I enjoyed the long horizons and distances as far as I could see, but I lived where the land was private and all the plant and animal life domesticated. I wanted to see vegetation other than farmers' crops of alfalfa, milo, and dryland wheat. I wanted to see public wildlands with large mammals such as mule deer, elk, and bears. And I did.

At sixteen I hitchhiked north into Yellowstone National Park and then across western Canada and down to Olympia, Washington. What got me started, and what urged me on to my first solo backpacking experience into remote southern Colorado canyons, was Terry and Renny Russell's book *On the Loose,* which my brother received for Christmas and promptly gave to me because he was an urban dweller from Chicago just home for the holidays.

I was sixteen that Christmas. The book struck me like a revelation. As a light snow fell outside our southwestern-style home and a log shifted in the fireplace grate, I read the whole book in half an hour and then I read it again, as I have all my life. The book's premise is simple: two guitar-playing brothers from California in a battered Willys Jeep pickup truck leave home in search of wilderness settings, and in finding wilderness, they find themselves. The boys grew up near Berkeley and knew David Brower of the Sierra Club, who published the book in 1967 at exactly the right time—the beginning of the environmental movement.

With its careful calligraphy, poignant quotes, color photos, wilderness insights, and youthful exuberance, the book became an instant hit and eventually sold more than a million copies. Terry Russell wrote that he and his brother traveled "not to escape from but to escape to: not to forget but to remember: We've been learning to take care of ourselves where it really matters. The next step is to take care of the places that really matter. Crazy kids on the loose; but on the loose in the wilderness. That makes all the difference."[3]

I was electrified by the promise of wild settings far different from the flat farm and ranch land all around me. I had to get out and get gone, but how? My friends all wanted to chase girls and drive faster cars. Being outdoors meant nothing to them except putting on irrigation boots to change a set of water flows for farm fields or saddling up horses to push cows from one pasture to the next. I wanted to explore, be on my own, on the loose.

After school I worked in a printer's shop feeding envelopes into an old handpress and doing other odd jobs. The printer, wearing khaki shirt and pants, always chain-smoking Pall Mall cigarettes, would tell me stories about the high plains when I worked Saturday mornings. If I kept listening he'd keep talking, and I wouldn't have to work as much. I asked him about local history and remote places, and he spoke about wild turkeys in a distant area named Jesus Canyon in Baca County, Colorado, southwest of Comanche National Grassland.

I became excited and started looking for maps. Finally, in the local title and abstract office I found a Baca County topographic map and realized that where I wanted to go there were no roads. The fact that it was all private land didn't occur to me, and it really made no difference. The ranches were so remote that if I came close to the right canyon I could be gone for days and no ranch hand would ever find me. The canyons drained south into New Mexico and the east-flowing Cimarron River. No one lived there.

In my little town there were farm implement stores but no outdoor recreation stores, yet somehow I found an old canvas pack and filled it with canned goods. I located an ancient, smelly, U.S. Army surplus goose-down sleeping bag with feathers poking out of the material, a couple of Boy Scout canteens, and an aluminum mess kit. I didn't take a tent or a sleeping pad or a camp stove. I didn't think I'd need them, and I couldn't buy those items, anyway. I'd slept out on our 168 acres, but I'd never done a solo hike before. Yet I was inspired, so I borrowed the family's Plymouth Fury station wagon and took two-lane blacktop and dusty, gravel roads south toward wild turkeys, adventure, and a hike that changed my life.

Closing the car's tailgate, rolling up the window, looking across wildflowers at the first sign of a descending canyon, I knew I'd arrived. Just finding this place meant my trip was a success before I even began. There were no trails to follow, only cattle paths. I had driven southwest into a part of southern Colorado where dryland farms gave way to ranches and then nothing but short grasses and finally piñon-juniper trees. Even barbed-wire fences seemed to have disappeared in this, one of the least settled areas in the American West.

At the last small town where I'd stopped, just a dot on the map, really, a handful of buildings had been abandoned in the 1930s. I found an open gas station with one pump and a battered, bruised mechanic, up to his elbows in grease. In the filling station's office on a dark, scarred desktop, I laid out the only map I had. "Jesus Canyon?" he said. "Never heard of it."

Deeply disappointed after having driven two and a half hours and determined not to go home a failure, I urged him on. "But it must be here somewhere. Will you look at this map?"

Clearly not used to reading, he squinted and stared, then smiled and laughed. "Ah, now I know. *Si, comprende.* You meant Hayzeuss Canyon, *porque, no?*" he said, giving the Spanish pronunciation to the English word "Jesus." Then he laughed again, shook his head, and pointed me down a dirt road.

So I'd made it to the rancher's gate. I was in a different ecosystem with juniper trees and cacti on south-facing slopes. I began to walk, occasionally swigging from the canteens banging against my sides. Several hours later I'd still not seen any wild turkeys, but I'd dropped deeper into the canyon, with evidence of abandoned Hispanic homesteads, the occasional cabin with fallen roof, collapsed corrals, and above me turkey vultures slowly circling in the wind.

In a small one-room cabin, on a creaky, unpainted wooden tabletop amid years of dust, I found an offering, a gift, and a memorial. In a bleached-white cow bone, one of the large, lower vertebrae, someone had placed a small bouquet of flowers and grasses. As I came upon it the bouquet was lit by a shaft of sunlight beaming through a low-slung doorway. The tenderness of that feminine gesture touched me. As I turned in the silence I wondered what had happened to the family who had lived there, worked so hard to wrestle a livelihood from the soil, gone broke, and moved on.

Climbing up out of the narrow valley I found an ancient, rusted, double-bitted hand ax with a weathered oak handle. What a prize! I tied it to my pack next to my sleeping bag, but it worked loose. By the time I reached the rim it was twilight, and somewhere along the game trail I'd walked, the canyon reclaimed the ax. As the Russell brothers had written, "Adventure is not in the guidebook and Beauty is not on the map. Seek and ye shall find."[4] In those quiet, abandoned Colorado canyons, I was alone and I was looking.

As the sun set I made a small wood fire to cook canned stew. I moved a few stones and laid out my sleeping bag, and as darkness came up the canyon walls and shadows increased, I could see opening after opening in side canyons that stretched forever. I'd walked into New Mexico and seen no one all day—just the occasional cow and frightened, fleeing female deer.

I was young. I was headed to college. I had no idea what I wanted to do or be, but that night sleeping under the stars, nothing mattered. Using a shirt as a pillow I stared into the bright, broad band of the Milky Way and thought about all the places I had yet to visit. I believed then, as I believe today, actor and race car driver Steve McQueen's motto: "I'd rather wake up in the middle of nowhere than in any city on earth."[5]

The rest of my solo time in Jesus Canyon remains a blur to me now, except for one powerful moment when I climbed out on the rim, circling back toward the car, and found a windmill, a stock tank, and an old, rusty Chevy pickup with a Colorado license plate on it valid the year I was born. How can that be? I thought, as I stopped in my tracks. For every year of my life this truck had sat there, rubber rotting, frame sinking, mice playing in the metal glove compartment. Stunned, I relived all the angst and emotion of being a high school student ready to leave home steeped in fear and wonder and nervous expectation. For every emotion I'd ever had, every argument with my parents or risky move with a girlfriend, this truck had been there silently waiting for me.

Soaking it all in, trying to understand my short, sweet life and my mystical relationship to this aging, dented truck, suddenly the windmill twenty-five feet above me began to slowly turn, and a rusted shaft rattled against the water tank, yet where I stood it was warm, hot even, without the faintest breeze. Something profound was happening to me here on the canyon rim, alone. No one knew where I was. I could feel no wind and yet the windmill had begun to slowly pump water. I wondered if the truck was magic, if I'd been too long by myself, if I would ever find the station wagon and drive safely home. Quickly, I backed away, headed north toward the ranch gate. I never looked over my shoulder and I've never returned.

If that old ranch truck had been waiting all my life for me to arrive on that canyon rim, the canyon itself had also been waiting. Out of that experience was born my love for distance, for long hikes, solo sunsets, and wide, western spaces without houses, farms, or fields. I came away with a few fears mastered and the personal promise of future trips into hidden landscapes where knowledge of nature lay waiting to be revealed. I'd gone on a vision quest without knowing it, and in those broken canyons I'd begun to find myself.

That truck stirred something profound in me. That rusty, dented pickup with a license plate the same year as my birth was standing by aging daily, sinking into prairie soil. Meanwhile I wanted to mature, to come of age, to step into a life filled with adventure. I wanted to roll down the highway and not stand still, broken, tired, waiting for life to happen.

I have come to believe what Terry and Renny Russell wrote in *On the Loose* about getting to know landscapes:

> One of the best-paying professions is getting a hold of pieces of country in your mind, learning their smell and their moods, sorting out the pieces of a view, deciding what grows there and there and why, how many steps that hill will take, where this creek winds and where it meets the other one below, what elevation timberline is now . . . which contour lines on a map mean better cliffs or mountains. That is the best kind of ownership, and the most permanent.[6]

We need wild country, and we also need to be alone, to go out solo, and to return with a renewed sense of purpose and a deeper commitment to the people and communities we love. I was sixteen then and didn't know much. I still don't, but I know what I need and it's always more time outdoors. The poet Walt Whitman understood. He wrote in "Song of the Open Road," "Now I see the secret of the making the best persons, / It is to grow in the open air and to eat and sleep with the earth."

~

Today, I still hike alone, although most of the time I'm not really solo because I have a trusty canine companion. It used to be my Border collie mix Charlie, but now it's my Springador (a springer spaniel–Labrador mix) named Finn. He's great. And I've promised my wife I'll never climb a peak, traverse a canyon, or enter an alcove where he won't go, but what she doesn't know is that he'll go anywhere because he has four-paw drive and a lower center of gravity than I do. Yet just having him around keeps me out of trouble—most of the time. A safer rule when hiking is about companionship: three is for safety, two is for caution, one is for fools. But as a college professor busy with classes I also need quiet time, alone time, and I find it in the canyons of southeastern Utah. I follow Ed Abbey's example in *Desert Solitaire* that the best of companionship is oneself.

On a blustery November day, seeking a route up a side canyon to the top of a mesa, I'd picked a horribly clogged and choked route with head-high tamarisk and willows. The side canyon desperately needed thinning; a little strategic lightning strike would have done the trick, because it was choked beyond belief and impenetrable even to local Hereford range cattle that seemed to have gone everywhere.

Finally, I found a route up, or I thought I did. Finn went first as dogs are wont to do, and as I followed, forty or fifty feet above the bottom, I slipped. Could have been loose gravel, I don't really remember, but it was a quick, sharp fall about halfway down that left a nasty bruise on my arm and an even sharper realization that I was, indeed, alone. I'd left no message on my truck's dashboard. No one knew where I was or when I'd be back. Dumb. I could have really hurt myself and damaged more than my pride.

Shaken, I descended, then found another way up. I topped out into late afternoon light and knew my exploration was almost over. Time to hoof it out before darkness, so we did. I'll never give up solo excursions, but I need to be more careful; we all do. And that's what this section is about: the issues related to solo adventure and important survival skills that we must have in

Summer clouds form over slickrock near Moab, Utah, home to both Arches and Canyonlands National Parks. Remote trails in Canyonlands provide superb desert hiking, especially in the Needles District; but be careful about carrying enough water. Hikers can get lost in the Maze. Photo by author.

the Southwest's backcountry. Perhaps the most important skill is attitude, not what's in your pack.

~

How do accidents happen? What's the difference between clear-headed decision making and thinking muddled by emotion? Experts in psychology and risk management have learned that survivors remain calm under pressure, do not panic, and have a particular mindset. They can deal with a drastically changed environment and adapt to conditions such as severe weather, injuries, or unexpectedly rising rivers. Survivors of accidents face reality first and foremost because fear is good, but too much fear is not.

Just like I rock scramble solo, risky business is fun for most who seek relaxation and challenge outdoors in the Southwest. But in wilderness settings there is an absolute need to pay attention, to remain humble and flexible, and to experience a Zen sense of openness to the world around you and rapidly changing conditions.

Because trivial events can shape an accident, you always need a bailout plan, an exit strategy. In his excellent book *Deep Survival: Who Lives, Who Dies, and Why,* Laurence Gonzales explains that accidents "are made up of conditions, judgments, and acts or events that would be inconsequential by themselves," but they cascade together—one simple mistake leading to other errors. Then at a critical time unexpected things create a serious problem.[7] Such wilderness tipping points require calmness and calculated actions, but only 10 to 20 percent of people can remain composed under stress.[8]

Experience may not help. Sometimes it's experience that creates the problem and betrays us, because we've done the same skill hundreds of times and don't think clearly about changed conditions or other factors. Wildland firefighter Peter M. Leschak explains that he waited too long to evacuate from a fast-moving fire because "I'd perhaps been too well trained. I was a victim of a common fire service mindset: Can do!" He had forgotten his instructor's admonition, "When in doubt, don't."[9] The clear lesson in wilderness and dangerous settings is to trust your instincts and to spend enough time outdoors so those instincts are raw and real and not smothered by too much time distracted by cell phones, iPods, and idle chatter.

Remember the rule of threes: a person can live only three minutes without oxygen, three days without water, and three weeks without food. We all have two brains, an older instinctual brain or our lizard brain, and a newer, modern neocortex that constitutes our consciousness. That's the wizard brain. In any true emergency, you'll get complicated and often conflicting messages from both the lizard brain or your instincts, and your wizard brain or your mind. Pay keen attention to both. Depending upon the circumstances, sometimes you might need to override either one brain or the other.

Accidents may also be caused by peer pressure and group dynamics in which individuals are cajoled into doing things against their better judgment and beyond their skill level. Often time is an issue—trying to accomplish a backcountry goal within a prescribed opportunity window only to have that window start closing because of bad weather, ground conditions, or misjudgments. Laurence Gonzales states, "Plan for everything to take eight times longer than you expect it to take. That allows for adaptation to real conditions and survival at the boundary of life and death, where we seek our thrills."[10] Also realize that the old metaphor of "conquering the mountain," or the ski run, or the rapids, is outdated. It's a far better idea to have humility and surrender yourself to the landscape rather than try to dominate it. Think clearly. Know where you are and where you've been.

Actual survival in dangerous conditions is often about the inner resources we develop in wilderness settings. To avoid getting lost, make mental notes of where you've been, keep maps in a notebook, carry a small pair of binoculars and stay tuned into your location, watch your backtrail, and always carry your own gear and map in case your group splits up. Remain open minded.

The single most important trait of survivors is their ability to quickly adapt to changed conditions. Whether it be a broken leg or a shattered ankle, they've planned ahead. In a situation in which an entire group is in danger, put the needs of the group ahead of your own. Get focused. Praying works as part of full-body alertness. Gonzales argues, "Starting from the moment of the accident it is necessary for a survivor to take control of his situation."[11] The experience of wildland firefighters also applies here; Standard Fire Order #10 is to stay alert, keep calm, think clearly, and act decisively.

Humor helps. Why not? You have to laugh at the absurdity of certain situations. If survivors can laugh at themselves, they also remain connected to a larger community of parents, friends, spouses, or children, and they draw strength from knowing that their loved ones expect them home even if a hospital stay will be part of the reunion. Survivors never consider themselves victims. They adapt to changing situations, assess their supplies and resources, become creative with what may be in the bottom of their packs, and plan routines and small tasks to both calm their minds and get them home.

Arizona photographer Lon McAdam planned a solo nine-day trip into Rough Canyon deep in the Superstition Wilderness. He shattered a kneecap when he tripped too close to a boulder. He dragged himself to water, he had all the supplies he needed, and he'd left a specific route plan with his wife, who alerted search and rescue. Seven days later a sheriff's helicopter arrived from Flagstaff. He stayed near water, kept his mind occupied, and took photographs. McAdam explains, "The rescuers said those types of rescue operations normally turn into body retrieval. They said I stayed alive because of a positive mental attitude, and I know that's true."[12] Some people make it out of wilderness and wild natural settings, but they never manage to return home.

There's a call of the wild that can be compelling, even overwhelming. Consider Everett Ruess from the 1930s, who hiked into Davis Gulch on the Escalante River in what is now Glen Canyon National Recreation Area and was never seen again.[13] Or think of Christopher McCandless, who took off on the Stampede Highway in Alaska for a solo jaunt that cost him his life. Too full of himself, convinced that he knew it all, when McCandless finally realized he was in deep trouble, it was too late. But then he learned a valuable lifesaving lesson, one I teach all my students. Wilderness experiences are about going out and coming back, about being solo and secure because of love and family ties that bind. Yes, we need to strike out on our own, but the most successful explorers do so within the warm matrix of family and friends. McCandless, who had shunned intimacy most of his short adult life, came to know that. In one of his last journal entries he wrote, "HAPPINESS ONLY REAL WHEN SHARED."[14]

There is, indeed, a wilderness within, and we need to be cognizant of our connections to other people, our responsibilities to ourselves and our communities. Sometimes outdoorsmen and women go too far and can't come back. Something happens and it's just too hard to face society and so-called civilization again.

Astronauts circling the earth, marveling at the fragile blue-green planet that we live on, call it reentry. And reentry from the quiet solitude of space can be as difficult as it is for an extreme skier who loves to bask in deep power, or a river guide who has spent weeks on the water being sung to sleep by Class III rapids. For Katie Lee, wooden boat river runner, naked canyon hiker, and folksinger, reentry has been a constant problem. She writes, "We riverphiles are plagued as soon as we leave the sounds of a living river behind. Since I can't heed the call but two, maybe three, times a year, the stimulus will begin a few days before takeout, along with a nagging apprehension: How long before I'll be here again? Soon? Next year? Never?"[15] She explains that the sense of loss in returning to mainstream America is because "for days—weeks if I'm on a long trip—I empty my brain and wash the decks of my mind to live within the moment, the hour, the present. . . . I don't calculate or plan, just take it all in, alerting my senses to respond to Nature and her stimuli; to accept it, become a part of it, and move blissfully along with the flow of the river."[16]

Katie Lee, the goddess of Glen Canyon, explains, "Because in the Glen's sensuous, gentle beauty and silence I had time—a soft ticking of the oars—to take a good look at where I was, discover its hidden secrets and allow the canyon's primitive spirit to spark a memory in my own genes." She adds, "I was familiar with the heart-stopping significance of 'being there' as opposed to 'been-there-done-that'. Adrenaline flowed, but it was no roller coaster ride; it was a lesson in how the earth was put together, how insignificant we are in the overall plan, how little we know and will ever know, and how the best we can do for ourselves, in our little time, is to try to discover who we are, then make the best of it."[17]

Some people discover who they are and also define themselves by ultimate outdoor challenges. Just as mountain climbers ache for first ascents and canyoneers long for first descents, river runners dream of being first down wilderness rivers. One man was. In the 1930s Buzz Holmstrom from Coquille, Oregon, built his own wooden boat, and when a friend begged off on a long trip down the Green to the Colorado and on through Grand Canyon, Buzz shoved off alone to become the first solo boatman to float the entire river system—impossible now because of late twentieth-century dams. He accomplished an enormous feat of endurance and yet he wrote in his journal, "the bad rapid—Lava Cliff—that I had been looking for, nearly a thousand miles,

with dread—I thought: once past there my reward will begin, but now everything ahead seems kind of empty and I find I have already had my reward, in
the doing of the thing. The stars, the cliffs and canyons, the roar of the rapids,
the moon, the uncertainty and worry, the relief when through each one." And
yet the relief did not remain. Nine years after his epic quest, on the Grande
Ronde River, Buzz took his own life at age thirty-seven.[18]

What is it about being face to face with raw nature, doing difficult tasks
involving split-second decisions, timing, pacing, agility, utter focus through
a rapids or on a cliff, and yet not having the ability to cope with day-to-day
trials and tribulations? In Telluride, Colorado, a forty-three-year-old writer,
skier, climber, and mountaineering guide died of an apparent suicide. According to the *Telluride Daily Planet,* Andrew Sawyer "was part of a new wave
of extreme skiers who'd decided to conquer the steep and avalanche-prone
peaks of the San Juans," including "a first descent of the ultra-steep Wire Couloir, among others." He'd cowritten a climbing guide, *Telluride Rocks,* and he
wrote newspaper stories about skiing the San Juans. His brother, Hugh Sawyer, commented that Andrew had battled depression, "but his best medication was being outdoors, being active and skiing, climbing, biking, bagging
peaks. Doing the things he loved."[19]

In a final essay, an ode to Telluride's extreme skiers, Andrew Sawyer wrote
about others but could have been describing himself with the lines, "Despite
the risks, there will always be an unquenchable pioneering spirit in someone, somewhere, that will lead us past new boundaries, and even those of us
who have faced death eye-to-eye are likely to be there, stepping out into the
unknown."[20]

Facing death may be the last great adventure, but there is no encore.
There's no second chance. What is it about being outdoors for long periods of
time that makes it hard to return from the wilderness? Hard to settle in for the
daily grind? River guides feel it, too. After months of being kings and queens
on the Colorado through Grand Canyon, with passengers depending upon
them for everything from food to personal safety, it's hard to be out of work in
winter, flipping burgers in Flagstaff, waiting for spring. Unneeded. Unwanted.
Some guides can't handle it. Author and guide Brad Dimock explains:

> For many of us, reentry is the hardest and most disturbing part of
> the river experience. Having just recently discovered (or rediscov-
> ered) an entirely different world, it is wrenchingly difficult to leave it,
> to return to the so-called real world. Which, one wonders, is the real
> world after all? The more one comes to know and love the River and

the solace it brings to the soul, the more miserable reentry can be. Those of us who spend our lives on the River experience the symptoms on an even greater scale. The end-of-the-season blues can be devastating, and worst of all is the time when a boatman must leave the river entirely for family, health or fortune. Many of us never fully reenter, but live out our lives trapped in some limbo, torn between the pain of parting from the River, and the joy and vision it has given us to carry through life.[21]

Legendary Colorado River guide Curtis Hanson, nicknamed "Whale," killed himself after countless river trips through the canyon. Rebecca Lawton writes, "Fall is when we've lost so many of the boatmen who have taken their own lives. Our community mourns them still, daring men have met their end that way—enough so you could call it an occupational hazard."[22]

In dangerous Crystal Rapid, Lawton had flipped her eighteen-foot raft in cold, high water. Hanson had been waiting below in an eddy and came to the rescue in his thirty-three-foot pontoon rig "in full control of his boat and the situation—a supreme look of concentration on his face, his blue eyes in a focused squint, his blond hair properly tousled and wild. He looked as brave as George Washington on the storm-whipped Delaware, as alert as a predator about to pounce, as unwavering as if he were my best friend."[23]

Yet if Curtis "Whale" Hanson had the cool and calm to save others, he could not save himself. "One of Whale's greatest attributes was his love for his friends and his willingness to listen to others as they talked through their troubles. Unfortunately, he rarely asked for any help in return," states a brochure for a nonprofit organization, the Whale Foundation, which works to help Grand Canyon river guides with health and employment issues as well as postseason depression.[24] Gonzales writes in *Deep Survival*, "To live life is to risk it," and "so intense is it for some that it seals their fate; once they've tasted it, they just can't stop. And in their cases, perhaps we have to accept that the light that burns brightest burns half as long."[25]

As for the romantic poet and artist Everett Ruess from Los Angeles, who vanished into Utah's Escalante country in 1934, one of his last letters to his brother is revealing of Everett's mindset. He wrote his brother Waldo:

As to when I shall visit civilization, it will not be soon, I think. I have not tired of the wilderness; rather I enjoy its beauty and the vagrant life I lead, more keenly all the time. I prefer the saddle to the streetcar and star-sprinkled sky to a roof, the obscure and difficult

Wilderness and wild landscapes inspire hikers, who sometimes go out but do not come back. In the Southwest mystery still surrounds the 1934 disappearance of young artist Everett Ruess, who was last seen as he headed into the rugged canyon country near what is now Lake Powell. His burros were recovered from a makeshift corral in Davis Gulch, off the Escalante River, but Ruess himself was never seen again. Ruess is pictured behind his burro from the Rainbow Bridge Expedition. Photo courtesy of the Center of Southwest Studies, Fort Lewis College.

trail, leading into the unknown, to any paved highway, and the deep peace of the wild to the discontent bred by cities. Do you blame me then for staying here, where I feel that I belong and am one with the world around me?[26]

For Everett, there was no reentry. He went out but did not come back.[27]

This section details solo experiences in the Southwest and some of the joy, exultation, and dangers that await those who venture forth alone.

Notes

1. Clifford E. Knapp and Thomas E. Smith, eds., *Exploring the Power of Solo, Silence, and Solitude* (Boulder, CO: Association for Experiential Education, 2005), 6.

2. Quoted in Knapp and Smith, *Power of Solo,* 3.

3. Terry and Renny Russell, *On the Loose* (Layton, UT: Gibbs Smith, 2001), 9.

4. Ibid., 85.

5. Ibid., 20.

6. Ibid., 37.

7. Laurence Gonzales, *Deep Survival* (New York: Norton, 2003), 102. For other survival stories from a medical perspective, see Peter Stark, *Last Breath: The Limits of Adventure* (New York: Ballantine Books, 2001).

8. Gonzales, *Deep Survival,* 24.

9. Peter M. Leschak, *Ghosts of the Fireground,* cited in Gonzales, 112.

10. Gonzales, *Deep Survival,* 122.

11. Ibid., 184.

12. Quoted in Kelly Kramer, "Man vs. Wild," *Arizona Highways,* November 2008, 18–19.

13. To learn about Ruess, see his *A Vagabond for Beauty and Wilderness Journals,* ed. W. L. Rusho (Logan, UT: Gibbs Smith, 2002).

14. Jon Krakauer, *Into the Wild* (New York: Villard, 1996), 189.

15. Katie Lee, *Sandstone Seduction: Rivers and Lovers, Canyons and Friends* (Boulder, CO: Johnson Books, 2004), 120.

16. Ibid., 122–23.

17. Ibid., 123.

18. See the award-winning biography by Vince Welch, Cort Conley, and Brad Dimock, *The Doing of the Thing: The Brilliant Whitewater Career of Buzz Holmstrom* (Flagstaff, AZ: Fretwater Press, 1998). After traveling eight thousand miles in two years and opening the West, Captain Meriwether Lewis also could not adjust to American society and killed himself at the age of thirty-four. See Stephen Ambrose, *Undaunted Courage* (New York: Simon & Schuster, 1996).

19. Patrick Healy, "Andrew Sawyer, Writer and Hard-core Skier, Dies at 43," *Telluride Daily Planet,* May 28, 2008, 3.

20. Ibid. For an extended discussion of suicide versus accidental high-altitude death, see Eric Blehm, *The Last Season* (New York: Harper Collins, 2006).

21. Cited in Lee, *Sandstone Seduction,* 124.

22. Rebecca Lawton, "Faith in the Dry Season," in Christa Sadler, ed., *"There's This River . . .": Grand Canyon Boatman Stories* (Flagstaff, AZ: This Earth Press, 2006), 183.

23. Ibid., 184.

24. Brochure for the Whale Foundation, P.O. Box 885, Flagstaff, AZ 86002-0855, www.whale-foundation.org.

25. Gonzales, *Deep Survival,* 278.

26. Quotation from Everett's last letter home to his brother Waldo Ruess, November 11, 1934, Escalante Rim, Utah, in Ruess, *Vagabond.*

27. See Andrew Gulliford, "Everett Ruess: Lost and Found in the Southwest," *Mountain Gazette*, July 2009. For recent scholarship see David Roberts, *Finding Everett Ruess: The Life and Unsolved Disappearance of a Legendary Wilderness Explorer* (New York: Broadway Books, 2011), and Philip L. Fradkin, *Everett Ruess: His Short Life, Mysterious Death, and Astonishing Afterlife* (Berkeley: University of California Press, 2011).

Goddess of Glen Canyon

Jerome, Arizona

There's a rumor in the historic copper mining boomtown of Jerome, Arizona, that river runner, rabble rouser, and eco-activist Katie Lee celebrated her eightieth birthday by riding naked on her mountain bike through town. "But that's not true," smiles Katie as we sit barefoot on her back porch. "I was only seventy-eight."

I made the pilgrimage to Jerome to interview this five feet four petite blond who crafted a unique life bouncing between Tucson, Hollywood, Utah's Canyon Country, and coffee shops and nightclubs across America. I'd come to talk with a living legend who beginning in 1954 rafted and floated the Colorado and San Juan Rivers two dozen times before floodwaters rose behind Glen Canyon Dam, creating Lake Powell and inundating one of the loveliest canyon systems on the continent.

Lee was one of the early women to run the Grand Canyon in wooden boats, and she reveled naked in the warm waters of the Glen exploring nameless sandstone canyons. Northern Arizona University library intern Bonnie Roos explains, "She's a gun-toting, guitar-strumming canyoneer and a lace- and high-heels wearing Hollywood starlet" who grew up in Tucson hiking Sabino Canyon and hunting buckskin on Mount Lemmon. In the 1940s from Tucson's Little Theatre she gravitated toward film and radio roles in Hollywood and wild all-night excursions into cantinas in Nogales, Mexico, to add to her folk song repertoire.

Katie worked for NBC, both on radio and daytime television, and performed in USO shows across the nation with Bob Hope. But by 1953 she realized Hollywood was not for her and became a full-time folksinger. During the McCarthy communist witch hunt she refused to be an FBI informer against other actors and singer/songwriters, and she assumes the FBI started a file on her. Lee comments, "By now it would contain several protest songs . . . many appearances at rallies and marches against nuke tests, mines, dams, air pollution, gravel companies, uranium dumps, wilderness depletion, logging, paving, fencing . . . hell's fire, you name it. Now the whole earth needs our help, not just my poor old rivers."

Between her Hollywood days and her folksinging success, she discovered river running and it changed her life. She's been married three times. She's a Scorpio on the cusp of Libra and freely admits that her first love is Navajo sandstone and the seductive, sinuous way that water shapes rock. For three consecutive years, beginning in 1955, she went down the Glen on "We Three Trips" with photographer Tad Nichols and boatman Frank Wright.

Often wearing only tennis shoes, Katie Lee, the goddess of Glen Canyon, personally explored all ninety-six side canyons before rising floodwaters covered them. She told me, "Every single canyon had a different personality. That first year I was so amazed by the forms." Katie explains, "We never carried water on our hikes thru Glen. The streams ran cool and clear." Over time her amazement and wonder became acute anger as the mysteries of Glen Canyon disappeared under Lake Powell. She's never forgiven the Bureau of Reclamation, which she calls the Wreck the Nation Bureau.

Terry Tempest Williams notes, "Katie Lee is a joyful raconteur, a woman with grit, grace, and humor. She is not afraid to laugh and tease, cajole and flirt, cuss, rant, howl, sing, and cry. Katie Lee is the desert's lover. Her voice is a torch in the wilderness." Lee's first book, *Ten Thousand Goddam Cattle,* documented cowboy songs of the West. Her second book, culled from her journals, is an elegy to Glen Canyon titled *All My Rivers Are Gone,* now reprinted with more photos and additions as *Glen Canyon Betrayed.* She's also written *Sandstone Seduction: Rivers and Lovers, Canyons and Friends,* where she remembers, "I think back on the time when each canyon devoured me, pulling me ahead of the others to clamber over obstacles that would reveal whatever the next bend held in secret . . ."

Sitting on her back porch, looking out at Jerome's vast copper pits, she says, "I've written hundreds of letters. I've done the best I could. I had a talent and I used it. If I've changed anybody's attitude, I've done my part." In her kitchen a plaque states, "Old guitarists never die, they just lose their pluck," and above her front doorstep, weathering in the Arizona sun, are the letters SING. Katie Lee's colorful living room contains wooden snowflakes, sculpted lizards and snakes, brightly lit stained glass, first-edition books on the Southwest, and guides to plants and birds. Her garden produces a hundred tomatoes yearly.

If her soul is still in Glen Canyon, the documentation of it is down in the basement on shelves lined with books, CDs, old posters, backpacks, suitcases, and photographic slides in their original boxes stored in leather cases. Her archives, her stories, and her hundreds of photos will go to the Cline Library at Northern Arizona University. The eventual sale of her house will create a small endowment for the Katie Lee Collection. Future generations of scholars and students will be moved by her life to make the Southwest a better place, more in balance with our desert environment.

Katie Lee inspires. Young women who've spoken with her and heard her play guitar write, "Thank you for doing what you do and being the wild spirit that you are." And Katie's advice to all of us? "Get out and walk. Don't get a guidebook. Find out where the quiet places are and explore." That's sound advice that has kept her in perpetual motion for ninety years. Keep it up, Katie. We need your wit and wisdom.

A Turquoise Trap in Glen Canyon

Katie Lee

Katie Lee did numerous Glen Canyon trips with Frank Wright, whom she named Big Feets, and Tad Nichols. Tad she called Tadpole and E. T. She referred to his busy eyebrows as caterpillars.

————————

I

Journal Note: September 28 (Afternoon), 1955

Watch the ball in the roulette wheel, how it hugs the sides at high velocity, then drops to the bottom when it slows down.

That's us. We've dropped to the bottom in a tangled heap and are laughing so hard we can't get up. Moki Canyon has a short side piece about a mile up from its mouth, alveolated with bowls eight to ten feet deep, oval to round, sides not too steep to stick to *if* we move fast enough. We speed around the sides in a nearly horizontal position, both arms out for balance, and don't fall in until we run out of breath. I never thought Frank could move that fast,

From *All My Rivers Are Gone* by Katie Lee. Copyright © 1998 by Katie Lee. (Boulder, CO: Johnson Books, 1998). Republished as *Glen Canyon Betrayed: A Sensuous Elegy* (Flagstaff, AZ: Fretwater Press). Reprinted by permission of the author.

and I was *sure* Tadpole couldn't, yet here we are like six-year-olds, trying out our wings of freedom. Back in the prehistoric days, this canyon must have fairly buzzed with activity. Its great length, many springs, side canyons, and abundant ruins give testimony, and I get the sensation that we're not the first little kids that played around these water pockets when they were empty. But I'm hot and sweaty after all this zooming, and I know where there's a full one, clear and cool, just a little way—in sight even.

"You guys go on back and start lunch, huh? I'm gonna do what comes naturally in the cool, cool water up yonder," I say, thumbing the direction over my left shoulder.

Bigfeets' eyebrows raise and he starts to say something, but changes his mind and waves. They head back to the boat. When I reach the pothole, I'm glistening with sweat, my face burning hot, salt running into my mouth. Not wasting a moment, I flip off my tennies, undo my shirt, pull the scarf from my head, run down and jump in.

The clear, untouched pool accepts me into its emerald depths like a big drop of water. I am part of it . . . it is part of me . . . surely I was once a fish. I dive down again and again, feel the water-fingers softly caressing my hot face, tracing my underarms, my neck and breasts—nipples raised hard against the cold. Its roiling crisscrosses my back and bottom, moves between my legs and up through my toes like feathers, tickling. I bubble up from the depths, many degrees colder than the sun-warmed upper layer, yet with all my motion, no sand has stirred from the bottom. Looking down, treading slowly, the spectrum around my head flickers and waves in many shades of green, like an aurora. The pool lies half in, half out of the sun, and though the water is not going anywhere, it seems to move against me still, even as I lie immobile on its surface. I flip and turn, purring to the sensual caress. I have dipped into a private treasure and am wrapped in the arms of the True Gods.

Maybe ten, maybe fifteen minutes.

Cooled to a most pleasant temperature I swim back to the sunny side to climb out. Foot slips and I fall back in . . . try another place close by, but slip again. There are no handholds on the dry, smooth sandstone above me. The pool is not full to its sloping rim, so from above, the sides seemed to slope gently, yet from down here they are quite steep. Far *too* steep! I suck in a quick breath of panic. Frank and Tad have probably not even reached the boat, a mile away.

Cool it, girl! Get hold of yourself. There *has* to be a foothold somewhere. Anxiously, I swim around the sides, checking every spot, then notice that in so doing I've made slick those grips that might have been possible when dry, yet I go at them all again only to compound the problem.

I swim back to the place where I ran down and jumped in; it is no longer in the sun. My tennis shoes lie just out of reach, my scarf trailing over the nearest one.

"*I'm not alone,*" I say aloud. "They'll come back for me when I don't show up for lunch."

Then with sheer stupid hope that Tad has stopped along the way to take more pictures, that they are still within earshot, I yell as loud as I can. . . .

"Fra-a-nk! Ta-a-ad! Big-fe-e-ets! E. T.! Come back!"

The sound echoes obediently from the vaulted wall six hundred feet above—then silence, stubborn and absolute. You stupid, *stupid* little fool! You knew better than to get yourself into this fix. Dumb, incautious idiot! How long? How long before they'll realize something's wrong? How long can I hold on? The sun is leaving the pool altogether and I am suddenly *very cold.* The few places where I can grip the slick wall are inadequate if I'm going to shiver . . . and I'm starting to shiver now. There's a fingerhold I can stick to with much effort, but I must t-tread water m-most of the time . . . legs so c-cold . . . feel like they might cramp. Float on my back . . . but I stirred up the cold from down deep . . . no warm water . . . on top . . . anymore . . . need to keep moving . . . keep moving.

Bigfeets . . . hurry! Tad . . . please!

I tell myself I must not cry. But the only warmth in my whole body is spilling unrestrained from my eyes.

"Goddess and bitch . . .

. . . carnal glory . . .

. . . *killing loveliness.*"

II

Oh-o—oh-oh, poor me. . . . I have loved and treasured your canyons beyond any other place on earth; I've trumpeted your magnificent beauty, mystery and wildness. How can you do this to me? All my hard work gone to pot . . . pothole! Those wrangle-tangle days, the sadness (now I'll never be able to bring my son here), the hope, the pressure, the seeking to understand my worth—trying to find the real me, through you. . . .

THE VERY REASON I CAME HERE!

Too bad, cutie—the lurching walls call back to me—watch your step next time. Been here three years, heard all sorts of tales about my inviting-but-treacherous potholes, and think you're so "in step with the stone" you can walk straight up my walls, huh? Think again, stupid. Serves you right!

Does not! I trusted you (can ever a love be trusted?), you deceptive, tempting, teasing. . . . You're like the Sirens; you made it *easy* to walk in, and now, you sonofabitch. . . .

Whoa, wait a minute . . . walk in . . . *walk* out? Maybe . . . if I can. . . .

Then I get mad. Teeth-grinding furious. Totally pissed. I'll be damned if I am going to drown in your pot. . . . ⚬

I goddamn well will not!

Journal Note: Wednesday Afternoon, September 28, 1955 (Continued)

Half an hour later, when I hear them coming, I am sitting in the sun up from the pool, putting on my tennies.

The blue scarf spread beneath me nearly matches the color of my bod. I pull on shorts and halter, teeth chattering noisily, more now from nervous exhaustion than the cold. Bigfeets takes in the scene, cocks his head, and sucks in the corners of his mouth, deliberating. "Well, thank the Lord!" he says, a smile dissolving his puzzled look.

E. T.'s reaction is different. "What in bloody hell are you up to? You like to scared us to death. We thought. . . ."

"You lookin' for Indian ruins," I chatter, "that why you're up here?"

"When you didn't come for lunch. . . ."

Frank grips Tad's arm to silence him, looks at me, then at the pothole and asks simply, "How'd you manage to get out?"

"You'll never guess."

Tad kneels and touches my leg with the back of his hand.

"My god, woman, you're an icicle! How long have you been in there?"

"Until about ten minutes ago."

"Why didn't you call?" asks Tad.

"Holy sh . . . nuts, I *did* call. Every thirty seconds at first—takes a bunch of energy to holler, and I was getting thin on that."

"We were too far away to hear you by that time, anyway," says Frank, shaking his head.

Still chattering, my legs trembling, I hold out my hand for Frank to pull me to my feet. Tad begins to rub my back and arms vigorously. "We need to get your circulation going. You do her legs, Frank; she's the color of a blue heron."

He kneels on the slanting sandstone, takes on the rubbing task, and reminds me: "Thought I taught you about jumping into strange potholes last year."

Folksinger, writer, and eco-activist Katie Lee, now 93, lost and found herself in the beauty of Glen Canyon, exploring and naming many of the side canyons before waters began to rise at Lake Powell in 1963. She is now shocked and chagrined at the motorboat traffic that frequents Dangling Rope Marina. *The Pagan, Katie Lee in Glen Canyon, 1957* by Martin D. Koehler, photo courtesy of Katie Lee.

Giving him a shamefaced look under dripping hair, I admit, "I thought you did too, Bigfeets. Obviously I failed to get the message, but after this one you don't have to worry."

"Tell us how you got out," Tad insists.

"You get in there and see if you can tell how I got out."

"I'll be damned. . . . you crazy?"

"I'll clue you it doesn't help to get the sides wet."

"You didn't find any footholds?"

"Nary one."

Frank, whose mind works at solutions through observation, not deductive reasoning, begins to hone in on the solution. He notes the scarf lying at my feet. "Your scarf . . . it had something to do with your escape, right?"

"You're getting warm . . . me too. Thanks, guys, you can stop rubbing now, before I look like a pink flamingo."

"Where were your tennis shoes?" queries Frank.

"Way out of reach."

"How far?" "Right here." Kneeling, I show them, some four feet above the pool's surface. Then I go after my shirt, which has almost blown into the water.

E. T. twiddles his cowlick and mutters. "The scarf. Mm-m, did you wrap it around you to get purchase on the rim?"

"What makes you think I had the scarf? I didn't. It was lying on top of my tennies . . . one of them."

"Then why is it wet?"

"Okay. After screaming for you, and crying, and cussin' out this canyon and this pool like you wouldn't believe . . ."

"I would," smirks Tad.

". . . the wind whipped its tail through here and blew one end of it closer, where I could just barely reach it."

"So you wrapped it around you to get purchase on the slope."

"I tried that, but it didn't work. First, with my hands just laying it across there, it slipped; then around my boobs trying to flutter kick and spring out. No way, slid back and scraped hell outta me poor knockers besides."

Frank, still on the observation track, asks, "How come only *one* of your shoes is wet?"

"Ah-ha!"

"Did it blow into the pool?"

"Nope."

Bigfeets picks up my scarf and stretches it out between his hands. It is over a yard long and wrinkled at one end.

"You tied a knot in this, didn't you?"

"Un-huh."

"Let's see." Tad takes the scarf from Frank, reties the knot, goes down to the pool, and wets it again. "Ah-ha!" he triumphantly concludes. "You flipped the knot at the shoes and somehow got one to you, put it on, and were able to get purchase and climb out! *Ole!*"

"No."

"Did you get *both* shoes?" asks Frank.

"Yup."

"Like Tad said?"

I nod. "Did one fall in the water?"

"Wow! I'll say, and I almost lost it. I made about twenty passes with that scarf. The shoe would roll over and stop, roll again and turn vertical, then on the last fling it really came a-runnin'. Plop . . . and down it went. I got it just before it sank past my toes."

While they try to imagine the rest of my scene, I unknot the scarf, tie it around my head and sigh, "Let's get out of here while we still have some of the afternoon left to explore. Besides, fellas, I'm hungry!"

We circle the pool and climb to the saddle of the bowl. E. T. stops and looks back. With long, slender fingers, he rubs his cheek and chin whiskers, now starting to itch with a five-day growth, and pulls his fighting caterpillar brows together in puzzlement. "How'd you get your shoes on and manage to keep one of them dry?"

I raise my eyebrows, blink, and say nothing.

"Okay, then, how would I get my shoes on if I were in there and still keep one foot out of the water while . . ."

"You wouldn't."

"Aw, c'mon, Kay. Are you going to tell us how you got out of there or not?"

"No. You have to use your noggin; might find yourself in the same fix someday and need to figure a way out. Hugh Cuttler told me he nearly drowned in one like this, and he's no dummy. You're a fart smeller—scuse me [snicker], I mean a smart feller, so . . ."

Frank interrupts with his ear-wiggle. "Maybe she didn't put the shoes on *her feet.*" "Right!" I shout.

"On your boobs?" he blinks.

"Ohferkrissake, E. T., be serious."

"On your *hands!*" Tad's caterpillars unlock. I nod and smile. "On your hands. Well, I'll be damned. And you must have gotten the purchase by kicking up out of the water with your hands *in your shoes* under you."

"You got it. Know what a flange is? We used to do it at the beach on parallel bars—rest your hip bones on your elbows, body and legs straight out. That's why I've got a skinned nose, or haven't you noticed? From the flange, I fell forward into the sandstone." I poke my nose under his and cross my eyes.

He smiles, says, "I'm sure glad it was no worse," gives me a pat and little hug. "Ouch! My boobs."

"Oh . . . uh . . . sorry."

I have a last look at my prison—an emerald eye, quiet now, reflecting the sky, bright rainbow colors from the oil on my body twisting on its surface. An innocent and beautiful intaglio jewel, ten feet across, set in pink sandstone—no longer lethal, not even enticing now that it's out of the sun and I'm no longer hot and sweaty. There it will lie, unruffled except by passing wind and birds dipping to drink; sinking a bit each day as evaporation and seepage shorten its life, until only waterbugs and strange, primeval shrimp are left to lay their eggs in the mud and die with the pool, their progeny wiggling to life with the next filling.

I should still resent my captor, but I don't. A priceless canyon lesson has been learned for keeps. What I resent is my carelessness, not being more in tune with nature and her whimsical tricks. I need to sharpen those instincts dulled by civilization so that one glance will warn me: This is not a movie set, baby. This is the real thing. Watch it!

The Silk That Hurls Us Down Its Spine—Colorado Plateau

Ellen Meloy

The trouble seems to be this: Although I should be in my raft, at the oars, savoring a morsel of uncooked Utah, I am not in the raft. On hundreds of trips down Colorado Plateau rivers over a span of eighteen years, I have been in the water on countless voluntary swims, but I should not be in the water now. Although I have often been stupid, I have just been extremely stupid. My need to pursue absurdity has overwhelmed my need to stay out of trouble. Moments ago I rowed to shore to investigate a pair of bright yellow objects in a debris pile. I pulled the raft's nose up on the sand and clipped my life jacket to the frame. I walked away. While my back was turned the river nibbled the raft off the sandbar and carried it off in its swift current. The raft is empty. I am swimming after it.

Excerpted from Ellen Meloy, *The Anthropology of Turquoise: Meditations on Landscape, Art, and Spirit* (New York: Pantheon Books, 2002). Used with permission.

The boat holds life jacket, transportation out of the desert, drinking water, and food. . . . The ghost voices of everyone who taught me anything about river running have stopped screaming *Always tie up your boat* long enough to start screaming *Always stay with your boat*. I am staying with my boat—it happens to be a considerable distance ahead of me, careening down the canyon. I am alone. I might drown. I have not finished living yet.

This must be the moment for a split-second flashback of my entire life: learning to read, eating avocados, my hamster Ned, my flannel sleeping bag with the little green turtles, climbing Mount Whitney, falling in love. However, I shall go back only as far as morning.

⁓

The coyotes howled the sun up the canyon rim, and when it spilled into my camp, the songbirds surrendered such lovely notes they broke my heart. So fervently did they sing, it was impossible not to separate their songs from all the other sounds of daybreak and fix on them as I lay wide-eyed and broken-hearted in my burning bed.

The canyon already blazed with heat. Sleeping bag and clothing felt like tools of the Inquisition. I donned hat and sunscreen and flicked aside the bed tarp quickly, checking for scorpions. On the campstove I brewed coffee, then cooled it down and iced it, barely surviving this rigor of Life in the Wilderness. Major John Wesley Powell, who ran the Green and Colorado Rivers more than a century ago, never had block ice in a giant cooler lashed to his wimpy wooden skiff. While today's river runners would gag on the Powell diet of rancid bacon, moldy flour, and stale coffee, they would sell their mothers for a glimpse of the Colorado Plateau before the dams and the crowds. I bore no delusions that the river beside me still flowed through Powell's *terra incognita*. From Rocky Mountain headwaters to the Sea of Cortez, the Colorado shoulders the weight of our needs, the thirsts of our farms and cities, and the affection of thousands of recreationists who ply its waters.

I daydreamed as I broke camp and loaded the raft, a routine repeated many times in my gypsy life as a river ranger's wife who spends much of the season afloat with him on his bimonthly patrols through the canyon. The packing, hefting, loading, and strapping felt so reflexive that, even after the first night out, I forgot that I had left the ranger behind. I missed him, but I did not need him. Other than keeping my tasks well within my own strength, a solo trip did not seem like a big deal.

I untied the raft, pushed it into the water, and climbed aboard. After an easy ferry the raft slipped into the main current. With an abruptness that could detach your teeth from your head, a low-flying B-52 suddenly unzipped the air between canyon rims, followed by an ear-splitting roar. The military planes flew over the river daily, sleek and darkly Transylvanian, looking as if no one were in them but bombs and robots. Around the first bend I passed a party of river runners. They waved from their camp, obviously bearing up well under the stress of the Nuevo Powell style—rancid prosciutto, stale cappuccino, Utah beer. Then I had the river to myself. It belonged to me all day long.

The canyon walls rose high, voluptuous, and red. I felt the river's muscle beneath the raft, pulling *me* along with little effort from the oars. It came to mind how simple river life is: Surrender all human measure of the universe to the river's own gauge of time and distance. Shed reason and frets so that what is left is a lean asceticism, a looking not at the world but into it. Let the morning serve up, as every slice of desert river will, a great blue heron.

The morning's heron stood in the shallows ahead, toes planted like twigs in the sandy bottom. It stared its Pleistocene stare. One foot lifted so slowly, the droplets that fell from it barely disturbed the water's surface. In a lightning motion the heron's stare disappeared underwater then reemerged. A few rope-like jerks of the bird's neck sent a silvery fish down its gullet. You can never get close enough to hear a heron's throat, nor can you easily identify the meal before it slides down that hose of a neck. Exotic and native fish swim these silty waters, natives whose endemism to the Colorado River basin is ancient (several million years) and now precarious. Biologists call the endangered Colorado pikeminnow, humpback and bonytail chubs, and other natives *obligate species* tied to a certain condition of life—that is, this river in which they evolved. In an ecology dramatically altered by humankind, some have become extinct, others hang on by a fin. Unless you have been dead, you know that this is a land replete with consequence and complications. We know our own history: Modern humans came to this arid, fissured, difficult place blinded, seeing not its particularities but our own aims. Because of this blindness, the shackles were severe, our covenant with nature set in terms of conquest rather than compatibility. "Taming the menace," in the words of the U.S. Bureau of Reclamation, has transformed the Colorado into a push-button river with a queue of dams and diversions in the lower basin and a flood-poor river in the middle basin. We reap the bounties of a watershed plumbed from headwaters to mouth, and we know the environmental costs, among them the loss of native fish, the drowning of spectacular canyons under enormous reservoirs, the alteration of riparian communities. We know that our urban desert culture is quickly outstripping the Colorado's ability to support it. What we do not know is this: Have we learned anything? Would we do it all over again?

In hundreds of side canyons and washes, on semiwild pieces of main-stem bracketed by the hardware, fluid gravity still more or less makes its own decisions and follows the path of its own weight, taking with it worn-down pieces of the continent grain by grain. It is in these reaches that you are most likely to glimpse the river's fight for eternity. To witness that persistence is why many of us make our home here. For me the bond between self and place is not conscious—no truth will arrive that way—but entirely sensory. Instinct and intimacy bring the feast closer, the river celebrates things we forget how to celebrate: our own spirits, the eternity of all things.

Watching the heron brought to mind a bird-watcher's story from the much reengineered lower Colorado, where a meandering swath of sand and scrub overgrew an old, dewatered channel. Instead of flying in a straight line across the flats, a great blue heron followed the dry, serpentine curve of the ghost channel, unable—or unwilling—to disobey an ancient avian wisdom, the imperative to match its flight to the shape of a river.

As the raft approached, the morning's heron took wing and flew the river bends as I did. The bird paid no attention to the unlikely yellow objects set against a gray-brown stack of logs jammed against the bank. The attention was mine. I pulled on the oars to make shore.

∼

I could use about twenty herons now, herons to pluck me from this roiling sandstone gravy and drop me into the runaway raft like a wet noodle. The water is not cold, but the flow is swift—no rapids yet, few rocks to bash myself against. In the shallows, without a life jacket for buoyancy and padding, the river bottom could shred me like a cheese grater. I struggle to stay in the deepest current, to reduce the distance to the boat, but my legs move like Gumby limbs, too weary to kick much longer.

What happens when I surrender to this aloof, silken creature that hurls me down its spine? What happens when I exhaust my strength and can swim no more, no matter how hard I try or how desperate I am? What happens if I let go?

How very familiar these waters feel, waters brought in from all directions over broad stretches of desert, through sinuous canyons to join their downward run to the sea. Every leaf, every riffle, every russet sweep of sandstone is saturated with memories, cut through and through with my own history. Along the river are strewn stories that make me who I am, that tell me what binds my life together, what to value and what to lay aside. We know few ways to tell the river's story other than through our own. Yet here it flows, making beauty a fact of existence, visible in its presence and absence, in flood and in washes as parched as old bones. To witness it you are grateful to have senses, to feel this one exquisite and dangerous thing that holds you to all life.

Shadows carve bands of mauve into the sun-bright terra-cotta of the canyon walls. Ripples of heat quiver against the high rims and disappear into a vault of azure sky. Ahead the water's surface splinters into a million fragments of sunlight. I try to match my swim to the shape of the river.

The river carries the raft into an eddy and slows it down. The oars no longer spin wildly in the oarlocks. If you observe stream hydraulics carefully, you will know that most eddies move in circles. The main current meets the eddy's slower water and pushes it in the opposite direction—the river flows upstream. It curls back, then meets the current again. At the top of the circling eddy I tread water and wait for the river to deliver the raft to me.

Never have I been so happy to become one with a gray bubble of inflated Hypalon. From water level the pontoon looks as high as a blimp. I find a strap end and use it to haul myself up and into the boat. Like bedraggled kelp, my dripping body drapes over the fat tube. A sudden anger rolls through me. I kick the sides of the dry box, the oars, the aluminum frame. I kiss my life jacket. I bite the bowline to shreds. I squint and growl, *Stupid, stupid, stupid.* All around me lies the sumptuous Colorado Plateau feast. In the cooler lies a normal dinner. In the pocket of my soaked shorts lie items scavenged from a debris heap. Bathtub toys. Two yellow plastic ducklings.

Havasu—Grand Canyon

Edward Abbey

One summer I started off to visit for the first time the city of Los Angeles. I was riding with some friends from the University of New Mexico. On the way we stopped off briefly to roll an old tire into Grand Canyon. While watching the tire bounce over tall pine trees, tear hell out of a mule train, and disappear with a final grand leap into the inner gorge, I overheard the park ranger standing nearby say a few words about a place called Havasu, or Havasupai. A branch, it seemed, of Grand Canyon.

What I heard made me think that I should see Havasu immediately, before something went wrong somewhere. My friends said they would wait. So I went down into Havasu—fourteen miles by trail—and looked things over. When I returned five weeks later I discovered that the others had gone on to Los Angeles without me.

Reprinted by permission of Don Congdon Associates, Inc. Excerpt from *Desert Solitaire* Copyright © 1968, renewed 1996 by Clarke Abbey.

That was fifteen years ago. And still I have not seen the fabulous city on the Pacific shore. Perhaps I never will. There's something in the prospect southwest from Barstow which makes one hesitate. Although recently, driving my own truck, I did succeed in penetrating as close as San Bernardino. But was hurled back by what appeared to be clouds of mustard gas rolling in from the west on a very broad front. Thus failed again. It may be however that Los Angeles will come to me. Will come to all of us, as it must (they say) to all men.

But Havasu. Once down in there it's hard to get out. The trail led across a stream wide, blue and deep, like the pure upper reaches of the River Jordan. Without a bridge. Dripping wet and making muddy tracks I entered the village of the Havasupai Indians where unshod ponies ambled down the only street and the children laughed, not maliciously, at the sight of the wet white man. I stayed the first night in the lodge the people keep for tourists, a rambling old bungalow with high ceilings, a screened verandah and large comfortable rooms. When the sun went down the village went dark except for kerosene lamps here and there, a few open fires, and a number of lightning bugs or fireflies which drifted aimlessly up and down Main Street, looking for trouble.

The next morning I bought a slab of bacon and six cans of beans at the village post office, rented a large comfortable horse and proceeded farther down the canyon past miniature cornfields, green pastures, swimming pools and waterfalls to the ruins of an old mining camp five miles below the village. There I lived, mostly alone except for the ghosts, for the next thirty-five days.

There was nothing wrong with the Indians. The Supai are a charming cheerful completely relaxed and easygoing bunch, all one hundred or so of them. But I had no desire to live *among* them unless clearly invited to do so, and I wasn't. Even if invited I might not have accepted. I'm not sure that I care for the idea of strangers examining my daily habits and folkways, studying my language, inspecting my costume, questioning me about my religion, classifying my artifacts, investigating my sexual rites and evaluating my chances for cultural survival.

So I lived alone.

The first thing I did was take off my pants. Naturally. Next I unloaded the horse, smacked her on the rump and sent her back to the village. I carried my food and gear into the best-preserved of the old cabins and spread my bedroll on a rusty steel cot. After that came a swim in the pool beneath a great waterfall nearby, 120 feet high, which rolled in mist and thunder over caverns and canopies of solidified travertine.

In the evening of that first day below the falls I lay down to sleep in the cabin. A dark night. The door of the cabin, unlatched, creaked slowly open, although there was no perceptible movement of the air. One firefly flickered in and circled my bacon, suspended from the roofbeam on a length of bailing wire. Slowly, without visible physical aid, the door groaned shut. And opened again. A bat came through one window and went out another, followed by a second firefly (the first scooped up by the bat) and a host of mosquitoes, which did not leave. I had no netting, of course, and the air was much too humid and hot for sleeping inside a bag.

I got up and wandered around outside for a while, slapping at mosquitoes, and thinking. From the distance came the softened roar of the waterfall, that "white noise" as soothing as hypnosis. I rolled up my sleeping bag and in the filtered light of the stars followed the trail that wound through thickets of cactus and up around ledges to the terrace above the mining camp. The mosquitoes stayed close but in lessening numbers, it seemed, as I climbed over humps of travertine toward the head of the waterfall. Near the brink of it, six feet from the drop-off and the plunge, I found a sandy cove just big enough for my bed. The racing creek as it soared free over the edge created a continuous turbulence in the air sufficient to keep away all flying insects. I slept well that night and the next day carried the cot to the place and made it my permanent bedroom for the rest of July and all of August.

What did I do during those five weeks in Eden? Nothing. I did nothing. Or nearly nothing. I caught a few rainbow trout, which grew big if not numerous in Havasu Creek. About once a week I put on my pants and walked up to the Indian village to buy bacon, canned beans and Argentine beef in the little store. That was all the Indians had in stock. To vary my diet I ordered more exotic foods by telephone from the supermarket in Grand Canyon Village and these were shipped to me by U.S. Mail, delivered twice a week on muleback down the fourteen-mile trail from Topocoba Hilltop. A little later in the season I was able to buy sweet corn, figs and peaches from the Supai. At one time for a period of three days my bowels seemed in danger of falling out, but I recovered. The Indians never came down to my part of the canyon except when guiding occasional tourists to the falls or hunting a stray horse. In late August came the Great Havasupai Sacred Peach Festival and Four-Day Marathon Friendship Dance, to which I was invited and in which I did participate. There I met Reed Watahomagie, a good man, and Chief Sinyala and a fellow named Spoonhead who took me for five dollars in a horse race. Someone had fed my mount a half-bushel of green figs just before the race—I heard later.

The Friendship Dance, which continued day and night to the rhythm of drums made of old inner tube stretched over #10 tomato cans while ancient medicine men chanted in the background, was perhaps marred but definitely not interrupted when a drunken free-for-all exploded between Spoonhead and friends and a group of visiting Hualapai Indians down from the rim. But this, I was told, happened every year. It was a traditional part of the ceremony, sanctified by custom. As Spoonhead told me afterwards, grinning around broken teeth, it's not every day you get a chance to wallop a Hualapai. Or skin a paleface, I reminded him. (Yes, the Supai are an excellent tribe, healthy, joyous and clever. Not only clever but shrewd. Not only shrewd but wise: e.g., the Bureau of Indian Affairs and the Bureau of Public Roads, like most gov-ernment agencies always meddling, always fretting and itching and sweating for something to do, last year made a joint offer to blast a million-dollar road down into Havasu Canyon at no cost whatsoever to the tribe, thus opening their homeland to the riches of motorized tourism. The people of Supai or at least a majority of them voted to reject the proposal.) And the peach wine flowed freely, like the water of the river of life. When the ball was over I went home to my bunk on the verge of the waterfall and rested for two days.

On my feet again, I explored the abandoned silver mines in the canyon walls, found a few sticks of dynamite but no caps or fuses. Disappointing; but there was nothing in that area anyway that required blowing up. I climbed through the caves that led down to the foot of Mooney Falls, two hundred feet high. What did I do? There was nothing that had to be done. I listened to the voices, the many voices, vague, distant but astonishingly human, of Havasu Creek. I heard the doors creak open, the doors creak shut, of the old forgot-ten cabins where no one with tangible substance or the property of reflecting light ever entered, ever returned. I went native and dreamed away days on the shore of the pool under the waterfall, wandered naked as Adam under the cottonwoods, inspecting my cactus gardens. The days became wild, strange, ambiguous—a sinister element pervaded the flow of time. I lived narcotic hours in which like the Taoist Chuang-tse I worried about butterflies and who was dreaming what. There was a serpent, a red racer, living in the rocks of the spring where I filled my canteens; he was always there, slipping among the stones or pausing to mesmerize me with his suggestive tongue and cloudy haunted primeval eyes. Damn his eyes. We got to know each other rather too well I think. I agonized over the girls I had known and over those I hoped were yet to come. I slipped by degrees into lunacy, me and the moon, and lost to a certain extent the power to distinguish between what was and what was not myself: looking at my hand I would see a leaf trembling on a branch. A *green* leaf. I thought of Debussy, of Keats and Blake and Andrew Marvell. I remembered Tom o'Bedlam. And all those lost and never remembered. Who would return? To be lost again? I went for walks. I went for walks. I went for walks and on one of these, the last I took in Havasu, regained everything that seemed to be ebbing away.

~

Most of my wandering in the desert I've done alone. Not so much from choice as from necessity—I generally prefer to go into places where no one else wants to go. I find that in contemplating the natural world my pleasure is greater if there are not too many others contemplating it with me, at the same time. However, there are special hazards in traveling alone. Your chances of dying, in case of sickness or accident, are much improved, simply because there is no one around to go for help. Exploring a side canyon off Havasu Canyon one day, I was unable to resist the temptation to climb up out of it onto what corresponds in that region to the Tonto Bench. Late in the afternoon I realized that I would not have enough time to get back to my camp before dark, unless I could find a much shorter route than the one by which I had come. I looked for a shortcut.

Nearby was another little side canyon which appeared to lead down into Havasu Canyon. It was a steep, shadowy, extremely narrow defile with the usual meandering course and overhanging walls; from where I stood, near its head, I could not tell if the route was feasible all the way down to the floor of the main canyon. I had no rope with me—only my walking stick. But I was hungry and thirsty, as always. I started down.

For a while everything went well. The floor of the little canyon began as a bed of dry sand, scattered with rocks. Farther down a few boulders were wedged between the walls; I climbed over and under them. Then the canyon took on the slickrock character—smooth, sheer, slippery sandstone carved by erosion into a series of scoops and potholes which got bigger as I descended. In some of these basins there was a little water left over from the last flood, warm and fetid water under an oily-looking scum, condensed by prolonged evaporation to a sort of broth, rich in dead and dying organisms. My canteen was empty and I was very thirsty but I felt that I could wait.

I came to a lip on the canyon floor which overhung by twelve feet the largest so far of these stagnant pools. On each side rose the canyon walls, roughly perpendicular. There was no way to continue except by dropping into the pool. I hesitated. Beyond this point there could hardly be any returning, yet the main canyon was still not visible below. Obviously the only sensible thing to do was to turn back. I edged over the lip of stone and dropped feet first into the water.

Deeper than I expected. The warm, thick fluid came up and closed over my head as my feet touched the muck at the bottom. I had to swim to the farther side. And here I found myself on the verge of another drop-off, with one more huge bowl of green soup below. This drop-off was about the same height as the one before, but not overhanging. It resembled a children's playground slide, concave and S-curved, only steeper, wider, with a vertical pitch in the middle. It did not lead directly into the water but ended in a series of steplike ledges above the pool. Beyond the pool lay another ledge, another dropoff into an unknown depth. Again I paused, and for a much longer time. But I no longer had the option of turning around and going back. I eased myself into the chute and let go of everything—except my faithful stick.

I hit rock bottom hard, but without any physical injury. I swam the stinking pond dog-paddle style, pushing the heavy scum away from my face, and crawled out on the far side to see what my fate was going to be.

Fatal. Death by starvation, slow and tedious. For I was looking straight down an overhanging cliff to a rubble pile of broken rocks eighty feet below.

⁓

After the first wave of utter panic had passed, I began to try to think. First of all, I was not going to die immediately, unless another flash flood came down the gorge; there was the pond of stagnant water on hand to save me from thirst, and a man can live, they say, for thirty days or more without food. My sun-bleached bones, dramatically sprawled at the bottom of the chasm, would provide the diversion of the picturesque for future wanderers—if any man ever came this way again.

My second thought was to scream for help, although I knew very well there could be no other human being within miles. I even tried it but the sound of that anxious shout, cut short in the dead air within the canyon walls, was so inhuman, so detached as it seemed from myself, that it terrified me and I didn't attempt it again. I thought of tearing my clothes into strips and plaiting a rope. But what was I wearing?—boots, socks, a pair of old and ragged blue jeans, a flimsy T-shirt, an ancient and rotten sombrero of straw. Not a chance of weaving such a wardrobe into a rope eighty feet long, or even twenty feet long.

How about a signal fire? There was nothing to burn but my clothes; not a tree, not a shrub, not even a weed grew in this stony cul-de-sac. Even if I burned my clothing, the chances of the smoke being seen by some Hualapai Indian high on the south rim were very small; and if he did see the smoke, what then? He'd shrug his shoulders, sigh, and take another pull from his Tokay bottle. Furthermore, without clothes, the sun would soon bake me to death.

There was only one thing I could do. I had a tiny notebook in my hip pocket and a stub of pencil. When these dried out I could at least record my final thoughts. I would have plenty of time to write not only my epitaph but my own elegy.

But not yet.

There were a few loose stones scattered about the edge of the pool. Taking the biggest first, I swam with it back to the foot of the slickrock chute and placed it there. One by one I brought the others and made a shaky little pile about two feet high leaning against the chute. Hopeless, of course, but there was nothing else to do. I stood on the top of the pile and stretched upward, straining my arms to their utmost limit, and groped with fingers and fingernails for a hold on something firm. There was nothing. I crept back down. I began to cry. It was easy. All alone, I didn't have to be brave.

Through the tears I noticed my old walking stick lying nearby. I took it and stood it on the most solid stone in the pile, behind the two topmost stones. I took off my boots, tied them together, and hung them around my neck, on my back. I got up on the little pile again and lifted one leg and set my big toe on the top of the stick. This could never work. Slowly and painfully, leaning as much of my weight as I could against the sandstone slide, I applied more and more pressure to the stick, pushing my body upward until I was again stretched out full length above it. Again I felt about for a fingerhold. There was none. The chute was smooth as polished marble.

No, not quite that smooth. This was sandstone, soft and porous, not marble, and between it and my wet body and wet clothing a certain friction was created. In addition, the stick had enabled me to reach a higher section of the S-curved chute, where the angle was more favorable. I discovered that I could move upward, inch by inch, through adhesion and with the help of the leveling tendency of the curve. I gave an extra little push with my big toe—the stones collapsed below, the stick clattered down—and crawled rather like a snail or slug, oozing slime, up over the rounded summit of the slide.

The next obstacle, the overhanging spout twelve feet above a deep plunge pool, looked impossible. It *was* impossible, but with the blind faith of despair I slogged into the water and swam underneath the drop-off and floundered around for a while, scrabbling at the slippery rock until my nerves and tiring muscles convinced my numbed brain that *this was not the way.* I swam back to solid ground and lay down to rest and die in comfort. Far above I could see the sky, an irregular strip of blue between the dark, hard-edged canyon walls that seemed to lean toward each other as they towered above me. Across that narrow opening a small white cloud was passing, so lovely and precious and delicate and forever inaccessible that it broke the heart and made me weep like a woman, like a child. In all my life I had never seen anything so beautiful.

The walls that rose on either side of the drop-off were literally perpendicular. Eroded by weathering, however, and not by the corrosion of rushing floodwater, they had a rough surface, chipped, broken, cracked. Where the walls joined the face of the overhang they formed almost a square corner, with a number of minute crevices and inch-wide shelves on either side. It might, after all, be possible. What did I have to lose? When I had regained some measure of nerve and steadiness I got up off my back and tried the wall beside the pond, clinging to the rock with bare toes and fingertips and inching my way crabwise toward the corner. The water-soaked, heavy boots dangling from my neck, swinging back and forth with my every movement, threw me off balance and I fell into the pool. I swam out to the bank, unslung the boots and threw them up over the drop-off, out of sight. They'd be there if I ever needed them again. Once more I attached myself to the wall, tenderly, sensitively, like a limpet, and very slowly, very cautiously, worked my way into the corner. Here I was able to climb upward, a few centimeters at a time, by bracing myself against the opposite sides and finding sufficient niches for fingers and toes. As I neared the top and the overhang became noticeable I prepared for a slip, planning to push myself away from the rock so as to fall into the center of the pool where the water was deepest. But it wasn't necessary. Somehow, with a skill and tenacity I could never have found in myself under ordinary circumstances, I managed to creep straight up that gloomy cliff and over the brink of the drop-off and into the flower of safety. My boots were floating under the surface of the little puddle above. As I poured the stinking water out of them and pulled them on and laced them up I discovered myself bawling again for the third time in three hours, the hot delicious tears of victory. And up above the clouds replied—thunder.

I emerged from that treacherous little canyon at sundown, with an enormous fire in the western sky and lightning overhead. Through sweet twilight and the sudden dazzling flare of lightning I hiked back along the Tonto Bench, bellowing the "Ode to Joy." Long before I reached the place where I could descend safely to the main canyon and my camp, however, darkness set in, the clouds opened their bays and the rain poured down. I took shelter under a ledge in a shallow cave about three feet high—hardly room to sit up in. Others had been here before: the dusty floor of the little hole was littered with the droppings of birds, rats, jackrabbits, and coyotes. There were also a few long gray pieces of scat with a curious twist at one tip—cougar? I didn't care. I had some matches with me, sealed in paraffin (the prudent explorer); I scraped together the handiest twigs and animal droppings and built a little fire and waited for the rain to stop.

It didn't stop. The rain came down for hours in alternate waves of storm and drizzle and I very soon had burnt up all the fuel within reach. No matter. I stretched out in the coyote den, pillowed my head on my arm and suffered through the long, long night, wet, cold, aching, hungry, wretched, dreaming claustrophobic nightmares. It was one of the happiest nights of my life.

Study Questions

1. What is it that we can find in the wilderness that can be found nowhere else? Why?
2. Terry Russell wrote in *On the Loose* that the reason they traveled was "not to escape from but to escape to: not to forget but to remember." What did Terry Russell mean by this?
3. It seems that there is a significant difference in the power of a solo expedition vs. one with a group. What makes the experience of a solo trip in the wilderness so powerful?
4. It is obvious that we need air, food, water, and sleep for survival. Many have argued that nature is also necessary. Why do we "need wild country"?
5. Why is attitude much more important than "what's in your pack" while in a wild setting?
6. Despite the fact that those who experience adversity in the backcountry can find themselves in a tough scenario, "Survivors never consider themselves victims." Why is this?
7. Why is fear good for survival?
8. Why must we remain humble while in the backcountry?
9. If the remains of Everett Ruess were found, would he lose his power as a symbol of southwestern wilderness? Why or why not?
10. How do you deal with climbers that just want to "conquer a mountain"? How do you explain to people that the landscape is greater and deserves an attitude of respect and humility?
11. How do you cope with the "end of season blues" and "reentry"? Why is it hard for people?
12. "Going out" is important, but so is coming back. How do you connect yourself to both worlds so that you don't lose yourself in either?
13. Describe your ideal solo experience. Where would you go? How long would you stay? And what would you do?
14. What landscapes help you "celebrate your own spirits" and notice the "eternity of all things"?

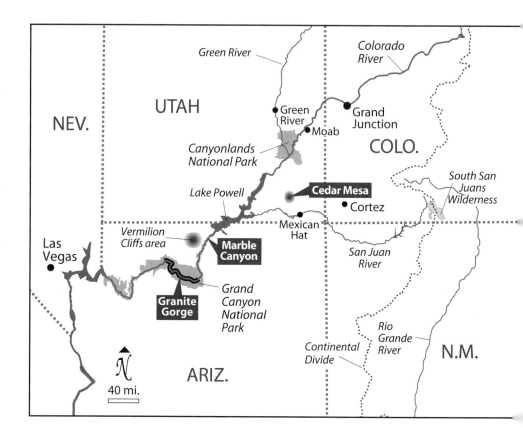

CHAPTER 7

Animal Encounters

We must learn, finally, that wilderness is not, as our history has insisted, a threat to be conquered but, in fact, a protection to be embraced. For in wilderness, as in the eyes of wild creatures that inhabit it, we find something that binds us firmly to the long history of life on earth, something that can teach us how to live on this cooling cinder of a planet, how to accept our limitations, how to celebrate the love we feel when we let ourselves feel it for all other living creatures.

—T. H. Watkins, *Testimony*

These landscapes nourish and teach and heal. They help keep us sane, they give us strength, they connect us to our roots in the earth, they remind us that we share in the flow of life and death. We encounter animals in their native place and they look into our eyes with the amalgam of indifference and companionship that separates us from and unites us with other creatures.

—Stephen Trimble, *Testimony*

All of us who hike, raft, climb, and backpack in the Southwest love to encounter animals along trails and river corridors. Seeing animals in their natural habitats adds excitement to backcountry trips and lets us know that we're being careful and quiet as we move through their territories. One morning on the Green River I remember seeing a beaver crossing the current, swimming with his own ferry angle and heading toward a beaver lodge on the river's far side.

In our large raft we stayed in the middle of the channel, but we must have come too close because he made a loud splash with his tail and then dived. Our passengers loved that encounter and were even more impressed half an hour later when we came upon a dozen reintroduced bighorn sheep, males and females, drinking at the river's edge. Their dark eyes watched us carefully as we floated by, but they made no effort to flee because bighorns have no natural predators that come from water.

Such encounters brighten the day for all backcountry travelers who feel a little closer to the earth and its natural processes when we can quietly observe animals. We remember that we're not the only species in the Southwest and that we're a part of the community of life—a web of biotic relationships dependent upon sun, food, water, shelter, and sleep. I enjoy observing mule deer mothers and fawns, as they rest on ponderosa pine duff, hidden under the trees and waiting for a summer thunderstorm to pass.

Once climbing a ridgeline in the La Plata Mountains in late October, I made fresh tracks in new snow as I headed into the aspens and the top of the ridge. As it grew dark and I descended, halfway down the mountain I was stunned to see large black bear paw prints exactly inside my size 12 boot prints. A bear had stepped in the tracks I made going uphill. I froze. Adrenaline flowed through my body. I stopped, dry-mouthed, pivoted slowly, and listened intently for the bear. A quiet late afternoon hike had become an encounter with a large mammal getting ready to den for winter. Was it a male or female? Was he or she in a good or bad mood in the struggle to put on food prior to a long winter's nap?

Within seconds the lackadaisical attitude I'd had climbing the slope changed into one of intense awareness as I walked back to the truck. I moved slowly, carefully, checking behind me and listening intently. Animal encounters in the Southwest will do that to you. They heighten your senses, deepen your awareness, broaden your humility, and let you know that you're in their home and only passing through.

We need animals. We need them to put us in our place, but that hasn't always been the prevailing philosophy. At one time farmers and ranchers dominated wildlife policies in the Southwest. Paid bounty hunters severely limited the number of mountain lions on the North Rim of Grand Canyon. Wolves and grizzly bears were exterminated throughout the nineteenth and into the early twentieth centuries because of their occasional attacks on domestic sheep and cattle grazing public lands. It took until the 1930s when a far-seeing ecologist and public lands manager, Aldo Leopold, began to understand that perhaps we should leave landscapes and habitat alone. Perhaps there were other more intrinsic values to the public domain besides grazing, mining, and lumbering.

The wolf has frequently been a touchstone of heated discussions of animal life in the Southwest. Biologist Daniel Botkin writes, "The wolf represents a powerful symbol of the character of wild nature. In its wariness of people, the wolf epitomizes our predominant contemporary image of nature: nature as separate from human beings and human beings as divorced from nature. Where we are, there are no wolves; where the wolf lives, there is wilderness."[1]

In one of the most famous essays ever written about animals in the Southwest, Leopold wrote about wolves. In this essay, published posthumously in *A Sand County Almanac*, Leopold philosophized about our need to "think like a mountain" and not just consider animal life and habitat from a human-centered perspective. Having worked in the wild backcountry of Arizona and New Mexico in the 1920s, Leopold wrote about having shot a wolf and later he came to regret that decision. He wrote, "I was young and full of trigger-itch," but what he did was entirely commensurate with federal policy at the time. Later, he would help to change that policy and become the father of wildlife management. He wrote:

> A deep chesty bawl echoes from rimrock to rimrock, rolls down the mountain, and fades into the far blackness of the night. It is an outburst of wild defiant sorrow, and of contempt for all the adversities of the world. Every living thing (and perhaps many a dead one as well) pays heed to that call. To the deer it is a reminder of the way of all flesh, to the pine a forecast of midnight scuffles and blood upon the snow, to the coyote a promise of gleanings to come, to the cowman a threat of red ink at the bank, to the hunter a challenge of fang against bullet. Yet behind these obvious and immediate hopes and fears there lies a deeper meaning, known only to the mountain itself. Only the mountain has lived long enough to listen objectively to the howl of a wolf.

He explains about wolves and men and how he shot a wolf. He writes,

> We reached the old wolf in time to watch a fierce green fire dying in her eyes. I realized then, and have known ever since, that there was something new to me in those eyes—something known only to her and to the mountain. I was young then, and full of trigger-itch; I thought that because fewer wolves meant more deer, that no wolves would be a hunter's paradise. But after seeing the green fire die, I sensed that neither the wolf nor the mountain agreed with such a view.[2]

Though Leopold had had a change of heart, it would be decades before federal policy evolved about the killing of predators or "varmints."[3]

One of the turning points in the discussion was the decimation of mountain lion populations in the Arizona Strip in a mass slaughter advocated by former president Theodore Roosevelt, implemented by professional mountain lion hunter "Uncle" Jimmy Owens, and endorsed by novelist Zane Grey.[4] The eventual result of their campaign of death was the elimination of mountain lions, but then the Kaibab National Forest and Grand Canyon's North Rim became overrun by mule deer, which starved by the thousands because their natural predators had been killed off. The excess deer also caused significant environmental damage to the forest. The balance of nature had been disrupted, and man's best intentions had proven to be disastrous.

We have yet to implement Leopold's vision across America's vast landscapes, but perhaps there is hope on wildlands in the Southwest. Biological diversity would include not only the survival of existing plant and animal communities but also the reintroduction of species that have vanished. We may never see grizzly bears back in the Southwest, though they were certainly here in the mountains, high meadows, and even desert playas. The last grizz trapped was in the eastern San Juans in 1952—but then a hunter killed a grizzly in the rugged South San Juans Wilderness, south of Pagosa Springs, in 1979. David Petersen, author of *Ghost Grizzlies,* writes, "Our legends are quartered in the landscape of dreams. . . . Each time an 'extinct' grizzly shows up, they are once again proclaimed dead and gone forever."[5] Are more of the great bears living deep in the mountains? Perhaps. One can only hope. Because of the huge hunting territories they need, to avoid inevitable human-bear conflicts, grizzlies will never be reintroduced. But wolves are returning to the Southwest, with Mexican wolves reintroduced in Catron County, New Mexico, in the Gila Wilderness, and gray wolves moving slowly down into Colorado from Wyoming and Yellowstone National Park.[6]

Today we better understand ecology and ecosystems. Hikers and backpackers traveling throughout the Southwest see animals in their own habitats, which proves that those habitats are healthy—both for animals and for two-legged human visitors. Leopold eventually distilled his ecological wisdom into a land ethic and the belief that "a thing is right when it tends to preserve the integrity, stability and beauty of the biotic community. It is wrong when it tends otherwise."[7] American cities and suburbs represent the antithesis of this ideal, because land is converted into habitat for only a few species: us and our pets. But Leopold would be pleased with how far we've come. His ideology and thinking helped inspire the Endangered Species Act (1973), which gave the U.S. Fish and Wildlife Service broad powers to protect existing species and to reintroduce species back onto their home ranges.

~

Eco-failures include the loss of warm-water habitat for endangered fish such as the humpbacked chub, razor-backed sucker, bonytail chub, and the Colorado pikeminnow. The latter, North America's largest minnow, grew to six feet long and were called "white salmon" by pioneers. But dams and canals along the Colorado River system have severely impacted the fishes' warm-water breeding areas. Aquatic species that took three million years to adapt may not survive the twenty-first century. The fourteen native Colorado River fish, which evolved in warm-water habitats, now must compete with forty nonnative species, especially trout, which thrive at the bottom of deep dams. "These fish are the West's heritage and are found nowhere else in the world," states literature from the Recovery Program for the Endangered Fishes of the Upper Colorado.[8]

If warm-water fish have not done well in the Southwest, peregrine falcons on the Colorado Plateau are thriving because of a successful stabilization and reintroduction program at Dinosaur National Monument. The year before Congress passed the Endangered Species Act in 1973, it banned the pesticide DDT, which bioaccumulates or stays in fatty tissues, resulting in weak egg-shells for raptor species. Songbirds had ingested DDT from dusted plants, and falcons pursued and ate songbirds. By 1963 peregrines, the fastest animals on earth, were gone from the eastern United States with only a few breeding pairs in the West.[9]

In 1976 one of the last breeding pairs in Colorado was found in Dinosaur, atop Steamboat Rock on an aerie or scrape. They had no nest, just twigs and the remnants of food that the pair had brought their young. Working with the National Park Service, intrepid climbers repelled off the top of the rock and brought a clutch of eggs to Colorado State University to safely incubate and hatch. The breeding pair then promptly double-clutched, or had a second set of eggs to replace the first set mysteriously snatched. Other researchers armed with spotting scopes in Echo Park gave the signal for climbers to scale the cliffs and take the second batch out. As eggs hatched, researchers feared that the young birds would imprint on them and think they were the birds' mother, so scientists used peregrine puppets to feed the young. Imagine the consternation of the peregrine parents when eggs one day disappeared, then magically, weeks later, climbers returned to the nest with fledgling teenage birds!

Though peregrines lay two eggs in nature, only one survives. To save the species in its natural habitat, a four-foot plywood wooden hack box was placed at the end of Split Mountain and Yampa Canyon, where biologists came three times a day with broken-up pieces of food. With no parents to teach them, the fledglings would not fly, making them midnight snacks for great-horned owls hunting at night. After too many owl attacks, the fledglings were locked in for their own safety. Thanks to those extra eggs and healthy falcons, peregrines have repopulated the Southwest with twenty-five pairs in Dinosaur National Monument, fifteen to sixteen pairs on the Yampa River alone, and more than a hundred pairs feasting on pigeons in major cities such as Denver and Salt Lake City.[10]

Unlike the threatened fish, by 1999 the U.S. Fish and Wildlife Service had taken peregrines off the Endangered Species list. Across the United States we now have 1,600 pairs, including 500 pairs at Lake Powell in Utah, where they're doing especially well because of miles of steep sandstone cliffs. I've enjoyed seeing falcons on the Green and Yampa; to view these incredibly fast birds dive-bombing their prey is to experience wild nature.

Climbing guide Jack Turner argues passionately for wildness and wild creatures to be left alone. He laments, "So we fight to preserve ecosystems and species, and we accept the diminished wildness. This wins the fight but loses the war, and in the process we simply stop talking about wildness." He adds, "What counts as wildness and wilderness is determined not by the absence of people, but by the relationship between people and place."[11] In *The Abstract Wild*, Turner states, "We are left with the vital importance of residency in wild nature and a visceral knowledge of that wildness, as the most practical means of preserving the wild. What we need now is a new tradition of the wild that teaches us how human beings live best by living in and studying the wild without taming it or destroying it."[12] In the Southwest one of the best places to experience such a wildlife/wild place interphase is on top of the Vermilion Cliffs National Monument on the edge of the Paria Wilderness.

In this location a Pleistocene-era bird, the California condor, has been rein-troduced. When you're standing on the Vermilion Cliffs at sunset, looking south toward Grand Canyon, if you're lucky you might see the huge, dark shape of a California condor. As it glides over the three-thousand-foot cliffs, the condor's ten-foot wingspan is unmistakable. To hike the Vermilion Cliffs on the edge of the Paria Wilderness is to experience a place out of time, especially when the giant birds dip and soar above you. When you're standing beneath this ancient bird, the largest in North America, comparisons inevitably come to mind. What's the difference between a California condor and a Boeing 747 jet? The condor doesn't serve pretzels.

In other places along the rim of the Paria Canyon–Vermilion Cliffs Wilderness, the sheer size of the landscape dwarfs the great birds. Visitors lose perspective. Looking out across the heart of the Colorado Plateau toward Navajo Mountain and Flagstaff, Arizona, even the largest birds on the continent seem like black receding dots. The deep, incised lines of canyons such as Echo Cliffs and Marble Canyon seem to stretch forever, which is why visiting Vermilion Cliffs National Monument in the remotest part of Arizona is like being on top of the world.

John Nielsen, author of *Condor,* believes that "the condor is the soul of the wilderness."[13] Environmentalist David Brower exclaimed, "I could wonder what it would be like to think the way a condor does, to sweep so much of creation at one glance, to know the wind." He added, "A condor is [only] five percent feathers, flesh, blood, and bone. The rest is *place.* Condors are a soaring manifestation of the place that built them and coded their genes."[14] To stand on the rim of the Vermilion Cliffs is to experience one of the wildest places in America.

Managed by the Bureau of Land Management, Vermilion Cliffs is not for the faint of heart. The BLM advises, "Visits to the area require special planning and awareness of potential hazards such as rugged and unmarked roads, poisonous reptiles and insects, extreme heat or cold, deep sand and flash floods." My kind of place! I agree with the BLM's recommendations to bring "a spare tire, and plenty of water, food, and gasoline." Extra gasoline and shovels are a necessity, as is car caravanning because of miles of treacherous sand. On a five-day car-camping visit, we saw no one.

The remoteness of the Vermilion Cliffs on the east side of the Arizona Strip is exactly why federal agencies used the cliffs as the perfect location to reintroduce endangered California condors, which may be eleven million years old. Grand Canyon guide Wayne Ranney believes that California condors evolved with Paleo-Indians. He thinks that before the extinction of megafauna such as wooly mammoths, when early man killed large beasts, condors cruised in for the banquet. Their affinity for human-killed carrion has gotten them into trouble. The birds almost became extinct due to lead poisoning they contracted from eating animals killed by modern-day hunters.[15] Other condors were themselves shot by these sportsmen. By 1982 there were only twenty-two birds left in the wild, and five years later biologists captured the last wild condor in California.

Now, on the southwest corner of the rim, holding and feeding pens have allowed young condors to acclimate. Trained specialists with the U.S. Fish and Wildlife Service use hand puppets to feed roadkill to juvenile birds. Begun in the mid-1990s, this reintroduction has brought the giant birds back to the Southwest, where their presence can surprise visitors. While eating lunch on the rim, one couple watched a young juvenile condor with number 43 attached to both wings land fifty feet away and then hop closer. At fifteen feet the bird ducked its head like it was bowing, dipped its wings, and, in condorese, begged for sandwiches. He was later taken back for "re-education" and a healthier diet of dead rabbits.

The birds released on the Vermilion Cliffs routinely glide over to the South Rim of Grand Canyon to watch tourists. The birds also practice aerial acrobatics below Navajo Bridge above Marble Canyon. A pair of condors even flew as far north as Grand Mesa near Grand Junction, Colorado. But to truly see them in their element, dipping, diving, swooping, and gliding, walk the rim of the Vermilion Cliffs. I saw no. 25. The bird silently drifted over us, white patches under its wings, feathers at the wing tips splayed out like spread fingers— a vision from another epoch. In late autumn light, as shadows stretch deep into canyon bottoms and that lovely orange-gold light climbs cliffs, look out over the vastness of northern Arizona. When you start to see the shadow of a low-flying jet, it's probably just a Pleistocene bird back from the brink of extinction.[16]

This is a bird that knows solitude. They don't flap their wings; they just leave them outstretched to soar with their legs dangling below. To drop from the sky the big birds simply fold or curl their wing tips to lose lift. Both the bird and its setting are magnificent, and on the Vermilion Cliffs I've spent an entire afternoon watching seven birds dip, soar, land, and preen. On one condor aerie we watched three birds face each other like black-robed monks in prayer—heads down, shoulders hunched forward, beaks in the air. Perhaps they were singing an ancient condor hymn, or muttering to each other a quiet condor prayer.

Late one afternoon we reluctantly returned to camp, walking out of the Paria Wilderness and turning our backs on the big black birds. After searching for days for condors it was hard to depart, but we left the condors in peace to return to their natural rhythms and their proper place on the Plateau. Jack Turner believes, "Instead of a vast machine, much of nature turns out to be a collection of dynamic systems, rather like the mean eddy lines in Lava Falls." He adds, "Life evolves at the edge of chaos, the area of maximum vitality and change."[17]

Now the condors are back in the southwestern ecosystem. At sunset, sometimes I dream of them soaring over the cliffs, dark shadows above a red landscape. They've returned to us from an ancient age, and I can only imagine what canyon country looks like from their eyes.

～

Navajo Bridge spans fifty-mile-long Marble Canyon almost five hundred feet above the swirling Colorado River. Building the bridge, now listed as a National Historic Civil Engineering Landmark, in 1927–1928 had been an epic task. Then in the 1960s professional beavers at the Bureau of Reclamation sought to place dams in Marble Canyon. But the public said no, especially after Sierra Club executive director David Brower launched an effective media campaign in the *New York Times*. The dams would have flooded the canyon and permitted power boaters to motor close to the canyon's rim. Outraged, the Sierra Club inserted full-page ads in the *Times* with the memorable slogan "Should we also flood the Sistine Chapel, so tourists can get nearer the ceiling?"

On a visit to Marble Canyon I was touched by commemorative plaques on both sides of the historic bridge, but it was something under the modern 1994 highway bridge that caught my eye. Walking across the historic span and looking over to the new bridge, I saw a black plastic garbage bag suspended on one of the bridge girders. Then I thought to myself, "That's not a garbage bag—that's one helluva big raven." I reached for my small birder's binoculars, and finally what I saw made sense. I yelled to my wife across the bridge, "Come here! Come quick!" She thought I'd gone nuts. In a way, I had.

To the northwest of Navajo Bridge the vivid escarpment of the Vermilion Cliffs towers above Marble Canyon. I'd spent days on top of Vermilion Cliffs National Monument exploring, hiking, and scanning the skies seeking endangered California condors released into the wild. So you can imagine my shock to spy one of my feathered friends actually below me, hunkered down on a cold metal bridge girder and looking like a punk rock star in need of a hot latte.

There was no. 69, according to the tag attached to his wing, with his shaved fluffy head, his red condor neck, and a rather morose look. Occasionally he'd tuck his head under his wing. It was an overcast morning and clearly he needed a breakfast burrito—or perhaps half a toasted mastodon, like the good old Pleistocene days when condors would swoop down after Paleo-Indians finished feasting. But that had been ice ages ago, long before this bridge was built, and here I was staring at the largest bird in North America just back from the brink of extinction. I yelled again for my wife.

Then I saw the others. No. 76 sat on a stone ledge where the bridge connected to the canyon. A third one, perhaps no. 54, stayed in seclusion against the rocks. We watched them for nearly half an hour as they used sharp beaks to preen their feathers, then they took off, quickly becoming tiny black eyebrows flying away against the immensity of Grand Canyon.

Yes, Navajo Bridge is an engineering marvel that united southern and northern Arizona, but too much of the American West in the twentieth century was about building, changing, and manipulating the environment for human benefit. We learned restraint when we stopped needless dams in

Marble Canyon, but our real accomplishment was the Endangered Species Act, which puts humanity in its place as a member of the vast community of life, not as the preeminent ecobully that we've become. I respect the bridge's bronze memorials, but even more I treasure the living feathered memorial of Ice Age California condors again flying above their ancient turf.

∽

Across the Southwest environmental changes and lead poisoning from hunters' bullets found in carrion almost doomed the California condor to extinction. In southwestern Colorado, the lynx also disappeared, but the same species was thriving in Canada. So staff from Colorado's Division of Parks and Wildlife (CPAW) sought to restore nature's balance by bringing back the silver-haired cat. Though I have yet to encounter one, my students have, and they've described it as an awe-inspiring, transcendent experience watching a lynx glide through a snowbound winter landscape.

When Kip Stransky retired after working thirty years for the Colorado Division of Wildlife (DOW), his last five years on lynx reintroduction, his colleagues gave him shit, literally. Poop on a plaque. And he could not have been happier. Kip's so proud of his unusual retirement gift that "It hangs on my living room wall and it's quite a conversation piece," he says. The plaque reads, "The fruit of your labors." Covered with a light coat of shellac is genuine lynx poop glued to mahogany and naturally imbedded with rabbit hair, "probably from a bunny that I purchased somewhere," Kip says with a smile.[18]

Working with lynx can be like that. You get dedicated to the three-foot-long, twenty- to thirty-pound cats with their beautiful silver and gray coats, huge ear tufts, and black-tipped tails. Kip's job was bunnies—lots of bunnies. Stransky was the rabbit man. In the complicated world of reintroducing an endangered predator, Kip's position as wildlife technician was to find food to keep Canadian lynx alive as they adjusted to Colorado in a secure DOW Rehabilitation Center near Monte Vista. It wasn't easy.

He had to convince bunny breeders across four states to sell him between 1,500 and 2,000 four-pound rabbits a year. In Price, Utah, Shiprock, New Mexico, and Grand Junction, Colorado, he would meet rabbit raisers with a horse trailer full of cages to buy live bunnies to stockpile for the approximately fifty lynx a year the DOW wanted to release into the San Juan and Rio Grande National Forests, which had been the southern range of lynx before they had been trapped almost to extinction.

Started with the best of intentions under DOW director and conservation biologist John Mumma, lynx reintroduction began poorly. Captured Canadian lynx, released in the spring, died: three starved in the wild, and one was badly malnourished when it was recaptured. At the University of Colorado, students held candlelight vigils to mourn the lynx loss. There had been almost no research on lynx reintroduction, and wildlife biologists had not adequately prepared the lynx. The biologists learned their lesson. That put Stransky in the bunny business looking for fresh food for furry friends. The failure of the "hard release" resulted in a dramatic rethinking of how to put lynx into the wild with the goal of fattening them up to adjust to their new mountain home.

But feeding captured lynx rabbits and roadkill was the least of DOW's worries. There were angry farm and ranch groups terrified of these small, elusive, gray-and-white cats with their huge back paws up to eight inches wide—perfect for traveling in snow in the same deep powder that has made Colorado an international ski destination. There were irate loggers, worried ski industry executives, and even arsonists and ecoterrorists, who in 1998 fire-bombed a ski lodge near Beaver Creek, Colorado, close to the location of the last illegal lynx trapping, in Vail in 1973.

Clearly, this small, stunningly beautiful cat with its oversized paws and its large, pointy ears stirs controversy, even though it is rarely seen. It's the mystery cat of the southern Rockies and a vital link in the predator-prey food chain, which conservation biologists seek desperately to maintain despite increasing habitat fragmentation. No stranger to controversy, Mumma supported his staff in bringing back the lynx. It was a fateful decision, and one of the best he ever made.

On a DOW float trip down the Dolores River in May 1997, Mumma and his staff talked about wild animals that had disappeared in their lifetimes. Late into the second night, sitting around a campfire and passing a bottle of bourbon, six biologists and game wardens discussed bringing one species back. John Mumma recalls, "I just made the decision right then that yes, we were going to do it. Let's just settle this argument once and for all about whether there are any lynx in the state. Let's go get 'em and bring them back in and then we'll have 'em." The plan for lynx reintroduction was born.

But lynx live where skiers ski. The felines prefer habitat between 8,500 and 11,000 feet, and they've been known to den in timber above 11,000 feet. They like the krummholz or the low-growing vegetation just above timberline. By reintroducing lynx, DOW staff knew they were about to make their professional lives more difficult. They knew there'd be long days tramping through deep snow or riding in small airplanes trying to catch faint signals from the cats' radio-tracking collars.

The biologists knew there'd be shouts of criticism as well as applause, but they did it for the lynx, and out of a belief in Aldo Leopold's land ethic and the understanding that biodiversity means having as many species as possible in their original habitat. No one thought it would be easy, but no one imagined the piles of paperwork or the professional protocols necessary to put a small predator back onto spruce-fir slopes in wilderness settings. Now backcountry travelers could anticipate rare animal encounters with the legendary lynx.

Rather than plan for a ghost species that may or may not have been slinking around the state's multimillion-dollar ski resorts, Mumma and the DOW decided to capture Canadian lynx, bring them to Colorado, and let them adjust to transportation corridors, logging and ranching industries, and downhill skiers. It was a high-stakes gamble complete with lawsuits and outraged farm and ranch groups, including the Farm Bureau and the Colorado Guide and Outfitters Association. Misinformed hunters were convinced that thirty-pound lynx would damage the state's healthy deer and elk herds. In an unprecedented alliance, animal rights and sportsman's groups aligned together out of fear that the small cats would develop a taste for venison or elk.

Successful restoration of the species to its former habitat had to coincide with the ten-year predator-prey food cycle with snowshoe hares in Canada. Instead of having Canadian trappers catch and kill lynx for their pelts, trappers were paid a higher amount to use live traps. Living lynx were then flown from Canada, where they are abundant, to the United States, where they had virtually disappeared. But it had to happen during an upswing in the lynx population, because nature rules.

When the snowshoe hare population plummets in a natural decade-long cycle, so do numbers of lynx. Catching live lynx, getting them through customs as an endangered species, bringing them hundreds of miles south to Colorado, and letting them go again required intense consultation, federal and state permits, and a dedicated and committed staff. Mumma had the staff; now he needed the lynx.

By 2005, 218 animals had been released. After eating Kip Stransky's dead bunnies, lynx have found their ecological niche and now munch on snowshoe hares, grouse, ptarmigan, squirrels, and other small game including mice. In turn, lynx are eaten by coyotes. A few lynx have had difficulty adjusting to the San Juan Mountains. Lynx never were numerous in the southern Rockies. Ute Indians have lived in the San Juans for hundreds if not thousands of years, and there's no Ute word for the small felines.

～

Though the goal had been for released lynx to survive, establish territories, find mates, and have kittens, in 2007, for the first time, no new kittens were found. Nada. Nothing. Zero. Where were the missing lynx? Even the experts didn't know, but the species has since recovered its birth rate.

Like other professionals securing a future for Colorado lynx, Kurt Broderdorp of the U.S. Fish and Wildlife Service is passionate about the prospects. He says, "The state has reintroduced a top-tier predator, which brings an ecosystem back into balance. From an ecological perspective we're bringing this predator back where it occurred, and this has positive psychological benefits to Colorado residents." In other words, we like our wilderness wild, and we like to know that somewhere out there silky gray and white cats are softly walking on pine needles and spongy moss at the edge of treeline.

Kip Stransky has lynx poop on a plaque. He'd love to see one in the wild, gliding ghostlike through an aspen grove on a winter's day. What happened to the kitten crop, the missing lynx? Will lynx survive in the mountains and become ever more popular for all-season visitors? Only the lynx know, and they're not telling. Perhaps half a century from now, we'll know more.

~

There are many stories to tell about animal encounters in the Southwest. There's much to say about habitat, about predators and prey, wildlife and wildlands. The Mexican grey wolf is trying to make a comeback in northern New Mexico and northern Arizona. Rare jaguars have been seen on the Arizona-Mexico border. To be outdoors in the Southwest and to not experience animals is to miss out on nature's diversity.

I'll never forget a glorious mid-September afternoon, driving on a forest road through a canopy of oak brush and ponderosa, and stopping to watch with binoculars a harem of cow elk move silently through the autumn colors to stand beside a huge bull elk almost invisible in the fall foliage. I'd never seen a larger elk or one with more females around him. His antlers perfectly matched the nearby tree limbs, and his brown coat blended with the dark bark. We watched for several minutes and then quietly drove on, leaving him to his reproductive duties, and leaving us with a deep appreciation for natural camouflage and the mystery of wildlife in wild places.

Enjoy the following essays. Keep a lookout for songbirds, raptors, and lizards, especially leopard lizards or collared lizards with their iridescent blue-green necks pulsing during mating season. My hero, President Theodore Roosevelt, said, "Be practical as well as generous in your ideals. Keep your eyes on the stars and keep your feet on the ground." I would add, Keep your eyes open for animals, too. In a kayak or canoe, concentrating on a river's rapids only makes sense, but also look to the shoreline. There may be a beaver or a bighorn staring back at you.

Notes

1. Daniel Botkin, *Our Natural History: The Lessons of Lewis and Clark* (New York: Berkley Publishing, 1995), 132. For other standard references on wolves, see Barry Lopez, *Of Wolves and Men* (New York: Scribner's, 1978); Bruce Hampton, *The Great American Wolf* (New York: Henry Holt, 1997); Gary Wockner, Gregory McNamee, and SueEllen Campbell, eds., *Comeback Wolves* (Boulder, CO: Johnson Books, 2005).

2. Aldo Leopold, "Thinking Like a Mountain," from *A Sand County Almanac* (1949; New York: Ballantine Books, 1970), 137–41.

3. Michael J. Robinson, *Predatory Bureaucracy: The Extermination of Wolves and the Transformation of the West* (Boulder: University Press of Colorado, 2005).

4. Because of a lack of predators, with so many extra deer on the North Rim, a wacky idea emerged to drive some of those deer down off the rim, across the Colorado River, and up to the South Rim where there were few mule deer. See Brad Dimock, "Jack Fuss and the Great Kaibab Deer Drive," *Boatman's Quarterly Review* 17, no. 2 (Summer 2004).

5. See David Petersen, *Ghost Grizzlies* (Boulder, CO: Johnson Books, 1998). Other important grizzly books include Frank Craighead, *Track of the Grizzly* (San Francisco: Sierra Club Books, 1979); Doug and Andrea Peacock, *The Essential Grizzly* (Guilford, CT: Lyons Press, 2006); and David Knibb, *Grizzly Wars: The Public Fight over the Great Bear* (Cheney: Eastern Washington University Press, 2009).

6. For wolves and a conservative perspective from ranchers, see Tom Findley, "The Wolves of Gooseberry Creek," *Range Magazine*, Summer 2004. For information on wolves and their native habitat, see Douglas Gantenbein, "Fire Away," *Outside*, December 2007; John Dougherty, "Last Chance for the Lobo," *High Country News*, December 24, 2007; Daniel Glick, "Still Howling Wolf," *High Country News*, November 10, 2008; and Tom Wolf, "World Champion Wolfer," *Inside/Outside Southwest*, March 2009.

7. Leopold, *Sand County Almanac*, 237–61.

8. Colorado River Recovery Program, U.S. Fish and Wildlife Service, P.O. Box 25486, Denver Federal Center, Denver, CO 80225.

9. See P. Barrows and J. Holmes, *Colorado's Wildlife Story* (Denver: Colorado Division of Wildlife, 1990). According to the U.S. Fish and Wildlife Service, in 1970 the peregrine was listed as endangered under the Endangered Species Conservation Act of 1969, which preceded the Endangered Species Act of 1973.

10. Other Colorado sites vital to peregrine reintroduction included Perins Peak and Chimney Rock.

11. Jack Turner, *The Abstract Wild* (Tucson: University of Arizona Press, 1996), 111, 112.

12. Ibid., 90.

13. John Nielsen, *Condor* (New York: Harper Collins, 2006), 2, 27. Also see Sophie A. H. Osborn, *Condors in Canyon Country* (Grand Canyon, AZ: Grand Canyon Association, 2007).

14. Quoted in Turner, *Abstract Wild*, 17, 13.

15. Mitch Tobin, "Getting the Lead Out," *High Country News*, March 5, 2007.

16. See Andrew Gulliford, "Condors—the Best Air Show in the West," Writers on the Range, *High Country News*; appeared in the *Salt Lake Tribune*, November 10, 2007.

17. Quoted in Turner, *Abstract Wild*, 123.

18. Andrew Gulliford, "The Missing Lynx: A Ten-Year Eco-Update on the Lynx Reintroduction to Colorado," *Inside/Outside Southwest*, August/September 2007.

In Search of Grizzlies in the South San Juans Wilderness

Platoro, Colorado

Thirty years ago the last grizzly bear in Colorado was killed in the South San Juans. Supposedly. On the chance that a big bruin or two had been hiding in the remote wilderness all these years, a friend and I backpacked in late one summer to take another look. Yes, I was afraid of actually meeting a grizz on the Continental Divide Trail, but my strategy was to push my six-foot-two hiking buddy in front to stand by the bear and wave for perspective while I took a photo. Then I'd turn and run.

Actually, I was even more afraid of collapsing under the weight of my backpack, since it had been years since I'd shouldered it for such an extended hike. So I jettisoned extra gear, including a tent. Starting at Platoro Reservoir in Conejos County on the eastern side of the divide, we hit Rito Azul Trail and began the hike up to Blue Lake, the headwaters of the Navajo River, and some of the finest grizzly habitat in the lower forty-eight states.

In the Weminuche Wilderness I'd ridden horseback into La Rincon de la Osa, or "the Hiding Place of the Bear," near La Ventana, ("The Window"). The last grizzly trapped in Colorado was killed there in 1952 in a place appropriately named by the Spanish two hundred years earlier.

After Lloyd Anderson trapped that bear, everyone assumed it was the last. And it was, until another grizz showed up in 1979. Guide and outfitter Ed Wiseman killed it with an arrow under questionable circumstances. He claimed he caught an old sow in her daybed and, in self-defense, stabbed it with a hunting arrow. What really happened is hard to say. Area Division of Wildlife Manager Patt Dorsey believes, "The true story is locked forever in the heart of the San Juans." I figured if grizzly bears showed up every twenty or thirty years, it was time for an encore. So up the trail we went.

The first day we hoofed it around Blue Lake, picked up the Continental Divide Trail, then left the smooth path with its stone cairns to drop over the edge into the headwaters of the Navajo River and highcountry paradise. That first night I was so tired that if a grizz had come into camp I'd have cuddled next to it and used it for a pillow.

Deep in the heart of the 158,790-acre South San Juan Wilderness, on the second day we shifted from backpacks to daypacks and set out on Fish Lake Trail in search of the wily grizz. At one time in Colorado there were hundreds if not thousands of grizzly bears with nicknames such as Old Clubfoot, Old Four Toes, Old Saddleback, and Old Mose. To this day you'll find dozens of place-names such as Grizzly Creek and Grizzly Peak. Even after the "last" grizz was killed in 1979, big bear sightings continued.

District Wildlife Manager for Pagosa North Mike Reid states, "The absence of proof isn't proof of absence." Reid adds, "Some hikers and hunters think they've seen a grizz because they've spotted a large brown bear. The remaining Colorado bear species is a black bear, but in our state the largest number of black bears are brown in color—like chocolate or cinnamon. Without photos, tracks, or other evidence, there's no way to tell what they've seen."

My friend and I hoped to see a slow-moving brown lump with a dished or flattened face, a distinctive hump, and tracks made from long claws. Instead we saw miles of mountains, clear Colorado blue skies, and perfect habitat for grizzlies.

I knew that grizzly bears needed at least a hundred square miles each to roam and romp, but as the days went by I came to understand what Patt Dorsey had told me: "Our wilderness is a lot of peaks, and that's not the best wildlife habitat to provide all the needs for big bears. The Colorado of a hundred years ago doesn't really exist. We have a hard time coexisting with black bears." With a note of resignation she had added, "Grizzlies have their own survival strategies, and there's too many of us and not enough wilderness."

Still, we scanned the horizon looking for well-muscled bears, long fur rippling in a breeze. We searched for tracks on the tundra among the bluebells, daisies, clover, and a dozen tiny alpine flowers. I wanted to see a grizz playing in the snowfields, holding its toes and tobogganing down a north-facing slope. Instead there was only wind and a slow-moving storm as we crested the Continental Divide Trail and camped below Gunsight Pass.

The next day we cleared the pass and hiked along the rim to look down into the turquoise waters of Lake Ann. At one point high on the divide we looked northwest into the awesome jumble of pines and cliffs at the head of the Blanco River basin. "Down there," we said. If there's any grizz left in the state they must be between the headwaters of the Navajo and Blanco Rivers in some of the wildest, most remote country we'd ever seen.

The skull of the last grizzly killed in Colorado is at the Denver Museum of Nature and Science. Though the hunter claimed he fought the bear in self-defense, Craig Childs writes in *The Animal Dialogues*, "Years later someone admitted that the hunting party had come upon the grizzly as it foraged in the tall grass of a meadow. She had been killed without warning. Her teeth had been worn to smooth bulbs. Her claws were flat."

I'd like to tell you I dreamed of grizz on our last night in the wilderness. I'd like to say that as we hunkered down in the dark pines like wet trolls for another rainy night, our dogs howled and a huge shape slipped through the trees. But no bears came. After twenty-six miles of backpacking, we'd seen awesome country but no grizzlies. Still, they could be there. I want them to be there.

Pirates of the Granite Gorge—Grand Canyon

Creek Hanauer

> At Carbon Creek we feed the pet raven, Sam,
> While we curse the Bureau and we curse the dam.
> Swamper throws a mudball at that old black crow
> Stuart says, "Now we're jinxed for down below."
> —Vaughn Short, "Seldom Seen and his Macho Crew"
> from *Raging River Lonely Trail*

Ravens (*Corvus corax*): shiny, ebon black, loud, bold beyond belief. They can be more than two feet tall with fifty- to sixty-inch wingspans. The principal adjective that comes to mind when describing the raven: *Ubiquitous*. Ever present, everywhere, far and wide, in other words All-Over-the-Effing-Place!

Ravens fascinate me. My daughter's middle name is Raven. Around my home at the mouth of Knownothing Creek on the South Fork of the Salmon River, in northern California, ravens are loud, bold marauders, soaring on the late-afternoon air currents above the mouth of the creek, raiding nests and generally making sure every other living thing in range of their abrasive, cawing voices was aware these plunderers were in the hood.

From *There's This River . . . Grand Canyon Boatman Stories,* edited by Christa Sadler (Flagstaff: This Earth Press, 2006). Reprinted by permission of the author.

Roadkill, compost, somebody else's empty nest, unattended picnic table . . . all prime Salmon River raven targets.

But by far the most audacious of the raven species make their homes along the Colorado River through Grand Canyon. They are the pirates of the Granite Gorge.

At the beginning of Grand Canyon river trips we remind each other to secure our camp gear against the intrusion of a host of nefarious potential pests: mice, fire ants, scorpions, ringtail cats, and rattlesnakes, to name a few. But even though river rangers have been known to warn groups that "you will be assigned two ravens," it's not until we encounter our first ravens in a camp farther on downriver that caution is halfheartedly adhered to. Folks tend to be a bit skeptical: "I mean really, a mouse might chew through my dry bags in search of hidden goodies. Scorpions, ick! A rattlesnake, sure, they'll kill ya! But a raven? Come on, man, it's a bird!"

The biggest, boldest swashbucklers of Grand Canyon inhabit a popular lunch spot and camp at the mouth of Carbon Creek, river right a couple of miles below the Little Colorado River. Woe to you if you dare leave even the slightest morsel unattended for the briefest moment. You *will* lose it to the gigantic, taunting black raven strutting brazenly through camp, just beyond reach. There is often a shout and mad dash to the kitchen at some point during a meal to chase away the big devils that have sneaked in while we were engaged by the more social decoys. The only time I've failed to see ravens at Carbon Camp were the days we've ducked into camp because the wind was blowing so hard both the kayaks and rafts were being blown back upriver, despite all efforts to the contrary. Hell, we could barely keep camp in camp. Don't know where the ravens hunkered down.

On a private trip in '97 we arrived at Carbon Creek a little before midday, too early for lunch but with plenty of time for a hike. We went up Carbon Creek to the top of the canyon, where it breaks open into the Great Unconformity. There used to sit a big ol' hunk of stromatolite about the size of a VW Beetle, called the Brain Rock (now broken and strewn the length of the canyon after being picked up and beaten to gravel by a flash flood in 2002). It was a warm, sunny day, no ravens in evidence, so pretty easy to overlook their probable presence. Thinking ahead, our food organizer decided to get a jump on dinner and pulled the partially frozen halibut steaks from the cooler to defrost them on the raft tubes while we hiked up the canyon: bad move #1. Bad move #2: everyone went on the hike. I remember glancing at the baggies of halibut steaks thawing in the sun and having the fleeting shadow of a discomfiting thought cross my mind before I turned upcanyon and immediately

Ravens and river runners have several things in common including their love for Grand Canyon beaches. Very intelligent birds, ravens can work in teams to steal food and small objects and even open zippers. Here a pirate raven is poised near rafts along the Colorado River in Grand Canyon, waiting to see what tasty morsel river guides might bring out of the coolers for lunch. Photo courtesy of Creek Hanauer.

forgot anything but the adventure ahead. When we returned a couple hours later, the warmth of the summer sun coaxed us back to the river, very pleased with our day. That is, until someone finally woke up to the fact that every one of our baggies full of halibut was missing! Dinner was gone before lunch!

To the ravens sitting in the rock crannies above, we must have looked a lot like a colony of ants that had lost its queen. We jumped about the boats cursing as we scrambled to look in the bilges, under ropes, straps, and duffel, to no avail. Probably too stuffed to move, the ravens politely refrained from rubbing it in with their infamous cawing laughter.

~

At lower flows 122 Mile Camp is large. It's got a big ol' sandbar expanse where folks camp far and wide. On one trip a young fella had spread his sleeping kit out on the upper reaches of the sandbar. After he had bathed in the river and spruced up, he went off to the kitchen to grab a brewski and snag some munchies before dinner. He had stuffed some of his gear back in his dry bag, but he hadn't secured it. (Not much of a challenge either way, as ravens have been seen unzipping closed tent flaps and unclipping Fastex dry bag buckles.) Feet crossed and lying back up in camp, he was startled by a cry from the sandbar and looked up to see another boater pointing to a raven with a baggie of stuff in its beak struggling to fly off with its ill-gotten gains.

"Oh my God! That's my wallet! My ID!" he shouted as he sprang from his beach chair and took off across the sandbar after the fleeing raven. The raven was laboring mightily, dragging the cache across the sand, never quite able to lift its treasure off the ground. But it was unwilling to quit trying, so our young fella was closing in on the tenacious buccaneer. Another realization had crossed the young man's mind that caused him to greatly accelerate his pace with the cry, "Shit! That's my stash!" Almost wish the raven had won this one, but with this new dawning our young hero, with a herculean burst of speed, overtook the scoundrel and its swag at river's edge. Then the raven fled the clutches of its pursuer at the last second by dropping the weighty booty in the river, luckily just within reach of our desperate dupe. Up in kitchen, there wasn't a dry eye to be found; the whole camp was rolling around holding their sides with laughter!

$\sim$

On days when we have long hikes planned, our morning camp activity raises the bar far above the normal levels into ostensible chaos. We prepare for the river and put together a hiking kit, which includes making sandwiches and snagging fruit and cookies for a sack lunch. A few years ago, the morning our group would be hiking the Tapeats–Thunder River hike was such a day. With the camp scene in a tizzy, two ravens from across the river made their move. They flew into camp together. Cawing loudly to announce their arrival, one raven made a feint toward the gear piling up by the boats at the river's edge, preventing the easily distracted resident humans from noticing that the other raven had made a beeline for the lunch table and snatched a package of cookies in its beak. It quickly swung out over the river and landed on a ledge on the other side. It momentarily fought off its partner for the prize, but a beak full of cookie leaves a bird vulnerable to the snitch move. Their taunting cries of victory followed us downriver as we departed camp that morning.

That was a great blow to the trip that put it into jeopardy. We were running dangerously low on cookies too early in the trip for comfort! Then a couple days later at Havasu Creek, we were saved! A guide from a motor trip already hiking Havasu Canyon said their group had plenty of cookies and he could let us have a couple of packages! Eureka! Since they'd be pulling out before our folks were back from hiking, their guide said he'd stash them in a shirt and stuff them in one of the nooks in the riverside rock shelf. Usually there's someone in the vicinity of the raft areas at Havasu, but this time, apparently not near enough. What were we thinking? As the first hikers returned to the mouth of Havasu that afternoon, they witnessed two ravens pull the T-shirt–wrapped cookie packages from the rock shelf. The dismayed hikers looked on in open-mouthed horror as the cookies tumbled down the rock, free of the T-shirt. Quicker than expected, the ravens had both packages snatched up, and once again our cookies disappeared in plain sight across the river.

~

The canyon ravens are like pirates on the Spanish Main; they need a port of call, a safe haven to fly to in the off hours between raiding innocent river travelers.

We lay helter-skelter in the late afternoon silence, flat on our backs in the basalt amphitheater of Nautiloid Canyon, lost in private thoughts. Six of us silently stared up the steep, vertical canyon walls to the narrow slit of blue sky directly above us. We were listening to silence, a startling lack of sound we don't get on the main canyon's corridor. But there off the river, with the river's sound blocked by the canyon's serpentine twists, we had the silence of God's original cathedral. We separately, together, became aware of a whispering sound, more like a compression of air than a noise; more in harmony with silence than allied with the thunderous tumult of the river. It was a muffled sound, a melodic tone like a mellow alto saxophone. A lone raven flew into the canyon from the river. As it approached we could hear the bird's soft cawing gently echo off the canyon walls as it slowly flew into our sanctuary. In the sanctum of such profound silence the sound was almost startling. Days later (was it only moments?) we became aware of a hushed whisper of air softly shed from the wings of the raven as it left the recess of Nautiloid on imperceptible currents, the air beneath the raven's wings now sighing softly as it floated out of our reality and returned to the river beyond. We let out our collectively held breath.

We didn't speak as we returned to camp. We had no need. We were blessed.

Grand Canyon river guides are more than a little superstitious about the Colorado River's ravens. We all curse the stealthy devils when appropriate, but, not so secretly, we all admire the freebooter's brazenness.

River guides and ravens—it must be the pirate thing.

A Ghost in the Night—Cedar Mesa

David Petersen

Exhausted from the day's explorations, I sag into camp at dusk, drop my pack, and slump down to the living heart of this particular Cedar Mesa oasis—a drip-spring tucked away in a shaded slickrock grotto at the head of a small side canyon. Uncapping my two canteens, I place them on the sand beneath twin slow trickles of sparkling water droplets emerging, as if by magic, from a seam in the sandstone wall. There is no sweeter music, wrote Ed Abbey, than the *tink-tink-tink* of desert water dripping into a tin cup—or, in this instance, into aluminum canteens. And there is no sweeter taste, I would add, than cool spring water and a splash of good bourbon whiskey spiced by the tangy smoke of a piñon/juniper campfire in the American Southwest on a gentle spring night such as this one promises to be.

As the day dims and the drip-spring drips, drips, in no hurry whatsoever to satisfy my raging thirst, I stand staring in wonder at this blessed anomaly. Here, as in uncounted similar oases flung by geologic happenstance all across the sun-parched Colorado Plateau, appear fecund riparian plant communities utterly dependent for their survival on scant water emerging improbably—one glimmering droplet at a time—from solid rock. Like the biblical burning bush, desert drip-springs are miracles in the wilderness—miracles you can *drink*.

Here, as in so much canyon-country elsewhere, enlivening the damp grotto wall along and below the horizontal seep-line are lush green folds of moss. Directly below, in and around the pellucid little pool, thrives a refreshing desert garden of cattails, bracken ferns, Indian rice grass, and one saucy, red-lipped, perplexingly named, unbearably beautiful monkey flower (*Mimulus eastwoodiae*).

At my feet (blessedly bare of boots again), the damp sand rimming the pool provides a guest register of recent visitation. From the clear fresh prints I read that a cottontail rabbit, various tiny rodents, a fox, and an adult mule deer, the usual lot of thirsty desert mammals, have been here recently.

Nor—by George!—is that all.

Nearby, in the grotto's slickrock bottom, in the failing light, at the periphery of my vision, at a place where rainwater runoff has washed a few inches of sand into a depression and left it damp, I discern an odd imprint, eerily

From *Cedar Mesa: A Place Where Spirits Dwell* by David Petersen (Tucson: University of Arizona Press, 2002). Copyright © 2002 David Petersen. Reprinted by permission of the author.

Unlike wolves in the Southwest, mountain lions were never exterminated, and now their numbers have grown. The sleek cats live in both suburban and wilderness settings, and they have been known to follow backpackers and hikers. Drawing © Veryl Goodnight.

familiar yet enigmatic. After fumbling in a pocket for my mini flashlight, I move closer to investigate. There, the pale yellow beam cuts through the graying twilight gloom to reveal a track as big as a big man's palm—much larger than any coyote, though not so big as an adult bear—and no claw marks. The bilobed front edge and trilobed rear of the wide palm pad are clearly distinguished in the impressionable sand and irrefutably indicative of . . . cougar. The single print is sharp-edged, moist, chillingly fresh. I search all around but find no others. Apparently, the big cat ventured just this one step off the slickrock toward the spring, then inexplicably withdrew.

My skin prickles with the knowledge that one of the most sublime megapredators in North America has been here, *right here,* and not so long ago—a beast of the elite clan popularly, and rightly, referred to as "charismatic megafauna."

Back at the track, I drop to my knees and study the print from every angle, then stand again and point the little flashlight all around. But the batteries are weak, and the limping beam is all but useless. Too soon, both twilight and flashlight will fade completely, and I'll be left here in the dark (as my father liked to say) "like Moses when the lights went out." And utterly alone—or, more worrisome yet, *not* alone. A tingle crawls up my spine and I feel my pulse accelerate.

Be cool, I counsel myself. Like the old saw says, there's nothing to fear but . . . what? Why is it we tend to fear the unseen more than the visible, the unknown more than the known, the uncertain more than the absolute?

Statistically, you are several hundred times less likely to be attacked by a mountain lion than to be struck by lightning. Yet, *you* aren't here, *I* am. There isn't a storm cloud in sight and statistics don't count for shit when the biggest lion track I've ever seen is fresh at my feet and my heart is hammering in my throat.

Wasting time no more, I snatch up the two sloshing, half-filled canteens in one hand—the quart they hold between them will have to do until morning—clutch the increasingly impotent flashlight in the other hand, and scurry back to nearby camp and the comforts of home and hearth. While it's only a couple of hundred yards from the spring, camp is up and out of the darkling grotto and in the relative open and thus, perhaps falsely, reassuring.

After replacing the spent flashlight batteries with spares from my pack, I distract myself with evening chores: retrieve ground cloth, sleeping pad, and bag from the piñon in which they've hung all day to freshen in the fragrant shade; arrange them neatly on the soft sand—a bit nearer the fire than last night; kindle a companionable blaze; boil water for tea; then scorch and devour a big bloody elk steak brought from home—still frozen yesterday but way past thawed tonight. We sure don't need any lion bait lying about.

Much later, following the usual flame-gazing, whisky-sipping, and internal campfire philosophizing, I toss a final club of wood atop the shimmering pool of red-orange coals, then strip and slide into the cocoonlike comfort of my sleeping bag. Just me, ten thousand desert stars above (the most, I read somewhere, the unaided human eye can discern), and two butterfly-sized bats—Mexican free-tails, I presume—flitting and diving amongst the confused multitude of moths circling the fading edges of firelight. Unavoidably, my mind keeps traveling back to that big round track down by the spring, and sleep is a long time coming.

$\sim$

Around midnight, my fitful sleep is happily interrupted by a family of coyotes, yammering maniacally, sounding (I know from long experience) much closer and more numerous than they are. How I love that wild, uncensored music! That anthem of freedom, self-reliance, and joy!

The fire, once so warm and cheering, has grown cold as worn-out love. I manage to hold my eyes open just long enough to witness one green-tailed shooting star making an ambitious rush for the western horizon, only, like so many human dreamers, to burn out and die in the trying.

Sometime later, when the dream comes, it is shapeless, blind, and haunting. There are no visual images but only eerie, suspiring, susurrus sounds—like the guarded footfalls of a prowler, breathing shallow and fast. Feeling vaguely threatened by this spooky chimera, I come wide awake and rise on my elbows. Though I'm warm in my bag, my arms are pimpled with gooseflesh. I peer into the swampy darkness but see only black. I listen, but no sound comes. All is quiet in the anthracite desert night. The stars have dimmed, the coyotes gone quiet, even the owls and crickets have hushed, predicting incipient dawn. I consider switching on the flashlight for a good look around, but don't, for fear I'll think myself a coward come morning.

Finally, feeling foolish, reminding myself it was only a dream, I lie back and hope for sleep to return.

～

In the amber glow of morning, I wake bleary-eyed and groggy to discover that the night's eerie dream was no dream at all. There, in the powdery sand just a body's length out from my sleeping place and imprinted over one of my own bare footprints, is a big round track.

I unzip my bag, struggle out, stand and peer around. The prints are everywhere. Over there, the lion approached from the sage. And those odd marks show where he, or she, sat back on bony haunches, long tail sweeping an arc in the desert dust. From that reflective repose I imagine the prowler staring at me with huge nocturnal eyes, listening, sniffing my acrid, sweaty scent, panting softly, pondering the innocent sleeper in inscrutable feline fashion.

As best I can read the jumbled sign, it appears the cat then moved to the far side of the fire pit and haunch-sat again. And over there, its curiosity apparently satisfied—or maybe I startled it with my sudden awakening—the spectral visitor padded back into the sage from which it had come. Perhaps it remains nearby even now, watching and waiting, biding its time, biding mine.

Succumbing to a reckless urge, I pull on shorts, lace boots over sockless feet, and follow the departing trail. But the prints soon strike slickrock. And that is that.

Warmed by strong camp coffee and growing increasingly relaxed under a brilliant morning sun, I sit and reflect. Had the cat been looking to make a meal of me, it likely could have. Pumas are predation perfected, capable of bringing down not just deer, but creatures as large as elk, cattle, even horses—and on very rare occasion, people. Stalking close, then pouncing after a short rush, the cougar kills by sinking long canines into the skull or neck of its startled prey, then clamping, viselike, with powerful jaws while ripping and shredding with the fanglike dewclaws inside both forearms. It's a high-risk way to earn a living—those sharp, flying deer hooves thrashing in your face— and most lions show the scars of their profession. By comparison, a naked snoring man would be cake.

Obviously, predation was not the cat's intent. Or perhaps it was, but drawing near, the keen-nosed animal was offended by my unwashed, unappetizing aroma. But far more likely, I spooked it from the spring last night, and it's been lurking nearby ever since, curious as a cat, innocent of ill intent.

Was I in any danger? I'll never know for sure. And just as well.

Which is to say, with all my introductory carrying on about magic and spirituality, I am not a spiritual person in any mystical, otherworldly sense of the term. Magical thinking of any stripe sends me sprinting for the nearest exit to reality. What I can see, hear, smell, taste, and caress is plenty good enough for me, here and hereafter. Yet, out here in the ancient dust, out here among Anasazi ghosts and nocturnal dream creatures, out here in the pulsing heart of the living Old West—here in this place where spirits dwell—I feel that I've been touched by magic.

Counting Sheep: Desert Bighorns Earn Their Wings— San Juan River

Lynell Schalk

The weather was not cooperating. For the past twenty-four hours, late January snows mixed with sleet had driven the residents of Bluff, Utah, indoors. Roads leading out of town were slick with ice. Nike's shout came as I was walking to the corral early that morning to feed my horse. "Lynell, the helicopter pilot says it's a go! We're leaving in ten minutes." Nike Stevens is my neighbor and a wildlife biologist. Under contract to the Navajo Nation, she and her husband, Dave, have been studying the population dynamics of desert bighorn sheep for nearly twelve years along the San Juan River between Bluff and Glen Canyon.

Today we would be starting a four-day desert bighorn sheep transplant operation. The herd along the San Juan River corridor now numbered 160 sheep, enough to make it possible for some of the animals' relocation. Any

---

Originally published in *Inside/Outside Southwest*, June–July 2008, 38–40. Used by permission of the author.

A bighorn ram descends
a steep cliff. Drawing
courtesy of Colorado Parks
and Wildlife.

more than their current numbers and the habitat would be overgrazed. Unlike bighorn in some areas of the American Southwest, this rare indigenous herd seems to be healthy and thriving. Over the past century, bighorn habitat has been reduced by competition from domestic livestock. Wild sheep are particularly vulnerable to disease contracted from neighboring domestic sheep, pneumonia being the most common. Biologists speculate that the desert bighorn sheep along the San Juan River corridor seem to have built up some sort of disease resistance to the nearby presence of their domestic cousins. Or it may simply be that pneumonia is contracted by nose-to-nose contact, and thus far, there has been minimal transference of the disease.

Nike and Dave track the herd's movements through the sheep's radio collars, observing them during the rutting season, witnessing birthing ewes caring for their lambs, and noting the herd's ever-increasing numbers each spring. It's one of those dirty jobs that someone has to do: lazily floating down the San Juan River in the spring, or perched high on the red sandstone cliffs above the river bottom, watching through their binoculars as bighorn forage hundreds of feet below. For Dave, this is a second career, having retired from the National Park Service after working for thirty years as a wildlife biologist in Rocky Mountain National Park. Nike has her Ph.D. in wildlife biology from Colorado State University and has worked as a research biologist for several federal agencies. For this couple, married eighteen years, studying the sheep is a shared passion.

The bitter cold weather of midwinter was chosen for the timing of the capture as it is less stressful for the sheep than hot weather, and the ewes, though pregnant, had not lambed yet. The biologists planned to capture thirty sheep from along the San Juan River and move them to the south side of Lake Powell. Nike and Dave would be in charge of the project. They had spent most of the previous week busily preparing for this transplant operation. Laid out on their living room floor, they carefully bagged an assortment of ear tags, ID microchips, and colored radio collars. Each sheep would be given a different colored collar and ear tags so they could be recognized from a distance.

When Nike asked for volunteers, I readily signed on. There was a limited selection of jobs. Mostly she needed sheep handlers, a crew who would do the controlling of the sheep during their processing. She also needed a data recorder, a position for which my neighbor, Ann Brabrook, volunteered. Ann's husband, Bob, had worked as a veterinarian on the Navajo Reservation for a few years while she worked alongside him as a vet technician. Used to whatever was thrown at her, she would fit right into the project.

Me? That presented a dilemma. "What about someone to be the project photographer?" I had asked, thinking I could take 35mm photos with my thirty-five-year-old Pentax SLR camera. "That would be great! Dave and I generally don't have much time to take photographs during these operations. You can use Dave's 10.2-pixel digital camera." Afterward, I smacked my forehead realizing that I had now obligated myself to learn how to operate a digital camera. I had only days to learn how to use Dave's camera—and my new, still-in-its-box digital camera, which came in a package deal with my new computer. Being a *digital dinosaur,* the pressure was on.

With this morning's break in the weather, the transplant operation was a "go." I tossed a couple of flakes of alfalfa in the feed barrel and hurried back to the house to get my gear and a thermos of hot tea. It was going to be a long, cold day.

The parking lot looked like a used government vehicle sale yard as I pulled my truck into the staging area in the shadow of the world-famous Mexican Hat Rock. I noted the logos on the vehicle doors. Navajo Department of Fish and Wildlife, U.S. Fish and Wildlife, Navajo Department of Agriculture—Veterinarian Services, the Navajo Natural Heritage Program, Arizona Department of Game and Fish, Arizona Desert Bighorn Society, Inc. A large flatbed truck sat along the edge of the staging area containing eight wooden crates, each weighing 350 pounds and able to hold up to three sheep. Four pickup trucks sat tailgate to tailgate. Specially constructed patient litters, each with four leg holes sewn into the canvas, stretched across the tailgates like some sort of jury-rigged wilderness emergency room, awaiting the first chopper-load of patients to arrive.

We stood in the cold morning air, a vigorous wind making it even colder than the twenty-four degrees registered on my truck's thermometer. A biologist from the Navajo Nation shouted out, "Where are the handlers?" A group quickly gathered around him to receive their instructions. "Watch their legs when they are in the litter. You don't want to get kicked, unless you want your voice raised an octave or two. One of you needs to hold the horns. When we move to the crates, on the count of three drop the litter to the ground and shove the animal in the crate."

Just then someone yelled out, "The helicopter's coming!" Two dozen people converged on the staging area to await its arrival. The helicopter swooped in low over the ridge, just south of Mexican Hat Rock. Two bags hung from the belly of the ship. The pilot, a New Zealander working for Pathfinder Helicopter Wildlife Management out of Salt Lake City, dropped in over the snowy field in front of us, hovered momentarily, and gently set the two bagged sheep down on the ground. The line was released and the ship moved swiftly away to land and refuel.

It suddenly became a scene out of an army MASH unit, the ground crew racing to the landing zone with their litters. The specially designed brilliant-blue bags were quickly unlaced, and the sheep were lifted out and placed on the litters, still hobbled and blindfolded. The crews carried the animals to the trucks, where each of the litters was suspended between two truck tailgates. As the hobbles were removed from their legs, one handler held onto the sheep's horns. The other handlers carefully but firmly directed each leg through a hole in the litter. The sheep's legs and feet now dangled in the air, kicking, looking for purchase.

With the animals fully immobilized, the medical personnel approached and took over the next stage of the processing. Dr. Scott Bender, a veterinarian with the Navajo Department of Agriculture based in Chinle, Arizona, worked like a man used to crisis situations, moving swiftly from one procedure to the next, quietly giving the handlers direction as needed. Bender inserted a needle in the sheep's neck, aiming for a vein to draw blood. Some of the blood samples would be provided to Washington State University in Pullman, Washington, for a sheep DNA testing study. The remainder would be frozen and kept on hand for various research requests.

When he finished with the blood, Dr. Bender inserted a specially designed metal tongue depressor down the sheep's throat to take a swab sample, followed by a quick dab from its nose. The swab would be analyzed to determine the presence of either pneumonia or sinusitis. Sinusitis is a disease caused by nose bots and, like pneumonia, is also contracted from contact with domestic sheep. Dr. Bender finished his procedures by implanting an identification microchip under the skin in the sheep's head, carefully positioned between the horn and ear.

Assisting Dr. Bender was Dr. Robert Heyl, a physician from Cortez, Colorado, who volunteered his services for the day, a constant grin on his face, unable to hide his excitement about being a participant in this rare opportunity. He, too, handled the sheep as efficiently as if they were his average office patients, smoothly giving one injection after another in the sheep's rump. A total of five shots would protect the sheep from fourteen different diseases. As the doctors finished their work, other assistants sprayed each sheep's ear for ticks, then attached ear tags and radio collars. While the animals awaited each step, the handlers became bighorn whisperers, gently holding the animals, quietly talking to them, leaning close and stroking their bristly taupe-colored coats to calm them. The medical process was now complete; each sheep had been collared, microchipped, and ear-tagged. The last step was to safely load them into the awaiting crates.

The frenzied mania of the last fifteen minutes abruptly died down. We stood around in the frigid cold with our gloved hands stuffed in our pockets, some of us ducking behind trucks to shelter ourselves from the icy wind. Sheep jokes were tossed back and forth. We waited.

At times we could hear the helicopter in the river canyon to the south of us, looking for more sheep. This part of the capture posed the greatest risk. The pilot flew with the ship's doors removed. He was accompanied by two assistants or sheep muggers. One mugger, with his leg perched on the copter's skid for balance, served as the net gunner, using a rifle to shoot a fine-meshed net over the sheep below him. When the animal was spotted, the pilot dropped the ship down into the canyon and aerially directed the sheep to an area where it could be safely netted, hobbled, blindfolded, and bagged before sling-lining it out of the canyon bottom and back to our staging area.

Sometimes the pilot was unable to land to unload his muggers. As one skid hit the ground, the crew had seconds to bail out before the helicopter lifted off again. They approached the netted sheep, placing a blindfold over its head. This immediately had a calming effect on the struggling animal, enabling the mugger to hobble all four feet together. The animal was then laced into the long-line bag to transport it out of the canyon.

The second helicopter load brought in three sheep, followed by two sets of four each. With the second set of four, the pilot flew in four healthy-looking adult rams with large curled horns. Bighorn paparazzi swarmed around the

Bighorn sheep are making a comeback across the Southwest on their traditional ranges. Individuals from healthy herds are transplanted to create new herds in their original bighorn habitats, which are often identified by prehistoric sheep petroglyphs. This bighorn ewe, from a Navajo Nation herd south of the San Juan River, is masked to keep her calm while she has a medical inspection. Photo courtesy of Lynell Schalk.

operating area like buzzing gnats as the crew worked, trying to capture a few stereotypical trophy shots—but with one exception. These rams were alive. With luck, they wouldn't end up as one of the three permitted hunts the Navajo Nation awards each year. One permit goes to a tribal member, and the other two are sold. These latter two permits fund the transplant operation and the biologists' continuing study of the reservation herd: a few sacrificed for the good of the others.

By early afternoon, the winds had increased the chill factor, which was beginning to take its toll on the crew. As the last sling-line of sheep came over the ridge, the helicopter was swaying in the gusting wind, almost staggering to the landing zone with the bags of heavy sheep swinging pendulously underneath. It was time to call it a day.

Twenty-two sheep were gathered the first day. Another eight remained to be captured and processed in the next few days. That night the animals would be driven south to Kayenta, Arizona, and held overnight in their crates. At daybreak they would be driven out to Lake Powell, where the helicopter would sling-line each crate eleven miles to the sheep's release site. A new herd would now be established, security against a die-off that could otherwise extirpate the herd.

It had been a long and brutally cold day. The crew was chilled to the bone, and my thermos of hot tea was emptied. Time to call it a wrap. One more sheep joke, I thought to myself as I climbed stiffly into my truck and fumbled the ignition key with my cold-numbed fingers: "Let's make like sheepherders and get the flock out of here."

Study Questions

1. What has been your wildest animal encounter? What emotions were going through your head? Did you feel that in some way you could communicate despite the human language barrier?
2. What is your view on reintroduction of once-native species? What precautions need to be taken before a reintroduction effort?
3. As an outdoor educator, how do you prepare students for wildlife encounters? What do they need to know related to at least three species prevalent in your area?
4. What is your opinion on the "Pirates of the Granite Gorge"? Are they pests? Teachers? Tricksters? Something else? What other "pirates" do you know, perhaps in different ecosystems?
5. Have *you* seen the elusive San Juan grizzly? Do you think they might still be out there? Or do only grizzly ghosts remain? Also, do you *want* them out there?

CHAPTER 8

Wilderness Tithing
Giving Back to Public Lands

We make a living by what we do, but we make a life by what
we give.

—Winston Churchill

Never doubt that a small group of thoughtful, committed citizens can change the world; indeed, it's the only thing that ever
has.

—Margaret Mead

The nineteenth-century naturalist Henry David Thoreau wrote, "Dwell as
near as possible to the channel in which your life flows." For many of us that
means trying to bring our avocation and our vocation into close harmony
with this southwestern landscape that we love—towering peaks, deep canyons, wild rivers, miles of sagebrush, ponderosa pines, mesa tops with prehistoric ruins, and cowboy camps on forgotten stock trails. We play and recreate
on public lands, which are so much a part of living in the West, but we don't
often give back.

Sure, we pay plenty of fees and the occasional fine. There are fees for cutting Christmas trees; fees for floating the Green, the Yampa, the Colorado;
and plenty of campground fees even if you are just living out of a tent. There
are entrance fees for national parks and additional paperwork for backcountry hikes. It seems we're always being dunned to play on land that as public
citizens we should have every right to access. And we do have those access
rights, but administering public lands, even managing wilderness, as odd as
that sounds, takes additional dollars.[1]

Federal agencies are pinched, as in the case of the U.S. Forest Service.
They have decreased revenue from the decline in visitation as well as a radical

shift in their budget toward more and more expensive wildland firefighting.[2] So for economic as well as moral reasons, it's time for us to give back to public lands, and there are wonderful opportunities to do so. Colleges now offer outdoor service learning opportunities and a variety of internships. Work-related elderhostels do the same thing. There are also exciting options to be a VIP or volunteer-in-the-parks, as I've done at Glen Canyon National Recreation Area at Lake Powell. Regardless of our age, it's important to give back. Scott Slovic explains, "As many environmentalists have noted, attachment to place (to home) typically leads to a sense of responsibility, a desire to protect particular places and the inhabitants."[3]

We need to pass on our environmental values and continue to press for land conservation, but we also need to educate a younger generation. *New York Times* columnist Nicholas D. Kristof notes, "One problem may be that the American environmental movement has focused so much on preserving nature that it has neglected to do enough to preserve a constituency for nature." He adds, "It's important not only to save forests, but also to promote camping, hiking, bouldering, and whitewater rafting so that people care about saving those forests."[4]

Across the Southwest public lands are used for dozens of wilderness therapy adventures, vision quests, and healing retreats. In *Landscape of Desire*, Greg Gordon describes a two-month field studies program and notes, "I've witnessed how extended time spent in a small group in the wilderness engenders a fundamental shift in the way we regard ourselves and our place in nature. . . . More than anything else the wilderness teaches us how to live in community, as citizens of the biotic community as well as a human community that we actively create."[5] Others go solo through guided therapy programs, as described by Mary Beath in *Hiking Alone* and Bill Plotkin in *Soulcraft*.[6] That's great for the individuals involved; psychological insight and transformation can be profound, but if the land gives us so much, what do we give the land?

Ginger Harmon, canyoneer, climber, guide in Nepal, is a founding member of Great Old Broads for Wilderness, which defends congressionally designated wilderness and wilderness study areas across the American West. Ginger coined the term "wilderness tithing" as the obligation we should all feel for the lands that have given our lives so much meaning, excitement, adventure, solitude, and satisfaction. We need and use wildlands as playgrounds, sanctuaries for the soul, and places to retreat and revitalize before returning to the workaday world.

I agree with Ginger that we need more ties that bind us to the land and landscape. Some of those ties can come from our own sweat: building trails, cleaning beaches along wild rivers, picking up trash, and acting as site

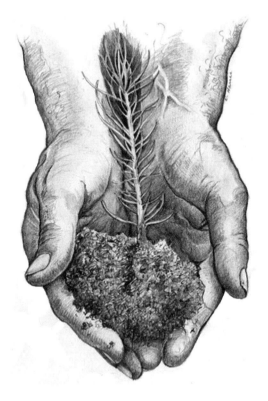

If the environmental and conservation movements are to have a future in the twenty-first century, American youths must get involved in preserving wild places and giving back to public lands. A pine tree seedling is cupped in a pair of hands prior to planting it. Drawing © Krista Harris.

stewards at archaeological and historic sites. Ed Abbey urged us to defend the West against developers, but it's never that simple. As the cartoon figure Pogo stated, "We have met the enemy and he is us."

We leave impacts on public lands despite trying to adhere to the "Leave No Trace" concept, the cornerstone of environmental ethics in the backcountry. Kurt Hahn, the founder of Outward Bound, urged students to learn compassion. Expedition leadership and group travel in wild places is important, but so are service activities and "experiencing the value of compassion through direct action on behalf of the community or specific people in need."[7] In Hahn's day, during World War II, that meant training for rescue service on the coast of England and Wales to save ships and passengers in distress. It meant, and still means, to merge one's ego and identity with larger group goals. For students in the Outdoor Leadership Program at Western State College in Gunnison, Colorado, that means serving on the search and rescue team, which is nationally certified for alpine rescue.

Thomas James explains in an essay on Kurt Hahn, "A thread running from Plato through Hahn and through Outward Bound is the responsibility of individuals to make their personal goals consonant with social necessity. Not only is the part subordinated to the whole, but the part cannot even understand its own identity, its relations, and its responsibility, until it has grasped the nature of the whole."[8] Ecological literacy is a case in point. We need to create more public land advocates, and in order to do so, we have an ecoresponsibility to lead by example.

Great Old Broads for Wilderness

Where on Durango's College Avenue do you see a lavender size 40D bra hanging in a street-side window? Why, the national office of Great Old Broads for Wilderness, of course. Like San Francisco, Boulder, and Flagstaff, Durango has evolved as one of the epicenters of the environmental movement in the West. But there's no group in town, or across the country, quite like Great Old Broads for Wilderness, which will celebrate their twenty-fifth anniversary in 2014.

"We're the junkyard dogs of the environmental movement," quips former executive director Ronni Egan. Now with four thousand members nationwide, the little environmental group that could continues to capture headlines and financial support. The Broads have found their own eco-niche among the stalwart Sierra Club and Audubon Society. How do they do it? With humor, grit, and grace, and a conviction that women fifty and over have an abiding interest in the health of American landscapes. Great Old Broads believe the heart of our nation is our roadless wildlands, which according to Egan "have never been more threatened."

But the group doesn't practice age or sex segregation, either. If you're a young woman under fifty you can join—by becoming a "Broad-in-Training." And if you're a guy like me, you can be a "Great Old Bro." I like that title a lot. I admire their belief in "wilderness tithing," a phrase coined by founding member Ginger Harmon. With some environmental groups you send them a check and wait for the next financial appeal, but with Great Old Broads for Wilderness you get personally involved. That's the recipe that brings American women together from all walks of life and from all parts of the United States for work projects or "Broadwalks." No couch potatoes here.

These are fit, active women eager and ready to hike, document public land issues with digital cameras and GPS units, and push the eco-envelope in the name of natural resource protection. Many Great Old Broads members classify themselves as ecofeminists, but they're not content to drink white wine and complain about pollution; they'd rather assist with work projects at national monuments, camp out in tents, and monitor all-terrain vehicle (ATV) abuse on federal lands in Utah.

Great Old Broads want federal agencies to manage western lands for the health of ecosystems. Their three focus areas are oil and gas leasing, overgrazing, and off-road vehicles. To that end, the group created one of the most important and up-to-date databases on public lands in the West with sixty thousand data points useful to land managers or judges when environmental issues go to federal court. Volunteers document illegal traffic on public lands and the resulting erosion and litter. Then the photos, complete with latitude and longitude coordinates, are uploaded to an online database to create, in Egan's words, "a picture over time of what's happening on the land." She feels strongly that "citizens have to do the work. We have to be the eyes on the land for the understaffed federal agencies."

Great Old Broads for Wilderness began in 1989 in Escalante, Utah, when after several hard days of hiking and backpacking, half a dozen weary women were having lunch in a local café only to read in the newspaper that Utah senator Orrin Hatch (R) stated that we didn't need any more wilderness lands because senior citizens couldn't visit them. Federal wilderness regulations require access only on foot or on horseback, and Hatch felt that the elderly needed lands they could get to in cars, trucks, Jeeps, recreational vehicles, or ATVs. I wasn't there for the ladies' comments, but apparently the discussion got boisterous with recommendations about where the senator could go and how he could get there. When one of the women rose to use the restroom, a male patron remarked, "Now there goes a great old broad." The name stuck and so did the conviction that western women over fifty didn't need a male U.S. senator to tell them what they did or did not want.

After standing up for National Park Service employees getting gassed by snowmobiles idling in West Yellowstone and joining several lawsuits for environmental causes, the feisty group has earned its share of respect. Now the group's membership is booming with local chapters known as Broadbands. The objective is for Broads to pass on their eco-advocacy to another generation of stewards of wilderness and wildlands.

Egan encourages us all to "protect your favorite wild places in the spirited company of kindred passionate souls," because she believes that represents "Broads at their best." She's right. There's nothing I like better than hiking new trails with old friends.[9]

～

Another example of on-the-ground stewardship is the Colorado Fourteeners Initiative, whose motto is "Get out, get up, give back." Because of increased interest in summiting Colorado's highest peaks, trails need realigning and rebuilding, and campgrounds need cleaning. It's one thing to climb a tall peak with your friends and take photos of everyone giving a high five as proof of a successful summit, but it's quite another to make trails to Fourteeners more ecologically safe with less runoff and reduced high-altitude soil erosion.

If a wilderness is a wild place with opportunities for silence, solitude, and darkness, can you improve upon it? Yes! Durangoans from the San Juan Mountains Association canoed the Gunnison River into the Dominguez-Escalante Wilderness and camped along the mouth of Dominguez Creek. With a crew from Volunteers for Outdoor Colorado, and logistics and cuisine provided by Centennial Canoes, they spent a long, hot day removing invasive tamarisks and making the area more accessible for watercraft. Along the river, crews used chainsaws to remove tamarisks at two campsites and handsaws within the wilderness study area. Volunteer Dianne Donovan saw "a remarkable change in just two days." In addition, the next day volunteers planted cottonwood trees along the river, which will eventually provide shade for future generations of wilderness visitors. Donovan says, "It's a beautiful, dramatic canyon."[10] All visitors are urged to walk down to the river and fill a bucket of water to pour on the young native trees. Eco-advocacy can be that simple.

~

And then there's Lake Powell. It's hardly a wilderness with its multistory houseboats—some with hot tubs and interior fireplaces—frenetic Jet Skiers, and noisy motorboats going in swift circles, but it's a vast landscape worthy of protection. The visitors here desperately need to adopt the "Leave No Trace" ethic. I know because I've been there in hundred-degree August heat, wearing river sandals, and walking the shores of Lake Powell through cockleburs, thistles, tumbleweed, and tamarisk. What was I doing? Why, trolling for trash, of course! I had joined Volunteers-in-Parks for the Glen Canyon National Recreation Area, and we were aboard the sixty-five-foot-long *Trash Tracker* houseboat patrolling the coves and bays of Lake Powell. We collected everything from cigarette butts to junk the size of refrigerators.

Our fleet included the houseboat, complete with gas barbeque grill, two bathrooms, and two refrigerators; an aging, aluminum National Park Service flat-bottomed barge named the *Eliminator;* and a battered fiberglass motorboat christened the *Minnow.* With two captains, Bruce and Pat George from Camp Verde, Arizona, and a four-person crew, our goal was to scour the shoreline of Lake Powell in a unique ecovacation whose goal was to give back to public lands.

Supported by Lake Powell Resorts and Marinas and ARAMARK, Lake Powell's concessionaire, the Trash Tracker program has been enormously successful in cleaning up what environmentalists have dubbed "Lake Foul."

ARAMARK provides the houseboat, the runabout, and all gas, ice, and coffee; the sturdy NPS *Eliminator* contains brushes, shovels, sledges, hammers, wrenches, hacksaws, grabbers, and long-handled nets. Volunteers provide the enthusiasm and muscle on five-day trips. In summer the *Trash Tracker* moors out of Stateline Marina at the southern end of the reservoir; in spring and fall it's located at the upper end at Bullfrog Marina.

Volunteer and third-grade teacher Eric Martinez from Yucaipa, California, smiles and says, "*Trash Tracker* launch day is my favorite day of the year. We're on a houseboat with a captain and it's free." Martinez explains, "We like to find things that are unusual," and Captain Bruce George adds, "The bigger the better." Indeed, it's a lot like treasure hunting, and beers found floating in abandoned ice chests do taste better.[11]

The Colorado River drains 246,000 square miles into Lake Powell, whose 1,960-mile shoreline is longer than the entire coast of California, Oregon, and Washington. Plastic water bottles abound, and Pat George notes, "We've found every kind of toy you can imagine and it's amazing how many different kinds of balls there are." Every day brings excitement for new finds, whether twenty yards or so above the water line or a mile back into side canyons. On previous trips in 113-degree heat, the crew found a fifty-five-gallon drum full of sand and muck, a houseboat waterslide a mile away from water, the rusty drive chain off a Dodge half-track truck, refrigerators, Ping-Pong tables, boats, and a full set of golf clubs. Golf balls are as ubiquitous as beer cans. One trash-tracking season garnered 964 of them.

Unlike environmentalists, who cry foul about Lake Powell and avoid the place like the plague, we wanted to reduce some of the collateral damage. The lake's here for the foreseeable future. With its vast shoreline, trash tracking can be truly monumental, because the Colorado River, dammed and damned at Glen Canyon, drains so much of the West. Each morning we had breakfast, boarded the *Eliminator,* and headed out to locate debris from *Americanus slobvius*, that unique human species who frequents Lake Powell, illegally sets off fireworks, builds and abandons numerous fire rings, and leaves human feces on sandbars and beaches.

His tracks are easy to find. Despite rigorous enforcement of "Leave No Trace" backcountry ethics on western wilderness rivers, where Porta Potties and fire pans are mandatory and used by river runners, anything goes at Lake Powell, and it shows. The amount of garbage recovered annually by the Trash Tracker program averages between fifty and sixty thousand pounds.

Tiffany Mapel, an eighth-grade teacher from Durango, believes, "Some people shouldn't be allowed outdoors." Yet she doesn't get disheartened. On our shift we patrolled Gunsight and West Canyons, Friendship Cove, and the

Main Channel. We found busted water balloons, air mattresses, sandals, sunglasses, tent stakes, bras, bullets, caps, cigars, and vintage fishing lures. Our biggest find came on our first day out, and we were as excited as pirates who'd just boarded a cruise ship. Off the Main Channel a flash of white plastic reflecting the sun meant a quick turn into a small rocky outcrop where we hit the jackpot—the entire top of a houseboat, the flying bridge, had blown off in one of Lake Powell's legendary windstorms. There it was. A twisted pile of fiberglass, metal supports, wiring, plastic, and even the upper bridge complete with steering wheel. What a catch! We fairly flew off the aluminum barge to gather up the debris, and it took four of us to wrestle the longer pieces out of the sand. I was prepared for rattlesnakes hiding in tamarisk along the beaches, but no one had warned me of rats. When a brown rodent came out of the muck and quickly crossed my Teva-clad foot, I jumped back, yelling.

Our sense of teamwork and camaraderie was cemented that morning when we filled the *Eliminator* with our first load. We worked as an efficient corps, jumping off boats with trash bags in hand, walking beaches and sandstone ledges at different levels, splitting up, meeting again, eager to share our finds. Enduring the afternoon heat, volunteer Dave Hauswald from Louisville, Colorado, laughed and said, "Lake Powell is about the only place where cold water tastes better than cold beer."

And it wasn't all work. There was time to splash and swim in the eighty-degree lake under a deep blue sky. At night we slept on the houseboat roof with an unimpeded view of the Milky Way. There was time to stop and catch striped bass when a school of them boiled the water directly in front of us, and time to enter a narrow grotto and explore side canyons. Other boaters helped us locate trash and shared their Gatorade and ice.

Lake Powell isn't the sole habitat for *Americanus slobvius;* the species leaves its mark on federal lands across the country. And not everyone intends to leave their trash behind. With 1.5 million annual visitors at Lake Powell, some things just blow off boats. But it's way past time for the National Park Service to require a "Leave No Trace" ethic for all boaters. Fire pans should be mandatory and provided with each houseboat rental, and the lake needs a serious recycling program. Hopefully, the next generation of houseboats will have their own onboard can crushers and shredders for plastic bottles.

Eco-activist Ed Abbey hated Glen Canyon Dam, and he called flooding Glen Canyon an abomination. Indeed, the lake is an artifact of mid-twentieth-century governmental hubris, built before the national Environmental Policy and Endangered Species Acts. River runners and environmentalists may deplore Lake Powell while houseboaters and fishermen may think it's heaven on earth. Whatever you believe, you can either be part of the problem or part of the solution.

~

Getting Trashed at Lake Powell

Most folks get trashed at Lake Powell. They consume cases of beer, bags of Wonder bread, quarts of sunblock, and gallons of soft ice cream at the Dangling Rope Marina. In between large bouts of drinking, they fall off boats, sunburn themselves, drive Jet Skis in tight little circles, and occasionally jump off sandstone cliffs to their deaths. But we were back for another exciting session of trash tracking.

The large seventy-five-foot triple-deck houseboats such as the *Odyssey* rent for $12,000 a week and include air-conditioning, multiple refrigerators,

In June 2013 six environmental studies students from Fort Lewis College participated in the Trash Tracker program at Lake Powell. They lived on a sixty-five-foot-long houseboat for five days. In an aluminum National Park Service barge named *The Eliminator* they picked up a whopping 3,500 pounds of trash, including the hull of a twenty-two-foot-long wooden boat, which they dug out of the sand at Padre Butte. Photo by author.

plasma TV, and a hot tub—as if you needed it in the scorching desert. Add another $5,000 for gas and rental fees for the ski boat and two Jet Skis and you've got a party for a dozen of your closest friends. Houseboat names personify owners' attitudes: *No Pressure, Lovin' It, Moonlight Sonata, Classic Voyageur, Half-Quacked,* and *Sotally Tober.*

Summer insanity thrives at Lake Powell where it's anything goes. Visitors routinely whack golf balls off the roofs of houseboats. They set off illegal fireworks, burn plastic in sandstone fire rings (fire pans are unheard of), and carve graffiti on 200-million-year-old Navajo sandstone walls. In one weekend two people were arrested for "boating under the influence." Deputies also wrote three citations for open containers and sixty-seven for safety violations, and 123 boaters received warnings. You're much safer going through Class III white-water rapids than risking your life boating with *Americanus slobvius* at Lake Powell.

Some folks in the West volunteer to pick up trash to gain good karma and make the planet a better place. Others do it under a judge's orders. We were doing it for the camaraderie, for the hell of it, for the National Park Service, for an ecovacation, and for the free sixty-five-foot-houseboat dubbed the *Trash Tracker.*

On previous excursions in the lake's main channel we picked up pounds of garbage, but this time, our team of teachers, entrepreneurs, and computer geeks, five volunteers and two captains, sought the mother lode of Lake Powell trash. We went for the big one: the fifty-mile-long San Juan arm of the lake. We wanted to set a record for how many bags of garbage we could collect.

Without access to boat fuel or facilities of any kind, the San Juan River is legendary for debris and rolling trees. It is without safety buoys, channel markers, or an easy place to moor at night. Captain Pat George said, "I don't like the San Juan. It's too dangerous. Too many floating debris fields that can nail boat props and sink ships." But we were determined to tackle the job. We wanted to make a difference.

We started out small—cans, bottles, bobbers, tennis shoes, sandals, shotgun shells, clay targets, boat seats, but we worked our way up to the harder stuff. Ever try to pull a rusted-out, doorless refrigerator onto a boat while slip-sliding in mud and goo? In the dark thick soup of mud, ooze, and millions of clogged tamarisk seeds we found every kind of ball, battered propane bottles, abandoned medical vials, pounds of Styrofoam, and one black hand grenade—plastic. We found coolers, microwaves, children's chairs, helium bottles, metal water coolers, broken glass, and fire extinguishers. But the big story on the San Juan River, above the main Lake Powell channel and below, where river runners take out at Clay Hills Crossing, are tires and rims. They bounce out of Aztec, Farmington, and Shiprock, New Mexico. They roll down creeks, gullies, and canyons off the Navajo Rez, and sooner or later, they float in the lake. So the race was on. Could we set a new record for trash tracking in one week on the San Juan arm? Easy.

There are thirteen canyons on the San Juan arm; we went into Nasja, Bald Rock, Cha Bay, Piute Canyon, Neskahi Wash, and Alcove Canyon on the Great Bend. All totaled we collected seventy-six large, full garbage bags of trash, one refrigerator, one marine battery, a whopping twenty-four tires and rims, and a box of shit. Yes, that's right, a floating groover or .50 caliber machine gun or metal rocket box that some river runner had "accidentally" lost. Our river booty included one Perception kayak paddle, one toy boat, a soaker squirt gun, and a blue plastic fish with thick lips. It was a good haul, but we'll be back. It's always easy to get trashed at Lake Powell.[12]

Scrubbing Graffiti on the True GRIT

There's another houseboat on Lake Powell that volunteers use to address an equally important problem across the Colorado Plateau and at Glen Canyon National Recreation Area: modern graffiti.

Historian and guide Fred Blackburn has found that within any site, including thousand-year-old cliff dwellings, "when one person signs, especially on beautifully plastered walls, other people then record their names." The original inscriptions are valuable historic information, attests historian and canyoneer Steve Allen. He says, "Back then there was a story to be told. With those signatures and inscriptions we can follow pioneer paths."[13] But understandable behavior during the exploration and settlement phase of the American West centuries ago in no way condones recent writing on rocks. Wanton graffiti mars the Colorado Plateau, because each year hundreds of thoughtless people carve on rock and deface public lands, which can result in a misdemeanor charge and a $6,000 federal fine. Across the Plateau the "Leave No Trace" ethic has a long way to go. At Glen Canyon National Recreation Area on the shores of Lake Powell, the National Park Service recruits volunteers to remove graffiti by scrubbing sandstone. So I joined up. I became a member of the Graffiti Removal Intervention Team (GRIT) and six of us lived for a week on the fifty-two-foot houseboat named the *True GRIT*.

As an avid hiker, giving back to public lands by scrubbing sandstone seems an important part of "wilderness tithing." I spend a lot of time on public turf, so why not give back? Bill and Carol Williams and Bob and Vicki Schwartz gave back by donating the vintage 1980s Skipperliner houseboat now named the *True GRIT*. The first few days we learned safety procedures, followed up on tips from a previous crew, and got into the graffiti removal groove. I like traversing canyons with a backpack and climbing sticks, but working with the GRIT group we carried blue buckets with squirt bottles of water, hammers, wire and bristle brushes of different sizes, safety goggles, and work gloves. The hammers were to smash signatures a half inch or more in depth prior to smoothing over the rock with the wire and bristle brushes. Captain Gene Longo taught me that "the final strokes should go with the grain to leave as little mark as possible." We learned to tell from the sandstone's patina how new the graffiti is.

After positioning the houseboat we took the Park Service's runabout to explore other areas. One morning, bucket in hand, I went into the cool shade of a narrow canyon, reflecting on what Glen Canyon must have been like a century ago, and after rounding a point and coming back toward water I saw four names scrawled on rock. Historic inscriptions have detail and context, but on the lake 90 percent of the graffiti constitutes first names only with no context whatsoever.

Following standard procedure, I drew the names on a pad, photographed the graffiti, and then with relish reached for a steel brush. Within minutes the names were gone. With the softer bristle brush I tidied up the surface using the spray bottle of water to soften the stone. Feeling deeply satisfied that I'd eliminated names from a quartet of Lake Powell morons, I rejoined the GRIT group. Capt. Longo and his wife Cyndy explain, "Our goal is to get as much of the lake's canyons as natural as possible."

The next day was the same—a little graffiti here, a scrub-a-dub there. We were doing our job, but we had yet to encounter the true tracks of *Americanus slobvius*, known to carve on the 1,960 miles of Lake Powell shoreline. With only a few days to go, we motored up West Canyon into a small slot canyon. Not thinking we'd find anything, we stepped off the boat with trash bags and walked up the slot. Soon I found a dinosaur image someone had chalked on the canyon wall. As I was preparing to retrieve my brush bucket, I heard shouts from deeper in the slot.

In that warm and sacred light, beneath steep ascending walls, I walked up the canyon with reverence as in entering a cathedral. I love the light in slot canyons and how their beauty evokes hushed tones. I walked toward the quiet voices of my crew. When I got to the end I was mesmerized.

It's hard to describe my feelings and how quickly they changed. At first I was stunned by the beauty of the miniature canyon and the size of the choke-stone caught in a crack at its end. Then I was dumbfounded to see dozens of senseless names sprawled all over the dark, sensuous sandstone covering more than a hundred square feet and thirty feet in height. Party boats had found this slot, and mindless minions had left their spoor beginning with a name and a 1992 date. Shock at the amount of graffiti turned to intense anger then doubt as to whether we could clean it all off. But we began with our secret weapons—long-handled broken oars with four steel brushes secured by duct tape. We even had a smaller, banjo-sized paddle with its own brushes to exert maximum torque when we leaned into the sandstone to scrub, scrub, scrub.

As I pounded on the deeper names with a hammer, then brushed and sanded, I thought about the most historic inscription ever found at Lake Powell, the 1776 Dominguez and Escalante inscription, and how two vandals named Rob and Kathi had gouged their names over it in 1994. The damage was so deep and the patina on the eighteenth-century inscription so fragile that the graffiti cannot be removed. A digital photographic process can reproduce the original carving, but the inscription itself is now covered over. As a historian, I was incensed by that act of vandalism, and that had led me to join the *True GRIT*.

That anger gave more power to my arms and shoulders as we worked in the slot canyon to remove sixteen years of mindless letters and gouges—some 1¼ inches deep and others only a month old. On previous GRIT trips, in just one year, 1,400 volunteer hours of graffiti removal at Lake Powell eliminated 17,280 square feet of paint and rock carving. In our week we sanded 195 square feet, but like the plague, you have to stop graffiti at its source.

Some families put their initials on rocks as part of annual houseboat vacations. As GRIT volunteer Jean Schwarz explains, "Once somebody starts, it snowballs." Ada Hatch agrees. She says, "Once they see two or three names then they want to carve theirs," which is why on the Escalante Arm, at the base of Rainbow Bridge, on Delicate Arch, along Capitol Reef and at Wahweap Window, you find lots of graffiti.

Historical inscriptions with names and dates fifty years and older have value and context as part of the archaeological record. They're protected under federal law. On two-hundred-million-year-old Navajo sandstone, modern graffiti defaces and disfigures the beauty and mystery of the Colorado Plateau. So we scrubbed away, trying to remove traces from vandals to avoid copycat graffiti scribblers.

～

Giving back to public lands is a simple concept. Because we use and abuse public lands in the West, it's time to share a little of ourselves and give back.

We need to clean up Anasazi ruins defiled by vandals shooting paint pistols; build trails, water bars, and bird houses; and weed-whack tamarisk wherever it can be found. Volunteers can stabilize historic and prehistoric structures and leave the landscape a little cleaner, a little greener, than what we found. Volunteers can assist in national parks and national monuments, be site stewards and monitor historic sites in canyons and on alpine trails, and plant young cottonwood trees along riparian corridors. Giving back connects us to the land we love, and by sharing our respect for wildlands, perhaps we can lead by example.

Aldo Leopold urged us to adopt a land ethic, to become one with the community of life in a distinct ecosystem. We can do that. We can share our time, our talents, our resources. Wilderness tithing is about connecting people and place with intrinsic ties that bind—the bonds of landscape restoration and habitat preservation.

What follows are other stories about giving back to public lands in the American Southwest and on the Colorado Plateau. It's not enough to use public lands for adventure, exploration, psychological insight, and wilderness expeditions. It's important to tithe a little, too.

Notes

1. See John C. Hendee, George H. Stankey, and Robert C. Lucas, *Wilderness Management*, USDA Forest Service, Publication No. 1365, October 1978, USDA Forest Service.

2. Will Sands, "Vanishing Visitors: Forest Service Reports Drop in Recreation," *Durango Telegraph*, July 30, 2009, 9.

3. Scott Slovic, ed., *Getting over the Color Green: Contemporary Environmental Literature of the Southwest* (Tucson: University of Arizona Press, 2001), xxiv.

4. Nicholas D. Kristof, "American Kids Are Raised Far Too Disconnected from Nature," *Durango Herald*, August 4, 2009.

5. Greg Gordon, *Landscape of Desire: Identity and Nature in Utah's Canyon Country* (Logan: Utah State University Press, 2003), x.

6. Mary Beath, *Hiking Alone: Trails Out, Trails Home* (Albuquerque: University of New Mexico Press, 2008), and Bill Plotkin, *Soulcraft: Crossing into the Mysteries of Nature and Psyche* (Novato, CA: New World Library, 2003).

7. Karen Warren, Mitchell Sakofs, and Jasper S. Hunt, Jr. eds., *The Theory of Experiential Education* (Dubuque, IA: Association for Experiential Education and Kendall/Hunt Publishing, 1995), 41.

8. Thomas James, "Sketch of a Moving Spirit: Kurt Hahn," in Warren et al., *Theory of Experiential Education*, 89.

9. Andrew Gulliford, "Great Old Broads Marks 20 Years of Hiking, Advocacy," Writers on the Range, *Salt Lake Tribune*, July 24, 2009.

10. Andrew Gulliford, "'Geography of Hope' Alive in Proposed Dominguez Canyon Wilderness," *Grand Junction Daily Sentinel*, July 20, 2008.

11. Andrew Gulliford, "Trash Tracker at Lake Powell," *San Juan Record*, Monticello, Utah, November 12, 2008.

12. Andrew Gulliford, "Getting Trashed at Lake Powell," *Mountain Gazette* 160 (October 2009).

13. Andrew Gulliford, "Historic Inscriptions on the Colorado Plateau and Tales from the *True GRIT*," *Inside/Outside Southwest*, February 2009.

Life's a Beach: Citizen Science and Stewardship in Grand Canyon

Lynn Hamilton

Imagine Grand Canyon as an anthropomorphic being, with the Colorado River as its lifeblood and the ancient rocks as its bones; then surely sediment must be the sinew that binds it together. Sediment supports riparian life along the river corridor—plants, animals, and birds. Wind-blown sand helps slow erosion of fragile and irreplaceable archaeological sites. Suspended sand improves the ability of some fish to avoid predators. Sediment also plays an important role in creating backwater habitats that benefit aquatic species such as the endangered humpback chub. And of course, the health of the recreational resource in Grand Canyon is dependent upon camping beaches that are used by more than 26,000 people who run the river each year.

In predam times, enormous spring floods pulsed down the Colorado River, distributing literally tons of sediment that preserved and protected the natural and cultural resources along the river corridor. In fact, river runners in those early days swore that the muddy Colorado was "too thick to drink, too thin to plow." Now fast-forward to 1963, when Glen Canyon Dam began to fill, forming Lake Powell behind it and blocking that rejuvenating sediment, not unlike an enormous man-made plug. Instead of a warm, muddy, free-flowing river, the flows from the dam were now clear and cold.

Grand Canyon River Guides (GCRG), a nonprofit educational and environmental organization with more than 1,600 members, was formed in 1988 to give river guides and the broader river-running public a collective voice in resource management issues. From the beginning, we felt that we had a long-term vision for Grand Canyon and the Colorado River, but more than that, as guides who work here and visitors who care, we realized that it was our *responsibility* to help preserve, protect, and defend this special place and the magic it continues to bestow upon us all. The day-to-day well-being of the canyon and the river are in our care—we are their passionate stewards.

GCRG's significant involvement in the passage of the Grand Canyon Protection Act and the subsequent Glen Canyon Dam Environmental Impact

Statement (EIS) process deepened our advocacy role. As the years passed, it became increasingly evident that sediment resources in Grand Canyon were becoming severely depleted, jeopardizing the health of multiple resources along the river corridor. But what could be done? In March 1996 Glen Canyon Dam's penstocks and two of the outlet works' bypass tubes were opened to maximum capacity, mimicking the natural spring floods—an unprecedented effort to utilize dam operations not for the sake of hydropower but to attempt to rectify damaged conditions in this fragile, compromised ecosystem. The following year, the Glen Canyon Dam Adaptive Management Program (GCDAMP) was established, charged with advising the Secretary of the Interior on how to best protect downstream resources and meet the intent of the Grand Canyon Protection Act.

GCRG also realized that this historic moment was indeed the time to "get off the boat" and take action. We sensed that the "flood flow" might not be a miracle cure but could be a step in the right direction. And we felt that we were in a unique position to document those changes, make those results public, and actively work to effect change.

Before the flood flow, GCRG sent volunteer guides down the river with cameras. Their task was to carefully document our dataset of more than forty camping beaches distributed throughout the Colorado River corridor where beaches are in highest demand, smallest in size, and/or fewest in number. Our Adopt-a-Beach program was born—a long-term monitoring, comparative photographic effort documenting and analyzing changes in sand deposition as a key indicator of ecosystem health in Grand Canyon.

Since 1996, hundreds of volunteers have enthusiastically participated in the program, including river guides from all of the commercial river outfitters, private boaters, National Park Service personnel, independent science trips, and even experiential learning programs such as Grand Canyon Youth. As an exemplary "citizen science program," Adopt-a-Beach brings these diverse constituencies together to keep tabs on the resource of common concern: the Colorado River through Grand Canyon. As one participant so aptly observed, "Anytime you get involved in this program, you take the time to analyze the beaches and how they might be affected, whether by flow regime regulations of the dam, natural flash flooding, or visitor use in an already fragile environment. It is one thing to talk about it and another to actually *see* what is taking place."

The beauty of the Adopt-a-Beach program is its simplicity. Volunteer adopters sign up for a beach (or beaches) of their choice, affording them a sense of "ownership" and investing them in the success of the program. The adopters are then provided with a packet that includes a disposable camera, a photo location (showing where you stand to take the photo), a beach photo (showing the exact view to match), user-friendly datasheets, an instruction sheet, pens, and Sharpies. Adopters are asked to photograph their beach each time they pass it during the regular commercial boating season and answer questions on their datasheets about its condition and appearance, including observations about the processes that may have caused evident changes. At the end of the season, the adopters mail their camera and datasheets back to GCRG. Photographs for each beach are then compared to assess changes and are entered into a database along with adopter comments. In this way, a detailed database is built by beach and date photographed, and an analysis of systemwide changes in beach condition can be made, demonstrating trends and changes over time.

Adopt-a-Beach provides the necessary documentation to effectively voice our concerns about the effects of dam flows on Grand Canyon beaches. A detailed state-of-the-beaches report that includes data, trends, causalities, and recommendations is disseminated to strategic river managers: Grand Canyon National Park, Grand Canyon Monitoring and Research Center, stakeholders from the GCDAMP, and other interested parties. In other words, the program results and recommendations are provided directly to decision makers to assist them in developing well-informed management decisions for Glen Canyon Dam. Additionally, the extensive photographic record of beach evolution is incorporated into the GIS Campsite Atlas project developed by Grand Canyon Monitoring and Research Center in cooperation with Grand Canyon National Park. This ensures that the Adopt-a-Beach photo record will continue to be an effective tool for researchers and scientists as they study beach change, vegetation encroachment, critical riparian habitat, and impacts on cultural sites.

GCRG is firmly grounded in the belief that change starts from the bottom up. Therefore, in addition to targeting the policymakers themselves, we place emphasis on highlighting the Adopt-a-Beach results more publicly, through a number of strategic venues: in our publication, the *Boatman's Quarterly Review*; in our annual Guides Training Seminar; on our website, www.gcrg.org; and most importantly, through the adopters themselves as they interact with the river-running public. Each time adopters perform their Adopt-a-Beach duties, they are in a unique position to further the environmental education of those around them. The program itself creates invaluable "teachable moments" about the complexities and challenges of dam management, the effects of dam flows, the importance of monitoring, and the distinct challenges facing the GCDAMP.

But how do adopters pique the interest of their passengers? One guide smiled as he remembered his clever method: "I stop and take a photo with no explanation, to raise their curiosity, and make them *make* me explain. . . . Once the door is open, look out!" Another adopter added, "In the big picture of their river trip, the Adopt-a-Beach program might be forgotten against the fun of swimming in the Little Colorado or running Lava Falls, but it definitely helped educate my passengers and, in a subtle way, enhanced their experience. I also feel that such a specific task is easily grasped, and it makes them feel they took part in caring for the Canyon."

In the simplest sense, the Adopt-a-Beach program is essentially "taking care of our own backyard," allowing us to give back to the place that has meant so much to us. In doing so, this citizen science program clearly demonstrates the stewardship ethic of river runners in Grand Canyon, highlights the shared responsibility we have for resource protection, and strengthens our obligation to take action in its defense. Ultimately, this long-term monitoring program also provides us with unique opportunities for constituency building, public outreach, environmental education and awareness, and a direct-action agenda.

Not surprisingly, the Adopt-a-Beach program has become a model for other monitoring programs in the West. For example, Adopt-a-Beach served as the specific model for "Adopt-a-Camp: Cooperative Resource Stewardship on the Middle Fork Salmon River." This program was submitted to the U.S. Forest Service for their consideration in 2005. We've also received inquiries from individuals interested in protecting the Gunnison River as well as an inquiry geared toward developing a novel way to study penguins in Antarctica.

The tenets of Adopt-a-Beach are simple: observe, document, analyze, generate public support, and effect long-term change. This model can be used anywhere, from a simple stream to a roaring river to a fragile wetland. The possibilities are endless. The necessary components are a proactive approach, a long-term vision, and a commitment to protect and preserve our resources for future generations. We fervently believe that education, stewardship, and advocacy go hand in hand. Simply put, people must understand before they will care, and they must care before they will defend.

Again, it all comes down to responsibility—our *collective* responsibility. The natural world has the ability to change people's lives in lasting and positive ways. Consequently, it must be our profound responsibility to ensure that the wilderness experience and its inherent resource values are carefully preserved. We urge you to get inspired, come up with an idea, and find a meaningful way to give back. Who will be the caretakers of our public lands, if not you and me?

Note: The Adopt-a-Beach program has been funded over the years through a variety of sources: The Grand Canyon Conservation Fund, a nonprofit grant-making program managed by the Grand Canyon River Outfitters; the U.S. Geological Survey; the Bureau of Reclamation; and individual contributors. And of course, the program would not be possible without the wonderful volunteers who give generously of their energy and enthusiasm, and the outstanding principal investigators who have infused the program with their expertise over the years.

The Southwest Conservation Corps: String Becomes Rope

Harry Bruell

I arrived just after dinner and spent the evening with a crew camping out in Great Sand Dunes National Park. This group, made up of six 16–21-year-old corps members and two 21–25-year-old crew leaders, was midway through an eleven-day camping hitch maintaining trails in the national park. We sat around the campfire reliving the day's and week's adventures: the sight of bear prints along the trail, the terrific dinner of the night before followed by the "cardboard" pizza of tonight, the laughter of who snored the loudest, the group sharing as the rancher from Kansas and the Navajo youth from Tohatchi learned about each other's lives. I was almost asleep in my tent while I could still hear the chatter from the shared tents of the corps members. In the morning, after breakfast and a "stretch and safety circle," we got our tools and walked in a line to the trailhead.

"Todd," walking in front of me, spoke about the Southwest Conservation Corps (SCC) shirt that he and the rest wore daily on the crew. These shirts had been bright blue and red a few weeks ago, but now they were badly faded with seemingly permanent dirt stains on the creases. "I'm going to wear my SCC shirt every day when I get back to school," Todd told me. And I could tell that he meant it. Todd was in foster care and had bounced around from home to home and from social worker to social worker. He was a "client" and receiver of services and had been so his entire life—until now. Now he was needed to give back to our public lands. SCC—with support from Great Sand Dunes National Park—paid him for his work. For probably the first time in his life, he was needed. His services were a valuable contribution to his public lands and a part of something bigger than himself. He would certainly be wearing that T-shirt every day, and with pride.

Each year SCC engages approximately a thousand young men and women across the Southwest who contribute more than 300,000 hours of service work on public lands. Like Todd, they work in crews, often in remote locations, to maintain trails, protect communities from wildfire, restore habitat, save energy, and remove invasive plants. The Corps Network—the national membership association of conservation corps organizations—reports that 158 corps are operating in multiple communities across forty-six states and the District of Columbia. These corps annually enroll more than 33,000 young people and mobilize 265,000 community volunteers, who provide their communities with nearly 15.3 million hours of service. Eleven of these 158 corps operate in the Four Corners states.

Launched in California in 1976, the Corps Network reports that the modern-day corps are heirs to the tremendous legacy of the Civilian Conservation Corps, a Depression-era program that engaged six million young men in conservation work. From 1933 to 1942, President Franklin D. Roosevelt's "CCC Boys" dramatically improved the nation's public lands, while also receiving food, shelter, education, and a precious $30-a-month stipend that saved many of their families from hunger in tough times. Like the legendary CCC of the 1930s, the Corps Network reports that today's corps engage young people as resources to restore our nation's public lands while also receiving paid work, job skills, and an opportunity to serve.

Unlike the original CCC, corps today face a myriad of issues that did not exist in the 1930s. Educating them about the outdoors builds a deeper connection, as does using the outdoors as a medium to provide challenges, such as rock climbing or backcountry hiking. However, the deepest and strongest connection comes when young people—or any of us—feel a sense of ownership that comes through stewardship of the land. For some, this leads toward careers working with public lands, while for others it builds a lifelong appreciation and connection to these lands.

Many of the youth who join SCC—aside from those from ranching families—have their first experience with hard, physical work on an SCC crew. It is not unusual to have corps members talking about going to bed at 7:30 P.M. after a day of hard work the first week on the job. In 2005 SCC did pre- and post-program weight and body fat tests on twenty-seven random crew leaders and corps members. After a four- to eight-week program, the average participant lost eight pounds, and their body fat went down 3.4 percentage points. The three most obese participants lost an average of 23.3 pounds, an astounding three to six pounds per week.

Through living together on the crew and through a purposeful team-building program (e.g., a chore chart, shared tents, crew-based project work,

There are many opportunities for young people to practice "wilderness tithing" or giving back to public lands in ways such as trail building. Here, Southwest Conservation Corps workers use hand tools to build a trail. Photo © Southwest Conservation Corps.

team-based decisions on everything from purchasing food to setting up camp), participants learn effective offline communication skills. Most importantly, through providing service to the public lands, the participants gain a sense of ownership. It is not unusual to have corps members take pictures of their project work to share with friends or to bring their families back out to the project sites to walk "their" trail or cross "their" trail bridge. After a season of work, each corps member now owns a small piece of a myriad of public lands across the Southwest. That ownership is a permanent, unending connection between the young person and his or her public lands.

Global climate change is affecting our world now and threatens greater impacts through glacier and sea ice melt, increased intensity of extreme weather events, rising sea levels, species extinction, and changes in agricultural yields. It has the potential—in the most dire models—to threaten the survival of the human race. The disconnection between communities and their environments can contribute to climate change. The changes seen across the globe can be traced to human causes, such as population growth, fossil fuel burning, and deforestation. We are using essential natural resources faster than they can be replenished.

Conservation corps—and other similar programs—reconnect people to people, communities, and nature, which begins the process of reconnecting communities and their environments. Each conservation corps graduate has a greater understanding of the importance of living in balance with the natural world as well as a sense of ownership of that natural world. They have lived in the backcountry with a team of peers. They have worked the land, protected communities from wildfire, built a trail so that others can experience the wilderness, promoted biodiversity by protecting wildlife, and saved natural resources by installing energy-saving measures for low-income people. These graduates become a beacon in their spheres of influence (family, friends, communities), promoting and living a balanced life. The work of creating more and more conservation corps graduates has never been more important than it is now.

I got a call a little bit ago from a local bank vice president who offered to take me to lunch, presumably to solicit business from us as he knew we were looking for loans to purchase a new building. However, when we got to lunch he really just wanted to talk to me about a time many years ago when he spent a week volunteering on a trail project in the backcountry. That week—among the thousands of weeks in his long life—had had a huge impact. It was a transformational experience. He was out of his comfort zone, living in a beautiful place, being challenged physically in ways he had never been, participating in a group, and getting new perspectives on the world by being in the wild. Knowing that SCC does similar work, he wanted to relive that experience with me. He felt that I could relate to this monumental time in his life. Our conversation about a potential loan lasted five minutes, while our conversation about living and working in the backcountry took more than an hour.

If you are twenty years old, you've lived more than a thousand weeks. If you are forty, you've lived more than two thousand. Among all of these weeks, which week affected your life the most? A week—or more—of stewardship can be transformational in ways that so few other experiences in our daily lives can. A year, six months, twelve weeks, or a month on a conservation corps crew or another stewardship group is the type of experience that stands out. What's more, the impact of this experience can bring you—and your crew mates—closer to each other and to others in your community. It can then help reconnect your community with its environment. Each person who makes those connections ties a small piece of thread between community and environment. As more people tie these threads, we have a piece of string and then a piece of rope. One day that piece of rope will be strong enough to pull our society back into balance with its environment. This work is critically important, and every person matters.

Walking the Distance: Finding the Advocate's Path in a Warming West

Phil Brick

> Be the change you want to see in the world.
> —Mahatma Gandhi

> This is a wonderful time to be progressive and to be alive. Fighting for democracy. In fact it's just about as much fun as you can have with your clothes on.
> —Jim Hightower

If you have this book in your hands, chances are you are one of the lucky ones. You have had the good fortune to live and learn in the great outdoors, most likely somewhere in the wide-open spaces of America's public lands. You have had the opportunity to experience the deep silences found only in big country, you've heard the shrill cry of a soaring osprey and the soft, descending call of a canyon wren. Your self-propelled travel deep in the backcountry has given you a new sense of freedom, purpose, and empowerment. You have no doubt also had some fun, perhaps even with your clothes on.

In any case, these lands—the deep canyons, desert rivers, and sky island mountains—have become a part of who you are. Now you want to give something back. You want to make a difference. After all the challenges you have faced while on the trail, this one seems the most daunting, as your studies no doubt have also made you aware of the relentless threats to public lands. Perhaps you have learned that oil and gas companies are eyeing one of your favorite places for new exploration. Reactionary chants of "drill, baby, drill" on the national stage make the situation seem even more glum. I will never forget a story I heard from a Wyoming rancher who flew Air Force missions over Iraq during the first Gulf War: "There are places we carpet-bombed in Iraq that look better than some of the oil and gas fields out there on the public lands," he said.

And that's just the old news. Now, with climate change threatening to transform the character of ecosystems across the West, new threats are emerging. Farms and cities are looking for new sources of water, threatening what few free-flowing streams and healthy aquifers remain. Energy developers are proposing to level hundreds of square miles of fragile desert lands to install huge solar thermal power plants. Many plant and animal species are predicted to disappear as the region becomes hotter and drier. According to an exhaustive summary of more than fifty scientific studies done by the Natural Resources Defense Council, the West is already warming 70 percent faster than the rest of the world. In the Colorado River Basin, the situation is even more dire. The area has warmed 120 percent faster than the twentieth-century global average, which is already producing water shortages, devastating pine beetle infestations in the region's upland forests, and disrupting plant and animal phenology in a way that threatens the region's biodiversity.

How can we reconcile our desire to defend the places we love with climate change, a problem so large that no single person, group, or even nation can alone solve? Although fights to protect wilderness were never easy, those battles seem small compared to today's challenges. We can't put a bubble over wilderness areas. Climate change makes everything we do, both in the outback and in our towns and cities, intimately intertwined. Perhaps this has always been so, and we've been leading what Brooke Williams calls "half lives"—half in the city, and half in the wilderness, and never the twain shall meet. So as daunting as climate change might seem, perhaps it is also an opportunity to rethink how we go about conceptualizing our places in the world, and to develop skills and strategies that will help us honor and defend those places.

⁓

For nearly two decades, I have been taking college students out in the field to develop what southwestern writer Ellen Meloy calls "a deep map of place." Our group had the good fortune to take a writing workshop with Ellen just before her sudden and untimely death. As our group sat silently in a circle on Comb Ridge slickrock, the vast expanses of desert unfolded before us. Sleeping Ute Mountain, far to the east, seemed to absorb the purple winter sky. Ellen then told us, "In the desert there is everything and there is nothing. Stay curious. Know where you are—your biological address. Get to know your neighbors—plants, creatures, who live there, who died there, who is blessed, cursed, what is absent or in danger or in need of your help. Pay attention to the weather, to what breaks your heart, to what lifts your heart. Write it down."

This is certainly a good place to start. Writing is a powerful way to share the experience of coming to know wild nature with others who might not venture as far afield. To care about places, one must know them, the more intimately the better. Certainly, it is hard to conceptualize the conservation and environmental movement without such writers as John Muir, Rachel Carson, and Edward Abbey. Good nature writing is good conservation strategy if it gets people to know more about our public lands, and presumably to care about them. It's important to get the word out, to give people a reason to care.

But is just knowing and caring enough? Many people care about our public lands, and even profess to love them. Ironically, we might love them too much, as some places (like Moab, Utah) have been literally overrun by desert enthusiasts, threatening fragile soils and the solitude that once characterized the red-rock canyon country. Mary O'Brien, a longtime public lands advocate now working for Grand Canyon Trust, once told another group of my students, "Knowing is not the same as caring, and even truly caring isn't really enough. To make a difference in this world, you have to know, you have to care, and you have to be ready to commit yourself to the life of an advocate." These are tough words, and for more than just a few students, bewildering ones. "Advocate" sounds a little too much like an "activist."

David Brower, a towering figure in the conservation movement in the late twentieth century, was fond of saying that "environmental activists make great ancestors." But in the present tense, he admitted, they can seem tedious and even insufferable. My students tend to admire activists, but they view them with suspicion. Activists are too singular in their thinking, too demanding, and too self-righteous. One student told me that most conversations she's had with hard-core environmental activists seem to last just a little too long. It's a bit like being cornered at a cocktail party by a Bible-thumping, New England preacher.

It's not that my students somehow lack green credentials or enthusiasm for all things environmental. They recycle and compost religiously. They are keenly interested in local foods, vegetarianism, and alternative modes of transportation, and they disdain conspicuous consumption. "Sustainable" is a regular part of their vocabulary, and they envision themselves being part of a much greener society in their lifetimes. At the same time, most reject the suggestion that they are activists. "I consider myself to be environmentally aware and active," says one student, "but I'm *not* an activist."

How can this be? It's not that recycling and local foods are a bad thing—far from it. But these activities are highly individualized, consumer preferences that do little to transform the larger structures of global capital that might actually bring about meaningful change. Gandhi's advice to "be the change you want to see in the world" is good advice if one is looking for individual moral guidance. But as a roadmap for the kind of economic, social, and political change that will be necessary to meaningfully address environmental challenges in the twenty-first century, individualized behavior, even if widespread, will clearly be inadequate.

Gandhi faced the British Empire, a formidable but already overextended opponent. Today's opponent, global capital, is much more nimble. What first appears as dissent is quickly converted into convenient commodities, effectively silencing meaningful dissent. Feeling guilty about your car? Here's a Prius. Want organic food? Here are some organic tomatoes (they might have traveled five thousand miles to get to you, but they are organic). Feel guilty about your spring break adventure on Maui? Click here to purchase a carbon offset. Many students recognize this, but they still insist their individual choices will somehow produce the change they want to see in the world. One student writes, "I know my recycling by itself won't make much difference, but it's something I *can* do. . . . The problems are just too big and complicated for one person to take on. If I can do the right thing, perhaps others will see this and follow, then, we will have the critical mass to really change the system." Well, no. Marginal changes in individual behavior, however virtuous, can at best produce marginal changes in existing systems of production and consumption. There has to be a better way.

This emphasis on individual action, however virtuous, is not without costs of its own. First, backsliding is both easy and common, inducing a pervasive and destructive sense of guilt. Second, that pesky New England preacher problem remains. The only thing worse than a moralist, of course, is a moralist with a backsliding problem. Third, and perhaps most importantly, the emphasis on individual virtue essentially cedes important strategic territory to opponents. Back in 2001, when Vice President Dick Cheney unveiled the Bush administration's energy plan, he belittled conservation as an essential, commonsense component of a national energy plan. Instead, his plan (developed in secret with oil and gas executives, coal lobbyists, and nuclear power advocates) emphasized (surprise!) more oil and gas, coal, and nuclear energy production. He then famously added, "Conservation may be a sign of personal virtue, but it is not a sufficient basis for a sound, comprehensive energy policy." During his tenure, oil and gas exploration exploded across the West, and environmental groups were mostly powerless to stop it. At the same time, consumers moved to larger cars and trucks, fueled by cheap gasoline.

Politics is a strategic activity, and a necessary one. As nauseating as the Bush administration was, it was not the time to retreat from politics, hoping that individual consumer and conservation activities might catch on. Dick Cheney is a shining example of *New York Times* columnist Thomas Friedman's plea to the electorate prior to the 2008 national election: "Change your leaders, not your light bulbs." While on the campaign trail, Barack Obama was once asked what he *personally* had done recently on behalf of the environment. He struggled for an answer, then remembered he had installed some compact fluorescent bulbs, and he had taken part in a tree-planting day. Later, he regretted his answer: "You know, this is a stupid question . . . what I'm thinking in my head is, 'Well, the truth is, we can't solve global warming because I f—ing changed light bulbs in my house. It's because of something collective."

For all his shortcomings once in office, President Obama still gets it. Personal action alone can't walk the long distances we need to travel together. Only collective action can take us where we need to go in a warming world. To work collectively, however, will require some adjustments. Isolated individual consumers, moralists, and preachers don't tend to play well with others. A new, reinvigorated environmental era will be populated by new alliances of pragmatic people who can work together to solve common challenges. In the West, this will be difficult, as environmental disputes have been so polarized in recent decades by battles over logging, grazing, wilderness, and oil and gas development. As necessary as many of these battles have been, I believe they will soon be eclipsed by climate change, which challenges all sides to think about our public lands in new and perhaps more creative ways.

~

A couple of years ago a group of students and I spent a morning with Doug McDaniel, a rancher who is spending tens of thousands of dollars of his own money to restore meanders in a stream that flows through his ranch. The stream was straightened by the U.S. Army Corps of Engineers in the 1950s as part of an effort to conserve farmland and water. Because meanders are essential habitat for native fish, our group wonders aloud how people back then could have been so short-sighted. Doug then tells us, "Look, no one wakes up in the morning and says, 'Gee, how can I screw this place up today?' We didn't know then what we know now. But casting blame isn't going to bring back the fish. We have to roll up our sleeves and find ways we can work together."

Doug's story is a good parable for what's coming as the West becomes much hotter and drier. Although environmentalists and ranchers have often found themselves shouting at each other from opposite sides of the fence, climate change is likely to make the fence itself less relevant. Instead of traditional battles between preservation and use, we will see more emphasis on new ways to enhance ecosystem services such as carbon sequestration, water supply, and species diversity. Ranchers, for example, are unlikely to give up their grazing privileges without a fight. But what if a way can be found to pay ranchers to ranch carbon (by restoring native grasslands) instead of cattle? What if former loggers were enlisted to put more trees in the ground, and keep them healthy, to sequester carbon? Such efforts are already under way, the dawn of a new era for our public lands.

Fresh from the trail, you might be wondering, quite understandably, how you can be part of this. There will be many opportunities. One of the great things about public lands is that they are open to public discussion and involvement. Anyone can participate in the process of public land management, and the only real price of admission is a commitment to participate in the oftentimes arduous public policy process. To influence the process, you don't need a lot of money. But you will need a willingness to sit down and engage in the give and take of public lands politics. You don't need to run for office—volunteering to sit on a local public lands advisory committee is a good place to start.

You will need to be ready to attend lengthy meetings, to listen, to do your homework, to bring new ideas to the table, and to do the research necessary to back up your ideas with solid evidence. You will need to figure out ways to build alliances with those whose interests might overlap with yours in only a few places. Success will come when you have a relationship *with* others across the political spectrum, not when you somehow convince others you are right. Finally, if public lands advocacy is not your thing, there is plenty of other good work to do in the climate movement. Local communities everywhere are convening to find ways to reduce local carbon footprints and to design greener civic futures. Local civic groups are always looking for energetic young people to join them. The aphorism "The world is run by people who show up" is surely right, and to that I might add: The world is changed by people who keep showing up, no matter the odds. You can't dance unless you keep coming to the party. Politics is messy, and results are always uncertain. But politics is good work, and the life of the advocate is never dull or sedentary. It's one of those special places in life, next to your favorite desert canyon or mountain trail, where walking the distance with others you have come to know and respect, despite your differences, will be its own reward.

Study Questions

1. Lynn Hamilton writes about the "Adopt-a-Beach" program in the Grand Canyon. If you could adopt anything related to the environment, what would you adopt? How could you create a meaningful program/relationship that would better the health of your adoptee?

2. How do we interact with the people sometimes labeled *Americanus slobvius*? What are some ways we can relate to them and educate them (without preaching) on subjects such as "Leave No Trace" and ecosystem health? How can we work to help them clean up their act?

3. Many of us hate politics and avoid it like the plague. But what if you were a politician? What changes would you make (like paying loggers to *plant* trees) that would help us restore balance and reduce our impact on the earth?

4. What is your "biological address"? How well do you know your home in terms of plants, animals, and ecological interactions? What changes have you noticed since you've lived at your current address? What will you do to keep your home livable for future generations of all species?

5. What has been your most meaningful week? Did it relate to any of the three things Harry Bruell talks about in the conservation corps world of reconnecting to the outdoors, reconnecting with physical work, and reconnecting with each other? How so?

GLOSSARY

aerie: The high platform nest of a large bird such as an eagle; this can refer to a high difficult to access cliff ledge.

arroyo: A ditch or gulch, usually dry, but which can be dangerous in a flash flood.

atlatl: A prehistoric Indian spear thrower. The shaft of the spear would detach giving the hunter more thrust than by heaving a single shaft of wood.

balaclava: A face-, neck-, and shoulder-covering useful in cold and windy conditions.

belay: A method of safeguarding climbers' ropes by applying friction using either a mechanical device or a sitting hip belay in which the belayer's body provides the friction.

biner blocks: a technique sometimes used to ensure that a rappel rope can be pulled in only one direction. If used incorrectly, biner blocks can be dangerous.

bivi sack: A large, lightweight, water-repellent sack one can use when bivouacing. Smaller than a tent, this is an enclosed shelter just large enough for a climber and a sleeping bag.

bivouac: A bivouac is an often uncomfortable and usually temporary outdoor camp where the usual niceties are not available. Bivouacs can be either planned or unplanned. The act of camping in a bivouac.

blow-sand: The scourge of desert hikers, sand blown in the wind—often in spring—can not only cover one's sleeping bag and camp, but frequently finds its way into food, ears, and eyes.

boatmen: River runners, either male or female; a proud, fun-loving, expert group.

brachiopod: A mollusklike marine animal having a dorsal and ventral shell found in layers of rocks across the Colorado Plateau.

bunny strap: A sling used for hanging your pack below you when chimneying a narrow portion of a slot canyon.

cairn: Stacks of rocks that can be seen from a distance used to mark a trail or route. Native Americans also built cairns to demarcate tribal and clan boundaries for hunting and fishing areas.

caliche: Dry, light gray or brown clay soil that can be notoriously slick when wet.

chimney: A rock climbing and canyoneering technique in which one uses cross-pressure to either ascend or descend a wide crack. The technique usually entails pressing one's back against one wall and feet against another. If the crack or chimney is especially wide, one may have hands on one wall and feet on the other. Also called bridging. In canyoneering the technique is called Mae Westing.

chokestone: (also called chalkstone) A boulder that is caught in a crack or chimney. In canyoneering they are often used as perches or anchors.

cholla: A spiny and treelike type of Southwestern cactus.

couloir: A steep crack or gully running up a mountainside, often filled with loose rock, or snow. Exactly the place where avalanches occur.

crampon: Metal edges strapped to hiking boots for extra traction in snow, particularly used on icefields.

cryptobiotic soil: (also called microbiotic soil) A type of desert soil that is a conglomeration of lichens, mosses, bacteria, and algaes. It forms a black crust that helps in the propagation of other plants and helps check erosion. Small individual mounds of the dark soil, a few inches tall, found in sandy desert environments, represent an important desert life form because they catch and store water, prevent soil erosion, and can be demolished easily by careless hikers or uncaring cows. On the Colorado Plateau it may represent 70 percent of the ground cover—it holds the place in place.

cyanobacteria: Bacteria that occur as single cells in the cryptobiotic crust, usually of the filamentous type, they join loose soil particles together and are important for fixing nitrogen in cold-desert ecosystems and helping to prevent wind erosion.

drag bag: Often found behind rubber rafts, drag bags let one's beer chill prior to evening consumption.

duckie: A fabulous form of watercraft that is, in essence, an inflatable one- or two-person kayak capable of bouncing off rocks, zooming through waves, and providing high times in rapids. Unlike in kayaks, water flows out the bottom of duckies, so paddlers get wet rather than sunk. A duckie can vary from eight to sixteen or more feet in length and are usually quite narrow. Duckies can be used on both flat water and in big rapids.

dugway: A historic Mormon term for a road descending precipitously from a canyon's edge. One of the most dramatic is the Moki Dugway between Bluff and Mexican Hat, Utah, which drops dramatically from Cedar Mesa to the desert below. Originally, dugways were hand-built by pioneers.

epic: Southwestern slang for an outdoor sequence of events that goes from bad to worse and may result in injuries but not fatalities. Epics make for bragging rights at local brew pubs.

étrier: A webbing ladder that attaches to a jumar in order to ascend a fixed rope in climbing.

federal wilderness: Lands approved by Congress to be protected under the 1964 Wilderness Act, "where man is a visitor who does not remain" and access is primarily only by human power or on horseback.

ferry angle: A river-running term whereby you point your boat at an angle of approximately 40 degrees to the river's current in order to cross the main channel. If you crossed at a straight 90-degree angle, the current would carry you downstream below your intended destination. Historically, ferry operators went upstream at a ferry angle to cross a river to arrive at a spot directly across from where they started.

fire pans: Small pans in which river runners may construct fires so that all ashes and charred wood can be carried out. These are mandatory on permitted rivers.

fireman's belay: A method used in rock climbing and canyoneering to help protect a person rappelling down a rope. If the rappeller loses control of the rappel and starts descending too fast, a person at the bottom can pull hard on the ropes, providing more friction and slowing the rappeller's rate of descent.

free soloing: Climbing a rock face with no protection, not tied in to another individual.

gaiters: Nylon and waterproof materials worn over boots or shoes to keep pant legs dry and to prevent snow or ice buildup on boots, useful for cross country skiing or high altitude treks in deep snow.

giardia: The short name for *giardia lambia*, a nasty internal parasite picked up from polluted streams, which can cause extreme stomach cramps, dehydration, and diarherra. These can be found everywhere in the American West, so it's best to filter all water not coming directly from rock or a pipe at an encased spring. Cases can vary from mild to deadly.

gorp: A high-energy mix of nuts, dried fruit, and chocolate often carried by outdoorspeople. The name is perhaps short for Good Old Raisin and Peanuts, but many add M&Ms, too. Recipes vary.

herradura: The archaeological term for a horseshoe-shaped roadside shrine of small stacked stones found near Chacoan roads built by Ancestral Puebloans around 1100 A.D.

hogan: A traditional Navajo home constructed of stacked logs or tree branches, always with a door facing east. A wood and mud dwelling that can vary in size from quite small to large enough to hold a family. They are still sometimes used as linecamps. They are usually gendered spaces with women only allowed on the left side.

javelina: Small, wild, desert pigs with thick hair bristles found in Sonoran or Chihuhuan desert ecosystems.

jug lines: The use of jumars to ascend ropes.

jumar: A mechanical device that once clamped on a rope will slide up, but not down, used for ascending climbing ropes.

KED: A spinal immobilization device used in search-and-rescue operations where back injuries may have occurred.

kiva: An underground ceremonial and religious space built next to room blocks by various cultures across the Southwest. Usually round, but occasionally square, kivas feature a smoke hole in the flat roof, a short stone wall to deflect cold air coming down the air vent, a hearth, and a sipapu or small hole representing the emergence of ancestors. Kivas are still in use by modern Pueblo Indian tribes.

Krummholz: Wind-blown vegetation and small trees found at or near timberline. They grow slowly because of the altitude and intense weather and usually only grow in the direction opposite to prevailing winds.

Leave No Trace®: A concept, program, and ethic with rules varying by altitude, location, and ecosystem, but whose main premise is to travel through wild country and "leave only footprints, take only photographs."

lithics: The archaeological term for chipped and shaped stone modified by humans for tools such as spear points, arrowheads, scrapers, etc. These may include broken or chipped debris as in a lithic scatter.

manky anchors: Anchors used for belays and rappels in rock climbing and canyoneering, which should be strong enough to comfortably hold a person's weight, with a wide margin for error. If there is little margin for error, and if one fears that the anchor may fail, it is called "manky." A manky anchor is not a good thing.

mano: The Spanish word for hand. At Southwestern archaeological sites, this refers to a smooth, horizontally shaped, rounded stone; small ones fit easily into one's hand, or larger stones could be held with both hands, and were used to grind corn and seeds into flour by prehistoric women and girls.

metate: A flat, horizontal stone onto which seeds or corn would be placed prior to being ground with a mano. Often, metates were set in groups of three so that women would grind flour into coarse, medium, or fine gradations. Because small chips of stone were eaten with the ground flour, prehistoric Native Americans often lost their teeth prematurely.

Mogollon: The last name of a New Mexican Spanish governor, and a place-name used in Arizona and New Mexico, as in the Mogollon Rim, as well as the name for one of the four main prehistoric Indian cultures in the Southwest. In the vernacular, pronounced as *mugyown*.

moki steps: Hand- and footholds chiseled into steep rock walls by Puebloan and pre-Puebloan Indians. *Moki* (or *moqui*) is the way early explorers misunderstood the word *Hopi*. Using the word *moki* in reference to hand-carved stone steps refers to dramatically steep prehistoric cliff routes often with exposure or dangerous angles of ascent. In actuality the word *moki* refers to the dead in the Hopi language.

paho: Small wooden sticks, painted with colored bands, adorned with feathers, and placed at shrines by native people, often on religious pilgrimages. The practice continues today in the Southwest.

PFDs: Short for *personal flotation devices*, the new term for life jackets.

put-in: The launch site for river trips, sometimes muddy, sometimes crowded, always fun.

quakies: The local nickname for aspen trees whose leaves shimmer, or quake, in the breeze.

rimrocked: To be stuck on a cliff edge with no discernible way to go up down or sideways, an occasional occurrence among Southwestern hikers. Sometimes even reversing one's course seems impossible.

scree: Loose stone on a mountain ridge that slips and slides and can make for interesting walking.

sitting hip belay: *See* belay.

slickrock: Navajo and Entrada sandstone, found across the Colorado Plateau but with concentrations at Bluff and Moab, Utah, and at Lake Powell. It makes for superb hiking unless wet; then it earns its nickname as *slickrock*.

sling-line: Similar to rope, sling-line is inch-wide, lightweight material with great tensile strength that climbers easily carry.

SPOT device: An emergency beacon that, once pushed, sends a message via satellite to the nearest search-and-rescue responders worldwide. Unfortunately, the GPS message only indicates location and does not indicate the extent of injuries or other difficulties, so first responders do not know how to react. They have a location but no other information.

stromatolite: Precambrian life forms in a sedimentary rock layer of fossilized algae and microbes that represent some of the earliest evidence for life on earth. These ancient living organisms can be found in Grand Canyon, specifically at Carbon Camp. They are lavender-hued and look like primitive brains that have become rocks.

taking out: Where river trips end and boats are placed on trailers. Hug your friends and, if it's a commercial trip, tip your guides.

travois: The Native American method of transport using two crossed poles and a small wooden platform pulled by horses to carry personal possessions.

water ouzel: Any of several aquatic birds. It may be stocky and has a funny jerking movement as it walks.

wickiup: A type of residence used by Ute and other Indians, formed from dead tree branches, sometimes placed around a tree but often free standing.

wilderness tithing: A concept of giving back to public lands by helping with a variety of outdoor projects from trail building to trash cleanup.

BIBLIOGRAPHY

ORAL INTERVIEWS BY THE AUTHOR

Allen, Steve. Interviewed at his home, August 18, 2008, at 665 Oakcrest Drive, Durango, Colorado.

Anderson, Arden, Recreation and Wilderness Specialist, Bureau of Land Management. Interviewed at the May 2008 meeting of the Southwest Colorado BLM Resources Advisory Council, and November 12, 2008, at the Gunnison, Colorado, BLM Field Office.

Bruell, Harry, Executive Director, Southwest Conservation Corps, Durango, Colorado. Interviewed in his office, May 6, 2008.

Dewitz, Ron, Visitor Information Specialist, USFS and San Juan Mountains Association. Interviewed in Silverton, Colorado, at the Visitor Center, July 24, 2008.

Foti, Pam, Professor and Chair, Department of Geography, Planning and Recreation, Northern Arizona University. Interviewed at Flagstaff, Arizona, September 22, 2008.

Franz, Ed, Outdoor Recreation Planner, Montrose, Colorado, Bureau of Land Management. Interviewed on the Gunnison River, May 29, 2008.

Hutt, Fred, La Plata County, Colorado, Search and Rescue. Interviewed December 10, 2008, at Fort Lewis College in Durango, Colorado.

Karls, William, Psychiatrist and Grand Canyon River Guide. Interviewed at his home, December 8, 2008, at 3350 East Fourth Avenue, Durango, Colorado.

Kime, Bruce, Professor/Coordinator, Outdoor Education, Colorado Mountain College, Spring Valley Campus, Glenwood Springs, Colorado. Interviewed in his office, March 6, 2008.

Lee, Katie, Singer/Songwriter and Eco-Activist. Interviewed September 23, 2008, at her home in Jerome, Arizona.

Lloyd, Leo, RN, Emergency Medical Services Captain, Durango Fire and Rescue, La Plata County Search and Rescue, Durango, Colorado. Interviewed December 4, 2008, at Fort Lewis College, Durango, Colorado.

Morse, Dan, Public Lands Director, High Country Citizens' Alliance. Interviewed in his office, November 14, 2008, 716 Elk Avenue, Crested Butte, Colorado.

Munsell, Steve, Faculty Coordinator, Outdoor Education Program, Adventure Education Faculty, Prescott College. Interviewed on campus, September 24, 2008, Prescott, Arizona.

Nelson, Kevin, Chair, Outdoor Leadership and Resort Management, Western State College, Gunnison, Colorado. Interviewed in his office, October 11, 2008.

Ross, Janet, Executive Director and Founder, Four Corners School of Outdoor Education, Monticello, Utah. Interviewed at the Four Corners School, October 10, 2008.

Stetson, Andre, Former Outward Bound Boundary Waters canoe instructor. Interviewed at her home, October 2, 2008, 3280 East Fifth Avenue, Durango, Colorado.

DOCUMENTS

"Biological Soil Crusts: Webs of Life in the Desert." "Don't Bust the Crust," handout, USGS Forest and Rangeland Ecosystem Science Center, Canyonlands Field Station, no date.
"Defining traditional cultural properties." National Register Bulletin #38.
Hendee, John C., George H. Stankey, and Robert C. Lucas. *Wilderness Management*. USDA Forest Service, Publication No. 1365, October 1978.
Presidential Executive Order 13007 Protecting Native American Sacred Sites. 1996.
Roehm, Gerald W. "Draft Management Plan for Endangered Fishes in the Yampa River Basin." Denver: U.S. Fish and Wildlife Service, July 2003.
"Swimming Upstream: The Endangered Fish of the Colorado River," and the newsletter "Swimming Upstream for the San Juan River Basin Recovery Implementation Program and the Upper Colorado River Endangered Fish Recovery Program," November 2008.
USDA Forest Service, Wilderness Management School Notebook, May 21–25, 1990, Gila Wilderness/Willow Creek, New Mexico.

JOURNALS/MAGAZINES

Ambinder, Marc. "Beating Obesity." *The Atlantic*, May 2010.
Fayhee, M. John. "The Great Fourteener Debate." *Mountain Gazette* 156 (June 2009): 34.
Findley, Tom. "The Wolves of Gooseberry Creek." *Range Magazine*, Summer 2004.
Fish, Peter. "Old Faithful versus the Xbox." *Sunset Magazine*, July 2007, 104–106.
Gantenbein, Douglas. "Fire Away," *Outside*, December 2007.
Gulliford, Andrew. "Geronimo, Aldo, and Earth First! All Basked in the Nation's First Wilderness Area." *Trilogy Magazine*, May/June 1991.
———. "Ed Abbey: One of the Last Things He Ever Wrote." *Inside/Outside Southwest*, August/September 2006.
———. "When Progress Is No Progress: Echo Park and the Environmental Movement." *Inside/Outside Southwest*, September/October 2006.
———. "Reading the Trees: Colorado's Endangered Arborglyphs and Aspen Art." *Colorado Heritage*, Autumn 2007.
———. "The Missing Lynx: A Ten-Year Eco-Update on the Lynx Re-introduction to Colorado." *Inside/Outside Southwest*, August/September 2007.
———. "On Horseback in Search of the Ancient Ones: Following Cowboy Trails in Ute Mountain Ute Tribal Park." *Inside/Outside Southwest*, January/February 2008.
———. "Four Corners Odyssey: The Ill-fated 1892 Illustrated American Exploring Expedition." *Inside/Outside Southwest*, April 2009.
———. "Everett Ruess: Lost and Found in the Southwest." *Mountain Gazette*, July 2009.
Klinkenborg, Verlyn. "Our Vanishing Night." *National Geographic*, November 2008.
Kramer, Kelly. "Man vs. Wild." *Arizona Highways*, November 2008, 18–19.
Maestas, Amy. "Corner Posts." *Inside/Outside Southwest*, August/September 2008, 10.
McAvoy, Leo H., and Daniel L. Dustin. "The Right to Risk in Wilderness." *Journal of Forestry* 79, no. 3 (1981).

McDonald, Mathew G., Stephen Wearing, and Jess Ponting. "The Nature of Peak Experience in Wilderness." *Humanistic Psychologist* 37, no. 4 (2009).

Menand, Louis. "Comment: The Graduates." Talk of the Town, *New Yorker*, May 21, 2007, 28.

"Online Trend: Is There Room for Nature in a Digital Age?" *Nature Conservancy,* Autumn 2008, 15.

"Out of the Wilderness." *Economist*, July 10, 2008.

Pergams, Oliver R. W., and Patricia A. Zardiac. "Is Love of Nature in the US Becoming Love of Electronic Media?" *Journal of Environmental Management* 80, no. 4 (September 2006): 387–93.

———. "Evidence for a Fundamental and Pervasive Shift Away from Nature-based Recreation." *Proceedings of the National Academies of Science* 105, no. 7 (February 19, 2008): 2295–2300.

Pohl, Sarah. "Technology and the Wilderness Experience." *Environmental Ethics* 28, no. 2 (2006).

Springer, Craig. "Riding the Storm Out: Living Outdoors with Lightning, Wind and Hail." *Inside/Outside Southwest*, July 2009, 8–9.

Waring, Lance. "A San Juan Mountains Mini-Epic: Scouting the Hardrock 100." *Adventure Guide to the Western San Juans*, Summer 2008, 13.

Wolf, Tom. "World Champion Wolfer." *Inside/Outside Southwest*, March 2009.

BOOKS

Abbey, Edward. *Desert Solitaire*. New York: McGraw-Hill, 1968.

———. *Down the River*. New York: Dutton, 1982.

———. *The Journey Home*. New York: Plume, 1991.

Aitchison, Stewart. *A Guide to Southern Utah's Hole-in-the-Rock Trail*. Salt Lake City: University of Utah Press, 2005.

Akens, Jean. *Ute Mountain Tribal Park: The Other Mesa Verde*. Moab, UT: Four Corners, 1995.

Allen, Steve. *Canyoneering 2: Technical Loop Hikes in Southern Utah*. Salt Lake City: University of Utah Press, 1995.

———. *Canyoneering 3: Loop Hikes in Utah's Escalante*. Salt Lake City: University of Utah Press, 1997.

Ambrose, Stephen E. *Undaunted Courage: Meriwether Lewis, Thomas Jefferson, and the Opening of the American West*. New York: Simon & Schuster, 1996.

Backes, David. *Sigurd Olson: The Meaning of Wilderness: Essential Articles and Speeches*. Minneapolis: University of Minnesota Press, 2001.

Baetz, Ruth. *Wild Communion: Experiencing Peace in Nature*. Center City, MN: Hazelden Press, 1997.

Barrows, P., and J. Holmes. *Colorado's Wildlife Story*. Denver: Colorado Division of Wildlife, 1990.

Bayers, Peter L. *Imperial Ascent: Mountaineering, Masculinity, and Empire*. Boulder: University Press of Colorado, 2003.

Beath, Mary. *Hiking Alone: Trails Out, Trails Home*. Albuquerque: University of New Mexico Press, 2008.

Bechdel, Les, and Slim Ray. *River Rescue*. Boston: Appalachian Mountain Club Books / Globe Pequot Press, 1985.

Belknap, Bill, Buzz Belknap, and Lois Belknap Evans. *Belknap's Waterproof Canyonlands River Guide*. Evergreen, CO: Westwater Books, 2008.

Blackburn, Fred M., and Ray A. Williamson. *Cowboys and Cave Dwellers: Basketmaker Archaeology in Utah's Grand Gulch*. Santa Fe: School of American Research Press, 1997.

Blehm, Eric. *The Last Season*. New York: Harper Collins, 2006.

Borneman, Walter R. *14,000 Feet: A Celebration of Colorado's Highest Mountains*. Pueblo, CO: Skyline Press, 2005.

Botkin, Daniel B. *Our Natural History: The Lessons of Lewis and Clark*. New York: Berkley, 1995.

Buzzell, Linda, and Craig Chalquist, eds. *Ecotherapy: Healing with Nature in Mind*. San Francisco: Sierra Club Books, 2009.

Callicott, J. Baird, and Michael P. Nelson. *The Great Wilderness Debate*. Athens: University of Georgia Press, 1998.

Cameron, Catherine. *Chaco and After in the Northern San Juan*. Tucson: University of Arizona Press, 2009.

Carson, Rachel. *Silent Spring*. New York: Houghton Mifflin, 1962.

Cassells, E. Steve. *The Archeology of Colorado*. Boulder: Johnson Books, 1988.

Chesher, Greer K. *Heart of the Desert Wild: Grand Staircase–Escalante National Monument*. Bryce Canyon, UT: Bryce Canyon Natural History Association, 2000.

Childs, Craig. *Soul of Nowhere*. Boston: Little, Brown, 2002.

Clark, H. Jackson. *The Owl in Monument Canyon*. Salt Lake City: University of Utah Press, 1993.

Cole, Sally J. *Legacy on Stone: Rock Art of the Colorado Plateau and Four Corners Region*. Boulder: Johnson Books, 1990.

Cordell, Linda S. *Prehistory of the Southwest*. New York: Academic Press, 1984.

Cornell, Joseph. *Listening to Nature: How to Deepen Your Awareness of Nature*. Nevada City, CA: Dawn Publications, 1987.

Cosco, Jon. *Echo Park: Struggle for Preservation*. Boulder, CO: Johnson Books, 1995.

Craighead, Frank C. *Track of the Grizzly*. San Francisco: Sierra Club Books, 1979.

Crawford, Suzanne J., and Dennis F. Kelley, eds. *American Indian Religious Traditions: An Encyclopedia*. Santa Barbara, CA: ABC-CLIO, 2005.

Crenshaw, Larry. *The Outward Bound Earth Book*. Asheville: North Carolina Outward Bound School, 1990.

Crimmel, Hal, and Steve Gaffney. *Dinosaur: Four Seasons on the Green and Yampa Rivers*. Tucson: University of Arizona Press, 2007.

Cutright, Paul Russell. *Theodore Roosevelt: The Making of a Conservationist*. Urbana: University of Illinois Press, 1985.

deBuys, William. *Enchantment and Exploitation: The Life and Hard Times of a New Mexico Mountain Range*. Albuquerque: University of New Mexico Press, 1985.

Dimock, Brad. *Sunk without a Sound: The Tragic Colorado River Honeymoon of Glen and Bessie Hyde*. Flagstaff, AZ: Fretwater Press, 2001.

Dolnick, Edward. *Down the Great Unknown: John Wesley Powell's 1869 Journey of Discovery and Tragedy through the Grand Canyon*. New York: Harper Collins, 2001.

Douglas, David. *Wilderness Sojourn: Notes in the Desert Silence*. San Francisco: Harper & Row, 1987.

Dustin, Daniel L. *The Wilderness Within: Reflections on Leisure and Life*. 2nd ed. Champaign, IL: Sagamore, 1999.

Egan, Timothy. *The Big Burn: Teddy Roosevelt and the Fire That Saved America*. Boston: Houghton Mifflin, 2009.

Ehrlich, Gretel. *A Match to the Heart*. New York: Penguin Books, 1994.

Ellis, Ruben, ed. *Stories on Stone: Tales from the Anasazi Heartland*. Boulder, CO: Pruett, 1997.

Emmitt, Robert. *The Last War Trail*. Boulder: University Press of Colorado, 2000.

Engelhard, Michael. *Hell's Half Mile: River Runners' Tales of Hilarity and Misadventure*. Halcottsville, NY: Breakaway Books, 2004.

Fagan, Brian. *Chaco Canyon: Archaeologists Explore the Lives of an Ancient City*. New York: Oxford University Press, 2005.

Farabee, Charles. *Death, Daring and Disaster: Search and Rescue in the National Parks*. Lanham, MD: Taylor, 2005.

Fletcher, Colin. *River: One Man's Journey Down the Colorado, Source to Sea*. New York: Alfred A. Knopf, 1997.

Foreman, David. *Confessions of an Eco-Warrior*. New York: Harmony Press, 1991.

Fradkin, Philip L. *Everett Ruess: His Short Life, Mysterious Death, and Astonishing Afterlife*. Berkeley: University of California Press, 2011.

Fredston, Jill, and Doug Fesler. *Snow Sense: A Guide to Evaluating Snow Avalanche Hazards*. 4th ed. Anchorage: Alaska Mountain Safety Center, 1994.

Gerke, Randy. *Outdoor Survival Guide*. Champaign, IL: Human Kinetics, 2010.

Gomez, Art. *Quest for the Golden Circle*. Salt Lake City: University of Utah Press, 2003.

Gonzales, Laurence. *Deep Survival: Who Lives, Who Dies, and Why: True Stories of Miraculous Endurance and Sudden Death*. New York: Norton, 2003.

Gordon, Greg. *Landscape of Desire: Identity and Nature in Utah's Canyon Country*. Logan: Utah State University Press, 2003.

Greenlee, Bob. *Life among the Ancient Ones: Two Accounts of an Anasazi Archaeological Research Project*. Boulder, CO: Hardscrabble Press, 1995.

Gulliford, Andrew. *Sacred Objects and Sacred Places: Preserving Tribal Traditions*. Boulder: University Press of Colorado, 2000.

———, ed. *Preserving Western History*. Albuquerque: University of New Mexico Press, 2005.

Hampton, Bruce. *The Great American Wolf*. New York: Holt, 1997.

Harvey, Mark. *A Symbol of Wilderness: Echo Park and the American Conservation Movement*. Seattle: University of Washington Press, 1994.

Heacox, Kim. *The Only Kayak: A Journey into the Heart of Alaska*. Guilford, CT: Lyons Press, 2006.

Hodgson, Michael. *Wilderness with Children: A Parent's Guide to Fun Family Outings*. Harrisburg, PA: Stackpole Books, 1993.

Huggard, Christopher J. *Forests under Fire*. Tucson: University of Arizona Press, 2001.

Hurst, Winston B., and Joe Pachak. *Spirit Windows: Native American Rock Art of Southeastern Utah*. Blanding, UT: Spirit Windows Project, 1989.

Ingersoll, Ernest. *Knocking around the Rockies*. 1882. Reprint, Norman: University of Oklahoma, 1994.

Jeffers, H. Paul. *Roosevelt the Explorer*. New York: Rowman & Littlefield, 2003.

Keen, Richard A. *Sky Watch: The Western Weather Guide*. Golden, CO: Fulcrum, 1987.

Knapp, Clifford, and Thomas E. Smith. *Exploring the Power of Solo, Silence, and Solitude*. Boulder, CO: Association for Experiential Education, 2005.

Knibb, David. *Grizzly Wars: The Public Fight over the Great Bear*. Spokane: Eastern Washington University Press, 2008.

Knipmeyer, James H. *Butch Cassidy Was Here: Historic Inscriptions of the Colorado Plateau*. Salt Lake City: University of Utah Press, 2002.

———. *In Search of a Lost Race: The Illustrated American Exploring Expedition of 1892*. New York: Xlibris, 2006.

Krakauer, Jon. *Into the Wild*. New York: Villard Books, 1996.

LaChapelle, Dolores. *Deep Powder Snow: Forty Years of Ecstatic Skiing, Avalanches, and Earth Wisdom*. Denver: Kivaki Press, 1993.

Lange, Frederick W., and Diana Leonard. *Among Ancient Ruins*. Boulder, CO: Johnson Books, 1985.

Lavender, David Sievert. *River Runners of the Grand Canyon*. Tucson, AZ: Grand Canyon Natural History Association, 1985.

Lee, Jeff, ed. *The Landscape of Home*. Boulder, CO: Johnson Books and the Rocky Mountain Land Library, 2006.

Lee, Katie. *All My Rivers Are Gone: A Journey of Discovery through Glen Canyon*. Boulder, CO: Johnson Books, 1998.

———. *Sandstone Seduction: Rivers and Lovers, Canyons and Friends*. Boulder, CO: Johnson Books, 2004.

Leemon, Drew, and Tod Schimelpfenig. *Risk Management for Outdoor Leaders: A Practical Guide for Managing Risk through Leadership*. Lander, WY: National Outdoor Leadership School, 2005.

Leopold, Aldo. *A Sand County Almanac*. 1949. New York: Ballantine Books, 1970.

Lewis, Michael, ed. *American Wilderness: A New History*. New York: Oxford University Press, 2007.

Lopez, Barry Holstun. *Of Wolves and Men*. New York: Scribner's, 1978.

Louv, Richard. *Last Child in the Woods: Saving Our Children from Nature-Deficit Disorder*. New York: Algonquin Books of Chapel Hill / Workman Publishing, 2005.

Loweay, Thomas Power. *Camping Therapy*. Springfield, IL: Charles C. Thomas, 1974.

Maclean, Norman. *A River Runs through It, and Other Stories*. Chicago: University of Chicago Press, 1976.

McAvoy, Leo H. *The Wilderness Within*. San Diego: San Diego State University Press, 1993.

McCarthy, Jeffrey Mathes, ed. *Contact: Mountain Climbing and Environmental Thinking*. Reno: University of Nevada Press, 2008.

McPherson, Robert. *Sacred Land, Sacred View: Navajo Perceptions of the Four Corners Region*. Provo, UT: Brigham Young University, Charles Redd Center for Western Studies, 1992.

———. *River Rising from the Sun*. Logan: Utah State University Press, 2000.

———. *Comb Ridge and Its People: The Ethnohistory of a Rock*. Logan: Utah State University Press, 2009.

Momaday, N. Scott. *The Way to Rainy Mountain*. Albuquerque: University of New Mexico Press, 1969.

Muir, John. *The Wilderness World of John Muir*. Edited by Edwin Way Teale. Boston: Houghton Mifflin, 1954.

Nabhan, Gary Paul, and Stephen Trimble. *Geography of Childhood: Why Children Need Wild Places*. Boston: Beacon, 1994.

Nash, Roderick. *Wilderness and the American Mind*. New Haven, CT: Yale University Press, 2001.

Nelson, Nancy. *Any Time, Any Place, Any River: The Nevills of Mexican Hat*. Flagstaff, AZ: Red Lake Books, 1991.

Nesbit, Paul. *Longs Peak*. 9th ed. Denver: Mills, 1990.

Nicholas, Lisa, Elaine M. Bapis, and Thomas J. Harvey. *Imagining the Big Open: Nature, Identity and Play in the New West*. Salt Lake City: University of Utah Press, 2003.

Nielsen, John. *Condor: To the Brink and Back—The Life and Times of One Giant Bird*. New York: Harper Collins, 2006.

O'Bannon, Allen. *Backpackin' Book: Traveling and Camping Skills for a Wilderness Environment.* Helena, MT: Falcon Guide, 2001.

Olson, Sigurd. *Reflections from the North Country.* New York: Alfred A Knopf, 1976.

Osborn, Sophie A. H. *Condors in Canyon Country: The Return of the California Condor to the Grand Canyon Region.* Grand Canyon, AZ: Grand Canyon Association, 2007.

Patterson, Alex. *A Field Guide to Rock Art Symbols of the Greater Southwest.* Boulder, CO: Johnson Books, 1992.

Peacock, Doug, and Andrea Peacock. *The Essential Grizzly: The Mingled Fates of Men and Bears.* Guilford, CT: Lyons Press, 2006.

Petersen, David. *Ghost Grizzlies: Does the Great Bear Still Haunt Colorado?.* Rev. and updated ed. Boulder, CO: Johnson Books, 1998.

———. *Writing Naturally.* Boulder, CO: Johnson Books, 2001.

Peterson, Freda. *Death in the Snow.* Silverton, CO: Ferrell, 2003.

Plog, Stephen. *Ancient Peoples of the American Southwest.* 1997. Reprint, London: Thames & Hudson, 2001.

Plotkin, Bill. *Soulcraft: Crossing into the Mysteries of Nature and Psyche.* Novato, CA: New World Library, 2003.

Powell, John Wesley. *The Exploration of the Colorado River and Its Canyons.* 1875. New York: Dover Books, 1961.

———. *Down the Colorado: Diary of the First Trip through the Grand Canyon, 1869.* Edited by Don D. Fowler and Eliot Porter. New York: Dutton, 1969. Print.

———. *Seeing Things Whole: The Essential John Wesley Powell.* Edited by William deBuys. Washington, D.C.: Island Press / Shearwater Books, 2001.

Priest, Simon, and Michael A. Glass. *Effective Leadership in Adventure Programming.* Champaign, IL: Human Kinetics, 1997.

Pritchett, Laura, ed. *Going Green.* Norman: University of Oklahoma Press, 2009.

Prouty, Dick, Jane Panicucci, and Rufus Collinson, eds. *Adventure Education: Theory and Applications.* Champaign, IL: Human Kinetics and Project Adventure, 2007.

Quammen, David. *Wild Thoughts from Wild Places.* New York: Scribner's, 1998.

Renner, Jeff. *Lightning Strikes: Staying Safe under Stormy Skies.* Seattle: Mountaineers Books, 2002.

Roach, Gerry. *Transcendent Summits.* Golden, CO: Fulcrum, 2004.

Roberts, David. *In Search of the Old Ones: Exploring the Anasazi World of the Southwest.* New York: Simon & Schuster, 1996.

———. *Finding Everett Ruess: The Life and Unsolved Disappearance of a Legendary Wilderness Explorer.* New York: Broadway Books, 2011.

Robertson, Janet. *The Magnificent Mountain Women: Adventures in the Colorado Rockies.* Lincoln: University of Nebraska Press, 1990.

Robinson, Michael J. *Predatory Bureaucracy: The Extermination of Wolves and the Transformation of the West.* Boulder: University Press of Colorado, 2005.

Roosevelt, Theodore. *Wilderness Writings.* Salt Lake City: Gibbs Smith, 1986.

Roszak, Theodore, Mary E. Gomes, and Allen D. Kanner, eds. *Ecopsychology: Restoring the Earth, Healing the Mind.* San Francisco: Sierra Club Books, 1995.

Rothman, Hal. *Devil's Bargain: Tourism in the Twentieth-Century American West.* Lawrence: University Press of Kansas, 1998.

Ruess, Everett. *A Vagabond for Beauty and Wilderness Journals.* Edited by W. L. Rusho. Logan, UT: Gibbs Smith, 2002.

Russell, Terry, and Renny Russell. *On the Loose.* Layton, UT: Gibbs Smith, 2001.

Sadler, Christa. *"There's This River . . .": Grand Canyon Boatman Stories.* Flagstaff, AZ: This Earth Press, 2006.

Sagstetter, Beth, and Bill Sagstetter. *The Mining Camps Speak: A New Way to Explore the Ghost Towns of the American West.* Denver: Benchmark, 1998.

———. *The Cliff Dwellings Speak.* Denver: Benchmark, 2010.

Schaafsma, Polly. *The Rock Art of Utah.* Cambridge, MA: Harvard University Press, 1971.

———. *Warrior, Shield, and Star: Imagery and Ideology of Pueblo Warfare.* Santa Fe, NM: Western Edge Press, 2000.

Scott, Doug. *The Enduring Wilderness.* Denver: Fulcrum, 2004.

Seuss, Dr. *Oh, the Places You'll Go.* New York: Random House, 1990.

Slovic, Scott, ed. *Getting Over the Color Green: Contemporary Environmental Literature of the Southwest.* Tucson: University of Arizona Press, 2001.

Smart, William B. *Old Utah Trails.* Salt Lake City: Utah Geographic Series, 1998.

Snyder, Gary. *The Practice of the Wild.* Berkeley: Counterpoint, 1990.

Stanton, Robert Brewster. *Colorado River Controversies.* 1932. Reprint, Boulder City, NV: Westwater Books, 1982.

Stark, Peter. *Last Breath: The Limits of Adventure.* New York: Ballantine Books, 2001.

Stegner, Wallace. *Beyond the Hundredth Meridian: John Wesley Powell and the Second Opening of the West.* 1953. Reprint, Lincoln: University of Nebraska Press, 1982.

———. *This Is Dinosaur.* 1955. Reprint, Boulder, CO: Roberts Rinehart, 1985.

———. *Marking the Sparrow's Fall: The Making of the American West.* Edited and with introduction by Page Stegner. New York: Holt, 1998.

Stiles, Jim. *Brave New West: Morphing Moab at the Speed of Greed.* Tucson: University of Arizona Press, 2007.

Stone, Michael K., and Zenobia Barlow. *Ecological Literacy: Educating Our Children for a Sustainable World.* San Francisco: Sierra Club Books / Collective Heritage Institute, 2005.

Stuart, David E. *Anasazi America.* Albuquerque: University of New Mexico Press, 2000.

Tejada-Flores, Lito. *Wildwater: The Sierra Club Guide to Kayaking and White Water Boating.* San Francisco: Sierra Club Books, 1978.

Thybony, Scott. *Rock Art of the American Southwest.* Portland, OR: Graphic Arts Center Publishing, 2002.

Trimble, Stephen, and Terry Tempest Williams, eds. *Testimony: Writers of the West Speak on Behalf of Utah Wilderness.* Minneapolis, MN: Milkweed Press, 1996.

Turner, Jack. *The Abstract Wild.* Tucson: University of Arizona Press, 1996.

Van Matre, Steve, and Bill Weiler, eds. *The Earth Speaks.* Greenville, WV: Institute for Earth Education, 1983.

Ward, Chip. *Canaries on the Rim.* New York: Capra Press, 2000.

Warren, Karen, Mitchell Sakofs, and Jasper S. Hunt, Jr., eds. *The Theory of Experiential Education.* Dubuque, IA: Association for Experiential Education and Kendall/Hunt Publishing, 1995.

Waterman, Jonathan. *Running Dry: A Journey from Source to Sea Down the Colorado River.* Washington, D.C.: National Geographic Society, 2010.

Webb, Roy. *Riverman: The Story of Bus Hatch.* Flagstaff, AZ: Fretwater Press, 2008.

Weiler Walka, Ann. *Waterlines: Journeys on a Desert River.* Flagstaff, AZ: Red Lake Books, 2000.

Welch, Vince, Cort Conley, and Brad Dimock. *The Doing of the Thing: The Brief, Brilliant Whitewater Career of Buzz Holmstrom.* Flagstaff, AZ: Fretwater Press, 1998.

Wockner, Gary, Gregory McNamee, SueEllen Campbell, and John Treadwell Nichols, eds. *Comeback Wolves: Western Writers Welcome the Wolf Home.* Boulder, CO: Johnson Books, 2005.

Wolf, Tom. *Ice Crusaders: A Memoir of Cold War and Cold Sport.* Boulder, CO: Roberts Rinehart, 1999.

———. *Arthur Carhart: Wilderness Prophet.* Boulder: University Press of Colorado, 2008.

Wright, Ken. *The Monkeywrench Dad.* Durango: Raven's Eye Press, 2008.

Wrobel, David M., and Patrick T. Long. *Seeing and Being Seen: Tourism in the American West.* Lawrence: University Press of Kansas, 2001.

Wuerthner, George. *Thrillcraft: The Environmental Consequences of Motorized Recreation.* White River Junction, VT: Chelsea Green Publishing / Foundations for Deep Ecology, 2007.

Zwinger, Ann. *Down Canyon.* Tucson: University of Arizona Press, 1995.

CONTRIBUTORS

Edward Abbey worked two seasons as a park ranger in Arches National Monument in the heart of Moab, Utah, in the late 1950s. When he returned, he was angered by "progress" in the parks. This formed the basis for *Desert Solitaire*, which is as acclaimed as his novel, *The Monkey Wrench Gang*. He also wrote *Black Sun, Fire on the Mountain, The Brave Cowboy, The Journey Home, Abbey's Road, Good News* and *Down the River*. Cactus Ed became godfather to an entire generation of Southwestern environmentalists. He died in March 1989.

Sue Agranoff lived in the Northeast for more than 30 years, until she found she needed to be near deserts and mountains and moved to Durango, Colorado. She spends most of her time playing in desert canyons, desert rivers, and the San Juan Mountains. She works and volunteers for several environmental nonprofits and is passionate about preserving and protecting wilderness and wild lands.

Steve Allen has been exploring the canyons of Utah for more than forty years. He is author of the *Canyoneering* series of guide books, and *Utah's Canyon Country Place Names: Stories of the Cowboys, Miners, Pioneers, and River Runners Who Put Names on the Land*. When not in the back country, he is active with several regional environmental groups.

Janice Emily Bowers is a botanist for the U.S. Geological Survey in Tucson, Arizona, and has written several books about southwestern flora including *100 Desert Wildflowers of the Southwest, 100 Roadside Wildflowers of Southwest Woodlands, Shrubs and Trees of the Southwest Deserts, Sonoran Desert Plants: An Ecological Atlas,* and *Desert: The Mojave and Death Valley*. She has also published collections of essays including *A Full Life in a Small Place and Other Essays from a Desert Garden* and *Fear Falls Away and Other Essays from Hard and Rocky Places*.

Phil Brick is Miles C. Moore Professor of Politics and Director of Environmental Studies at Whitman College in Walla Walla, Washington. In 2002 he founded Semester in the West, an environmental studies field program emphasizing the integration of ecology, natural resource policy, and environmental writing. Phil has received several awards for his pedagogy, including Washington State Outstanding Educator and the Robert Fluno Award for Excellence in Social Science Teaching.

Harry Bruell is CEO of the Southwest Conservation Corps (SCC), a nonprofit that provides service and work opportunities for a diverse group of individuals to complete important conservation and community projects for the public benefit. Operating out of regional offices in Durango, Colorado, Salida, Colorado, Tucson, Arizona, and Acoma Pueblo, New Mexico, the SCC engaged 997 corps members and crew leaders in 2010 and completed 350,000 hours of service. Bruell cofounded the national Public Lands Service Coalition and currently serves as chair of the Corps Network and treasurer of Veteran Green Jobs.

Craig Childs, a native of the Southwest, writes for *High Country News, Arizona Highways*, and other publications. His books include *Finders Keepers, The Animal Dialogues, The Desert Cries, Soul of Nowhere, House of Rain, The Way Out*, and *The Secret Knowledge of Water*.

Dean Cox has climbed all of Colorado's fourteeners during his forty years of exploring the state's high country. A Pagosa Springs resident, Cox retired from a career of resort property management. He has almost finished building his own cabin on a mining claim near Silverton, Colorado, where the high country is just out his back door.

Aussie Dave (David Booth) is a sixty-four-year-old retired engineer from Canberra, Australia. In the past ten years David has concentrated on solo section hikes of long-distance trails in the United States. He completed the Pacific Crest Trail in 2007 and is currently hiking the Continental Divide Trail. Over the past forty-five years he has hiked extensively in Australia, New Zealand, the United States, Great Britain, Sweden, and Spain.

Andrew Gulliford is a professor of history and Environmental Studies at Fort Lewis College in Durango, Colorado. He is the author of *America's Country Schools, Sacred Objects and Sacred Places: Preserving Tribal Traditions*, and *Boomtown Blues: Colorado Oil Shale*, which won the Colorado Book Award. *Preserving Western History*, which he edited, was voted one of the best books on the Southwest by the Tucson-Pima County Library. Gulliford has received the National Individual Volunteer Award for wilderness education from the U.S. Forest Service, and a certificate of recognition from the Secretary of Agriculture for "outstanding contributions to America's natural and cultural resources."

Lynn Hamilton was raised in St. Joseph, Missouri, and received her degree in Political Science from the University of California at Berkeley. Hamilton moved to Flagstaff, Arizona, with her husband and two sons in 1995 and had the great fortune to become involved with a wonderful nonprofit organization called Grand Canyon River Guides. As executive director, her passion is protecting Grand Canyon and the Colorado River experience while urging others to do the same.

Creek Hanauer lives with his wife, Betty Ann, their black Lab, Sadie, and an extended family on the remote Salmon River in northern California. Hanauer has worked as a white-water river guide and kayak instructor on the Salmon and Klamath Rivers and in the Grand Canyon since the early 1980s. He is a board member and a volunteer recreation consultant for the Salmon River Restoration Council.

Fred Hutt is a Volunteer Station Lieutenant with Durango Fire and Rescue, and he continues to serve as a member of La Plata County Search and Rescue. He works as a SharePoint Administrator for Mercury Payment Systems and participates in as many fire and mountain rescue calls as work and family commitments allow.

William Karls was born and raised in Nebraska, which gave him a special appreciation of and awe for landscapes that are not flat or dominated by cornfields. He pursued water sports through the Nantahala Outdoor Center in North Carolina and other rafting companies in the West. Karls did his psychiatry residency in Albuquerque and got hooked on the beauty of the Southwest. He currently lives in Durango, Colorado, with his wife, Maggie, and hopes to introduce his grandchildren to Grand Canyon.

Barbara Kingsolver lives in Arizona and the southern Appalachian mountains. Her novels include *Pigs in Heaven, Animal Dreams, The Bean Trees*, and *The Poisonwood Bible*. Trained as a biologist, her articles have appeared in *The New York Times, The Nation, Smithsonian, and National Geographic*. Her nonfiction writing includes *High Tide in Tucson: Essays from Now or Never* and *Holding the Line: Women in the Great Arizona Mine Strike of 1893*.

Jane Koerner has permanent damage to her right calf, but she still climbs mountains, although never on her own. Since her retirement from higher education, she has been writing a memoir based on her mountaineering adventures in the Colorado Rockies. Her articles, essays, and editorials have appeared in regional publications such as the *Denver Post, High Country News* and *Mountain Gazette*.

Katie Lee is a singer, songwriter, activist, and author who has spent half a century describing the loss of Glen Canyon, which lies buried beneath Lake Powell. Her books include *All My Rivers Are Gone* (republished as *Glen Canyon Betrayed: A Sensuous Elegy*) and *Sandstone Seduction: Rivers and Lovers, Canyons and Friends*. She has hiked most of the 125 side-canyons in Glen Canyon. Lee has been inducted into the Arizona Music and Entertainment Hall of Fame, and her most recent book is *The Ballad of Gutless Ditch*. She resides in Jerome, Arizona.

Leo Lloyd is an EMS Captain with Durango Fire and Rescue in Durango, Colorado, and has been an active paramedic/nurse involved in pre-hospital EMS since 1984. Lloyd has been a member of La Plata County Mountain Rescue since 1985. He has participated in many difficult and challenging technical rescues in and around the mountains of Southwestern Colorado.

Ellen Meloy, a recipient of a Whiting Foundation Award in 1997, lived in California, Montana, and Utah. Her book *The Anthropology of Turquoise* was a finalist for the Pulitzer Prize and won the Utah Book Award. Her other books include *Raven's Exile: A Season on the Green River; The Last Cheater's Waltz: Beauty and Violence in the Desert Southwest*, and *Eating Stone: Imagination and the Loss of the Wild*. Meloy spent most of her life in wild, remote places.

Chad Niehaus lives in Moab, Utah, with his wife, Emily, and their son, Oscar. He is a printmaker, painter, writer, teacher, and the owner of a company called Subvert®. You can learn more about Chad and his work at www.ChadNiehaus.com.

David Petersen is an outdoorsman, sportsman, and award-winning conservationist who enjoys writing about "wild places, wildlife, and wild people with wild ideas." He lives with his wife, Carolyn, in a hand-built cabin near Durango, Colorado.

Wayne Ranney is a geologist and trail guide based in Flagstaff, Arizona. Ranney became interested in geology while working as a backcountry ranger at Grand Canyon National Park and later received his bachelor's and master's degrees from Northern Arizona University. He subsequently worked as a geologic lecturer on shipboard expeditions to places such as Antarctica, Africa, the Amazon, and the North and South Poles. He is the author of eight books including *Ancient Landscapes of the Colorado Plateau* and *Carving Grand Canyon.*

Lynell Schalk retired as the Special Agent in Charge (SAC) of the Oregon/Washington Bureau of Land Management (BLM) in 2001 where she was responsible for administering a Federal law enforcement program on 16 million acres of public lands. Schalk previously worked as a ranger for the National Park Service and the BLM. She was the BLM's first female law enforcement officer and its first female SAC in the agency's history.

Steve Susswein began his love affair with desert canyons while living in Israel in the 1970s and has been hiking, rafting, and climbing throughout the Southwest for the past twenty years. He is an ardent supporter of the Southern Utah Wilderness Alliance (SUWA) and currently splits his time between his home in Salt Lake City and his sailboat in the Sea of Cortez.

Jack Turner was educated at the University of Colorado and Cornell University and taught philosophy at the University of Illinois. Since 1975 he has traveled in India, Pakistan, Nepal, China, Tibet, Bhutan, and Peru, leading more than forty treks and expeditions. He has lived in Grand Teton National Park for more than twenty years and teaches mountaineering during the summers. He is the author of *Travels in the Greater Yellowstone, Climbing and Contemplating the Teton Range, Teewinot: A Year in the Teton Range* and *The Abstract Wild.*

Terry Tempest Williams is a Utah native and an acclaimed naturalist who writes for a variety of publications including *Orion* and *High Country News.* Her books include *Red: Passion and Patience in the Desert, Refuge, Pieces of White Shell,* and *When Women were Birds.*

Ann Zwinger is a Colorado-based naturalist and artist whose many publications include *Wind in the Rock: The Canyonlands of Southeastern Utah, Run River Run,* and *Down Canyon.*

INDEX

References to illustrations are in italic type

Abajo Mountains, Utah, 78–79
Abbey, Edward, 8, 12, *13,* 15n35, 31, 358;
  Desert Solitaire, 17, 23, 139–40, 287,
  309–17; *Down the River,* 18
Accidents, 59, 170, 190, 290; avalanche,
  166–68; hiking, 163–65; lightning, 155–59;
  mountain climbing, 175–87
Adopt-a-Beach program, in Grand Canyon,
  366–69
Adventure, 8–9, 11, 12
Adventure degree program, Fort Lewis
  College, *128*
Adventure education, programs, 10, 18
*Adventure Guide to the Western San
  Juans* (Waring), 9
Akens, Jean, 196
Aldo Leopold Wilderness Area, N.M., *16,*
  18, 24, 25
Allen, Steve, 210; on Barrier Canyon rock art,
  91, 93–94
All-Terrain Vehicles (ATVs), 93. *See also*
  Off-road vehicles
American character, and wilderness, 21–22
Anasazi. *See* Ancestral Puebloan sites
Ancestral Puebloan sites, 81, 99, 133, 262; on
  Comb Ridge, 68–71; evidence of, 65, 67;
  types of, 71–72; in Ute Mountain Tribal
  Park, 195, 196–200
Anderson, Adrienne, 78
Anderson, Arden, 9, 10
Anderson, Lloyd, 333
Animals, 215; encounters with,
  319–20; endangered, 27–28, 323–24;

reintroduction of, 324–31. *See also by
  type*
Anselmo, Joan, 6–7
Antiquities Act (1906), 68
ARAMARK, Lake Powell cleanup, 356–59
Arborglyphs, sheepherder-made, 81–85
Archaeoastronomy, 110–11
Archaeological Resources Protection Act
  (ARPA; 1978), 67, 68
Archaeological sites and resources, 52, 65,
  90n3; aspen art as, 81–85; on Comb
  Ridge, 68–71; in Gila National Forest,
  72–76; in Gila Wilderness, 29, 40; in
  Grand Canyon, 262, 263; historic, 85–89,
  285–86; in the Maze (Canyonlands),
  119, 121–22, 123; peeled trees as, 76–79;
  trails as, 129–31, 133; treatment of, 67–68;
  types of, 71–72; Ute, 80–81; Ute Mountain
  Tribal Park, 195–200; visiting, 102–104
Arches National Park, Utah, 139–40
Arizona, 52, 141; condor reintroduction in,
  324–28; mountain climbing in, 149–54;
  sacred landscapes in, 132–33
Arizona Raft Adventures (AzRA), 262, 266,
  268, 270–71, 273, *279*
Arizona Strip, 322
Arkansas River: running, 264–65
ARPA. *See* Archaeological Resources
  Protection Act
Artifacts, 95, 191; Fremont, 97–98, 99, 101;
  treatment of, 67, 72–76, 86, 100–101, 103;
  in Ute Mountain Tribal Park, 195, 197–99
Aspens, sheepherder art on, 81–85

401